Just Your Type

Other Books by the Authors

Do What You Are

Nurture by Nature

The Art of SpeedReading People

Just Your Type

*Create the Relationship
You've Always Wanted Using the Secrets
of Personality Type*

Paul D. Tieger and
Barbara Barron-Tieger

Little, Brown & Company
New York   Boston

Little, Brown and Company
Time Warner Book Group
1271 Avenue of the Americas, New York, NY 10020
Visit our Web site at www.twbookmark.com

The people described in this book are composites. Names have
been changed to protect their privacy.

Library of Congress Cataloging-in-Publication Data
Tieger, Paul D.
    Just your type : create the relationship you've always
wanted using the secrets of personality type / by Paul D.
Tieger and Barbara Barron-Tieger.
        p.   cm.
    Includes bibliographical references (p.).
    ISBN 0–316–84569–8
    1. Man-woman relationships.   2. Couples.   3. Typol-
ogy   (Psychology)   4.   Interpersonal   communication.
I. Barron-Tieger, Barbara.   II. Title.
HQ801.T485   2000
306.7 — dc21   99–41532

QW-FF

Text design by Joyce C. Weston
PRINTED IN THE UNITED STATES OF AMERICA

This is dedicated to the one I love.

—PDT & BBT

If you don't like someone, the way he
holds his spoon will make you furious;
if you do like him, he can turn his plate
over into your lap and you won't mind.
—Irving Becker

♥

Contents

♥

Acknowledgments

♥

As with any book project, there are many, many people to recognize and thank for their support, encouragement, and assistance. This book is certainly no exception. We start by thanking the thousands of people who visited our Web site to take part in the extensive research project to gather data for this book. Thank you for your time, candor, and generosity in sharing your thoughts and experiences with us. Next, we are grateful to the hundreds of couples who allowed us to poke around in their relationships by participating in the in-depth interviews. It was a privilege and honor for us, and we thank you for sharing the joys and the frustrations of your relationships. We promised everyone anonymity, so we won't list your names here, but we are grateful beyond words, and we wish you all the best of luck and happiness.

There are also dozens of people who actively helped us recruit research participants, and their contributions and assistance were invaluable. They are Sandra Hirsch, Jane Kise, Linda Berens, Nicky Bredeson, Tom Carskadon, Jamie Johnson, John Golden, Steve Buttner, John Beck, Peggy Holtman, John Madigan, Gary Hartzler, Don Johnson, Susan Brock, Terry Duniho, Jean Whitney, Richard Grant, Sarah McNaughton, Sarah Sharman, Lou Loomis, Joyce Yarrow, Alice Gould, Glenn Orkin, Ed McKeon, Henry Milan, Robin Holt, Rona Branson, Bill Murray, Donna Denoon, Scott Blanchard, Jerry Vastano, Kevin Harrington, Irwin Nussbaum, John Knerling, James Francis, Ralph Braithwaite, Rhonda LoBruto, Eleta Jones, Carol Pfeiffer, Sandra Morgan, Gerry MacDaid, Margaret Fields, Bill Haddock, Mary and Brian Twill-man, Pat Swain, Sue Scanlon, Phyllis Reeds, Tad Graham-Hadley, Lou Sanders, Madeleine and Bill Swain, Peter Grandy, Alice Noyes, Sue Lucas, Helen Barron, and all the Association for Psychological Type (ATP) chapter coordinators.

We especially thank John Cubeta, Ph.D., our friend and colleague, for his assistance with the design and analysis of the survey. He crunched many a number and created uncounted charts and graphs to help us make sense of all the data we collected. And we are so grateful to our good friend Bert Miller, for his brilliant mind, the great survey design, and his superb Web master wizardry. But mostly we thank him for his constant friendship, support, and love.

We recognize again and always the people who have taught us so much about Personality Type through the years, including Mary McCaulley, Gordon Lawrence, Sue Scanlon, Terry Duniho, and Naomi Quenk. We are grateful to our many therapist friends for their advice and suggestions: Ruth Hofstatter, Ginger Blume, Nicky Bredeson, Francie Brown, Linda Chase Wayman, Barbara Hollender, and Jane Kimball.

We're grateful to our editor, Amanda Murray, and our other friends at Little, Brown, including Sarah Crichton, Carl Lennertz, Sairey Luterman, Jane Comins, Katie Long, and Gary Strauss. And we especially thank our great literary agent, Kit Ward, for her continued encouragement, support, and advice. Thanks for pushing us to write this book.

And we again thank our families and friends for their support and patience: Bob Baumwoll and

ACKNOWLEDGMENTS

Martha Heller, Jimmy and Trina Stafford, Joel Lavenson and Crista Cooper, George and Nancy Bacall, Jesse Stoner and Larry Zemel, Bob and Susan Stern, Kip Kolesinskas and Lesley Schurmann, Christy and John Burrmann, Evan Williams and Greig Shearer, La Donna Carlson, Marilyn and Mel Gallant, Don and Genie Street, Paul Chill and Brigid Donohue, Carolyn Koch, Gerry and Jan Smyth, Vera and Tony Tosoni, Gail and Ken Beare, Sheila and Irwin Nussbaum, Vincent and Kathleen Trantolo, Joan and Dave Kingdon, Ruth Hofstatter and Paul Selwyn, Jude Kauffman and Steve Kemper, Wendy and Rob Benson, Nina and Evan Fox, Jane and Ted Carroll, Robyne Watkin and Mark Anson, Thona McEnroe, Janet Penley, Daniel Oppenhiem and Julia TenEck, Cheryl Greenberg and Dan Lloyd, Keats and Joe Jarmon, Amy Mazur, Trisha and Dave Livingstone, Sue Piquera, Nancy Aronie, Greg and Cathy Garant, Marc and Judy Tieger, and Debbie Barron.

And, finally, thanks to our children, Danny and Kelly, for their endless love, enthusiasm, and patience during this very long writing process.

PART ONE

The Secret to Making Love Work

"I used to think my wife was just shy and needed to grow out of it. Now I respect her need to be alone, and I get some of my needs for action and socializing met on my own."

"We're both very careful with our relationship. We're never hurtful or impulsive. There's real security in knowing what to expect."

"My husband forces us to really discuss things and as a result, our relationship is much more meaningful and satisfying."

"We're not a 'warm and fuzzy' couple. We both really like the fact that this isn't a security blanket kind of relationship."

"Our challenge is to be present with one another. We each get seized by an idea and disappear inside our respective heads with it."

"One time I just mentioned that I wished we had a shelf above the washing machine. That night, my partner stayed up late and built one. No discussion — he just did it!"

Chapter 1

"You Say Tomato, I Say Tomahto"

Susan and Jeff thought they were perfect for each other. They met in college, enjoyed some of the same interests, came from similar backgrounds, and married after both had had time to establish their careers. Although they knew they were different in many ways, they felt a powerful attraction that they attributed to those very differences. Jeff was enthusiastic, outgoing, and creative; Susan was gentle, down-to-earth, and responsible. Each balanced the other's weaknesses, and together they complemented each other's strengths. But a few months after they were married, their bliss began to fade, replaced by a low-grade, constant tension. Susan's traditional nature surfaced. She was a conservative person at heart and wanted a stable, predictable life. Hardworking, quiet, and extremely diligent with all her commitments, she planned carefully for the future, saved their money to buy nice things, and was eager to settle down and raise a family in the town where she'd grown up. But Jeff was the quintessential Renaissance man — constantly reinventing himself and talking about his many creative ideas. A natural entrepreneur who kept busy developing new ventures — often on a shoestring — Jeff was outgoing, flexible, insightful about people, and curious about new experiences. Far from wanting to settle down, he longed to travel the globe with Susan, learning as much as he could about other cultures.

What was initially a strong attraction between Susan and Jeff was slowly becoming an inescapable source of frustration. Susan tried to get Jeff to commit to buying a house in their community, and Jeff tried to get Susan to consider borrowing a friend's camper so they could at least spend some time traveling and exploring the country. Instead of feeling supported and encouraged for his ideas and curiosity, Jeff felt undermined, criticized, and stifled. Try as she might, Susan couldn't help but see the practical problems with most of his ideas. Because she couldn't get Jeff to commit to a definite plan, Susan grew increasingly worried about their future and their financial stability.

Although they tried to talk about their frustrations, their inability to reach each other only led to more frustration and defensiveness. Feeling hurt and unsupported, Susan withdrew, while Jeff vacillated between trying to cajole her into giving it one more try and storming off to spend time with his friends. After three years of bickering, retreating, and building walls between them, they decided they were just too incompatible and joined the estimated 53 percent of marriages that end in divorce.

What might have happened if Susan and Jeff had had a better, more constructive way of communicating with each other? What if they had not only understood their differences but also viewed them positively and as a source of richness? And what if instead of trying to change each other, they had reveled in their individuality and worked together to establish common ground? Maybe they could have avoided some of the pain they both felt and saved their marriage. Perhaps.

Although not all couples are as seemingly mismatched as Susan and Jeff, many are. According to our latest research — an extensive couples survey project comprising a scientific survey and in-depth interviews — more than 40 percent of couples report experiencing regular relationship difficulties that range from vague dissatisfaction and frustration to outright misery. Most couples sincerely want things to be better between them, but because they don't even understand the problems, they can't figure out how to fix them. Why are so many people so dissatisfied? Why is it so difficult to make a relationship work? After all, doesn't "love conquer all"?

Obviously, there are many reasons relationships fail, but an important one is that most people enter into relationships when they're young and inexperienced and simply don't know much about themselves, let alone their partners. When you add to this the enormous pressure put on young people to "settle down" (and get married) by well-meaning parents, friends, religious institutions, and media, it's not surprising that so many jump into marriage assuming this is the way it's supposed to be. And despite the fact that the life expectancy today far outpaces that of only a couple of generations ago — when being married for life meant maybe twenty years — we still have the expectation that we'll live happily ever after with our one true love, even though that could be as long as sixty years. That's a long time, even for a great marriage!

And is it any surprise that we are attracted to people who are different from us? Like Susan and Jeff, most of us are inexplicably drawn to people who are very different than we are. The qualities that we find charming or exciting during the magical courtship period become much less appealing when we discover that our partners are like that *every day!* Rather than understand, accept, and appreciate our partners for who they are, we unwittingly turn the differences between

us into the chief source of our frustration, irritation, and dissatisfaction. Instead of celebrating our differences, we resist them; we try to make our partners more like us. And as we do, we chip away at the foundations of our relationships by constantly criticizing, complaining, blaming, and dismissing our partners' characteristics and natural tendencies. Most couples engage in this undermining campaign in very subtle and indirect ways; they rarely address the problem honestly and openly. They just stop talking — *really* talking. So the overwhelming reason relationships fail is poor communication.

This is hardly news. But given the abundance of advice available to people today, it's still amazing and sad that we haven't yet learned how to communicate more effectively with our partners. Many have offered their pet theories about why people have such a hard time finding and sustaining satisfying relationships. Most offer simple, quick-fix approaches, not unlike the latest fad diet that promises a twenty-pound weight loss in as many days. And some of these programs deliver, at least temporarily. But ultimately they fail, because they are based on bad science, fail to appreciate the way human beings really act, or both. A whole industry has been created around the notion that gender is to blame: men and women are so inherently different that they don't even come from the same planet! Since they don't, won't, and can't speak the same language, they can never be expected to understand each other, much less communicate well.

Debunking the Myth That It's All About Gender

There's no denying that those who espouse the viewpoint that gender is an inevitable barrier to good communication have struck a chord with millions of people who are frustrated with the way they deal with their partners. Most people would agree that men and women *are* different, and in some very profound ways. Some women do fit the female stereotype of being sensitive, emotional, nurturing, and open, just as some men fit the male stereotype of being tough, competitive, emotionally self-contained, and independent. But as our research study demonstrated, it turns out these men and women represent only between 30 and 40 percent of the American population. Although advice based on such gender stereotypes often is helpful to these individuals, it doesn't accurately describe the 60 to 70 percent of people who don't fit the stereotype.

So if it isn't gender that accounts for the communication failures between people that are the leading cause of conflict, what is it? It is our personality differences, our basic natures. People are not all the same. We have different energy levels, notice different aspects of the world around us, make decisions based on different criteria, and structure our lives in different ways depending on what makes us most comfortable. These important and fundamental characteristics combine to create the whole personality, a sum total that goes way beyond our gender. This is a comprehensive perspective we get through the powerful insights of Personality Type.

Welcome to the Wonderful World of Personality Type

Actually, there's a pretty good chance you're already familiar with Personality Type, and perhaps you've even discovered your own type by reading one of the many books on the subject, taking a psychological inventory called the Myers-Briggs Type Indicator (MBTI),* or attending a workshop or seminar. Over the past twenty-five years, Personality Type has helped more than thirty million people gain valuable insights into

themselves and others and become more successful in their personal and professional lives. Originally based on the work of Swiss psychologist Carl Jung, the popularity of Personality Type is due to the work of two remarkable American women, Katharine Briggs and her daughter, Isabel Briggs Myers. It is such an exceptional tool that it is used by thousands of counselors, therapists, and educators every day, and it is considered by many Fortune 500 companies to be the most effective tool for improving interpersonal communication.

So what is Personality Type, and how does knowing about it help people communicate better? Personality Type is a system of understanding human behavior. There are sixteen distinctly different personality types — all equally valuable, each with its own natural strengths and potential weaknesses. And although every individual is unique, people of the same type are often remarkably similar in important ways, such as how outgoing or private, realistic or imaginative, logical or emotional, or serious or playful they are. Rather than relying on limiting stereotypes about men and women, Personality Type paints a clearer and richer portrait of a person by enabling each individual to understand his or her values, drives, and motivations. In hundreds of in-depth interviews with couples of each combination who know and use Personality Type to better understand each other, it wasn't at all surprising that practically all of them echoed the same sentiment: "I only wish we had learned about Type *earlier* in our relationship. It would have made all the difference in the world!" And when asked what advice they would give to other couples of their same type combination, virtually all said the same thing: "Learn about Personality Type."

---

*The Myers-Briggs Type Indicator instrument and the MBTI are registered trademarks of Consulting Psychologists Press, Inc.

About the Authors

As avid students of this powerful model of human behavior, we've conducted research, written four books, and trained thousands of professionals in the use of Personality Type for more than twenty years. We began as career counselors and wrote the best-selling *Do What You Are,* a book that helped more than half a million people find more satisfying careers by matching work with their personality types. As parents, we next wrote *Nurture by Nature,* a guide that helps partners understand their children's types so they can be more respectful and nurturing parents and reduce the number of conflicts they have with their children. At the urging of many colleagues and readers, we next wrote *The Art of SpeedReading People,* a system that teaches how to size up other people instantly so you can speak their language. Now we tackle the important topic of helping couples better understand and appreciate each other so they might build more satisfying relationships.

The Research

Practically everyone who has any experience with Personality Type finds it immediately applicable to their personal relationships. Whether we're presenting workshops on team building or effective parenting or training career professionals, seminar participants inevitably ask us about their relationships: Is theirs a relationship that's destined to succeed or fail? Is there such a thing as one perfect type for them? Are some types naturally better suited to each other than others? Can opposites stay together? Although over the years we accumulated plenty of anecdotal information on the subject, until now, there hasn't been the kind of empirical and rigorous scientific research needed to test our hypothesis: The more similar two

people's types are, the more they understand each other and the easier the relationship is. And the less two people have in common, the harder they'll both have to work to understand each other — but they can still have a great relationship!

We began by designing a comprehensive research study — the first of its kind — to support the evidence we'd seen for twenty years among Type users, workshop participants, family, friends, and associates. We designed an extensive, anonymous, on-line survey to help us discover, among other things, what people of all sixteen personality types considered most important in a relationship. People also told us about the most common sources of conflict and what they believed was the secret of a satisfying relationship. Respondents shared their experiences, their hopes, and their disappointments. Specifically, they told us the kinds of things that brought them closer to their partners and what drove them apart. And they volunteered tips they'd picked up along the way to help make things easier, less contentious, and more gratifying. Well over a thousand people participated in the survey: they represented each of the sixteen types, all fifty states, all ages, all educational and economic backgrounds, and all different types of relationships — very new ones, second and third marriages, and unions that have lasted more than fifty years.

Next we interviewed hundreds of couples of every combination about their relationships either over the phone or in person. These generous folks candidly shared their observations about their joys and frustrations. They told us their hard-won secrets of success and what they thought made their relationships satisfying. And, most important, they offered valuable advice for other couples of the same type combinations.

Our research showed that of the more than one thousand people from all walks of life who answered all the survey items, a striking 91 percent cited good communication as the single most important aspect of a satisfying relationship. Poor communication was cited as the most frequent and serious cause of conflict. Our findings are very clear: the better the communication, the more satisfied couples are with their relationships. Understanding Personality Type is a powerful tool for helping couples communicate better. Results and discoveries like these are included throughout this book to give you the kind of practical advice you've always wanted — the kind that really helps you to understand yourself and your partner and to communicate in new, more effective ways. Solving communication problems will help alleviate many other important challenges that couples face, such as parenting conflicts and sexual compatibility issues. Understanding your partner's language makes those issues infinitely easier to manage and resolve. So *Just Your Type* is first and foremost a communication guide.

So, Who's This Book For, Anyway? And Do I Really Need It?

Unlike many of the dozens of other relationship advice books, *Just Your Type* is tailor-made for you and your partner. No matter your type (or your partner's type), this book is written specifically for you. Every one of the possible type combinations will find a section just for them. And it's designed for people in all stages of their relationships — couples just starting out as well as those who've been together for many years. And because people at different stages of development have different needs and face different challenges, we examined those age-specific concerns in our research. What we learned will help you no matter where you are.

Shopping for Mr. or Ms. Right

Learning about Personality Type will be helpful for young people who are looking for a partner or who are already involved with someone but aren't quite sure he or she is "the one." If you're one of these readers, this book will give you some important insights into your own needs and help you determine whether a potential partner is likely to meet them. Understanding Personality Type now will help you move forward with your eyes wide-open. And although there isn't just one right type for anyone, you will learn important things about yourself and what you need in a relationship for it to be fulfilling. This book may even save you from future heartache by helping you decide to end a relationship that's not right for you.

The Honeymooners

What if you're already involved with someone and things are pretty good? Why would you need this book? Our research indicates that 18- to 25-year-olds report the highest level of satisfaction in their relationships. For these people, their relationships are new and exciting, and typically their careers are starting to take off. Most young people have some money to spend on themselves — often for the first time in their lives. They enjoy plenty of freedom and few responsibilities (only about 6% of survey respondents in this age group have children). At this stage, many are still idealistic and have great optimism about the future. If you are at this age, learning about Personality Type now will give you the kind of self-awareness that will help you communicate your needs and make you more likely to get those needs met. It will help you appreciate the aspects of your relationship that work and provide insights into why certain issues always seem to result in conflict. If your difficulties are related to Type differences, as relationship conflicts almost always are, now is the time to deal with them, before they become entrenched patterns. Personality Type provides such accurate insights that thousands of counselors and clergy highly recommend (and in some cases insist) that couples learn about each other's personality types before they get married.

Twenty- to Thirty-Something, and the Beat Goes On

Most people in relationships during their mid-twenties to early thirties experience mounting pressure relating to career choice and advancement, and about a quarter of them have children. The courtship phase, in which both people were on their best behavior, may be a fading memory. Reality is setting in, and many of those quirky personality qualities they found so appealing are now a source of annoyance and a cause of arguments. In the midst of all this, individuals struggle to redefine themselves in a variety of new roles. In addition to being husbands and wives, they may be new parents and sons- or daughters-in-law. And many have to navigate this tricky journey without the benefit of good role models, since half their parents' marriages ended in divorce. Using the powerful tool of Personality Type strengthens and supports these relationships by giving them a common language and a new level of mutual respect.

The Stress Factory

Of all the different age groups, the people who claim they are the "least satisfied" are those in the 31- to 40-year-old range. They are arguably under the greatest amount of pressure, as these are the critical years for building careers, making major financial decisions (such as the purchase of homes and cars), and starting to invest for the future. Add to this becoming and being parents, which is perhaps the biggest source of stress on a couple. Although the overwhelming majority of parents consider children to be their greatest source of happiness, they are also the number one cause of stress. Since your personality type influences your values and your parenting style, it makes sense that parents of different types are more likely to experience great conflict over issues involving children, such as how demanding and how consistent or flexible to be. Good communication becomes even more important. Given the crushing pressure

on people in this age group, it's not surprising that they experience the highest rate of divorce. This is the critical time when relationships either sink or sail. Most people in this group have been together for seven to fifteen years; many haven't been especially happy for a long time, and they may secretly be wondering, "Is this all there is for me?" Others who are drifting apart may feel that if things aren't going to get any better, they may as well leave now, while they're still young (and attractive) enough to find another mate.

But there is reason to be optimistic for people who hang in there and honestly look at themselves and their partners, take responsibility for their shortcomings, and find compassion for their partners' imperfections. Since the two greatest sources of stress are career and parenting, our research shows that the more satisfied people are in these areas, the happier they are in their relationships. Knowing your type can help you make positive changes on both fronts, and those who are able to weather the storm often emerge with a much stronger, closer relationship than they had before.

It's Gettin' Better All the Time

But the news gets even better for people who stay together longer. People age 41 to 50 report more satisfaction, and those 51 to 60 report even more satisfaction due in great part to growing maturity, increased self-awareness and understanding of their partners, greater career stability and satisfaction, and less financial pressure. As couples become more realistic in their expectations, they are generally better able to accommodate the conflicts in their relationships, and, most important, they have learned how to communicate with their partners in ways that work. This is often true of people in second or third marriages as well, since they've learned much from their past experiences. And by age 61 to 70, many couples say they're having the best times of their lives — especially if they enjoy good health and don't have excessive financial concerns. Not only do they have relatively few responsibilities, but they also finally have the time to pursue interests they may have deferred during their working years. As couples, they have strengthened their bond through decades of life experiences and have come to know each other well. In essence, they have learned through decades of being together — and lots of tough times — the secrets that Personality Type can offer people earlier on: how to understand, accept, and appreciate their partners for who they are. This is the gift of Personality Type. So whether your relationship has been going on for two months or twenty years, this book will help you see and appreciate your partner in an entirely new light.

How to Get Started

Great rewards await you and your partner, but achieving them will require some pretty active participation on your part. Think of this as a workbook, an interactive guide for the two of you to share. We'll give you plenty of step-by-step instructions as you work through this exciting and thought-provoking experience. We know from conducting the interviews that the couples who answered our research questions together (even those who had been together for decades) learned important things about their partners that they had never known before. Many found a new appreciation for their partners, and most felt a renewed sense of hope, enthusiasm, and attraction for each other. And more than a few couples told us that it was as if they were finding each other for the first time.

Despite all our independence, human beings are at heart social animals. We seem to be designed to be part of a twosome. In fact, even though more than 50 percent of all marriages end in divorce, most divorced people remarry within a couple of years. It seems we all want to be in a satisfying relationship, even if different types define a satisfying relationship differently. By discovering how to make constructive and loving use of the natural differences between you and your partner, you can create the kind of relationship that works for both of you. Personality Type is a tool you can use to strengthen and perhaps save your relationship so it can grow and change with you over a lifetime.

Chapter 2

The Secrets of Personality Type Revealed

You are about to learn about — or perhaps expand your understanding of — a fascinating and well-respected tool that will give you powerful new insights into yourself, your partner, and all the important people in your life. Of the many systems that philosophers, psychologists, and all-around wise people throughout the ages have devised to understand people, we think Personality Type is one of the best. Since its rise in popularity in the early 1970s, it has enjoyed worldwide acclaim because it's easy to learn and understand, it has a host of practical applications, it explains a lot about why people do the things they do, and it recognizes the value and uniqueness of every person.

Based originally on the work of Swiss psychologist Carl Jung and the American mother-daughter team of Katharine Briggs and Isabel Briggs Myers, Personality Type identifies and explains the fundamental ways people behave naturally. It explains how we prefer to interact with the world, are energized, notice the world around us, make decisions, and organize our lives. By expanding upon Jung's work, Katharine and Isabel developed and published the Myers-Briggs Type Indicator (MBTI) instrument, the most popular and widely respected personality assessment instrument in the world. Uses of Personality Type are varied and include career counseling, management training, team building, personal therapy, training for educators, and parent effectiveness training.

By the end of this chapter, you will have a pretty good idea of your own personality type and, if you're in a relationship, of your partner's type as well. In fact, you'll find that going through this process together will be fun and probably will help you identify your "true" types more quickly. But before we get started, we'd like to share a few general principles about Personality Type:

1. We believe that everyone is born with one true personality type and that although we all change greatly as we develop and mature, our type remains the same.

2. All types are equally valuable. There are no better or worse, healthy or sick, intelligent or unintelligent types, and all have their own strengths and weaknesses.

3. Every individual is unique. Although people who share the same type have a lot in common, we all have different parents, genes, and experiences that exert a tremendous influence over what kind of people we become. And although Type provides invaluable insights, it doesn't explain everything! One hundred people of the same type will have a lot in common with one another, but they certainly won't be identical.

4. In the American culture, some personality type characteristics are more highly valued than others. Type is a great tool for helping people understand and appreciate people who may be very different from them in small and great ways.

There are four *dimensions* of Personality Type, each of which is an important aspect of our personalities. It's helpful to think of each of these dimensions as a continuum, with two ends and a midpoint, much like a scale.

Extraversion	**Introversion**
Sensing	**Intuition**
Thinking	**Feeling**
Judging	**Perceiving**

For each of the four dimensions, every person has a natural, inborn *preference* for one side or the other of the midpoint. By preference, we mean an essentially unconscious preference, not a conscious choice. It's the way that feels the most natural and comfortable to us — the way we automatically behave. For the first dimension, Extraversion or Introversion, if you fall on the Extraversion side, you are called an Extravert, and if you fall on the Introversion side, you are called an Introvert. People display these preferences to varying degrees, but for the time being, you don't need to be concerned about the strength of your preference on any of these scales. What's most important is to figure out on which side of the midpoint you (and your partner) fall.

One more important thing to keep in mind: although we all have a preference for one side or the other on each of these four type dimensions, everyone uses both sides of each dimension at certain times. In other words, one is *primarily* an Extravert, not *exclusively* an Extravert. The same is true for the other type dimensions.

Ready to Figure Out Your Type?

Figuring out your type is like putting together a puzzle: some pieces are harder to identify and some reveal more than others. And it's essentially a process of elimination. Your goal is to determine which of the sixteen types fits you best by eliminating those that don't fit you well.

As you read about each of the four Type dimensions, try to figure out which side of each one more ₋ₜly describes you and jot down your observations. These will come in handy when it's time to verify that you've identified your one true type. As you go through this exercise, you may notice that it's much easier for you to identify some of your preferences than others. This happens to most people. Don't worry about deciding absolutely all four of your preferences at this time; rather, think of them as a "working hypothesis" for now. And remember, there is no such thing as a pure Extravert or Introvert — we all use both sides of our personalities throughout the day, though not at the same time or with the same ease. We just have a natural preference for one side over the other. So let's take a look at the first type dimension: are you an Extravert or an Introvert?

Extravert or Introvert

Where Do You Get and Direct Your Energy?

"We threw a party for Jill but could invite only about a hundred or so of her closest friends!"

"Rob's like that old stockbroker commercial. He doesn't say much, but when he speaks, everyone listens."

When most people hear a person described as an *Extravert,* they picture someone who is outgoing and talkative, just as the word *Introvert* conjures up a quiet and perhaps even shy person. In fact, many Extraverts are talkative, and many Introverts are quiet. But the much more significant differences have to do with energy — where they get it and where they direct it.

Extraverts are more outwardly focused — that is, they direct their energy toward the world outside themselves. As a result, they are more aware of the external environment, almost as if they are equipped with radar and are constantly scanning to see what and whom it picks up. This explains why Extraverts tend to be easily distracted. Extraverts look at a situation and ask, "How do I affect that?" On the other hand, Introverts are more inwardly focused, directing their energy toward themselves and their own ideas or thoughts. Introverts tend to ask themselves, "How does that affect me?" They are more naturally self-centered, but in a literal, not a pejorative, sense. Another important difference is that when problems or issues develop in a relationship, Extraverts usually need to talk things out in order to understand or resolve them. Introverts, however, need to mull things over — sometimes only for a minute, other times for much longer, depending in large measure on how important the issues are.

Renee and James found themselves at a familiar impasse — once again. A simple misunderstanding during dinner had somehow mushroomed into a full-blown fight. Renee, the Extravert, wanted to deal with it now, hoping they could resolve the conflict before it escalated any further. But James, the Introvert, was nowhere near ready to discuss it. Although he really didn't understand what had happened to cause the rift, he knew he needed time by himself to think about it. So they sat in frustrated silence: Renee feeling forced to remain quiet, and James feeling pressured to speak before he was ready. The way they each needed to deal with the problem seemed to be the exact opposite of what their partner needed.

In this example, the woman is the Extravert and the man is the Introvert. In American culture, there is about an equal number of male and female Extraverts and male and female Introverts. Although this has been well documented in several studies over the past twenty years, proponents of the "gender myth" still contend that all women are Extraverts (people who need to talk in order to think) and all men are Introverts (people who need to mull over their thoughts in silence before they feel comfortable responding). The inaccurate stereotypes continue: women are open, and men are reserved; women like being with people, and men are primarily loners; women ask for help, and men have to do everything on their own. As you will soon see, it is really Extraversion and Introversion — not gender — that is responsible for these significant differences.

Another distinction between Introverts and Extraverts is the amount of social interaction each prefers. Typically, being around other people stimulates Extraverts. It seems to charge their batteries. As a result, they generally look forward to gatherings, even with people they don't know, and often have a large and varied circle of friends and acquaintances. Conversely, Introverts' energy is often drained by having to be with lots of people, especially for sustained periods of time. This is not to suggest that Introverts are recluses or are unable to interact with others. Instead, Introverts are generally more comfortable interacting one-on-one or being by themselves, whereas their Extraverted counterparts like and need to be around others and frequently feel lonely when they're not.

Understandably, Introverts choose to have fewer people in their lives, and they are more often close friends or confidants. Most Extraverts, however, "collect" people and often have a stable of friends and acquaintances with whom they enjoy spending time.

Tom, whose nickname was "Mr. Personality," was always at the center of the action — organizing social events, joining clubs, or just hanging out with his many friends. Laura was often described as a quiet, thoughtful girl, not easy to get to know but a person of real substance. When they met in college, predictably, Tom and Laura were drawn to each other. Laura was impressed with Tom's seemingly limitless energy and social ease in any situation. And Tom found Laura's calm energy and independence appealing. During their courtship, when both were on their best behavior and trying to be accommodating, things went smoothly. But after a while, the difference in their social needs began to surface. While Tom loved being out with people — his friends or clients — Laura preferred to spend their nights home alone together or occasionally hosting small dinner parties for a few close friends. It wasn't until several years, and many arguments, later that they realized they had such different social needs because he was an Extravert and she an Introvert. Now they've come to an understanding that enables them to accommodate these differences. Tom no longer pressures Laura to accompany him to the many social events his business requires, and when she does go, he makes sure to introduce her to strangers and stay with her until she finds someone comfortable to talk with. And they often take two cars so she can put in an appearance and then leave when she's had enough. To accommodate Laura's need for quiet togetherness, they have a standing dinner date — just the two of them — every Tuesday night.

Extraverts and Introverts have different gifts. For Extraverts, it's breadth of experience; for Introverts, it's depth of experience. Whereas Extraverts are often interested in a variety of subjects and ideas, Introverts are usually more selective about their interests and almost always prefer to explore them in greater depth.

When Kevin and Lorraine got their first home computer, it put an unexpected strain on their marriage. They were both excited about the endless possibilities that the Internet presented. Lorraine, an Extravert, found it fun to go on-line and explore lots of things for short periods of time. Kevin, an Introvert, could lose himself for hours at a time researching some esoteric subject in great depth. Many evenings Kevin would retreat to the den after dinner, and Lorraine wouldn't see him again until he came to bed. They finally decided to make some evenings computer nights and others computer-free.

The term "shooting from the hip" (or, perhaps more accurately, "shooting from the lip") was undoubtedly coined to describe an Extravert. When you ask an Extravert a question, he or she will usually start talking. This is because Extraverts think out loud. But with Introverts, the opposite is more often true. When you ask an Introvert a question, he or she will usually pause before answering. Introverts need to think things through before they are ready to speak. Their thoughtful, deliberate reasoning process often leads Introverts to be misunderstood and even underestimated. Not only do Extraverts speak first and think second, but they also tend to act before they think. As a result, they are usually quick to become engaged in new and interesting situations, they like being out in front, and they are comfortable in the spotlight. Introverts tend to be more selective about the activities they choose to get involved in and often like to maintain a lower profile.

Kathy and David, the parents of a second-grader, sat at the PTA meeting listening to the new principal outline some major changes in school policy. While both were unhappy with what they heard, how they expressed their displeasure was very different. David, the Extravert, was immediately up on his feet asking questions, making suggestions, and imploring that the policy decision be revisited. Kathy, an Introvert, sat listening carefully to several parents express their various points of view. Although she didn't speak at the meeting, Kathy agreed to be part of a small group of parents who would meet and discuss the issue in greater depth and then make recommendations to the PTA at its next meeting.

These descriptions and anecdotes should have helped you decide whether you are more of an Extravert or an Introvert. The following summary lists key aspects to help you further. One side of this list should already feel more like you than the other, but if you're not quite sure yet, reviewing this list may convince you of one side over the other. Here are a few things to keep in mind: Not every aspect is going to ring equally true for every person. Remember that we're all unique individuals. If one side sounds about 80 percent like you, that is probably your true preference. Your job here is to try to identify who you really are, not how you'd like to be or think you ought to be. Your partner or someone who knows you very well may provide a helpful reality check.

So what do you think? Are you more of an Extravert or an Introvert? Indicate your preference and mark where you think you may fall on the line below. If you're doing this exercise with your partner, have him or her mark the line as well.

Extravert   **Introvert**

Summary of Key Aspects	
Extraverts	**Introverts**
Prefer being around people	Are comfortable spending time alone
Are interested in many things	Are selective and like to focus on one or a few things
Have lots of friends and associates	Have a few very close friends
Jump into things pretty quickly	Think about things before they act
Are usually pretty talkative	Are usually fairly reserved
Are more public and easier to get to know	Are more private and harder to read
Are enthusiastic and outgoing	Appear calm and self-contained
Represent about 55% of the American population	Represent about 45% of the American population

Great! Now we're ready to look at the second dimension and discover whether you are a Sensor or an Intuitive.

Sensor or Intuitive

Do You Tend to Focus on the Facts or on the Possibilities?

"Jeanie is so down-to-earth. Her common sense has saved us from more catastrophes than I care to remember."

"Tom's creativity is astounding. I honestly have no idea where all his marvelous ideas come from."

People perceive the world primarily in one of two very different ways — either as *Sensors* or as *Intuitives*. Sensors take in information through their five senses, paying close attention to what something looks, sounds, feels, tastes, or smells like. That's why they're usually such realistic and practical people. In contrast, Intuitives look at the world quite differently. Rather than focus on what is, they see what could be, questioning the reasons why it is as it is and how it's related to other things. Rather than trust and rely on their five senses, it's as if they use their sixth sense to understand and make sense of things.

Naturally, there are special gifts unique to both Sensors and Intuitives. For example, Sensors tend to notice, remember, and be accurate about details. Intuitives often quickly forget the specifics of a situation and, in fact, aren't likely to notice many details unless they are unusual or out of the ordinary. On the other hand, Intuitives tend to easily imagine the possibilities and see subtle patterns, connections, and implications that may elude the more literal and practical Sensors.

Searching for a new home for months, Phillip and Diane had been through every available house in their town at least once. One of the first homes they'd seen was a huge colonial that was in such poor shape it had been on the market for almost two years. Although Phillip liked the size, to him, a Sensor, the dirty shag wall-to-wall carpet, grimy thirty-year-old wallpaper, outdated kitchen and bathrooms, and ancient heating and electrical systems spelled disaster. He had quickly dismissed the house and was surprised when Diane suggested they give it a second look. Whereas Phillip had seen discouraging realities, Diane, an Intuitive, had seen exciting and creative possibilities. She admired the beautiful original woodwork and could easily imagine what the house would look like with repainted walls, refinished oak floors, and inexpensively remodeled kitchen and bathrooms. She envisioned their eight-year-old daughter one day coming down the grand staircase dressed for her high school prom. Once Phillip realized that by pay-

ing so little for the house they could afford to hire contractors to make it just as they wanted it to be — and end up actually paying less than they would for a much smaller, less well-built house — he was sold.

Another key distinction between Sensors and Intuitives has to do with the way they view time. Sensors are very present-oriented, so whatever they are engaged in at the moment commands their full attention. As a result, they tend not to worry too much about possibilities that may or may not occur in the future, especially those things over which they have little or no control. By contrast, Intuitives are generally more future-oriented, so they tend to dream about tomorrow and imagine how present events will affect the future.

Ron and Ellen faced a classic Type dilemma when they needed to choose a new child care center for their two young children. There were two options, either of which would have adequately met their immediate needs. Ellen, a Sensor, argued for the first center on the basis that it had a nicer facility, had a bigger and newer play area, and was ten minutes from their house. She was particularly impressed with the qualifications and demeanor of the young woman who would be the lead teacher for her child. Although Ron agreed that the center would be fine for now, he stressed that many things were likely to change during the next few years. They would probably be moving to another part of town, so if they started their older child in this school and then moved, by the time the younger one was ready to attend, the older one would have to start all over someplace else. And although Ron also liked the teacher, he pointed out the typically high turnover rate in this field and noted that she might not be working at the center for more than a year or so. True to their types, Ellen focused on the here and now, and Ron focused on the future.

Another distinction between Sensors and Intuitives is their attraction to new ideas. Most Intuitives love ideas. To them, ideas are interesting in their own right and really don't need to have any practical utility to be worthwhile. Similarly, theories — proven or not — are worth considering because they represent a new or different way of looking at things. Sensors also like ideas, but only if they can be demonstrated to have some practical usefulness and can be used to address an immediate need or solve a real problem. And they tend to have little patience for theories unless someone can provide hard proof that a theory is valid and makes sense in some concrete way. Sensors also tend to be hands-on people who trust direct experience. Intuitives often forsake the lessons of history and rely on their own gut instincts.

Gina and Brian discovered they shared a love of science when they met in their premed college chemistry class. Years later, when they both became physicians, they were drawn to different — some would say opposite — philosophies of medicine. Gina, a Sensor, embraced the more traditional scientific model. In her view, good medicine was based on good science: a treatment or drug required rigorous scrutiny and replicable, double-blind studies to be proved effective. Anything less was foolish at best and irresponsible at worst. Brian, an Intuitive, was fascinated by, and became an enthusiastic proponent of, alternative therapies. His instinct told him that natural healing treatments and remedies, which have been practiced by various cultures for centuries, must have some value. Even in the absence of hard proof, there was much anecdotal evidence to support their effectiveness. Although it took several years, Gina and Brian were able to convince each other that each approach has merit. As more and more studies were published in Western medical journals showing the efficacy of certain natural treatments, Gina became more open to them, and as her patients began reporting good results,

she became even more of a believer. For his part, Brian came to appreciate the need to integrate more traditional approaches into his heavily alternative-oriented practice.

Sensors like to learn a skill, master it, and then use it. This is called being efficient. To make sure they do it right, Sensors read and follow directions as written. Regardless of the particular task, Sensors are at their best when they can replicate something they've done before, and they tend to like systems that enable them to do just that. Intuitives also like learning new skills, but they usually have little patience for following detailed directions, preferring to figure it out for themselves. And once they have mastered a particular skill, they are often easily bored and seek another, more creative or interesting way of doing the task.

Jim and Anne learned early on in their relationship that some jobs were better done separately rather than together. Their first experience came when they decided to wallpaper the dining room. Jim, a Sensor, had papered many rooms before and knew exactly how to do it. Anne, an Intuitive, had no experience but was eager to try something new. At first Anne dutifully followed Jim's instructions for measuring, pasting, and hanging the rolls — a system that worked well but was much too slow and mechanical for her taste. After thirty minutes, she was thoroughly bored and started thinking up more interesting ways to accomplish the task. Each of her suggestions was met with resistance from Jim, who had learned from experience the way it should be done. (And he knew Anne well enough to realize that even if they did try it a new way, she would soon be bored again and would want to try yet another way.)

On page 17 you will find a summary to help you decide whether your preference is for Sensing or Intuition.

Summary of Key Aspects	
Sensors	**Intuitives**
Focus on the facts and specifics	Focus on the possibilities
Are more concrete; like ideas to be practical	Are more abstract; like ideas and theories for their own sake
Trust their direct experience	Trust their gut instincts
Like to operate in the here and now	Like to imagine and think about the future
Are realistic and practical	Are innovative and imaginative
Like established ways of doing things	Like to create new ways of doing things
Think and talk in a step-by-step manner	Frequently jump around from topic to topic
Represent about 65% of the American population	Represent about 35% of the American population

Well, were you able to decide whether you're more of a Sensor or more of an Intuitive? Indicate your preference and approximately where you may fall on the line below. And if you're doing this with your partner, have him or her do the same.

Sensor   **Intuitive**

Two down and two to go. Next, to help you determine whether you are a Thinker or a Feeler, we'll look at the two different ways people tend to make decisions.

Thinker or Feeler

Do You Base Most Decisions on Logic or on Your Personal Values?

"As all the kids Pam teaches will tell you, she's tough, but she's fair."

"Larry's got to be the most thoughtful person I know. He always seems to know just the right thing to say."

Thinking and Feeling are the two very different ways people come to conclusions. As with the first two Type dimensions, everyone has an in-born preference for one or the other, and although no one is exclusively a *Thinker* or a *Feeler*, you are primarily one or the other. Also like the first two dimensions, there are great differences between Thinkers and Feelers. One challenge of understanding this is that most people think of these two words as signifying something quite different from their meaning with regard to Personality Type. Both Thinking and Feeling are rational decision-making processes. It's not that Thinkers have no feelings or that Feelers are incapable of being logical. But when faced with a decision, Thinkers tend to step back, look at the situation objectively, and decide based on impersonal analysis. In contrast, Feelers tend to step forward and decide based on their personal values, how they feel about the issue, and how others are likely to feel about them.

The Gender Connection

There is an interesting but complicating factor in describing Thinking and Feeling: it is the only Type dimension in which there is a gender difference. Although the American population is about evenly divided between Thinkers and Feelers, it appears that about 65 percent of Thinkers are men and about 65 percent of Feelers are women, so natural differences between Thinkers and Feelers are exacerbated by the fact that they are often different genders. As we mentioned in Chapter 1, some people think that males and females are so different that they must originate from different planets. Certainly, some obvious and important differences do exist. However, after using Type for twenty years and collecting significant evidence for this book, we believe that most behavior typically characterized as either male or female is really more a result of whether people are Thinkers or Feelers. Two Thinkers of different genders will be more alike in many important ways than a Thinker and a Feeler of the same gender.

For example, the prevailing stereotype is that men are more logical, objective, fair-minded, and competitive than women, and then generally have a thicker skin. Women are seen as more emotional, sensitive, cooperative, and nurturing and as having a thinner skin. However, the first group of words, the "male" words, more accurately describe Thinkers, and the second group of words describe Feelers, regardless of gender. Certainly, we all know people who don't fit the stereotypes — men who are sensitive and gentle, and women who are assertive and tough. Frequently, such men are described as "feminine" and such women as "masculine." More than likely, those men are Feelers and the women Thinkers.

Assuming that the stereotypes were accurate, you would expect women to place a higher value on intimacy than men. Our survey confirmed that this is true, but only by a slight margin. However, when we compared Personality Type instead of gender, we found a much more dramatic disparity: about 60 percent of Thinkers (both men and women) considered intimacy the most important aspect of a relationship, but 75 percent of Feelers (both men and women) expressed that opinion. In fact, by a slight majority, more male Thinkers than female Thinkers considered intimacy most important.

Another issue we examined was "intellectual stimulation" as an aspect of a satisfying relationship. Again, according to the stereotypes, you might expect intellectual stimulation to be more important to the logical and objective man than to the emotional and subjective woman. But by a wide margin (58% to 45%), more women than men rated intellectual stimulation as most important. And what part did Thinking and Feeling play? Predictably, more Thinkers than Feelers considered intellectual stimulation most important, but by a very significant margin (63% to 41%), more female Thinkers than male Feelers rated it most important. So much for the stereotypes!

To many people this, in and of itself, is an important new insight with many implications. However, the plot thickens a bit when you realize that (in American culture, anyway) girls are still socialized to be Feelers. They're dressed in pastel colors; given dolls and stuffed animals to play with; taught to smile, be nice, and get along; and encouraged to follow traditionally female career paths. In contrast, boys are socialized to be Thinkers. They're dressed in dark colors, given toy weapons to play with, and taught to be assertive and competitive and to avoid showing emotion ("Don't be a crybaby"). They, too, are encouraged to follow traditionally male career paths but are given a wider range of options.

There are, of course, consequences to this socialization. Male Feelers and female Thinkers often feel that they are out of sync with the world — that they are somehow different from the way they should be. Both tend to learn adaptive behaviors to make themselves feel better and fit in. But interestingly, Thinking women may receive an unintended benefit. Many Thinking girls grow up to have much more access to their Feeling sides, which means greater balance and greater competence. Although Feeling boys are still subtly discouraged from being too sensitive or gentle, it is much easier to be a Feeling male today than it was two or three decades ago. Yet it remains a serious challenge for Thinking women to speak their minds, be logical and tough in their decision making, and reject some or all of the more romantic expectations of society.

The more people discover their true types, the more free they feel to be themselves. It may be helpful to keep this phenomenon in mind as you try to decide your and your partner's types — especially if you are either a female Thinker or a male Feeler.

While cultural and environmental influences certainly play a part in how people live in the world, we believe that Type is predetermined genetically. So even if a child is a Thinker being raised by two Feeling parents, the child won't be turned into a Feeler. In all likelihood, however, the child will learn to model some Feeling behavior or even come to mistrust his or her natural way of making decisions. As parents, it's important that we recognize, accept, and appreciate our children's natural preferences rather than try to make them fit an increasingly outdated and limited mold. (For more about identifying children's types and how to parent them in their natural style, see our book *Nurture by Nature*.)

Ultimately, Thinkers are concerned about making decisions that are logical and fair, whereas Feelers are ruled by their own personal values and how others will be affected by their decisions.

Tanya, a Feeler, bounded up the front steps clutching an adorable but obviously neglected young dog that had wandered into the yard while she was gardening. She felt an immediate rush of sympathy for this dog and suggested to her husband, Richard, a Thinker, that they keep it. She knew it would probably be a tough sell. Although Richard didn't have anything against having a pet per se, his lack of enthusiasm was apparent from the start: "First of all, before you get all excited about this mutt, it probably belongs to somebody. And even if it doesn't, or if we can't find its owner, we don't know anything about this animal — whether it's sick, had its shots, has behavior problems, that kind of stuff.

Besides, what are we gonna do with it when we go on vacation in two weeks? And who's going to take care of it all day while we're at work? I think we should take it to the pound so its owner can fetch it there."

Thinkers feel an obligation to adhere more firmly to the principles they consider important. To be fair, an important principle to most Thinkers, one must be consistent and hold everyone to the same standard. Feelers are more often driven by their personal values. Since they are naturally concerned and aware of how other people feel, they are more inclined to look for and accept extenuating circumstances.

Steve and Liza are the parents of 14-year-old Nate and 13-year-old Amanda. Although Steve, a Feeler, and Liza, a Thinker, agree on many things, a recurrent source of conflict is their different parenting styles. In Steve's opinion, Liza is often too tough on the kids. She takes every opportunity to teach and challenge them. Liza values independence, so she often insists that they try to do things on their own. She believes that, to be fair, the house rules that apply to one must also apply to the other. Steve tends to disagree. He is clearly the more nurturing parent and helps his kids express their feelings. But he often makes excuses for why rules are bent or special circumstances allowed ("She's so tired tonight, let's let her skip her chores"). For the most part, their different styles serve to balance each other. Liza presses for consistency when Steve would too frequently give in, and Steve softens Liza's tough stand when it's really important. As long as Steve and Liza work out their compromises in private, their children will benefit from the strength of both approaches.

Because Thinkers tend not to take things as personally as Feelers, they often enjoy the give-and-take of a good debate. Using logic to analyze an

Summary of Key Aspects	
Thinkers	**Feelers**
Are more logical and analytical	Are more sensitive and sympathetic
Believe it's better to be truthful than tactful	Believe it's better to be tactful than truthful
Are fair and consistent; apply one standard to all	Like harmony; look for extenuating circumstances
Are motivated by achievements	Are motivated by being appreciated
Like to compete and win	Like to cooperate and create consensus
Easily see flaws; can be critical and brusque	Like to please others; express appreciation easily
Are thick-skinned and not easily offended	Get their feelings hurt more easily
Comprise about 65% males	Comprise about 65% females

issue and make a point is usually fun for a Thinker, a form of intellectual stimulation. This is especially true of Thinkers who are also Intuitives. However, Feelers rarely experience a debate in the same way. When two people argue and the goal is for one to convince the other of his or her position, one person is going to win and the other is going to lose. To most Feelers, this feels like disharmony, which is distressing and something to be avoided.

Kayla, a Feeler, was understandably nervous about bringing her new boyfriend, Marty, a Thinker, home for dinner for the first time. She was particularly concerned because she knew her father and Marty held very different political opinions. It didn't take long before the conversation turned to the topic of gun control, and, predictably, Marty and Kayla's father had opposite yet equally strong views on the subject. For the next forty-five minutes, Kayla sat anxiously, shooting her mother worried glances, as the two men engaged in a heated "discussion."

Although this exchange made Kayla extremely uncomfortable, she didn't realize until after dinner had ended, how much these two Thinkers had really enjoyed the debate and the evening.

Because Feelers are so sensitive to others, they will often go out of their way to avoid hurting people's feelings. This means they are usually very tactful and diplomatic, but it also means they can be less than 100 percent honest. They know what other people want to hear, so they may tell little white lies or be insincere in their compliments. Thinkers, however, place a high value on honesty and directness. As a result, they are more likely to offend someone unintentionally. What they see as being frank and forthright, others may perceive as being blunt and insensitive. And because Feelers value harmony and avoid conflict, they are not likely to confront a Thinker who offends them. Ironically, the Thinker may never know the effect his or her actions or words had on the Feeler.

Stuart, a Thinker, was surprised to learn that his sister Bonnie, a Feeler, had silently harbored hurt feeling for something he did when they were teenagers. Growing up, Bonnie had secretly had a huge crush on Stuart's friend Tom. Not realizing this, Stuart had embarrassed her in front of Tom by teasing her about something she considered very personal. Because she was so embarrassed, she never let Stuart know how she felt, and because she never dealt with it, the wound had remained open all these years. When Bonnie finally confessed, Stuart was dumbfounded. He said, "Obviously, I'm sorry I screwed up, but I wish you had told me then, when I could have done something about it. And then it wouldn't been a thing between us all these years.

You should know you don't have to worry about my being able to take it!"

In general, Feelers are much more comfortable dealing with emotions — their own and other people's — than are Thinkers. Feelers strongly value expressing their emotions and typically have an easier time showing affection, whereas Thinkers tend to be less aware of their feelings and often less skillful in dealing with others'. Perhaps the biggest conflict between Thinkers and Feelers is over how frequently they express their appreciation for each other. Feelers tend to tell their partners how much they love them all the time, hoping they will hear it in return. This classic example of a Thinker talking to a Feeler illustrates the point: "I told you I loved you when I married you. If anything changes, I'll let you know." Granted, this is an exaggeration, but in reality many Thinkers (especially male Thinkers) often consider it unnecessary, and even find it uncomfortable, to repeat the words "I love you."

When Feelers are confused or upset, they want their partners to listen supportively and compassionately. Thinkers tend to want constructive advice about how to fix the problem. And it's a sad truth of human nature that we usually give what we wish to receive rather than what our partners really want. Thinkers and Feelers in relationships struggle with this difference more than any other Type preference, and it creates the greatest challenge to open communication and a close connection.

Could you determine whether you are a Thinker or a Feeler? Once again, indicate your preference and approximately where you may fall on the line below. If you're doing this with your partner, have him or her do the same.

Thinker   **Feeler**

Now we're ready to look at the last type dimension and to determine whether you are a Judger or a Perceiver.

Judger or Perceiver

Do You Prefer to Be More Planful or More Spontaneous?

"If it weren't for Josh, we'd never start anything."

"Yeah, but if it weren't for Linda, we'd never finish anything!"

One of the key aspects of Judging and Perceiving has to do with the issue of closure. *Judgers* like things to be settled and often feel a certain tension before a decision has been made. Since making decisions relieves the tension, they typically take in only as much information as is necessary to make a decision and then move on. By contrast, *Perceivers* feel tension when they are forced to make a decision. To alleviate that tension, they avoid making decisions and try to leave their options open as long as possible. As a result, they are often (but not always) prone to procrastinating.

As you are about to see, Judging and Perceiving have much to do with the way we like to run our everyday lives. As a result, many couples experience their greatest frustrations when they're different in this type dimension.

Before continuing with this discussion, it's important to point out that just because a person is a Judger doesn't mean he or she is necessarily judgmental, any more than a Perceiver is especially perceptive. This dimension simply describes which way of deciding is more natural and comfortable for a person. Another thing to keep in mind when trying to decide whether you are a Judger or a Perceiver is that there is a lot of pressure in American culture to be a Judger, since so much of people's identities are tied up in their work. And regardless of their natural preferences, nearly everyone has to act like a Judger at work: we have to be there at a certain time, follow rules and procedures, meet deadlines, and be productive. To more accurately identify your preference, think of how you are in your home life rather than how you may have to behave at work.

Neither Lynn nor Fred looked forward to spending yet another Saturday shopping for a new car. In the three weeks they had been looking, they'd nearly driven each other crazy. Before beginning their search, Lynn, a Judger, had sat down with Fred, a Perceiver, and made a list of the features they wanted. Then they prioritized the list. Although Fred went along with the initial exercise, he was uncomfortable being forced to decide on features before he had a chance to see and experience them. By week 3, Lynn felt that they'd seen plenty of cars that met their agreed-on criteria. Although Fred liked certain things about many cars, he couldn't find one that had all the features he was hoping for, and he felt sure that if they spent a little more time looking, they would find the perfect car.

Judgers are planners, and they like to be prepared. Because they expect a set plan to be followed, they often have a hard time shifting gears when the plan unexpectedly changes. By contrast, Perceivers often are hesitant to commit themselves for fear that if they do, they may miss some great opportunity that will come along later. Besides, Perceivers like to act spontaneously and usually adjust well to surprises. These opposite preferences result in some predictable behaviors: Judgers are usually very time conscious, while Perceivers are more casual about time. Judgers make "to do" lists, cross off items as they are accomplished, and then make new lists. Perceivers may make lists but seldom accomplish all the tasks or even look at their lists again. Judgers are more likely to write appointments in ink and rely on their calendars to organize each day, whereas Perceivers are more likely to write things in pencil and try to respond to opportunities as they arise.

Married for only a few months, Joanne, a Judger, had put considerable thought into the special dinner she planned to cook that night for Jerry, a Perceiver, and herself. Having shopped earlier in the day, she was just getting ready to start cooking when the phone rang. Obviously excited, Jerry announced that he had invited David, an out-of-town client whose account he was trying to win, to join him and Joanne for dinner. They were leaving at that moment to stop by the hotel and pick up David's wife and would arrive home in about an hour. Joanne's immediate reaction was consternation. Since she hadn't prepared for company, she'd have to rush to the store and buy more food, quickly straighten up the house, and make herself presentable — all in one hour! She felt that Jerry was being extremely inconsiderate to pull this on her at the last minute. Joanne's reaction took Jerry by surprise. He couldn't understand why she was making such a big deal out of it. After all, it didn't have to be some big fancy feast, just a simple meal so the four of them could get to know each other. And if she didn't have enough time to shop, no problem — he would pick up some takeout, or they could just go out for dinner.

One of the hallmarks of Judgers is their penchant for organization. The expression "a place for everything and everything in its place" was no doubt penned by a Judger (and probably as an admonition to some perennially messy Perceiver). It is distracting to Judgers to live amid clutter, because it calls out to be put away. Although "mess equals stress" to many Judgers, the same is not usually true for Perceivers. Some Perceivers also like a neat and clean home, but they tend to have a more casual attitude. They often leave projects unfinished, clothes scattered on the bed, and unwashed dishes in the sink. And when it comes to keeping track of things — especially paperwork — Judgers tend to be "filers," while Perceivers are often "pilers."

In our conversations with couples therapists familiar with Personality Type, many expressed the belief that couples who are different on the Judging/Perceiving (J/P) scale seem to have the most conflicts. So in our survey, we paid close attention to whether couples were alike or different on the J/P dimension, but we found that couples who were alike and those who were different reported almost identical levels of satisfaction with their relationships. Although a difference in this dimension alone doesn't appear to affect the number of conflicts a couple will experience, it clearly affects which issues are the sources of conflict. One hot-button issue is who does the household chores. In our survey, the percentages of those who said they frequently experienced conflict on this issue were as follows:

Perceivers with Judging partners	33%
Judgers with Judging partners	25%
Judgers with Perceiving partners	24%
Perceivers with Perceiving partners	16%

The results were both consistent with our experience and with Type theory. Not surprisingly, more than twice as many Perceivers with Judging partners (33%) found household chores a frequent source of conflicts than Perceivers with Perceiving partners (16%).

After ten years of marriage, Carol and Gordon had come to an understanding regarding the habits each had that annoyed the other. Early in their relationship, they had many arguments over what Carol lovingly, but sarcastically, referred to as the "pig factor." Whereas Carol, a Judger, wouldn't think of leaving the house in the morning without making the bed, Gordon, a Perceiver, considered a corner of their bedroom his personal dirty laundry hamper. Among Carol's complaints: Gordon practically never *completely* finished a project. He started dozens, came close to finishing several, but rarely finished any. For his part, Gordon hated the fact that Carol was such a neatnik, practically washing the glass before he finished drinking from it.

Finally, realizing that neither was going to change the other, they decided to make a pact. They agreed that Gordon would respect Carol's need for order and keep the common areas, such as the living room, bedroom, bathroom, dining room, and kitchen, free of clutter. But Carol had no jurisdiction over Gordon's private spaces, so he was free to keep his den, his workroom, and the attic any way he pleased. Although there are occasional slips on both sides, by and large the arrangement has worked very well.

A central issue for many couples who are different on this dimension has to do with the issue of control. In their drive for closure, Judgers often believe a decision has been made when in fact it was only discussed. On the other hand, Perceivers often consider actual decisions as tentative agreements. Many Judgers have a strong need to be in charge of whatever situation they are in, and many Perceivers have an equally strong need to be free to do as they like. So when Judgers try to exert control, Perceivers often feel reined in and constrained.

Again, the potency of "power and control" issues was borne out in our research. We wanted to know the percentages of people who said they frequently experienced conflict in this area, and here's what we found:

Perceivers with Judging partners:	46%
Judgers with Perceiving partners:	36%
Judgers with Judging partners:	29%
Perceivers with Perceiving partners:	22%

Although 22 percent of Perceivers with Perceiving partners frequently experienced conflict around issues of power and control, more than twice as many Perceivers with Judging partners frequently experienced it. Add to the mix the Judgers' strong work ethic (work before play) and the Perceivers' strong play ethic (play before work), and you have the potential for enduring conflict.

Summary of Key Aspects	
Judgers	**Perceivers**
Like to make decisions; decide quickly	Like to keep options open; may procrastinate
Prefer to make and keep plans	Prefer to be free to act spontaneously
Are usually well organized	Are often disorganized
Like to be in control	Like to adapt to changing situations
Have a strong work ethic: work, then play	Have a strong play ethic: play, then work
Are more formal and conventional	Are more casual and unconventional
Tend to see things as black or white	Tend to see things as shades of gray
Are often better at finishing projects	Are often better at starting projects

Mark and Sarah were excited about hosting their first party as a couple, but soon after they sat down to plan it, the trouble began. Mark, a Judger, suggested they start by making a list of the potential guests. As the list grew, it became clear to him that, because of the small size of their apartment, they had to limit the number to twenty, including themselves. Sarah, a Perceiver, countered that if they had to limit the number to twenty, she at least wanted to have some leeway so she could invite friends she might run into at the last minute. After discussing the guest list, they agreed they would ask people to bring an appetizer or a dessert. Sarah wanted people to bring whatever they felt like making, but Mark insisted that they confirm what each guest planned to bring. "Otherwise," he explained, "we could end up with five Mexican layer dips and six plates of brownies." Next he suggested that they decide whether to plan games to play and which CDs they wanted to buy or borrow. The more things

he was able to nail down, the more comfortable he felt. Sarah had a different reaction. To her, the party was becoming too formal, overproduced, and not at all the spontaneous, "whatever happens, happens" type of event she enjoyed most.

Generally, Judgers prefer to handle their responsibilities well ahead of any deadline (real or self-imposed). It's very hard for most Judgers to enjoy themselves when there are still chores to be done or projects to be finished. By contrast, most Perceivers feel that there's always more time, so why not relax or take advantage of some unexpected opportunity?

Another difference is that Judgers tend to want to follow the rules and to do what is expected of them, whereas most Perceivers don't mind bending or ignoring the rules occasionally. They are especially likely to disregard rules that they think are unnecessary or restrictive.

Also, Judgers tend to make a lot of declarative statements and voice their strong opinions freely. Perceivers are much more inquisitive, so they ask a lot of questions. This can be a source of irritation between couples when one is a Judger and the other a Perceiver. Perceivers often feel that Judgers shut down discussions too quickly, make blanket statements that are oversimplifications, and are sometimes judgmental. Judgers sometimes find the endless questions from their Perceiver partners to be redundant and annoying. Many Judgers complain to their Perceiver partners, "You ask my opinion, I give it, and then you have to ask six other people for their opinions. Then you come back with the very conclusion I gave you in the first place! Don't you value my opinion?" From the curious Perceivers' perspective, they are merely answering the call for more information. They certainly don't mean to insult their partners.

Finally, the casual and spontaneous style of most Perceivers can be a nuisance to the more planful and serious Judgers. Many is the time a Perceiver distracts a Judger with some question, comment, or urge to do something fun. Most Judgers find it hard to leave what they're doing, and this sort of disruption is really irritating, even if they are faced with a great opportunity. Perceivers are equally annoyed when their uptight Judging partners can't or won't be flexible. What a Perceiver views as a fun impulse is often seen as being irresponsible by a Judger.

The summary of important distinctions between Judgers and Perceivers on page 24 will help you decide your natural preference and the preference of your partner.

Are you a Judger or a Perceiver? Once again, indicate your preference and approximately where you think you fall on the line below. And if you're doing this with your partner, have him or her do the same.

Judger   **Perceiver**

Congratulations! You have probably figured out your (and your partner's) personality type. We say probably because there's a little more information you need to verify your type. Most people who go through the exercise you just completed will have correctly guessed at least two or perhaps three of their four type preferences. And that's a great start! But to be certain you have all four right, or to clarify if you feel a bit torn, read on.

Your Type: More Than Just Four Letters

By this point, you probably accept the notion that everyone has a preference for one side or the other of each Type dimension (while understanding that each person still has the ability to use both sides when they need to). But no one is just an Extravert or just a Sensor. It's the combination of the four dimensions of one's type, represented by the first letter of each dimension, that tells the most about the whole person. To understand the subtleties of your type, it's helpful to look at certain combinations of preferences. In this book, we'll look at the two combinations that we think provide the greatest insights: The first is the middle two letters of each person's type, known as the *type functions*. The second is a combination of preferences called temperament (see the next section). Some people who have studied and used Type for many years consider the function approach best because this combination identifies the way a person prefers to perceive (through either Sensing or Intuition) with the way he or she likes to judge (through either Thinking or Feeling) — in other words, what the person naturally notices about the world and how he or she usually makes decisions.

To help make this clear, we've created a chart (page 26) that identifies some of the common strengths and possible blind spots people of these type combinations share. But remember, this function pairing has to do with only the middle letters, not the first or last ones. The information concerning these other two dimensions also will help you start to confirm your true type. Ask yourself (and your partner) how well each combination may or may not fit you. For example, if you're sure you're a Sensor but can't decide whether you're a Thinker or a Feeler, read the brief description of SFs (Sensors who are also Feelers) and STs (Sensors who are also Thinkers) in the chart to see which sounds more like you. A little later on, you will have an opportunity to read more in-depth profiles of the type or types you think you may be, and that information will help you confirm your hunches.

Perhaps this chart confirmed your original estimate, or maybe it made you question whether

At a Glance: Strengths and Blind Spots Based on Function Combinations		
Function Combination	**Potential Strengths**	**Potential Blind Spots**
Sensing Thinkers (*STs*)	Logical problem solvers Careful and realistic with facts Calm and steady in a crisis	Can be critical and tough May resist new ideas May not be sensitive or aware of feelings
Sensing Feelers (*SFs*)	Nurturing and supportive Helpful in tangible and practical ways Lots of common sense	May avoid conflict Not assertive and direct Easily hurt or offended
Intuitive Feelers (*NFs*)	Encourage open communication and understanding Supportive of others' growth and development	May be unrealistic Take everything personally Often vague and emotional
Intuitive Thinkers (*NTs*)	Encourage partners' intellectual development Creative problem solvers Interesting and stimulating	Demand high standards Often perfectionists Impatient with feelings

you'd guessed the middle letters of your type correctly. Either way, it is a good way to start verifying your true type. The second step involves learning about another important combination of preferences we call *temperament*.

Temperament: Four Different Human Natures

Throughout history, philosophers, writers, psychologists, and other observers of humanity have noticed four different "natures" in which all people seem to fit. Almost twenty-five hundred years ago, the Greek philosopher and physician Hippocrates described four dispositions. In the Middle Ages, Paracelsus described four similar natures that were influenced by four kinds of spirits. The American Indian medicine wheel refers to four spirit keepers (like temperaments), and Hindu wisdom postulates four central desires.

Enter California psychologist David Keirsey.* He was impressed with the remarkable similarity of these theories held by such diverse cultures and across vast periods of history. When he learned about Personality Type through the work of Isabel Myers, he discovered that the four temperaments

---

* Over the years, Keirsey and other temperament researchers have added to our understanding of the critically important way temperament influences our drives, motivations, and values. See David Keirsey and Marilyn Bates, *Please Understand Me* (Del Mar, Calif.: Prometheus Nemesis, 1978) and information on the Temperament Research Institute in the resources section of Chapter 14.

he'd been studying and observing bore a striking resemblance to the four combinations of personality types described by Myers. All sixteen types fall into one of these four temperament groups:

NT   (Intuition, Thinking)
NF   (Intuition, Feeling)
SJ   (Sensing, Judging)
SP   (Sensing, Perceiving)

Many labels are used to identify the four temperaments, but we've chosen the following — some borrowed and some original — because they seem best to describe each temperament's central characteristics: Conceptualizers, Idealists, Traditionalists, and Experiencers.

The Plot Thickens

All Conceptualizers are Thinkers, and all Idealists are Feelers. But in the next two groups, Traditionalists and Experiencers, Thinking or Feeling is not the crucial element of the temperament. Instead, all members of both groups are Sensors, but then each group is broken down according to a preference for either Judging or Perceiving. Now, you may be bothered by this apparent inconsistency. Why are the two middle letters of the Conceptualizer and Idealist temperaments consistent with the middle two letters of the type dimensions, while the second and fourth letters of the dimensions (Sensing with Judging and Sensing with Perceiving) make up the temperaments of the Traditionalists and the Experiencers? The answer is quite simple. When David Keirsey compared the sixteen personality types with the four temperaments, he found that the middle letters of the dimensions combined to explain the basic natures of the first two temperaments (NF and NT), but the combinations of Sensing and Judging (SJ) and Sensing and Perceiving (SP) better explained the natures of the other two temperaments. Therefore, what appears to be an inconsistency is really just a matter of a symmetry.

Some Personality Type practitioners consider the function approach (the middle two letters of one's type) the best way to understand types, but others are strong supporters of the temperament approach, which taps the broader themes of core motivations and values. Knowing your temperament will not only help you verify your type but also will shed light on your essential nature.

Conceptualizers (NTs)

Conceptualizers are people who have a preference for both *Intuition* and *Thinking*. Intuition allows them to see possibilities, the big picture, and patterns and relationships and to have a future time orientation. Thinking provides them with objectivity and an ability to analyze things logically. The combination of Intuition and Thinking (NT) means that Conceptualizers are people who are independent, love to learn and excel, and strive to be competent in all they do.

Conceptualizers want to be respected for their considerable knowledge and appreciated for their good ideas, opinions, and achievements. They crave intellectual stimulation and like to discuss many interests, new ideas, and important issues of the day with their partners. They are ambitious people who set high standards, but they also tend to be somewhat impatient with others who aren't as quick to grasp concepts or who need a lot of reassurance or emotional support. Conceptualizers often have ingenious solutions to problems but have little interest in or energy for routine or repetitive tasks, such as household chores.

Idealists (NFs)

Idealists are people with a preference for *Intuition* and *Feeling*. Their Intuition gives them original insights and the ability to see meaning, patterns, and connections. Like Conceptualizers, Idealists also have a future orientation and a tendency to focus on the big picture. But since they also prefer

Feeling, they tend to make more personal and value-based decisions and are typically very concerned about how other people feel. This combination of Intuition and Feeling (NF) makes Idealists naturally empathetic, gentle, and insightful about other people.

Idealists tend to search for personal meaning and authenticity in all they do and strive to create and maintain harmony in their many treasured relationships. Communication, emotional intimacy, and deep understanding are essential to most Idealists. They want loving, supportive relationships and often seek spiritual connections. They tend to avoid conflict or dealing with unpleasant issues that really need to be discussed.

Traditionalists (SJs)

Traditionalists are people who have a preference for both *Sensing* and *Judging*. The Sensing part makes them factual, realistic, and practical, while the Judging part makes them decisive, organized, and serious and gives them a strong work ethic. The combination of Sensing and Judging (SJ) makes them extremely responsible, hardworking, and conservative people. In general, all Traditionalists are realistic, practical, and dependable. They play by the rules and are respectful of tradition and authority.

But since a person's preference for Thinking or Feeling is such an important part of who they are, it's most useful to talk about two different kinds of Traditionalists — Traditionalists who are Thinkers (STJs) and Traditionalists who are Feelers (SFJs).

Thinking Traditionalists (STJs). Thinking Traditionalists are dependable, reliable, responsible, and often predictable. Committed to their relationships and true to their word, they tend to see things in terms of black or white, good or bad. They find comfort in maintaining their routines and can be put off when these are disturbed. Always efficient and consistent, they can also resist

new ideas and be inflexible when necessary changes occur. They are often great in a crisis — keeping their heads and making logical and analytical decisions — but can be tough and even insensitive when dealing with people's needs or feelings.

Feeling Traditionalists (SFJs). Feeling Traditionalists are responsible, devoted, and conscientious people. They live by their strong values of service and commitment to their obligations. Warm and helpful, they love to take care of other people and get satisfaction from fulfilling their duty to their families, friends, and communities. Typically cooperative, thoughtful, and polite, they strive to keep their families safe and happy.

Although SFJs are usually expressive and nurturing, their sensitivity makes them prone to being easily offended or hurt. Because they so dislike conflict, they sometimes avoid speaking up for themselves or confronting issues head-on. They live to please others and want their partners to acknowledge and appreciate the many tangible things they do to keep their homes running smoothly and efficiently.

Experiencers (SPs)

The final temperament group, the *Experiencers,* includes people who have a preference for both *Sensing* and *Perceiving*. The Sensing part makes them factual, realistic, and practical, while the Perceiving part makes them curious, casual, and impulsive. The combination of Sensing and Perceiving (SP) tends to make them free spirits — people who love to live in the moment and be free to respond to whatever new opportunities arise. Again, the distinction between Thinking Experiencers (STPs) and Feeling Experiencers (SFPs) is an important one.

Thinking Experiencers (STPs). Thinking Experiencers are pragmatic, adaptive, and very easygoing. They seem to be able instantly to assess what must be done and get it done with a minimum of effort or fuss. They are straightforward, direct, and logical thinkers who need a lot of freedom and action to be happy. They are excellent short-term problem solvers, but they don't tend to have a lot of patience for complicated ideas, and they often resist any structure they deem unnecessary or restrictive.

STPs are typically fun loving and playful and try to find the fun, action, or variety in every moment. Their live-for-the-moment ethic sometimes results in their being insensitive to other people's feelings or schedules. Casual and easygoing about almost everything, STPs sometimes don't take the time to share their feelings or seek to understand their partners' needs.

Feeling Experiencers (SFPs) Feeling Experiencers are warm, gentle, and unassuming. They are typically playful and fun loving but also deeply caring and devoted to their families and friends. Loyal and generous, they have strong values that guide their behavior. Accepting and accommodating, SFPs love to help others, enjoy the beauty and joy of nature, and follow their impulses.

SFPs are down-to-earth and unpretentious people who are usually supportive and affectionate partners. But they tend to see only the good in people and sometimes have difficulty disagreeing with others or standing up for themselves, especially if it will disappoint someone they care about. They may hold on to hurt feelings or grudges if they feel judged or criticized. Although they are very responsive and relaxed, they can become disorganized and overwhelmed by big or complicated projects.

Moving On to the Four Profiles

Now that you've read the descriptions of all four temperaments (and the two versions of SJs and SPs), you ought to have a good idea which is the best fit for you and your partner. Between the type preferences (the letters), the function combination (the middle letters), and the temperaments, you are now ready to read the individual full type profiles to confirm your well-developed hypotheses of your and your partner's types. Those profiles follow in Chapter 3, but first a word of explanation and caution.

It's likely that you won't agree with every word of your type profile, because each of us is a unique individual. But about 80 percent of the description should ring true for you. If you are still somewhat ambivalent about your true type after reading the profile, you should probably read at least one other profile to be sure. To determine which one(s) you need to read, start with what you're most sure of. For example, if you're confident that you're an Extravert (E), Sensor (S), and Thinker (T) but aren't sure whether you're a Judger (J) or Perceiver (P), you should read the profiles for ESTJ and ESTP. If you're sure of only two preferences — say, Intuition and Feeling (NF) — you need to read all four profiles containing these letters: ENFJ, ENFP, INFJ, INFP.

Since you will probably be figuring out your type with your partner, ask him or her to read the profiles you think might be yours and see what he or she thinks. Don't worry if it takes a while; some people need more time to find their true type than others. Now, on to discover your type!

Chapter 3

A Perfect Fit: Verifying Your Type

To help you verify your type and further your understanding of how Type really works, we'd like to take a few minutes to familiarize you with what is called the *type hierarchy*. This is essentially a blueprint that identifies each type's natural strengths and weaknesses.* Although there are four letters in each type and all are important, the middle letters, known here as the *functions,* have special significance. While only two functions (Sensing or Intuition and Thinking or Feeling) show up in a person's type, all people can and do use the other two functions, but typically not with the same frequency or competency. For example, with ESTJs, Sensing and Thinking are their preferred functions. Certainly, there are times when ESTJs use their Intuition and Feeling, but because those are not their preferred functions, those letters don't appear in the ESTJ's type.

We rank all four middle letters (the two you see in your type and the two you don't) in terms of their importance. For each person, the two functions that are most important are naturally more developed, since the person uses them most often. And of those two, the predominant function is that type's greatest natural strength, so we call it the *Lead,* or the dominant,† function.

The Lead is the most developed and most trustworthy part of a type. When Thinking is Lead, as it is for ESTJs, ENTJs, INTPs, and ISTPs, that person tends to be superlogical and objective. When Feeling is Lead, as it is for ENFJs, ESFJs, INFPs, and ISFPs, that person tends to be very sensitive and empathetic. When Intuition is Lead, as it is in the case of INFJs, INTJs, ENFPs, and ENTPs, that person is often extremely creative and imaginative. And when Sensing is Lead, as it is for ISTJs, ISFJs, ESTPs, and ESFPs, the person is ultrarealistic and detail-oriented.

The Second part of each type, also called the auxiliary, is the second-greatest strength and helps out the Lead by providing balance — either promoting sound decision making or encouraging accurate information gathering. The Third function, or tertiary, does not start to develop in most people until around midlife. Until then, it is often somewhat of a liability, but at midlife it can become an important strength. And finally there is the Least, also known as the inferior. This is the least developed, least trustworthy part of a person's type. It is always the opposite of the Lead. For example, in an ENFP, the Lead is Intuition and the Least is Sensing. ENFPs naturally spend more of their conscious energy using and developing

---

*For a more thorough explanation and discussion of this aspect of Type theory, see Paul T. Tieger and Barbara Barron-Tieger, *Do What You Are,* 2nd ed. (Boston: Little, Brown, 1995).

†People familiar with Type are used to referring to the functions in the hierarchy as dominant, auxiliary, tertiary, and inferior, as introduced by C. G. Jung in *Psychological Types* and elaborated by Isabel Briggs Myers and Mary H. McCaulley in *Manual: A Guide to the Development and Use of the Myers-Briggs Type Indicator* (Palo Alto, Calif.: Consulting Psychologists Press, 1985).

		The Most- to Least-Favored Functions			
		Organized by Temperament Groups			
	Type	**LEAD #1**	**Second #2**	**Third #3**	**LEAST #4**
SJs	ESTJ	Thinking	Sensing	Intuition	Feeling
	ISTJ	Sensing	Thinking	Feeling	Intuition
	ESFJ	Feeling	Sensing	Intuition	Thinking
	ISFJ	Sensing	Feeling	Thinking	Intuition
SPs	ESTP	Sensing	Thinking	Feeling	Intuition
	ISTP	Thinking	Sensing	Intuition	Feeling
	ESFP	Sensing	Feeling	Thinking	Intuition
	ISFP	Feeling	Sensing	Intuition	Thinking
NTs	ENTJ	Thinking	Intuition	Sensing	Feeling
	INTJ	Intuition	Thinking	Feeling	Sensing
	ENTP	Intuition	Thinking	Feeling	Sensing
	INTP	Thinking	Intuition	Sensing	Feeling
NFs	ENFJ	Feeling	Intuition	Sensing	Thinking
	INFJ	Intuition	Feeling	Thinking	Sensing
	ENFP	Intuition	Feeling	Thinking	Sensing
	INFP	Feeling	Intuition	Sensing	Thinking

KEY

TEMPERAMENT GROUPS
(A discussion of temperament is presented on page 26.)

Thinking: making logical, objective decisions

Feeling: understanding and relating to people

Sensing: being in the moment; seeing things realistically

Intuition: seeing possibilities and implications

SJs: Sensing Judgers or "Traditionalists"

SPs: Sensing Perceivers or "Experiencers"

NTs: Intuitive Thinkers or "Conceptualizers"

NFs: Intuitive Feelers or "Idealists"

their Intuition, so they don't use or pay much attention to their Sensing. Think of the Least as your Achilles' heel — that part which, when used, causes the most frustration and stress. Most people never fully develop their Least, and those who do usually don't start to develop it until late in their fifties.

The following metaphor is often used to help

31

people appreciate the importance of the Type hierarchy.* Picture a family of four taking a car trip. In the front seat are two adults. The Lead is driving, and the Second is sitting next to the Lead, navigating. In the backseat are two children, the Third (a 10-year-old) and the Least (a toddler). Clearly, you want the Lead to be driving (to be in charge) and the Second to be helping out. But you still have to pay attention to the "kids" in the backseat — feed them and maybe settle their fights. When we're operating at our best, we're using our Lead and Second functions. But when we're under stress, our Third and Least functions often kick in — as if the "kids" in the backseat climbed into the front seat and took control of the car. Not a good situation!

So why is it important to know your and your partner's type hierarchies? Knowing your partner's Lead enables you to appreciate what he or she does best, and knowing your partner's Least helps you understand why he or she might have trouble or become stressed doing other things. You'll know when and how to cut your partner some slack, and make him or her feel better about himself or herself, and strengthen your relationship in the process. How do you know the hierarchy for your and your partner's types? The chart on page 31 ranks the most- to least-favorite functions. As you review your Verifying Profiles in this chapter, you may find it helpful to review and discuss the Lead and Least functions for each of you. **At the end of this chapter (see page 57) is an exercise that you and your partner can do to gain new insights into each other.**

---

*We first learned this metaphor from Mary McCaulley in 1980 and gratefully acknowledge her insight. An excellent book that deals with the effects of Type dynamics, and especially the role of the Least function, is Naomi L. Quenk, *Beside Ourselves: Our Hidden Personality in Everyday Life* (Palo Alto, Calif.: Consulting Psychologists Press, 1993).

ESTJ: Extravert, Sensing, Thinking, Judging

Estimated to be between 12 and 15 percent of the American population*

Logical and analytical, ESTJs are natural leaders and quick decision makers. Their serious, no-nonsense approach to life inspires confidence and trust in the people with whom they live and work. Respected for their objectivity and fairness, ESTJs live by a code of behavior that includes working hard and always acting ethically. Consistent and impartial, they are seldom accused of playing favorites or acting capriciously. People of their word, ESTJs are thoroughly committed to their families and the organizations to which they belong, and they are willing to make tough decisions for the good of their families. ESTJs are consummate project managers, and regardless of the nature of the task to be accomplished or whether they do it as part of their job or for fun, these Lead Thinkers are talented at realistically sizing up a situation, setting goals, determining available resources, and organizing and supervising those around them to make sure the job gets done correctly and in the most efficient manner.

Because ESTJs' Least function is Feeling, they may inadvertently act insensitively at times. Because they are not focused on the emotional side of life, they sometimes don't stop to consider or find out how people feel about an issue before making a decision. They are often very outgoing and friendly, but ESTJs are also highly competitive and have a strong need to be in control. Typically

---

*For each type and temperament, we provide an estimate of the percentage of the American population with this type. These percentages were developed by Dr. Charles K. Martin of the Center for Applications of Psychological Type (CAPT), Gainesville, Florida.

strong-willed and very verbal, they frequently intimidate less assertive people.

Most comfortable in structured, organized environments, ESTJs like to establish strict ground rules and want all expectations to be clear and consistent. They are loyal team players who are more interested in maintaining than challenging the status quo. They respect authority and expect others to do the same. Practical and realistic, ESTJs consider it important to be accurate with facts and pay close attention to details. They are particularly good at using resources wisely, sticking to their budgets, and making informed, careful investments.

Very traditional and conservative, ESTJs prefer to stay with familiar and tested ways of doing things, so they rarely have much enthusiasm for experimental approaches. Since they don't adapt easily to change, they usually challenge the need for it, sometimes vehemently. Forceful and effective opponents, they are rarely convinced by anything other than hard facts and sound reasoning.

Because ESTJs focus primarily on the present, they may fail to appreciate how current actions may affect the future, and they are not particularly good at anticipating future needs or forecasting future trends. They tend to make quick decisions and sometimes rush to judgment before they have carefully and thoroughly considered all their options. Once they've made up their minds, they are difficult to convince otherwise. When ESTJs slow down and take the extra time to listen patiently to the suggestions of others, they often find the added perspective helps them make better choices for themselves and others.

Looking down the Road:
How ESTJs Change over Time

Up until about the age of 30, ESTJs are run by their Lead Thinking, supported by their Sensing. But as ESTJs reach their thirties and forties, they begin to trust the impressions that come from their Intuition. They may be less inclined to take things at face value, begin to wonder why things are as they are,

and start to take a longer view of issues. They also begin to examine and understand the patterns in their own lives. In their late forties and fifties, ESTJs begin to use their Least function, Feeling. This is their greatest weakness and where they are most vulnerable. By consciously working at it, they may be more motivated to understand their feelings and to forge stronger emotional connections with the important people in their lives. Although they're still best when using their superior Thinking, they often start to develop a gentler, more patient side.

ESTJs as Partners

Because ESTJs are great talkers with strong opinions, their partners seldom have to guess where they stand on any given issue. Dependable, responsible, and rock solid, they work hard to make their homes safe and secure havens and find comfort in family routines and traditions. They also have great energy and enthusiasm for family adventures and projects. They run an organized and orderly home and may exert considerable control over their partners. They can be rather inflexible about their schedules and unwilling to accept other points of view. But their impatience when dealing with their partners' feelings can be the greatest impediment to open communication, sharing, and intimacy.

ESTJs want to be appreciated for being trustworthy, efficient, and productive. They feel most appreciated when their partners notice and acknowledge all the tangible ways they keep their homes and lives running smoothly.

Relationship Satisfiers

Trust, good communication, and mutual respect are aspects of relationships that all types value highly. Here are the aspects that ESTJs report are most and least important to them.

Most Important Aspects	Least Important Aspects
Fidelity	Shared religious beliefs
Mutual commitment	Shared interests

Mutual support
Companionship
Shared values
Security
Having fun together

Spiritual connection
Similar parenting styles
Intellectual stimulation

ISTJ: Introvert, Sensing, Thinking, Judging

Estimated to be between 7 and 10 percent of the American population

ISTJs are responsible, reliable, hardworking people whose word is their bond. Literal, precise, and no-nonsense, they say what they mean and mean what they say. As Lead Sensors, ISTJs are especially attuned to the specific details of life. They are careful and accurate about facts and go about all they do in a thoughtful and meticulous fashion. Serious, conscientious people, ISTJs have a strong work ethic and always choose to get their tasks done before they take time to relax. ISTJs also have excellent memories for details and can usually recall with impressive clarity events that occurred in the past. Quiet and independent, ISTJs are often happiest when they have plenty of time alone without interruption. They know what they have to do and how to do it and seldom need or want any supervision or input from others. Even when they are relaxing, ISTJs are productive and often enjoy using their hands to do crafts such as woodworking, restoring antique autos, cooking, and needlepoint. Many also enjoy reading and being a part of nature by hiking, fishing, or camping.

ISTJs are happiest living with a familiar routine and may become uncomfortable or anxious when faced with new challenges. Because their Least function is Intuition, they are naturally mistrustful of unproven ways of doing things. Although they pride themselves on their efficiency, they tend to resist any change if they don't immediately see its practical benefits. And because ISTJs focus so completely on present realities rather than on future implications, their skepticism can sometimes impede real and needed progress.

Logical and objective, ISTJs are impersonal decision makers who carefully weigh the pros and cons and then decide what makes the most sense. They are not likely to be significantly influenced by how people will feel about their decisions, so they may at times seem aloof or uncaring. Although they like to be of service to their families and friends, they can also remain utterly objective and make the tough calls when necessary. ISTJs are eminently fair people, but appeals based solely on emotion may fall on deaf (or at least hard-of-hearing) ears.

Usually possessing great powers of concentration, ISTJs are not easily distracted from the task at hand, which they always approach in a systematic fashion. Their single-minded determination is one of their greatest assets, but it can also make them stubborn or inflexible when they are unexpectedly forced to change their plans or act spontaneously. Likewise, they are very conservative by nature and often reluctant to take even reasonable risks.

Looking down the Road: How ISTJs Change over Time

Up until about the age of 30, ISTJs are run by their Lead Sensing, supported by their Thinking. But as ISTJs reach their thirties and forties, they begin to get more in touch with their Feeling side, especially as it pertains to them but also in relation to how their decisions affect others. They tend to become more thoughtful and willing to examine their values and feelings about important issues. Sometimes they feel a desire to strengthen family relationships and make an effort to be more nurturing and supportive. In their late forties and fifties, ISTJs may begin to use their Least function, Intuition. Typically, this is their greatest weakness and where they are most vulnerable. ISTJs who consciously work at it may become more aware of subtleties, develop an interest in more theoretical subjects, or look for patterns and meaning in their own lives.

ISTJs as Partners

ISTJs are hardworking, dependable, and predictable, and they usually like things to be done in very specific ways — their ways. Traditional and conforming, they work hard to achieve the goals they set with their partners. However, because they are not usually comfortable sharing their feelings, they tend not to be as emotionally available as their partners might like. In their eagerness to be organized and productive, they can also be unwilling to examine and embrace alternative points of view.

ISTJs like to be appreciated for their practical contributions, their common sense, and the effort they put into maintaining their homes and keeping their families' lives on track. They feel most appreciated when their actions are noticed and acknowledged both informally, with a well-deserved thank you, and formally, with cards and gifts on appropriate holidays and anniversaries.

Relationship Satisfiers

Trust, good communication, and mutual respect are aspects of relationships that all types value highly. But here are the aspects that ISTJs report are most and least important to them.

Most Important Aspects	Least Important Aspects
Fidelity	Shared religious beliefs
Mutual support	Spiritual connection
Being listened to	Shared interests
Mutual commitment	Similar parenting styles
Shared values	Sexual compatibility
Companionship	
Security	

ESFJ: Extravert, Sensing, Feeling, Judging

Estimated to be between 11 and 14 percent of the American population

The saying "A friend in need is a friend indeed" could well have been inspired by an ESFJ, because ESFJs are often the first ones to volunteer their assistance. Friendly, outgoing, and sympathetic, these Lead Feelers are very sensitive and have a strong desire to please and an equally strong need to be liked and appreciated. ESFJs are traditional people who value their families' and friends' happiness and security above all else. Generous and loyal, they give freely of themselves, often committing large amounts of time and energy to local charitable, community, or religious organizations that reflect their values. Conscientious and hardworking, ESFJs usually have a well-defined code of behavior based on their strong value systems, which they often feel compelled to try to instill in others.

ESFJs tend to personalize everything and can have such a thin skin that their feelings get hurt easily and often. ESFJs who feel they have been wronged may take drastic actions, such as ending the relationship with the person who offended them — even if it has been a long-standing one. More often, ESFJs get into trouble by becoming overly involved and assuming too much responsibility for the feelings of others. In their effort to be good friends, they run the risk of actually making themselves sick by overburdening themselves with others' problems. Since ESFJs' Least function is Thinking, they are often unable to evaluate situations fairly and objectively. They rarely value an argument's logic and may consider objectivity to be an unappealing quality.

ESFJs are essentially down-to-earth, realistic, and practical. To many, life is serious business, so they attend to responsibilities before relaxation and fun. ESFJs often have a hard time taking a joke or being teased, especially in relation to something about which they care deeply. Many especially enjoy their physical possessions, are conscientious about maintaining their things, and are very careful to keep them neat and tidy. In their spare time, many ESFJs like to engage in physical activities — walking, biking, or playing sports. They also often enjoy working with their hands and doing crafts.

Typically well organized and productive, ESFJs are most comfortable following a familiar routine, so they may have difficulty shifting gears or doing things in different ways. This applies equally to both little things, such as taking an unfamiliar road on a car trip, and big things, such as changing jobs or moving to a new town. ESFJs also tend to see the world in absolute terms; things are either good or bad, right or wrong. ESFJs who are willing to accept extenuating circumstances manage to achieve a balance that keeps them from becoming too judgmental.

Looking down the Road: How ESFJs Change over Time

Up until about the age of 30, ESFJs are run by their Lead Feeling, supported by their Sensing. But as ESFJs reach their thirties and forties, they often gain better access to their Intuition, helping them become more open to and interested in new ideas and possibilities. They may become more adventurous in general. In their late forties and fifties, ESFJs may begin to use their Least function, Thinking. Typically, this is their greatest weakness and where they are most vulnerable. By consciously working at it, they may become more objective, especially about themselves. They may not take things as personally and may be better able to ignore some of the pressure to please others and fit in.

ESFJs as Partners

ESFJs are very supportive partners who work hard to nurture and protect their relationships. They go to great lengths to maintain harmony, are typically affectionate and expressive, and are generally motivated to resolve conflicts. ESFJs usually have very clear ideas about what's important to them and are most comfortable when their partners subscribe to the same values. They want their partners to be loving, committed, and willing to support their frequently overwhelming feelings and reactions.

ESFJs want most to be appreciated for their helpfulness, generosity, and hard work. They feel appreciated when their partners are kind, considerate, and helpful in return and when they notice and compliment them on their specific efforts, such as how nice the house looks or what a good purchase they made.

Relationship Satisfiers

Trust, good communication, and mutual respect are aspects of relationships that all types value highly. But here are the aspects that ESFJs report are most and least important to them.

Most Important Aspects	Least Important Aspects
Mutual commitment	Shared interests
Fidelity	Similar parenting styles
Being listened to	Spiritual connection
Mutual support	Shared religious beliefs
Shared values	Sexual compatibility
Companionship	Intellectual stimulation
Having fun together	

ISFJ: Introvert, Sensing, Feeling, Judging

Estimated to be between 7 and 10 percent of the American population

ISFJs have a strong need to belong, and the friends they choose to be with are lucky to attract these thoughtful, conscientious, and devoted people. As Lead Sensors, ISFJs focus all their energy on the problem or issue before them at the moment. They are painstakingly accurate with facts, attentive to details, and methodical in applying both. ISFJs like gathering practical data for some useful purpose and enjoy carefully documenting the results. In general, they have excellent memories and are especially good at remembering dates and events that pertain to the people they love. Consequently, they often fill the role of unofficial family or office historian.

Generally quiet and reserved, ISFJs are loyal and devoted family members and friends who take their responsibilities toward others very seriously. Sensitive and sympathetic, they are good listeners and eager to help people in practical ways, which they do best by drawing on their own personal experiences. Because ISFJs don't like confrontation and are uncomfortable when people are unhappy with them or those close to them, they usually try hard to accommodate others. They are very loving but also firm disciplinarians, and they go to great lengths to maintain harmony.

Because ISFJs' Least function is Intuition, they may have difficulty imagining possibilities or scenarios that don't exist. In problem solving, they are much more comfortable applying knowledge gained through direct experience than trying a new approach. ISFJs are very rooted in the present. They trust the lessons of the past, so when they look to the unknown future, they often feel apprehension or even dread. ISFJs may have trou-ble appreciating the interconnectedness of things, since they naturally pay more attention to specifics than to the big picture.

For relaxation, ISFJs often prefer activities that engage their senses, such as cooking, gardening, painting, or making things with their hands. While they enjoy the company of close friends, they are also comfortable spending time alone. ISFJs tend to dislike surprises and are most at ease when they are in familiar surroundings, enjoying activities they planned. They like to get their work done before relaxing and are most comfortable when they can stick to a predictable routine. When it comes to holidays and other special events, ISFJs love to organize them well in advance and pay careful attention to all the details. Then they love to participate with great gusto.

Looking down the Road: How ISFJs Change over Time

Up until about the age of 30, ISFJs are run by their Lead Sensing, supported by their Feeling. But as ISFJs reach their thirties and forties, they begin to get more in touch with their Thinking side, so they may develop more objectivity, especially as it pertains to them, people close to them, and their projects. Naturally sensitive and somewhat easily offended, they may begin to take fewer comments or actions personally. In their late forties and fifties, ISFJs may begin to use their Least function, Intuition. Typically, this is their greatest weakness and where they are most vulnerable. By consciously working at it, ISFJs may become more interested in and better able to see the patterns, connections, and complexities of issues.

ISFJs as Partners

Because ISFJs are so accommodating, generous, and gentle, occasionally they can be taken for granted. They do so much for their families and are so tireless in their efforts to maintain a happy home that they can run the risk of becoming exhausted or always putting their loved ones' needs ahead of their own. ISFJs frequently have trouble saying no and holding firm in the face of opposition or unhappiness.

Although they are warm and helpful partners, ISFJs are also quite private. They are most comfortable sharing their deepest feelings when they have plenty of support, encouragement, and time to prepare their thoughts ahead of time. They are especially sensitive to criticism and tend to withdraw rather than fight back.

ISFJs want to be appreciated for their loyalty and wholehearted nurturing. They feel most appreciated and supported when their values are respected and they are treated with consideration, thoughtfulness, and kindness.

Relationship Satisfiers

Trust, good communication, and mutual respect are aspects of relationships that all types value highly. But here are the aspects that ISFJs report are most and least important to them.

Most Important Aspects	Least Important Aspects
Mutual commitment	Shared religious beliefs
Fidelity	Shared interests
Mutual support	Intellectual stimulation
Being listened to	Spiritual connection
Shared values	Similar parenting styles
Companionship	
Intimacy	

ESTP: Extravert, Sensing, Thinking, Perceiving

Estimated to be between 6 and 8 percent of the American population

For ESTPs, life is one fun-packed adventure after another. Energetic, curious, and playful, these Lead Sensors are active participants in every aspect of their physical lives. Responsive and adaptable, ESTPs act first, rarely thinking about the possible consequences — especially the long-term implications of how their actions may affect others. Naturally impulsive, they immediately seize any exciting opportunity that presents itself. Super-observant and realistic, ESTPs notice everything as they constantly scan the environment and people around them. They learn best when they are physically engaged in the process, talking through what they are doing and commenting on the many details they see, feel, and hear.

Irrepressibly enthusiastic, ESTPs are great lovers of any kind of surprise. They willingly join in whatever is going on around them — as long as it doesn't get too complicated or emotionally intense. Because their Least function is Intuition, when conversations get too serious or theoretical, or when plans are tightly structured, they grow restless. To try to lighten up the mood, they may act irreverently or treat issues with too much superficiality. Most ESTPs love the outdoors, many are avid sports fans, and they are usually the first ones to try physical feats of daring or risk. Of all of the sixteen types, ESTPs are perhaps the most naturally athletic and coordinated, learning physical skills and tricks almost effortlessly. They typically have a host of interests and hobbies that they are ready to plunge into at a moment's notice. This is good because they often have trouble sitting still or remaining inactive for any period of time.

Happiest when they are immersed in the action of the moment, ESTPs may be unusually good at immediate problem solving, bringing logic and objectivity to their analyses. They are often quite pragmatic and are poised to change direction quickly if they think there is a better or more expedient approach.

Friendly, talkative, and outgoing, ESTPs love to laugh and joke and are naturally flirtatious. Easygoing and casual, ESTPs tend to know a lot of people and typically are the life of the party. In interpersonal relationships, they can sometimes give the erroneous impression that they are more emotionally invested than they really are. And they may have to work hard to overcome their tendency to move on to greener pastures once things become too familiar or predictable. ESTPs are often so eager for the next experience that they neglect to follow through on the projects they've already started and can wind up disappointing people who are counting on them. When they put their minds to something, however, they are usually able to pull it off with skill and style — even if it is at the last minute.

Looking down the Road: How ESTPs Change over Time

Up until about the age of 30, ESTPs are run by their Lead Sensing, supported by their Thinking. But as ESTPs reach their thirties and forties, they begin to become more aware of their Feeling side. Typically, they become more concerned about how their actions will affect others and become more sensitive to others' needs. This is a time when they also may begin to reexamine some of their own values and priorities, especially as these things relate to their partners or families. Many ESTPs grow considerably more conservative in their attitudes, and their political leanings usually emphasize self-responsibility. Most maintain a "forever young" attitude about themselves and their choices and lifestyles. In their late forties and fifties, ESTPs may begin to use their Least function, Intuition. Typically, this is their greatest weakness and the area where they are most vulnerable. By consciously working at it, they may begin to question the reasons things are as they are, start to see connections and relationships they haven't noticed previously, and develop new interests.

ESTPs as Partners

ESTPs are usually exciting partners who are willing to try anything once. They are often much more responsive to their mates' physical needs than their emotional ones. Because they don't usually have the patience for or see the need for long heart-to-heart talks, they tend to keep communication at a somewhat superficial level, which can prevent them from discovering the real sources of a conflict or making their partners feel that they truly understand them.

ESTPs want to be appreciated for the fun-loving, responsive problem solvers they are. They feel most appreciated when their partners acknowledge and respect their need for freedom and encourage them to be spontaneous and to enjoy fully life's many pleasures.

Relationship Satisfiers

Trust, good communication, and mutual respect are aspects of relationships that all types value highly. But here are the aspects that ESTPs report are most and least important to them.

Most Important Aspects	Least Important Aspects
Having fun together	Spending time together
Mutual commitment	Shared religious beliefs
Fidelity	Spiritual connection
Intimacy	Intellectual stimulation
Being listened to	Financial security
Mutual support	Similar parenting styles
Sexual compatibility	

ISTP: Introvert, Sensing, Thinking, Perceiving

Estimated to be between 4 and 7 percent of the American population

Independent, self-contained, and sometimes aloof, ISTPs are the ultimate pragmatists. They are supremely objective about all things, even-tempered, and unflappable. In times of crisis or high anxiety, they are able to focus on the demands of the moment and apply their Lead Thinking to solve problems with skill and dispatch. They are at their best when responding to challenges that arise spontaneously, preferring to skip a lot of discussion and get busy. Once they put out the fire, however, they may have limited energy for follow-through and little need to reap praise.

Resourceful and adaptable, ISTPs seem to possess an innate understanding of how things work, whether it be toasters or computers. They are especially effective when they combine their keen powers of observation with their talent for logical analysis to solve problems. But since people rarely act with the same predictability that things do, ISTPs are generally less skilled and effective at dealing with interpersonal conflicts. The inherent inconsistency and irrationality of human beings is so confusing and frustrating to ISTPs that they will frequently walk away from personal conflicts rather than be left feeling helpless and inept. Very private about personal matters, they rarely share their innermost feelings or fears, even with people they know well and trust.

Realistic and extremely practical, ISTPs are people of action and self-direction. They like to work alone or alongside other skilled and capable people, figuring things out without outside help or input. They seek fun and action in both their work and their personal lives and feel most alive when they are doing something independent, risky, or even dangerous. So strong is the allure of the adrenaline rush that they often seek occupations that place them in harm's way. And even those ISTPs whose jobs involve great risk, such as firefighters, police officers, and pilots, often seek additional thrills in their recreational activities by racing cars, riding motorcycles, or skiing expert slopes.

Direct, honest, and down-to-earth, ISTPs tend to be literal and explicit, and they find pretentious people or those with hidden agendas annoying. ISTPs also are cool and unemotional, and so easygoing that they rarely try to control others. Above all, ISTPs want to be left alone to live their lives as they see fit, and they have little interest in or energy for trying to change others. The people in their lives may find it difficult to develop and maintain a deep level of intimacy with ISTPs, because they are generally uncomfortable or even unwilling to let others in. Once they master the skills required to foster a healthy relationship, they are usually more invested in making it work.

Looking down the Road:
How ISTPs Change over Time

Up until about the age of 30, ISTPs are run by their Lead Thinking, supported by their Sensing. But as ISTPs reach their thirties and forties, they begin to get more in touch with their Intuitive sides. As a result, they may become interested in understanding how things are related to each other and the deeper meaning of experiences. In their late forties and fifties, they may begin to use their Least function, Feeling. Typically, this is their greatest weakness and where they are most vulnerable. By consciously working at it, ISTPs may develop a greater sensitivity toward people and a new appreciation for the important people in their lives. They also may find themselves examining their core values and reordering their personal priorities.

ISTPs as Partners

ISTPs are calm, handy partners to have around, especially when something goes wrong or needs fixing. They can be very responsive to their mates' immediate and obvious needs but are usually much less comfortable dealing with their emotional ones. They are fun, playful, and adventurous, and they may be patient teachers and coaches of physical experiences. But they are essentially loners and may resist exposing themselves by sharing their private thoughts.

ISTPs want to be appreciated for their often superb ability to size up a problem and solve it. They feel most appreciated when they are left to do their own thing, free to respond spontaneously to life's many adventures.

Relationship Satisfiers

Trust, good communication, and mutual respect are aspects of relationships that all types value highly. But here are the aspects that ISTPs report are most and least important to them.

Most Important Aspects	Least Important Aspects
Having fun together	Shared religious beliefs
Mutual commitment	Financial security
Fidelity	Shared interests
Companionship	Spiritual connection
Humor	Intellectual stimulation
Sexual compatibility	Security
Mutual support	

ESFP: Extravert, Sensing, Feeling, Perceiving

Estimated to be between 8 and 10 percent of the American population

ESFPs are natural performers who delight in surprising and entertaining people. Warm, outgoing, and friendly, they are usually vivacious and talkative. They know a lot of people, and as long as their acquaintances are nice and not too pretentious, ESFPs usually like everyone equally well. Animated and fun loving, ESFPs love to be at the center of the action, surrounded by other easygoing, optimistic, and considerate people, laughing, talking, or sharing a common interest or activity.

Enthusiastic, social, and spontaneous, ESFPs can find it hard to settle down and finish tasks because they are so easily distracted by other people and by spontaneous opportunities to relax or play.

Also very practical people, these Lead Sensors are typically focused on whatever they are doing at the moment. Since their Least function is Intuition, they do not naturally anticipate future events or stop to consider the possible consequences of their current choices. Realistic and literal, ESFPs appreciate the simple pleasures in life and tend to notice beauty everywhere. They often like to fill their environments with elements of nature, soft fabrics, bright colors, and great smells. They take pride in their appearance and may spend time and energy keeping themselves fit and attractive. Their busy social lives and many active, physical interests fill every free minute, and they often rush excitedly from one experience to another. Since they live completely in the present moment and rarely plan ahead, they may find themselves overextended. Because they hate to miss any experience, they tend to leave many options open and then have trouble eliminating any or focusing on one project at a time. Often running late or forgetting appointments in the flurry of their busy lives, ESFPs nonetheless feel very guilty if they unintentionally let people down.

Generous and eager to please, ESFPs are loyal friends and great companions. They are curious people who accept life as it is and rarely come to experiences with preconceived notions or agendas. Unpretentious and matter-of-fact, they also are very sensitive to other people's feelings and tend to take criticism and rejection very personally. They are generally open and expressive, but they tend to keep their most private feelings, especially fear and sadness, to themselves or to share them with only a select few. Since they find conflict between people uncomfortable, they will rarely initiate a confrontation and instead simply avoid overbearing or insensitive people. Eager to help others, they are most satisfied when they can make a tangible contribution and are most gratified to see and hear that their efforts have made a difference to someone in need.

Sympathetic and compassionate, they are sometimes disappointed by people, because they have refused to see anything but others' most positive attributes. ESFPs also may become overly involved in other people's problems and have a hard time breaking free of unhealthy relationships. Since they rarely apply objective analysis to their decision making, and instead rely solely on their personal feelings and values, they run the risk of being manipulated or disillusioned. Finding a balance between deciding with their heads and their hearts can be a lifelong challenge.

Looking down the Road:
How ESFPs Change over Time

Up until about the age of 30, ESFPs are run by their Lead Sensing, supported by their Feeling. As ESFPs reach their thirties and forties, they become more objective as they begin to trust their Thinking side. They often become more assertive about their needs and have an easier time being tough when they need to be. They also begin to take things less personally and to develop greater objectivity in general. In their late forties and fifties, ESFPs may begin to use their Least function, Intuition. Typically, this is their greatest weakness and where they are most vulnerable. By consciously working at it, they find themselves more interested in exploring the underlying reasons for things rather than just accepting them as they are. And they may develop new interests in more theoretical subjects and more patience with planning for the future.

ESFPs as Partners

ESFPs are usually fun and affectionate partners. Because they love socializing and have a large cir-

cle of friends and associates, they tend to lead very active lives. Naturally happy-go-lucky, they're supportive of their mates, try to make sure their families are happy and well cared for, and try to ensure that their homes are harmonious and fun places to be. Their dislike for confrontation, however, can result in a tendency to avoid conflict at all costs, even healthy discussion of problems. ESFPs tend to let things go, figuring they'll go away on their own if ignored long enough.

ESFPs want to be appreciated for being the sympathetic, friendly, and very helpful people they are. They derive great pleasure from being responsive to people in hands-on, immediate ways. ESFPs feel most appreciated when their partners are affectionate and acknowledge their good deeds but don't make a particularly big deal about them.

Relationship Satisfiers

Trust, good communication, and mutual respect are aspects of relationships that all types value highly. But here are the aspects that ESFPs report are most and least important to them.

Most Important Aspects	Least Important Aspects
Being listened to	Shared religious beliefs
Having fun together	Shared interests
Mutual commitment	Spiritual connection
Fidelity	Similar parenting styles
Shared values	Security
Humor	Sexual compatibility
Mutual support	

ISFP: Introvert, Sensing, Feeling, Perceiving

Estimated to be between 5 and 7 percent of the American population

Gentle, sensitive, and compassionate, ISFPs are typically the most unassuming and down-to-earth of all types. Characteristically people of few words, they demonstrate their deep commitment and unwavering loyalty first to their friends and families and second to the few select causes that are dear to them. They are people of loving action rather than words. Modest and reserved, these Lead Feelers feel all things personally and typically have extraordinarily strong values. Usually only their trusted friends are privy to their private thoughts and feelings, however. ISFPs are deeply affected by the pain and misfortune of others, but they tend to hide their vulnerability behind a veneer of detachment, appearing cool and removed to strangers. It can take a long time to get to know ISFPs, for they are intensely private people and highly selective about whom they take into their confidence.

ISFPs are so sensitive that they tend to take on the worries of those near them. Observant and curious, they are quick to notice what other people (or animals) need, and since they are highly motivated to help in any way they can, they often become overly involved. Because their Least function is Thinking, they can lose their objectivity and become exhausted in the process. Since they tend to be quite unassertive, they don't readily speak up in their own defense and are sometimes taken advantage of by others who are more dominating. In their desire to maintain harmony and please others, they also may be less than forthcoming about negative feelings, holding on to their hurts for longer than is healthy. Because they are so trusting, some ISFPs are vulnerable to fast-talking, charismatic, and unscrupulous people. Developing a bit of healthy skepticism will protect them from being disappointed by others.

Exceptionally patient and flexible, ISFPs are tolerant of other people and life, so they rarely criticize the actions or beliefs of others. They tend to follow the path of least resistance, responding to change rather than trying to control or resist it. Concerned with living life fully in the present moment, they find beauty and joy in simple plea-sures. Because they value inner balance, they like to keep their lives as uncomplicated as possible and rarely place a higher importance on their work than on their families or personal lives. But because they dislike planning, they are often taken by surprise by unpleasant situations that could have been avoided. Similarly, because they don't easily foresee what might be coming down the road, they may become pessimistic and discouraged if it looks as if they have no attractive options at the present moment. With their relaxed and easygoing style, ISFPs often have great difficulty getting and staying organized. Trying to manage complicated or long-range projects can leave them feeling overwhelmed, so they are usually much happier working quietly, behind the scenes, doing their best as part of a team.

Looking down the Road: How ISFPs Change over Time

Up until about the age of 30, ISFPs are run by their Lead Feeling, supported by their Sensing. But as they reach their thirties and forties, they begin to become more aware and trusting of their Intuition. They may become even more introspective as they ponder their purpose and priorities in life. In their late forties and fifties, ISFPs may begin to use their Least function, Thinking. Typically, this is their greatest weakness and where they are most vulnerable. By consciously working at it, these very gentle, accommodating people may begin to assert their own needs and develop a thicker skin.

ISFPs as Partners

ISFPs are nurturing, supportive partners who often put their partners' needs ahead of their own. But they tend to struggle when they feel anger or resentment, because the last thing they want to do is engage in confrontation. Only with patience, support, and encouragement can they discuss problems in constructive ways that are helpful to their relationships. Often very sensitive communicators, ISFPs want a deep and intimate connection with their partners.

ISFPs also want to be appreciated for their thoughtfulness, kindness, and willingness to help their partners, families, and friends. They feel most appreciated when their partners reciprocate with spontaneous and thoughtful acts that show they are really important.

Relationship Satisfiers

Trust, good communication, and mutual respect are aspects of relationships that all types value highly. Here are the aspects that ISFPs report are most and least important to them:

Most Important Aspects	Least Important Aspects
Mutual commitment	Shared religious beliefs
Fidelity	Spiritual connection
Having fun together	Similar parenting styles
Companionship	Financial security
Shared values	Sexual compatibility
Being listened to	Intellectual stimulation
Intimacy	

ENTJ: Extravert, Intuitive, Thinking, Judging

Estimated to be between 3 and 5 percent of the American population

ENTJs are natural leaders whose competence and strength inspires confidence and respect in others. Their Lead Thinking enables them to analyze problems logically and objectively, weigh the pros and cons, and then make efficient, sensible, and often tough decisions. ENTJs value honesty and directness; they speak their minds and express their strong opinions with fervor. Decisive and energetic, they usually get right to the point without mincing words.

Because their Least function is Feeling, ENTJs can be unaware of the impact their actions have on others. In fact, many ENTJs are so removed from their emotions that they may behave in ways that are insensitive to the needs or feelings of others. Although this is not intentional, they can be brusque and critical and can appear arrogant when they become impatient with people who don't grasp a concept quickly, take an opposing side, or express an illogical position. ENTJs also have the propensity to be bossy and may intimidate others into supporting their positions. And because they are often in a hurry to get things done and move ahead, they may fail to express their appreciation when others have helped them or have done a good job.

As talented strategic planners, ENTJs are capable of anticipating how current actions may affect future decisions. Creative and often innovative, ENTJs have great courage when it comes to making bold, sweeping changes, especially with respect to complex problems or issues. Not easily intimidated, they engender confidence in others and may have a commanding and even awe-inspiring presence. Great lovers of learning, ENTJs are always looking for ways to improve themselves and increase their expertise and power.

Typically friendly and outgoing, ENTJs like to be where the action is and are good at juggling several projects simultaneously. They are often very articulate, think quickly on their feet, and speak publicly with skill and confidence. ENTJs are usually not the least bit shy about sharing their ideas or expressing their strong opinions about any number of subjects. But because they are so eager to get one project completed and move on to the next one, ENTJs may not spend enough time reflecting and thoughtfully considering the immediate, practical, or personal consequences of their actions. And they may be surprised to learn that their good ideas are not as enthusiastically accepted as they expected them to be.

ENTJs are often very career-driven. Organized and productive, they like to work hard and eagerly take on challenges, the more complex the better. As a result of their competence and resourcefulness, they are usually able to accomplish or even exceed their goals. But once they have embarked on a course of action, they can be unwilling or unable to modify their plans and pursue a new direction, even if it's warranted. ENTJs sometimes have difficulty striking a healthy balance between their work and home lives, becoming so preoccupied with furthering their careers that they neglect their personal or family lives in the process.

Looking down the Road: How ENTJs Change over Time

Up until about the age of 30, most ENTJs are run by their Lead Thinking, supported by their Intuition. But as ENTJs reach their thirties and forties, they may begin to use their Sensing side and become more aware of the realities of everyday life. They usually focus more attention on the facts rather than on the big picture and implications for the future. And they may find themselves more engaged in the present moment and more able to take the time to enjoy life's simple pleasures. In their late forties and fifties, ENTJs may begin to use their Least function, Feeling. Typically, this is their greatest weakness and where they are most vulnerable. ENTJs who consciously work at it may become more sensitive to the needs of others and begin to examine their own feelings and values. Some ENTJs reach out as mentors or seek to reestablish past friendships. This new balance can help them become gentler, more tolerant people.

ENTJs as Partners

ENTJs can make inspiring, if sometimes challenging, partners. They have such a strong desire to be in charge and such a clear need to have their lives and homes organized that they can overwhelm their partners. Most ENTJs like to confront conflict directly, discuss problems unflinchingly, solve them, and then move on. However, they tend to be impatient or unwilling to take the time to listen patiently or to give their partners a chance to express themselves fully. In addition, ENTJs are uncomfortable dealing with emotions, so they may dismiss feelings as invalid when those feelings do not seem immediately logical.

ENTJs feel most appreciated when their partners ask for their opinions, take their advice, and rely on them to get a job done right. They want to be shown respect for their many capabilities and their individuality. ENTJs are happiest when their partners understand their need to demonstrate their competence and express their independence.

Relationship Satisfiers

Trust, good communication, and mutual respect are aspects of relationships that all types value highly. But here are the aspects that ENTJs report are most and least important to them.

Most Important Aspects	Least Important Aspects
Fidelity	Similar parenting styles
Mutual commitment	Shared religious beliefs
Mutual support	Spiritual connection
Shared values	Shared interests
Companionship	Humor
Intellectual stimulation	
Having fun together	

INTJ: Introvert, Intuitive, Thinking, Judging

Estimated to be between 2 and 3 percent of the American population

INTJs are global thinkers with original minds. Their Lead Intuition enables them to see connections and to understand the long-range implications of current actions and events. Ingenious and innovative, INTJs have a unique talent for looking at almost anything and seeing how it can be improved, whether it's the smallest product or household chore, or an entire organizational system. By far their favorite subject for improvement is themselves. Most INTJs are on a constant quest to increase their knowledge and, by extension, their overall competence.

Creative and imaginative, INTJs are intellectually curious and daring, even as they may be hesitant to try new things, particularly physical experiences. Able to grasp and analyze complex issues quickly, INTJs are excellent strategic problem solvers with highly developed critical thinking skills that allow them to perform incisive analysis. Constantly seeking new challenges, INTJs are independent people who set very high standards for themselves and usually reach or exceed their goals.

Because their Least function is Sensing, INTJs sometimes have difficulty operating comfortably in the real world. They tend to spend most of their time and energy in the inner world of ideas and possibilities, and they may be completely unaware of, or utterly uninterested in, the more realistic details of their physical surroundings. This can result in small consequences, such as absentmindedly bumping into the furniture or wearing mismatched socks, as well as larger ones, such as failing to realistically assess the feasibility of a project because they are unaware of the costs of necessary resources. And because they tend to be complex, abstract, and theoretical, they often have trouble communicating clearly with people who are not as technically oriented, and they may not be very patient in working to find common ground.

INTJs are most comfortable operating on an intellectual level, so they are sometimes unaware of or surprised by the emotional reactions of others. They may be insensitive or neglectful of those close to them, and they may need to be reminded to take time to appreciate and actively nurture those relationships. INTJs are perfectionists who often set impossibly high standards for themselves and their families. They are sometimes condescending or highly critical of those who fail to live up to their expectations and are parsimonious in their praise for the few who do.

Given their intense powers of concentration, INTJs often prefer to be alone or with a small group of equally competent colleagues. They are especially reluctant to take the time and energy to explain themselves or their ideas to people they perceive to be less competent or not genuinely interested. Because INTJs are so private, they are very difficult to get to know. They especially do not like to share their ideas or feelings until they can articulate them perfectly. Hard workers capable of persevering against great odds, INTJs have enviable focus and determination, and they will not be deterred from reaching their goals. Their single-mindedness comes with a price, however, as it may result in their being stubborn and inflexible. INTJs also may have trouble making the transition from one project to another. Usually it takes an even more fascinating, unique, or complex challenge to recapture their attention.

Looking down the Road: How INTJs Change over Time

Up until about the age of 30, INTJs are run by their Lead Intuition, supported by their Thinking. But as they reach their thirties and forties, they begin to use and trust their Feeling side more and to include their personal values in the decision-making process. This may become a time for serious reflection about their priorities and values, with special focus given to their important relationships. Family matters that often took a backseat to their careers may begin to attract more of their attention. And they may find they have more patience for the people they care about and a heightened desire to meet their needs.

In their late forties and fifties, INTJs may begin to use their Least function, Sensing. Typically, this is their greatest weakness and where they are most vulnerable. By consciously working at it, INTJs may find that they are more aware of things happening in the physical world around them and are less likely to lose themselves in their own thoughts. As a result, they may pay closer attention to the practical needs of others, get more in touch with the realities of daily life, and learn to relax and derive greater enjoyment from day-to-day pleasures.

INTJs as Partners

INTJs can be fascinating but demanding partners. Because they rarely feel compelled to express even their deeply held emotions, their partners can be unsure how they really feel. INTJs strongly dislike repeating themselves or listening to the often disorganized process of sorting out emotional conflicts. They see their own commitments as self-evident and may not understand the importance of expressing appreciation and affection. Harder still for most INTJs is admitting their vulnerabilities to their partners or even to themselves. Although INTJs enjoy intellectual and creative connections with their partners, they may have to push themselves to share themselves emotionally. They often need to be reminded to take the time to nurture their intimate relationships.

INTJs feel most appreciated when their partners admire the number and quality of their innovative solutions to problems and listen respectfully to their ideas and advice. INTJs also need plenty of quiet and space to explore their interests in the depth that gives them satisfaction.

Relationship Satisfiers

Trust, good communication, and mutual respect are aspects of relationships that all types value highly. But here are the aspects that INTJs report are most and least important to them:

Most Important Aspects	Least Important Aspects
Fidelity	Shared religious beliefs
Mutual support	Security
Mutual commitment	Financial security
Intellectual stimulation	Similar parenting styles
Being listened to	Spending time together
Shared values	Spiritual connection
Having fun together	

ENTP: Extravert, Intuitive, Thinking, Perceiving

Estimated to be between 4 and 6 percent of the American population

ENTPs usually make a great impression and often have a natural gift for getting people excited about their ideas. Charming, outgoing, and friendly, they are extremely perceptive and skillful at communicating with all kinds of people. As Lead Intuitives, they possess the ability to see the big picture and anticipate trends. They also exhibit great curiosity about the unknown and enormous confidence. Their enthusiasm is generally so infectious and their negotiating skills so accomplished that they are able to convince others to join them in their always innovative and frequently successful ventures.

But ENTPs can sabotage their most inspired plans by neglecting their Least function, Sensing. Many of their best ideas never come to fruition because they do not pay close attention to important details, grow bored after the initial, creative phase of any project has been completed, or ignore the important follow-through on the many commitments they make. For many ENTPs, it is definitely the thrill of the chase, not the prize, that is the most energizing and satisfying part of the experience.

Although they are logical decision makers, ENTPs also like to please people and have a strong need to be liked. Comfortable occupying center stage, they enjoy demonstrating their cleverness and sophisticated language skills, which usually include an impressive vocabulary and a penchant for puns. Eager to entertain their many friends and acquaintances, as well as strangers passing by, they are often funny and engaging storytellers. ENTPs are typically superb deal makers who know how to use their strategic thinking skills to get what they want. Despite their outward charm and facility with people, they are ultimately pragmatic decision makers, capable of analyzing situations dispassionately and making decisions that are politically expedient.

Because they are so personable, engaging, and outwardly sincere, ENTPs may disappoint or even alienate their friends and supporters when they fail to follow through on their commitments or when they talk a better game than they play. Other people often find this inconsistent behavior confusing and may come to mistrust them.

ENTPs are very flexible and adaptable; they're usually able to turn on a dime and go in a completely different direction if the situation calls for it. Neither particularly liberal nor conservative by nature, ENTPs are aware of the rules of the game and are masters at bending them to suit their purposes. Curious and open-minded, they like to collect information, especially the opinions of lots of people, and to keep their options open for as long as possible. Because they so dislike closing off options, many ENTPs have difficulty making decisions or sticking with them. Some ENTPs can run the risk of becoming chronic procrastinators, squandering their inspiration and never reaching their potential. They also may develop a reputation for being indecisive and untrustworthy. Fortunately, most ENTPs who have these tendencies are smart enough to recognize their destructive potential and learn to focus some of their considerable talents to reap great rewards.

Looking down the Road: How ENTPs Change over Time

Up until about the age of 30, most ENTPs are run by their Lead Intuition, supported by their Thinking. As they reach their thirties and forties, they begin to use their Feeling side and factor in their personal values when making decisions. ENTPs may seek a deeper and more intimate connection with some of the people in their lives, and they may develop an increased sensitivity to and appreciation for how others feel and are affected by their decisions and actions. In their late forties and fifties, ENTPs may begin to use their Least function, Sensing. Typically, this is their greatest weakness and where they are most vulnerable. Those who consciously work at it may become much more selective and discriminating about the projects they get involved in, and much more realistic about what it takes to make them successful. They also tend to become more careful and a bit less impulsive.

ENTPs as Partners

Flirtatious and energetic, ENTPs can be great playmates. They're fun, engaging, and inventive, and they're always looking for something unusual to try. In their enthusiasm, however, they may make promises they can't keep. Their competitive nature, combined with their strong need to be perceived as the expert, can be a bit overwhelming. They so enjoy the tug of a good argument that they sometimes act as if they don't take anything seriously or don't stand firmly for any principle. They are usually very supportive of and helpful to their mates, especially with regard to work, but they can be somewhat scattered and unable to devote their full attention to their partners.

ENTPs want to be appreciated for their great ideas, unusual perceptiveness, and ability to understand and communicate with people. They feel most appreciated when their partners encourage their strong need for lots of social contact and support their desire to respond to life spontaneously.

Relationship Satisfiers

Trust, good communication, and mutual respect are aspects of relationships that all types value highly. But here are the aspects that ENTPs report are most and least important to them.

Most Important Aspects	Least Important Aspects
Having fun together	Shared religious beliefs
Mutual support	Shared interests
Humor	Financial security
Intimacy	Similar parenting styles
Accepting each other's differences	Spiritual connection
Intellectual stimulation	
Companionship	

INTP: Introvert, Intuitive, Thinking, Perceiving

Estimated to be between 3 and 4 percent of the American population

INTPs are intensely private, logical, analytical people. Because they are Lead Thinkers, they are at their best when turning concepts and problems over in their minds like the tumblers inside a lock, rotating around until they click into the correct combination. Detached, intellectual, and complex, INTPs are constantly on the lookout for increasingly difficult challenges.

Independent, skeptical, and often brilliant, INTPs are innately self-assured. They possess an inner confidence that they can tackle any problem and logically work their way through it. In a crisis, they are generally unflappable, remaining amazingly calm and unnerved even when they are up against seemingly insurmountable odds. They are

fascinated with power and are rarely intimidated by anyone or anything.

INTPs are also easily bored with simple issues and tend to pay little attention to mundane facts or details. They are especially intolerant of redundancy in thought or discussion and may simply ignore things they consider trivial. This tendency can give them a rather arrogant demeanor, especially when they tune out people who may be struggling to understand something they have already figured out. Because Feeling is their Least function, they are generally less aware of, and have little interest in, the needs and feelings of others. Although they are usually patient with people who are genuinely eager and quick to learn, they may be demanding and condescending toward those who need more hand-holding.

Creative and often ingenious, INTPs see possibilities where other people do not. They have a global perspective and are quick to find subtle connections between things and to imagine far-reaching implications. Intellectual risk takers, they are usually very curious and eager to learn new things in an effort to become more competent. Although they are especially adept at almost anything they deem worth the effort, they are frequently not nearly as competent in the area of interpersonal relationships, as they keep their thoughts and feelings hidden, even from those who love them. Often they are not even aware of their own or others' feelings about important issues. Because they view their own commitment as self-evident, they do not understand other people's need for reassurance.

INTPs often spend much time in the world of ideas, and they can become so distant that it is difficult for them to communicate simply and effectively with others. And since they focus their impressive powers of concentration on possibilities rather than details, they may miss important realities that could make their ideas more workable.

INTPs absorb new information with incredible speed and can synthesize it almost immediately. They are good at seeing flaws in ideas and generating innovative solutions. But because they are energized by the creative process and working out problems, they usually have more energy for starting projects than they do for finishing them. Although they resist allowing others to help them implement their visions, when they occasionally do so, the results can be impressive.

Looking down the Road: How INTPs Change over Time

Up until about the age of 30, INTPs are run by their Lead Thinking, supported by their Intuition. But as they reach their thirties and forties, they begin to become more aware of their Sensing side and the everyday details around them. As a result, they can become more practical and realistic about themselves and their projects. In their late forties and fifties, INTPs may begin to use their Least function, Feeling. Typically, this is their greatest weakness and where they are most vulnerable. INTPs who consciously work at it may become more sensitive, gain new appreciation for the contributions of others, and become more willing to express their gratitude for the way others improve the quality of their lives.

INTPs as Partners

INTPs can be playful mates with great energy for getting things going, but they also can be somewhat casual when it comes to following through. And because they are not naturally tuned in to the emotional world, they can inadvertently hurt the feelings of those they care about by not sharing their own reactions and feelings. INTPs are often much more preoccupied with their own ideas and projects than with the events or experiences of their partners and families.

INTPs want to be appreciated for their ability to respond quickly and to fix problems creatively.

But they usually need plenty of time to themselves to work on projects or ponder their thoughts. To feel understood and loved, INTPs want their partners to respect their independence and originality.

Relationship Satisfiers

Trust, good communication, and mutual respect are aspects of relationships that all types value highly. But here are the aspects that INTPs report are most and least important to them.

Most Important Aspects	Least Important Aspects
Mutual commitment	Financial security
Fidelity	Shared religious beliefs
Mutual support	Spiritual connection
Being listened to	Security
Humor	Similar parenting styles
Intellectual stimulation	
Companionship	

ENFJ: Extravert, Intuitive, Feeling, Judging

Estimated to be between 3 and 5 percent of the American population

To ENFJs, maintaining harmony in relationships is a lifelong goal as well as a natural skill. Their Lead Feeling enables them to understand other people's feelings and drives them to make people happy. Warm, compassionate, and friendly, ENFJs are so naturally empathetic that they often anticipate others' needs, especially their emotional ones. They also are excellent at helping people solve personal problems in creative ways.

Articulate, vivacious, and enthusiastic, ENFJs are often talented public speakers who possess an innate sense of what an audience wants. They are blessed with a rare gift for making personal connections and thus are skillful communicators, both one-on-one and in groups. Tactful and diplomatic, they pride themselves on being able to make people feel good and go to great lengths to avoid offending others.

Because ENFJs' Least function is Thinking, they often suffer from a serious lack of objectivity. They may be overly sensitive and take things personally. For many ENFJs, the expression "constructive criticism" is an oxymoron. They may have trouble making decisions based solely on logic, often find it hard to know whether a particular behavior or action is fair, and may not trust themselves to make a just and impartial ruling. ENFJs are prone to idealize relationships, so they can be deeply disappointed when people let them down. And because they value diplomacy so highly, they sometimes trade honesty for what they perceive as immediate harmony.

Most ENFJs are highly productive and organized people who run on high energy. Any social interaction further boosts the energy level of these engaging conversationalists. They are often capable of juggling several thoughts or projects at the same time, giving each the attention it deserves. They are happiest when they have a plan and can work cooperatively with others to realize their goals; and they derive satisfaction helping others find ways to reach their full potential. Aware of and concerned about global issues, ENFJs usually have strong, value-based opinions that they feel free to share.

Sometimes ENFJs are in such a hurry to make a decision or complete a task that they discard options prematurely. As a result, they may fail to consider important factual information or may miss experiencing the process if it slows their pace. In their desire to get the job done as quickly as possible and according to the way they feel it should be done, ENFJs can become inflexible and resist acting spontaneously, even when the situation calls for it. Once they feel reassured of their worth and of the value of their contribution, ENFJs are usually able to regain a sense of balance and objectivity.

Looking down the Road:
How ENFJs Change over Time

Up until about the age of 30, ENFJs are run by their Lead Feeling, supported by their Intuition. But as they reach their thirties and forties, they often become more aware of their Sensing. As a result, they usually become more realistic about their projects, ideas, and expectations of other people. They also begin to pay attention to what is happening in their lives at the moment, rather than just dreaming about or planning for how they'd like things to be in the future. And although they still readily see the connections and possibilities, they are better able to temper them with a healthy dose of reality.

In their late forties and fifties, ENFJs may begin to use their Least function, Thinking. Typically, this is their greatest weakness and where they are most vulnerable. ENFJs who consciously work at it may gain important objectivity, the ability to evaluate situations dispassionately, and the ability to be more assertive about their own wants and needs.

ENFJs as Partners

ENFJs need to feel a deep and meaningful connection to their partners, and they go to great lengths to understand and please their mates. Since harmony is so important to them and being helpful is central to their natures, they often put their partners' and families' needs before their own. Ultimately, this can lead them to feel unappreciated and exhausted. They are their partners' most enthusiastic cheerleaders, supporting them in all aspects of their professional and emotional lives.

Most ENFJs have a very thin skin and are easily hurt. Although they strive for harmony, when their values are violated or their feelings are dismissed, they can be very emotional, confrontational, and even punishing. But since they're insightful about the underlying causes of conflicts, deeply motivated to resolve them quickly, and skillful communicators, they can usually help bring about a peaceful resolution.

ENFJs want to be appreciated for the thoughtfulness and compassion they show to others. They need their partners to make a real effort to get to know them and to understand their often spiritual or philosophical natures. Above all, they need to be able to express their feelings and have them taken seriously, and they need to be told how much their partners appreciate the many big and little things they do to make their mates happy.

Relationship Satisfiers

Trust, good communication, and mutual respect are aspects of relationships that all types value highly. But here are the aspects that ENFJs report are most and least important to them.

Most Important Aspects	Least Important Aspects
Mutual commitment	Shared religious beliefs
Being listened to	Financial security
Mutual support	Shared interests
Having fun together	Spiritual connection
Fidelity	Intellectual stimulation
Intimacy	
Accepting each other's differences	

INFJ: Introvert, Intuitive, Feeling, Judging

Estimated to be between 2 and 3 percent of the American population

The two words that best describe most INFJs are integrity and originality. Their Lead Intuition provides them with vision and creativity, and using both in the service of others gives them great satisfaction. They are usually excellent listeners, as they are naturally patient and insightful. Extremely perceptive and empathetic, they are especially

gifted at thinking up new and better ways to help people satisfy their needs and are usually eager to provide whatever support is necessary.

Typically gentle and reserved, INFJs do not like to call attention to themselves and often are content to work behind the scenes. As thoughtful, caring, and sensitive people, INFJs will usually go the extra mile to maintain harmonious relationships. But they can also be fiercely independent — willing to subject themselves to skepticism or criticism in order to make their vision, driven by their strong values, a reality. They are earnest and exude an unshakable faith in their beliefs that engenders trust and respect in others. For this reason, they often make inspiring leaders.

Because their Least function is Sensing, INFJs may fail to take into account the everyday realities that might prevent their ideas from working on a practical level. Preferring to focus on the big picture, they sometimes miss or choose to ignore important everyday details. Because they believe so deeply in the correctness of their positions, they can be somewhat judgmental or dismissive of competing views. INFJs' single-mindedness can become a liability if they are not flexible enough to modify their plans once they have embarked on a course of action — much like a person driving down the highway and making great time but, unfortunately, going in the wrong direction. INFJs' perfectionism also can result in a tendency to be stubborn and unyielding, especially on issues of morality. They usually find that sharing their vision with someone they trust helps them see the flaws and gain a more realistic perspective.

INFJs are decisive and organized, and they like living according to their plans. With their ability to focus and their strong determination, they are often extremely productive. They like to set goals and work tirelessly to achieve them. But sometimes in their haste to come to a conclusion, they miss out on experiencing and enjoying the process, and they can become so preoccupied with making their vision a reality that they lack the ability to act spontaneously.

Since INFJs are motivated by their values and deeply held convictions, they tend to take things personally or become offended when no hurt was intended. Unfortunately, their sensitivity can cause them to become defensive, to cut people off, or to reject ideas that don't meet their high standards. They may need a gentle reminder to take themselves less seriously so that they can enjoy some of life's lighter moments and laugh at their own foibles.

Looking down the Road:
How INFJs Change over Time

Up until about the age of 30, INFJs are run by their Lead Intuition, supported by their Feeling. But as INFJs reach their thirties and forties, they may start to let their Thinking influence their decisions. As a result, they usually develop the ability to be more critical and objective about everything, especially themselves and their ideas. Although they still trust their own personal values above all else, they often have an easier time being critiqued and factoring in outside suggestions.

In their late forties and fifties, INFJs may begin to use their Least function, Sensing. Typically, this is their greatest weakness and where they are most vulnerable. By consciously working at it, they may become more aware of the realities that affect their ideas. They also may gain a new appreciation of their bodies and of nature.

INFJs as Partners

INFJs can be supportive and insightful partners, encouraging their mates to have dreams and to work hard to make them come true. And because they're so creative, they frequently have a wealth of good suggestions to help their partners reach their goals. INFJs like and need harmony so much that they are driven to resolve conflicts quickly — but on terms that don't violate their ethics. Because

they are so ruled by their vision and sense of integrity, they may feel their view is the morally correct one and it would be unjust to yield or compromise.

INFJs feel most appreciated and loved when their partners admire and encourage their creativity, trust their inspiration, and respect their values. It's also vitally important that their partners be open and emotionally available to them and that their mates be willing to share themselves completely.

Relationship Satisfiers

Trust, good communication, and mutual respect are aspects of relationships that all types value highly. But here are the aspects that INFJs report are most and least important to them.

Most Important Aspects	Least Important Aspects
Mutual support	Shared religious beliefs
Mutual commitment	Shared interests
Being listened to	Sexual compatibility
Fidelity	Spiritual connection
Intimacy	Similar parenting styles
Companionship	
Shared values	

ENFP: Extravert, Intuitive, Feeling, Perceiving

Estimated to be between 6 and 7 percent of the American population

ENFPs love possibilities. Because their Lead function is Intuition, they are compelled to see beyond the obvious and are driven to understand the reasons things are as they are. But ENFPs are especially intrigued and energized by other people. They have an almost insatiable curiosity and a wide spectrum of interests. Enthusiastic, friendly, and energetic, ENFPs are generally fun-loving, easygoing people who seek to find meaning in all they do.

Unconventional and occasionally irreverent, ENFPs are seldom impressed by authority or rules. To the contrary! They pride themselves on their uniqueness and originality, they are talented at solving problems and overcoming obstacles, and they find creative ways to bend rules they consider unnecessary. One of ENFPs' greatest gifts is their belief that nothing is impossible. Brainstorming and bouncing new ideas off other creative people is one of their favorite pastimes.

Because ENFPs' Least function is Sensing, they are often inattentive to details. Frequently, they find themselves searching for some lost object. Tasks that require them to focus all their attention on a single activity for long periods of time, especially by themselves, can be extremely stressful. Although ENFPs are usually capable of generating a torrent of new ideas, they can lack the ability to determine whether any of them are practical or workable. And because they are driven by the idea rather than the logistics of making the idea a reality, they can become bored and may neglect to follow through on details once any project has moved past the energizing inspiration stage.

ENFPs are usually well connected, counting among their legion of friends and associates people from many different walks of life. Because they hate to close doors, they tend to maintain friendships for many years. They are enthusiastic and effective catalysts who derive great satisfaction from tapping into their huge network and putting people together for their mutual benefit. Perceptive, insightful, and empathetic, they are often gifted at understanding others' motivations. And they are usually good talkers, capable of persuading people of the merits of their positions. Because ENFPs dislike being tied down, they may experience difficulty making decisions and have a tendency to procrastinate. They have great enthusiasm for starting projects, but they are also easily distracted.

Warm, caring, and concerned, ENFPs have strong personal values on which they base most of their decisions, especially important ones. They are deeply committed to their relationships and are usually eager to help a friend at a moment's notice. Though generally cheerful, ENFPs can become withdrawn and moody when they feel frightened or overwhelmed. Under the influence of their gloomier side, their usual perceptiveness can become badly flawed, and they may misjudge others' intentions and motives and generally feel pessimistic and alone. Usually a change of scenery or the reassurance of a friend or partner helps restore their natural optimism.

Looking down the Road: How ENFPs Change over Time

Up until about the age of 30, ENFPs are run by their Lead Intuition, supported by their Feeling. As they reach their thirties and forties, they start to use their Thinking side more and usually develop a thicker skin. Comments or actions they previously would have taken personally are less likely to hurt their feelings. They become more assertive and generally less concerned about pleasing others. Along with their evolved Thinking comes more objectivity and an ability to temper their natural emotional reactions. And although they still make decisions based primarily on their personal values, they usually have an easier time seeing a more logical and fairer point of view.

In their late forties and fifties, ENFPs may begin to use their Least function, Sensing. Typically, this is their greatest weakness and where they are most vulnerable. ENFPs who consciously work at it may become more realistic, grounded, and selective about which projects or people to become involved with. They also may develop interests that engage their physical senses, such as gardening, cooking, woodworking, or enjoying nature. They frequently become more patient with details and more appreciative of the simple pleasures in life.

ENFPs as Partners

As partners, ENFPs need and love to talk about what's going in their lives. They are strong supporters of their partners' efforts to grow and change, and they encourage their mates to do whatever is necessary to be happier and more fulfilled. ENFPs want and need to feel the same level of support and encouragement they give others. Expressive, optimistic, and curious, they are eager to enjoy new experiences with their partners, whom they want to be their confidants and soul mates as well as their playmates.

Although ENFPs are expressive and loving, if their feelings get hurt, they are often uncomfortable sharing that fact, even with their partners. When they experience conflict with their mates, they initially tend to withdraw and process their feelings privately. But the tension they feel can take a toll, and before long most ENFPs need their partners' support to reestablish harmony.

ENFPs feel most valued and loved when admired for their creativity, accepted for their uniqueness, and seen as the compassionate people they are. They like and need to hear their partners tell them how much they mean to them and to do thoughtful, spontaneous things to demonstrate it.

Relationship Satisfiers

Trust, good communication, and mutual respect are aspects of relationships that all types value highly. Here are the aspects that ENFPs report are most and least important to them.

Most Important Aspects	Least Important Aspects
Being listened to	Financial security
Mutual commitment	Shared religious beliefs
Intimacy	Shared interests
Fidelity	Similar parenting styles
Having fun together	Security
Mutual support	
Humor	

INFP: Introvert, Intuitive, Feeling, Perceiving

Estimated to be between 3 and 4 percent of the American population

INFPs are on a lifelong quest for meaning and inner harmony. Their Lead function is Feeling, so they are driven by their deeply felt personal values and are passionately committed to making sure their beliefs and actions are in balance. Their need for authenticity and personal integrity is so strong that they can't do anything they don't believe in their hearts is right. Sensitive and caring, INFPs have great empathy for people and can be very nurturing and comforting toward those to whom they feel close. However, because they are so selective about what and whom they allow to enter their private world, they may appear rather cool and aloof to people who don't know them. It can take a long time to get to know an INFP, but they are utterly devoted to those few people they do take into their hearts.

Because INFPs' Least function is Thinking, they have very personal reactions and often have difficulty stepping back to consider things objectively. Their feelings frequently get hurt, and remarks that are not intended as critical can cause them pain. Rather than confront an offender, INFPs are more likely to keep their feelings to themselves, allowing the resentment to fester. Since they are often reluctant to discuss the matter even later, INFPs will sometimes simply drop people from their lives rather than make the effort to work things out. Ironically, because INFPs tend to idealize relationships, they are often disappointed when someone does not live up to their expectations.

Creative and imaginative, INFPs have great curiosity about the world and often have a passionate and lifelong love of the arts. They especially appreciate new and unusual forms of self-expression. Not bound by convention or traditional ways of doing things, INFPs do not follow the pack, and in fact often feel a little out of sync with the rest of the world. Open-minded and adaptable in small things, they are usually supportive and tolerant of others with alternative lifestyles, as long as these people's behavior or customs don't have a personal impact on them or force them to compromise their values. In those cases, INFPs become rigid and unforgiving.

INFPs' primary focus is inward, and many have highly developed and deeply meaningful spiritual components to their lives. Sometimes their preoccupation with self-awareness can keep them from noticing or participating in some of the more pedestrian activities in life. Although they naturally imagine possibilities and consider how things are related to each other, they don't tend to be especially realistic or practical. They may find the more mundane, day-to-day activities of life unfulfilling and may have to work hard to stay on top of things. INFPs often enjoy spending long periods of time alone, quietly reflecting, reading, or writing. They are happiest when they can immerse themselves in interesting and personally meaningful projects.

Looking down the Road:
How INFPs Change over Time

Up until about the age of 30, INFPs are run by their Lead Feeling, supported by their Intuition. As INFPs reach their thirties and forties, they begin to take notice of their Sensing. They are likely to start paying more attention to the practical realities of life, and tasks such as balancing their checkbooks may become easier. They also become more realistic in their expectations of themselves and others. In their forties and fifties, INFPs may begin to use their Least function, Thinking. Typically, this is *their* greatest weakness and where they are most vulnerable. By consciously working at it, INFPs may become more logical and better able to make decisions with clarity and objectivity. They also

tend to take fewer things personally and are less likely to get their feelings hurt. Although they remain deeply committed to their values and beliefs, this new balance can make them more tolerant and appreciative of other, equally valuable but different styles of decision making.

INFPs as Partners

INFPs are supportive and nurturing partners, but they are also highly individualistic and often preoccupied with their own projects and thoughts. Because harmony is so important to INFPs, they are very affected by conflict and tension, but they may resist confronting their partners directly about problems between them. When they become angry, they're likely to feel guilty and blame themselves rather than their partners. INFPs can also be stubborn and unyielding when they feel they're being criticized or mistreated. And because they may not verbalize those feelings, it may be hard for their partners to know when they've been hurt.

INFPs feel most appreciated and loved when their partners are patient and supportive and listen carefully. They need to be understood and want a partner who is sensitive to their feelings and respectful of their values. They also like to be reassured, often verbally, about how much they are loved.

Relationship Satisfiers

Trust, good communication, and mutual respect are aspects of relationships that all types value highly. But here are the aspects that INFPs report are most and least important to them.

Most Important Aspects	Least Important Aspects
Mutual commitment	Shared religious beliefs
Fidelity	Financial security
Mutual support	Shared interests
Intimacy	Similar parenting styles
Being listened to	Sexual compatibility
Accepting each other's differences	
Shared values	

An Exercise for All Couples

By all means, try this exercise at home.

1. Prioritize your list of relationship satisfiers and think of real-life examples of how each is true for you.

2. Ask your partner to review your list, then share specific ways in which he or she might better meet your needs.

3. Read your partner's profile and prioritized list of satisfiers. Compare both of your lists and discuss ways in which you might better meet each other's needs.

PART TWO

How to Love the One You're With: Introduction to the Couple Combinations

"Early on in our marriage, we'd wake up on a Saturday and I'd announce the plan for the day. He'd want to take a drive and see what happened. I thought he was insane!"

"Active pursuits are always best for us. Our best conversations are when we're outside, doing something rugged together."

"My partner is so optimistic. She seems to just believe things will be all right and makes it so with the sheer strength of her imagination!"

"Great spirited, theoretical debates are fun — they're what draws us together and what holds us together."

"We believe that it's not merely a human attraction but rather a spiritual command that we be together."

Now that you've discovered your type and your partner's type, it's time to get to the really good part — the reason you bought this book in the first place: to see how you and your partner mesh. The first step toward creating a truly satisfying relationship is to understand ourselves. The next is to be more aware of the ways we naturally, and to some extent automatically, interact with our partners. Then we can learn how to make some minor adjustments in our styles to be more accommodating and appreciative of each other. But before you read about your combination, we have some general words of guidance.

Do Opposites Really Attract?

You may have just read your type profile and your partner's type profile and feel somewhat discouraged because you are quite different. It might be reassuring to learn that many couples — about 35 percent according to our research — have only two type preferences in common. About 25 percent have one preference in common, 20 percent have three, and only 10 percent are either different on all four or alike on all four. It's true that the more alike two people are, the easier time they usually have understanding each another and communicating. But just because you and your partner may be very different doesn't mean you can't have a satisfying relationship. You may simply have to work harder to achieve understanding and satisfaction (not that this is news to you!).

Although relationships are often easier for couples who are very similar, the greatest opportunities for personal growth come from loving someone who is quite different. On some level, we're drawn to our partners precisely because of those differences. The old adage that opposites attract turns out to be true. We see things in them we don't have in ourselves, or at least don't have in the degree they do. They stimulate us to try things we might not ordinarily try, encourage us to open up and share on a deeper level than we're used to, or get us to slow down and have more fun than we normally allow ourselves. As Carl Jung wrote, "The meeting of two personalities is like the contact of two chemical substances; if there is any reaction, both are transformed."

Bear in mind that no one combination is either perfect or automatically doomed to failure. While every couple faces challenges based in great part on their type preferences, every relationship also is as unique as the two people in it. In addition to our types, a host of other factors — we think of them as overlays — make us who we are and influence how we behave in our relationships. Here are some of the important factors.

- Our memories and experiences from past relationships (Have we been hurt a lot before?)
- The impressions we have of our own parents' marriages (What's our concept of a marriage?)
- Our culture and heritage
- Our education and life experiences
- Our age and level of maturity (Is this our first relationship or our third marriage?)
- Our gender

Our research showed that gender is not nearly as important a factor as Type in understanding the conflicts couples experience, but we are each nonetheless still under societal pressures. For the most part, boys and girls still grow up with clear expectations of what each person's role in a relationship or marriage is supposed to be. Women, regardless of their type, are still expected to do more of the housework, child rearing, and nurturing of the relationship than men. And men are still expected to be more responsible for bringing in the money. This places a strain on people whose natural types run counter to those expectations. For example, most women Thinkers (but not all) have less of an urge to nurture than most Feeling women, but they grow up in a culture that tells them they should be mothers — and should enjoy it, too. So when a male Thinker marries a woman Thinker, he may be in for a bit of a surprise when she's not interested in being the stay-at-home mom he always pictured his wife to be. The same holds true for male Feelers. They may be less driven and more easily hurt than male Thinkers, but it may be hard for them because they've grown up believing that "real" men are always calm, cool, and collected. And it may be difficult for the women who love them to adjust to their very gentle natures as well.

Each of us brings myriad unconscious desires, fears, and patterns into a relationship. As any couples therapist will tell you, it's the unconscious stuff that plays out more dramatically in our relationships than anywhere else. Aside from the elements that make each of us unique, daily stresses provoke underlying emotions that affect our relationships. These are situations all or most of us have to deal with in addition to our partners' and our own natural styles. Some of the more universal ones are:

• The quality of the relationships we have with our parents and our in-laws
• Dealings with our ex-spouses

• Our financial stability and the enormous financial strain that comes with it
• Career pressures and our level of satisfaction with our work

And then there are more serious problems, such as substance abuse and poor health, and perhaps the granddaddy of all stressors — children.

Little Bundles of Joy?

Most parents know that having children is perhaps the single most profound experience of their lives. Just deciding whether or not to have children is a major stress-producing event, especially if we don't see eye to eye with our partners. And although children are an incredible blessing, they also add stress to even the best relationships. In addition to the energy and patience they demand of us, we have to figure out how to raise our children with someone who may have very different beliefs and values. Conflicting parenting philosophies can be a tremendous source of frustration, and it's no surprise that couples who share several type preferences, and especially the same temperament, usually have fewer arguments about child rearing. The two type dimensions that are most often the source of parenting disagreements are Thinking and Feeling, and Judging and Perceiving. Remember Steve and Liza from Chapter 2 (see page 19)? Liza is a Thinker and Steve is a Feeler. They often disagree about how consistent or lenient to be with their children. Usually the Thinking partner believes that the Feeling partner is too easily swayed by their children's feelings, and the Feeling partner believes that the Thinking partner is too tough and demanding. Consider another couple, Jake and Maureen, who brought together children from previous marriages.

Jake is an ESTJ and Maureen is an ENFP. Not only do they sometimes disagree about the same issues

Steve and Liza do, but they also have different temperaments and values. Jake takes his job as father very seriously. He believes it's his duty to raise responsible, polite, independent children. He's the disciplinarian, establishing and enforcing the rules of the house with calm consistency. Jake's kids will tell you that he's strict and demanding but that he shows his devotion to his kids by being an enthusiastic coach and never misses a swim meet, dance recital, or school play. Maureen is more concerned about her children's emotional well-being and self-esteem. She wants them to develop as unique individuals and strive to find personal meaning in their lives. She's clearly the fun parent, the nurturer, who is less worried about bedtimes and rules and more concerned about helping the children articulate their feelings and grow into compassionate and tolerant adults. For the most part, Jake and Maureen complement each other well, but they also have their share of disagreements about everything from how hard to push the kids academically to whether to pay them for doing chores. This hurdle is not insurmountable, but it is a strain on their relationship; it gives them one more thing to disagree and argue about. Fortunately, knowing about their types — and their children's types — has helped them figure out strategies to be more cohesive as a team and more sensitive and effective with their children.

The situation is made all the more complicated when some of the children are his, some are hers, and some are theirs. Blended families have to deal with yet another overlay that includes ex-spouses and step relations.

All these factors make us unique and provide the rich texture that makes our relationship different from everyone else's. But what if we and our partners are really very much alike? Is that the key to a blissful relationship?

Mirror, Mirror on the Wall — Why Are You Such a Pain in the Ass?

We all accept the notion that opposites attract. And it makes perfect sense that if you and your partner are very different, you'll probably experience your share of conflict. He's very talkative, and you're rather quiet; she's wildly imaginative, and you're super-realistic; he likes everything neat and tidy, and you couldn't care less about order, and so on. But frustrations also result from two people being alike. When you and your partner have the same strength (say, a take-charge attitude), you probably also have the same blind spot (maybe you're both a wee bit overbearing at times?). And although it's hard to recognize our shortcomings in ourselves, they're abundantly clear and generally much more difficult, annoying, or downright painful to see in our partners. When we share a type preference with our partners, it's like looking into a mirror and seeing our own flawed reflection staring back at us. And we don't like it. But instead of recognizing it for what it is, we turn it around and find fault with our partners, criticizing them for the very qualities we dislike in ourselves. Despite the frustration these insights cause, they also give us the opportunity to honestly appraise our own tendencies and make the kinds of changes we desire to become more effective, more tolerant, and more loving people. Growth comes with change.

You may find it helpful to review some of the pluses and minuses of sharing a type preference listed on page 64.

Through the Years

One of the fascinating and useful aspects of the Personality Type model is that it isn't static. Although people are born with type preferences, they grow, change, and develop over time, usually

The Pluses and Minuses for Couples Who Share Type Preferences	
The Good Stuff	**The Challenging Stuff**

Extraverts (E) with Extraverts (E)

Are big talkers — lots of discussion	May not listen well
Are active and busy	Interrupt each other
Are social — like to be around lots of people	May become overextended with outside activities

Introverts (I) with Introverts (I)

Listen well	May lose touch with the outside world
Are patient with depth of thought	See everything in terms of themselves
Respect each other's need for privacy and quiet	Don't speak up right away about issues, problems, and reactions

Sensors (S) with Sensors (S)

Share a realistic and practical view of the world	May not consider alternatives
Are literal and linear	May be skeptical of new ideas
Are unpretentious and down-to-earth	May be materialistic

Intuitives (N) with Intuitives (N)

Love to share ideas and discuss possibilities	May miss essential details
See alternatives	Can be sloppy with facts or money
Appreciate each other's uniqueness	May be vague and abstract

Thinkers (T) with Thinkers (T)

Are direct and honest	May be critical, blunt, or insensitive
Are consistent and logical	May not understand emotional causes of conflicts
Rarely compromise their principles	May not risk sharing emotionally

Feelers (F) with Feelers (F)

Are eager to understand each other	Take everything personally
Are warm, compassionate, and expressive	Are sensitive to criticism
Are eager to connect emotionally	Tend to avoid conflict

(continued)

(continued)	
The Good Stuff	**The Challenging Stuff**
Judgers (J) with Judgers (J)	
Make great teammates and partners	Struggle for control of agendas
Are decisive and organized	May be stubborn
Share a desire for order and neatness	Are unwilling to adjust plans
Perceivers (P) with Perceivers (P)	
Are easygoing and adventurous	Don't plan ahead or follow through
Are playful and have fun together	May be impulsive or mismanage money
Are curious and open to change	Procrastinate and miss opportunities

at predictable times and in fairly predictable ways. A 20-year-old INTJ is not the same person he will be when he's 50. Sure, his type will remain constant, and he will still notice possibilities and make decisions based primarily on logical analysis. But as we age, especially as we move through midlife, we tend to become more aware of the less-developed parts of our personalities. Thus our INTJ becomes more sensitive to the needs of others and eventually pays closer attention to details. This is great news for couples who are very different and is why couples who stay together for many years often find that they become more alike.

Meet the Connollys. Richard is an INTP, and Pauline is an ESFJ. They married when they were in their mid-twenties and candidly admit that the first ten years were pretty difficult. They disagreed about everything. Richard was intensely private, while Pauline was very expressive. Richard was a philosopher and Pauline a practical realist. Pauline was the consummate host and diplomat, and Richard loved to debate complex and abstract concepts — a polite way of saying he had to argue about everything! And Richard was low-key but disorganized, while Pauline

was productive but also a bit controlling. Pauline often felt that Richard was dismissive of her strong feelings, and Richard often thought that Pauline was illogical and too emotional. But over time, Pauline became better able to hear and accept constructive criticism without falling apart, and Richard became more sensitive and gentle. Now it's often Pauline who is the tough negotiator with contractors or who speaks her mind at meetings, while Richard spends more time volunteering and mentoring. Pauline says that Richard is much more appreciative and expressive, and Richard has found a very competitive tennis partner in Pauline. Friends who helped them celebrate their thirtieth wedding anniversary say that although they're still the individuals they've always been, they are much more alike now than when they were married. Richard and Pauline agree. It's been difficult at times for sure, but their differences have given them each the opportunity to help the other grow and develop in important ways. They're both more competent and well-rounded people today, and they understand each other much better.

So there's hope for all of us, whether we share all four type preferences or none at all!

16 x 16 = 136?

Are you ready to read about your combination? First you have to find it! As strange as it may seem, there are not 256 possible combinations (16 x 16) but rather 136. For those not mathematically challenged, 16 x 16 actually equals 256, but same-type combinations are reported only once. In other words, we don't count ESTJ with ESTJ as two different combinations. Also, each combination is reported only one way. For example, ESTJ with INFP appears once, not again as INFP with ESTJ. The math aside, here is how we organized the 136 combinations in the list beginning on page 67 and in the following chapters. To make them as easy as possible to reference, they are organized by temperament groups, starting with the Traditionalists, then the Experiencers, the Conceptualizers, and the Idealists. Within each temperament group, we list the Extravert before the Introvert, the Thinker before the Feeler, and the Judger before the Perceiver. In some cases, it will be easier to search under your partner's type. For example, if your type is INTP and your partner's type is ESFP, your combination will be listed as ESFP with INTP.

If you aren't completely sure of either your type or your partner's, we strongly advise that you go back and reread those profiles in Chapter 3 that you thought fit you best. (It will be much easier to sort through 16 descriptions as opposed to 136.) Because different types find different formats easier to use, in addition to the list, we've created a chart that contains the page number on which you will find your type combination (see page 69).

How to Use the Combination Descriptions

The information in the combination descriptions in the following chapters is the result of thousands of in-depth survey responses and hundreds of telephone interviews. We gleaned from our research the most common joys and frustrations couples of each combination routinely experienced. We also learned how people in each combination like their partners to demonstrate their appreciation. A majority of the couples we interviewed have been together for many years, and all spoke from lots of experience. We think you'll find almost all of what they shared to be true for you, too.

If you find yourself disagreeing with most of what you're reading, you are probably not reading the right combination. If that happens, double-check the types you came up with after reading Chapter 2 and the profiles in Chapter 3. If you or your partner was torn between two types back in Chapter 3, you may need to read a couple of the combinations before you find the one that describes you.

Finally, these combinations are not intended to take the place of professional therapy. If you and your partner are experiencing significant problems, this may not be the best time to try to figure out your type combination. People under great stress often find it difficult to be objective and, therefore, find identifying their types more difficult. These descriptions are intended to help you make the most of the relationship you have by understanding, accepting, and appreciating the ways you and your partner are alike and different.

As you read your combination, pay particular attention to the statements that ring especially true. Make note of the things that you really want your partner to understand about you and the insights you gain about why your behavior may be annoying or frustrating to your partner. After you've read the description and the advice we offer to help you reach your partner, turn to Chapter 14 for some suggestions about taking the next step. There we include an exercise that hundreds of couples have found thought provoking, powerful, and helpful in creating the relationships they've always wanted.

The Traditionalists		The Experiencers		The Conceptualizers		The Idealists	
SJ with SJ		**SP with SP**		**NT with NT**		**NF with NF**	
ESTJ with ESTJ	70	ESTP with ESTP	172	ENTJ with ENTJ	245	ENFJ with ENFJ	288
ESTJ with ISTJ	71	ESTP with ISTP	173	ENTJ with INTJ	246	ENFJ with INFJ	289
ESTJ with ESFJ	73	ESTP with ESFP	175	ENTJ with ENTP	248	ENFJ with ENFP	291
ESTJ with ISFJ	74	ESTP with ISFP	176	ENTJ with INTP	249	ENFJ with INFP	292
ISTJ with ISTJ	76						
ISTJ with ESFJ	78	ISTP with ISTP	178	INTJ with INTJ	251	INFJ with INFJ	294
ISTJ with ISFJ	79	ISTP with ESFP	180	INTJ with ENTP	252	INFJ with ENFP	295
ESFJ with ESFJ	81	ISTP with ISFP	181	INTJ with INTP	254	INFJ with INFP	297
ESFJ with ISFJ	82	ESFP with ESFP	183	ENTP with ENTP	255	ENFP with ENFP	299
ISFJ with ISFJ	84	ESFP with ISFP	184	ENTP with INTP	257	ENFP with INFP	300
SJ with SP		ISFP with ISFP	186	INTP with INTP	258	INFP with INFP	302
ESTJ with ESTP	86	**SP with NT**		**NT with NF**			
ESTJ with ISTP	88	ESTP with ENTJ	188	ENTJ with ENFJ	260		
ESTJ with ESFP	89	ESTP with INTJ	189	ENTJ with INFJ	261		
ESTJ with ISFP	91	ESTP with ENTP	191	ENTJ with ENFP	263		
		ESTP with INTP	193	ENTJ with INFP	265		
ISTJ with ESTP	93						
ISTJ with ISTP	95	ISTP with ENTJ	195	INTJ with ENFJ	266		
ISTJ with ESFP	97	ISTP with INTJ	197	INTJ with INFJ	268		
ISTJ with ISFP	98	ISTP with ENTP	198	INTJ with ENFP	270		
		ISTP with INTP	200	INTJ with INFP	272		
ESFJ with ESTP	100						
ESFJ with ISTP	102	ESFP with ENTJ	202	ENTP with ENFJ	273		
ESFJ with ESFP	104	ESFP with INTJ	204	ENTP with INFJ	275		
ESFJ with ISFP	106	ESFP with ENTP	206	ENTP with ENFP	277		
		ESFP with INTP	207	ENTP with INFP	278		
ISFJ with ESTP	107						
ISFJ with ISTP	109	ISFP with ENTJ	209	INTP with ENFJ	280		
ISFJ with ESFP	111	ISFP with INTJ	211	INTP with INFJ	282		
ISFJ with ISFP	113	ISFP with ENTP	213	INTP with ENFP	283		
SJ with NT		ISFP with INTP	215	INTP with INFP	285		
ESTJ with ENTJ	115	**SP with NF**					
ESTJ with INTJ	117	ESTP with ENFJ	217				
ESTJ with ENTP	118	ESTP with INFJ	219				
ESTJ with INTP	120	ESTP with ENFP	220				
		ESTP with INFP	222				

(continued)

How to Find Your Type Combination

1. Locate your type on the horizontal axis.
2. Locate your partner's type on the vertical axis.
3. The box where they intersect indicates the page number for your combination's description.

	ESTJ	ISTJ	ESFJ	ISFJ	ESTP	ISTP	ESFP	ISFP	ENTJ	INTJ	ENTP	INTP	ENFJ	INFJ	ENFP	INFP
ESTJ	70	71	73	74	86	88	89	91	115	117	118	120	144	146	147	149
ISTJ	71	76	78	79	93	95	97	98	122	123	125	127	151	152	154	156
ESFJ	73	78	81	82	100	102	104	106	128	130	132	134	157	159	161	163
ISFJ	74	79	82	84	107	109	111	113	136	137	139	141	165	166	168	170
ESTP	86	93	100	107	172	173	175	176	188	189	191	193	217	219	220	222
ISTP	88	95	102	109	173	178	180	181	195	197	198	200	224	226	227	229
ESFP	89	97	104	111	175	180	183	184	202	204	206	207	231	232	234	236
ISFP	91	98	106	113	176	181	184	186	209	211	213	215	237	239	241	243
ENTJ	115	122	128	136	188	195	202	209	245	246	248	249	260	261	263	265
INTJ	117	123	130	137	189	197	204	211	246	251	252	254	266	268	270	272
ENTP	118	125	132	139	191	198	206	213	248	252	255	257	273	275	277	278
INTP	120	127	134	141	193	200	207	215	249	254	257	258	280	282	283	285
ENFJ	144	151	157	165	217	224	231	237	260	266	273	280	288	289	291	292
INFJ	146	152	159	166	219	226	232	239	261	268	275	282	289	294	295	297
ENFP	147	154	161	168	220	227	234	241	263	270	277	283	291	295	299	300
INFP	149	156	163	170	222	229	236	243	265	272	278	285	292	297	300	302

Chapter 4

The Traditionalists[2]: SJs with SJs

ESTJ with ESTJ

The Joys

Whenever two people share all four type preferences, they tend to have a lot in common. ESTJ couples share the similar values of hard work and responsibility, and are both traditional and conservative people. They often hold strong and sometimes absolute opinions about right and wrong and strive to live their lives in ways that are consistent with their beliefs. ESTJ couples tend to be very active, friendly people with lots of friends and busy professional and social calendars. They are straightforward, unpretentious, and down-to-earth realists who communicate directly, honestly, and frequently! ESTJs tend to say what they mean and mean what they say. They are punctual, careful, and polite people who take all their commitments very seriously and are diligent about fulfilling their promises and finishing the many projects they begin. ESTJs tend to be careful with their money and willing to budget and save to afford the things they buy. They also take good care of their possessions and invest time in maintaining their homes and property. Since they both like a traditional life, ESTJs tend to be content to fill conventional gender roles. Most ESTJs believe in protecting the status quo, since they are uncomfortable with change, are skeptical of untested methods, and hate leaving things unsettled. ESTJs are often known to say, "If it ain't broke, don't fix

it" — an axiom that applies to all areas of their lives, including their relationships.

The Frustrations

Most of the frustrations ESTJs typically experience stem from the fact that they tend to make the same mistakes and share the same blind spots. They may both become so busy with their many business and civic commitments that they neglect to spend time together enjoying each other's company. As a result, they may find themselves too exhausted to fully share the events of their days. ESTJs also tend to be quite verbal and may irritate each other when they interrupt or finish each other's sentences. Regardless of how alike two partners are, they need to remember that they are still unique individuals and stay open to learning about each other over time.

Another frustration for ESTJ couples is that since they both tend to have very strong opinions about almost everything, they can be stubborn and a bit hardheaded when it comes to listening and accepting alternative points of view. They may also have a hard time backing down, since they see things in black-and-white terms and may equate compromise with selling out. Naturally skeptical of new or unproven approaches, ESTJs' first reaction to change is often a negative one, so they may need to be careful not to squelch their partners' enthusiasm simply because they don't share it. Since they are so naturally logical and thick-skinned, they can also be critical and negative with each other. Still, they can unintentionally hurt each other, and because neither is especially eager to admit that they feel upset, they may postpone important discussions of their needs, expectations, and disappointments that would ultimately strengthen their relationships.

Perhaps the biggest area of concern for ESTJ couples is their tendency to become stuck in conventional but restrictive roles. It can be easy for one or both partners to fall into such strict and limiting roles that they feel a little trapped. This can be a problem, especially when one partner feels the need to change and the other feels an equally strong desire to keep things the way they've always been. ESTJ women may struggle with the pressure to be competent at work and still keep their homes neat and well organized. And they may feel, justifiably, that they are doing much more than their fair share of the household chores. It may be difficult for male ESTJs to accept the inevitability of change and willingly take on responsibilities that their fathers never had. Whatever the division of labor, ESTJ couples do well to try to ignore the expectations of society and their well-meaning families, and instead make choices that are right for their particular situations and for each other.

Advice for ESTJs

- Be willing to give as well as to receive. Practice generosity and patience.
- Be careful to listen completely to your partner before jumping in, interrupting, or saying no.
- Watch your tendency to get stuck in a boring routine. Try something new together.
- Slow down and protect your private, quiet time together. Take vacations together or make regular dates for walks or adventures away from home.
- Watch your tendencies to fall into strict gender roles. Encourage each other to break free of limiting expectations.

ESTJ with ISTJ

The Joys

Because ESTJs and ISTJs share three of the four type preferences, they are alike in many ways. Their relationships are often easy and comfortable because they understand each other so well and strive to organize and run their lives in much the same way. They're both down-to-earth and utterly practical people, careful and accurate with facts and details. They each weigh the pros and cons of options and almost always trust their well-developed sense of what's logical to make a final decision. ESTJs and ISTJs both like matters to be settled, so they tend to be decisive and opinionated. Many enjoy direct and honest communication with each other, unlike that which they experience with many other partners. They find it refreshing to be able to speak their minds clearly and honestly without worrying that their partners will be offended. Since they share a desire for closure, they rarely leave things up in the air for long. They tend to be most comfortable when their homes and lives are organized and efficiently run. They like to plan activities in advance, like to stick to their predictable and consistent schedules, and don't like sudden change. Great teammates and partners, ESTJs and ISTJs are generally willing to pitch in and help each other with their projects so they can enjoy the sense of satisfaction they get from completing their work early.

Since they have so much in common, it's understandable that these couples often get along so well. In addition to their other similarities, ESTJs and ISTJs tend to have very similar values and are usually quite conservative and traditional. But ESTJs and ISTJs are also attracted to each other because of their differences. ESTJs are drawn to ISTJs because of their calm unflappability. ESTJs also like how responsible and focused ISTJs are and that they are attentive listeners. For their part,

ISTJs are drawn to the social ease and high energy of ESTJs. ISTJs admire how quickly ESTJs make things happen and how many things they get done with astonishing speed and competence.

Because of their similarities and their differences, ESTJs and ISTJs have the opportunity to help each other grow and develop in important ways. ESTJs help ISTJs get out in the world, broaden their horizons, discover new experiences, and widen their circle of friends and acquaintances. ISTJs are able to help their ESTJ partners focus some of their time and energy, slow down, and become more attentive listeners.

The Frustrations

Whenever two people are of very similar types and have many of the same blind spots, they often find those foibles irritating in their partners. ESTJs and ISTJs are quick to notice and point out flaws they see but are generally glad to receive honest feedback. After a while, though, constant criticism can wear them down. They need to consciously work at increasing their sensitivity to each other and to take the time to recognize their partners' accomplishments.

Another challenge for many ESTJs and ISTJs is that neither is especially interested in new ways of solving problems. Both tend to reject out of hand untested ideas and may miss out because they are unwilling to adjust their schedules to take advantage of unexpected opportunities. And ESTJs and ISTJs can individually or as a couple get into a rut and become bored with their carefully planned schedules. The somewhat more adventurous and active ESTJs may struggle to get their ISTJ partners to take even the most modest risks and try something new. This is especially true of social activities. But ESTJs can also easily get overextended and inadvertently leave their ISTJ partners out of the action.

Another area of frustration common to many couples is that since ESTJs and ISTJs are both so traditional by nature, they tend to fall into strict gender-based roles. This is especially true when it comes to housework. The woman, regardless of her type, tends to do more of the household chores than the man. Since equity is something that really matters to both ESTJs and ISTJs, the unfairness can breed deep resentment and undermine a healthy relationship.

Finally, although ESTJs and ISTJs are typically honest and direct, they can be reluctant to discuss emotional issues that cause them to admit their insecurities or vulnerabilities. Neither is comfortable with emotions, so they may avoid heart-to-heart discussions because they feel less than competent when articulating their true feelings. They may need to get outside assistance or commit extra time and energy to deepening the emotional intimacy in their relationships.

How to Reach Your ISTJ Partner

- Respect your partner's need for time alone and quiet, especially after a busy, stressful, or social day.
- Give your partner time to think things through before expecting a response, especially if it's an important issue or decision.
- Understand that your partner needs more time to consider making changes. Make a suggestion, then leave your partner alone to ponder it.
- Beware of your tendency to be negative and critical.
- Slow down and don't rush your partner to make transitions.

How to Reach Your ESTJ Partner

- Don't withdraw or give your partner the silent treatment when you get angry or upset.
- Share your thoughts and reactions with your partner. Don't make him or her guess what you're feeling.
- Encourage your partner to socialize only as much as he or she needs and wants to, and don't

hold your partner back from doing things without you.

• Initiate discussions or activities. Occasionally offer to host or attend social events.

• Speak up. Don't leave your partner guessing

ESTJ with ESFJ

The Joys

Since ESTJs and ESFJs share three of the four type preferences, they have a lot in common and usually understand each other quite well. They are both fundamentally traditional people who usually have conservative personal and political values. They are willing to work hard toward their mutual goals and tend to be careful with money and respectful of each other's professional responsibilities. ESTJs and ESFJs are very realistic, practical, and literal people who often enjoy working on household projects together because they like to plan things in advance and then proceed through the steps in a systematic fashion. Both like their homes to be neat and well organized and are usually quite willing to do their fair share of household chores. Like many other couples, the woman tends to do more around the house, but because ESTJ and ESFJ men share their partners' desire for an attractive and orderly home, they are often better at pulling their weight than men of some other types.

In addition to their many similarities, ESTJs and ESFJs are often attracted to each other because of their different ways of making decisions. Typically, ESTJs are drawn to ESFJs because of their genuine concern for other people, their big hearts, and their bubbly, affectionate personalities. ESTJs feel really loved and nurtured by their sympathetic and understanding ESFJ partners. For their part, ESFJs are often attracted to ESTJs because they are generally so stable, responsible, assertive, and willing to take charge of almost any-thing. ESTJs are usually so serious about their commitments that ESFJs feel that they are utterly trustworthy and dependable.

Because of their differences, ESTJs and ESFJs have the opportunity to help each other grow and develop in important ways. Typically, ESTJs are able to help ESFJs become more logical and objective in their decision making, and they are able not to take everything so personally. ESFJs also credit their ESTJ partners with helping them become less driven to please other people. Conversely, ESFJs are often able to help ESTJs develop genuine compassion, gain more patience with the problems and needs of others, and become more willing to express appreciation for the efforts of those with whom they live and work. ESTJs often say that their ESFJ partners encourage them to assess their personal values so they are better able to articulate them.

The Frustrations

Like other couples with so much in common, many ESTJs and ESFJs experience some frustrations due to their similarities. Since they are both very social and active people, they can find they quite easily become overextended from their many outside commitments. They often spend lots of time on the phone with friends or work longer hours than required. This can lead to a sense of disconnection between partners if they don't protect their quiet, private time together. And since they are both big talkers, they may have to struggle to be sure they are listening to each other without interrupting. ESFJs in particular may feel that their partners spend too much time working and not enough time with them or their families.

Another source of frustration for many ESTJ and ESFJ couples involves their mutual desire for control. They both like their schedules and routines to be respected. Given their many firm opinions about the right way to do things, they have a tendency to believe that their own ways are best.

As a result, ESTJs and ESFJs can quickly come to an impasse when neither partner is willing to back down or compromise. Whether they are deciding whose job it is to balance the checkbook or wrangling over possession of the TV remote control, ESTJs and ESFJs need to find ways to delegate responsibility and take turns so they aren't constantly struggling for control.

The largest source of frustration for many ESTJs and ESFJs is their very different decision-making styles. ESTJs are so utterly logical and objective that they can appear unfeeling. By contrast, ESFJs are very emotional and take things so personally that even the most innocuous observation is often perceived as personal criticism. ESFJs often feel that their partners are impatient with their feelings simply because they don't share them. For ESFJs, how they feel is paramount to whether an issue makes sense. ESTJs are firm and logical but can also be demanding and tough, while ESFJs are very empathetic and can be swayed by how they or others feel.

ESTJs and ESFJs handle conflict very differently. ESTJs tend to want to discuss problems as they arise and to quickly and calmly resolve them. ESFJs generally avoid unnecessary conflict, since it brings about too much tension and disharmony. ESFJs can often become upset and defensive, and they tend to bring up and rehash old issues. ESTJs can be insensitive and arrogantly accuse ESFJs of overreacting. After a cooling-off period, both partners need to listen carefully to each other in order to regain their balance and perspective.

How to Reach Your ESFJ Partner

- Listen, listen, and listen some more! Let your partner spill out his or her feelings without comment or criticism.
- Don't try to fix your partner's problems. Instead, be a supportive and concerned listener.

- Share your reactions and feelings readily so your partner doesn't have to wonder what you're feeling.
- Be patient with your partner's emotions, even when you don't fully understand them.
- Compliment and appreciate your partner for all the ways he or she makes life more comfortable and happy.
- Take a load off your partner by doing one of his or her chores.
- Emphasize the positive and be gentle with criticism.

How to Reach Your ESTJ Partner

- Try to remain calm and rational when presenting your feelings. Try not to exaggerate or overreact.
- Explain when you need your partner to listen without suggesting ways of resolving the problem.
- Once an issue is settled, don't bring it up again.
- Compliment your partner on his or her achievements. Thank your mate for all the hard work and the ways he or she makes life more secure and comfortable.
- Take a load off your partner by doing one of his or her chores.
- Tell other people how much you admire your partner. Third-party compliments are usually more credible and well received.
- Present your ideas or arguments logically. Ask your partner to help you see the natural consequences of actions.

ESTJ with ISFJ

The Joys

Because ESTJs and ISFJs share two type preferences and have similar traditional values, they often have a lot in common. They are typically very conservative people who trust their own experiences and are somewhat skeptical of new ideas or theoretical approaches. They tend to enjoy a stable and predictable life and are respectful of each other's schedules and routines. They generally like to plan activities and events well in advance and don't appreciate sudden changes. ESTJs and ISFJs also take good care of their possessions and like to maintain an orderly home. Sensible and practical, ESTJs and ISFJs are down-to-earth and unpretentious people. Meticulous and careful with their money, they are responsible and dependable, take their commitments very seriously, and enjoy the fact that they seldom give their partners reason to question their faithfulness. They are both very hardworking and take special delight in planning and observing the traditions of special holidays.

In addition to their similarities, ESTJs and ISFJs are often attracted to each other because of their differences. ESTJs are drawn to ISFJs because they are so gentle, sympathetic, and nurturing. ISFJs love to take care of ESTJs and are affectionate and eager to please. ESTJs like and admire ISFJs' polite demeanor and adherence to courtly behavior. ISFJs are attracted to ESTJs because of their energy and social ease. ESTJs exude strength and confidence, and they seem capable of managing almost anything. ISFJs admire their honesty, their directness, and the fact that they rarely become overwhelmed.

Because of their differences, ESTJs and ISFJs have the opportunity to help each other grow and develop in important ways. Typically, ESTJs help ISFJs stand up to resistance, speak up for themselves, and be less likely to be taken for granted. ISFJs often credit their partners with helping them get out into the world, meet new people, and expand their horizons. For their part, ISFJs help ESTJs develop increased sensitivity to and appreciation of others and to become less critical and

demanding. ESTJs also appreciate how ISFJs help them slow down and enjoy quiet times together.

The Frustrations

A common frustration for ESTJs and ISFJs stems from their different social needs. ESTJs are very outgoing people who come alive when surrounded by others. They tend to have a wide circle of friends and are often busy outside their homes, participating in a variety of projects and activities. But they are sometimes so involved elsewhere that they are inattentive to their partners' need for quiet time alone together. By contrast, ISFJs are much more private and reserved. They usually have a smaller group of trusted friends and want their relationships to be close personal ones. ISFJs also want their partners to keep their confidences and put them ahead of other relationships and commitments.

ESTJs are more eager to talk about issues or irritations as they come up and to take immediate action to fix problems. ESTJs take on life with a directness and logic that ISFJs can experience as overbearing and cold. ISFJs tend to be so sensitive and gentle that they are easily offended and hurt by what their partners intend as constructive criticism or merely an objective observation. ISFJs are very polite and respectful and rarely enjoy or initiate debates or arguments. They tend to hold on to hurts for a long time — much longer than seems rational to their more matter-of-fact ESTJ partners.

The biggest area of frustration for most ESTJs and ISFJs stems from their different ways of making decisions. More reflective and cautious, ISFJs generally need more time to think through their positions. ISFJs often feel pressured and intimidated into making decisions before they really feel ready, and ESTJs may get antsy in the meantime. Whereas ISFJs need to speak up for themselves, ESTJs need to make sure they don't finish their partners' sentences or make erroneous assumptions or snap decisions. ESTJs often feel as if they need to handle their partners with kid gloves, while ISFJs may feel overwhelmed and intimidated by their partners. Naturally, the more impatience ESTJs show with the depth or intensity of their partners' feelings, the more upset ISFJs become and the more they retreat. ISFJs need to be willing to stand their ground and explain clearly, calmly, and precisely what they need in order to make their partners understand. Since ESTJs don't always trust themselves to deal competently with their or others' emotions, they tend to avoid the kind of disclosure that makes them feel vulnerable and weak. Ironically, that is precisely the level of sharing ISFJs long for and what they feel helps forge a stronger bond.

How to Reach Your ISFJ Partner

• Be patient. Give your partner plenty of time to express his or her feelings. Listen attentively and respectfully.
• Ask about your partner's day and listen with your full attention.
• Demonstrate your interest by paying close attention to the people details of your partner's stories.
• Speak softly and remember to notice and appreciate the positive things before commenting on the negative.
• Be careful of your tendency to become so busy with work, other people, and outside activities that you neglect your partner.
• Don't pressure your partner to participate in social activities more than he or she wants to.
• Never share personal information about your partner with other people.

How to Reach Your ESTJ Partner

• Be clear and direct. Don't skirt around issues, but instead come right to the point.
• Try to stay calm even when you're feeling upset.

Explain why you feel as you do and try not to exaggerate.
• Ask for help rather than take on too much and then become exhausted and resentful.
• Be willing to try to join in some of the social activities your partner wants to enjoy. Be sure to encourage our partner to go without you when you're too tired.
• When you need time to think something through, be sure to tell your partner, then agree to a time when you will discuss it together.

ISTJ with ISTJ

The Joys

When two people have as much in common as two ISTJs, they typically experience a very comfortable and steady relationship. Both partners are so completely dependable that they know they can trust and take each other at their word. ISTJ couples are usually quiet, serious, and hardworking, each pulling his or her own weight and striving to keep their home lives stable and secure. ISTJs find that they can totally be themselves with each other, and their similarities create a familiarity that feels intimate and special.

Most ISTJs lead very traditional lives and share conservative values. They like predictability and take comfort in the routines and rituals of their lives. ISTJs are independent, but they enjoy participating in low-key activities such as sitting quietly, reading, or watching TV together. They generally maintain a traditional division of labor and often express their appreciation for each other by helping out with their partners' chores or doing household projects together. When conflicts arise, they usually take time alone to figure out what went wrong and then come back together to agree rationally and calmly on a fair compromise. One of the great sources of satisfaction for ISTJs (especially female ISTJs, who are susceptible to social conditioning that tells them not to speak their minds) is that they are usually able to discuss issues honestly or defend their positions without their partners taking offense. Their logic and objectivity are liberating elements of their relationships.

It's not surprising that ISTJs are typically attracted to each other because of the sense of familiarity, ease, and comfort they experience together. But ISTJ couples also have to help each other grow and develop in important ways. Together, they can broaden their horizons and try new things. They also may support each other's efforts to be flexible and adopt a slightly more relaxed and playful attitude. Finally, they may become more willing to try to express their deepest feelings and let themselves be vulnerable. When they do, they learn to be more patient with and sensitive to others.

The Frustrations

Perhaps the biggest challenge for contented ISTJ couples is keeping the relationship dynamic and interesting. Although neither partner needs wildly exciting times, they may find themselves stuck in routines that feel stifling. And since neither is especially effusive with his or her appreciation, praise, or expression of affection, they may come to take each other for granted. Also, because most ISTJs have exacting standards, they are highly selective about almost everything pertaining to themselves and their homes. When two people are both quite set in their ways and convinced that their own ways are the right ways, they can be somewhat bossy, controlling, and judgmental. Since they also tend to be a bit obsessive, they may get stuck on details that provoke resistance and resentment.

ISTJs' characteristic tenacity and precision can take the fun out of a debate. And when the tone of a discussion turns contentious and it becomes more important to be right than kind, they may unintentionally hurt each other's feelings. Since neither is likely to admit that fact right away, a rift may develop in their otherwise close relationships.

Finally, because ISTJs are driven to keep things as calm and constant as possible, they tend to make very quick and absolute decisions. They are very careful and hesitant about new things, and their inflexibility can sometimes make them miss fun and useful new experiences. Neither partner is especially inclined to ask a lot of questions or want to keep options open for too long. So in order to accomplish a resolution, they end up locking themselves into unpleasant situations. ISTJ couples need to work at being flexible about letting little things go and sharing the burden of unpleasant tasks, such as doing all the chores, asking for directions, researching options, and taking some risks. By actively cultivating outside friendships and activities, they can ensure that they don't become too isolated from the world and each other.

Advice for ISTJs

- Rather than being critical or demanding, be explicit when you explain what your partner does that hurts or offends you.
- Take time to really reflect on your feelings and emotions. Then agree to share them on a regular basis.
- Remember to protect the trust between you and your partner, which makes it possible for you to cultivate intimacy.
- Share the job of staying in touch with friends, family, and colleagues.
- Be sure to encourage each other to maintain separate friendships and interests. Try new things together.
- Don't avoid confrontations. Initiate discussions and risk vulnerability with your partner.
- Watch your tendency to be stubborn and unyielding. Remember the benefits of compromise and generosity, and temper your tendency to be critical of one another's idiosyncrasies.

ISTJ with ESFJ

The Joys

ISTJs and ESFJs have two of the four type preferences in common and share traditional values. Since they both enjoy a fairly conventional home life, they appreciate the responsibility and maturity each possesses. They tend to be conservative in their personal values and careful and accurate with their money. They are naturally organized, so they usually keep a neat and efficiently run home. They enjoy spending time as a family, and since neither ISTJs nor ESFJs like sudden changes or surprises, they place a high value on fidelity and the comfort that comes from living with a predictable partner. ISTJs tend to be planners and caretakers of their possessions, and ESFJs tend to initiate the couple's social activities and push their partners to get out in the world. These couples usually adhere to pretty clear divisions of labor, often according to traditional gender roles.

In addition to their similarities, ISTJs and ESFJs are initially attracted to each other because of their differences. ISTJs are often drawn to the warmth, vivaciousness, and enthusiasm of ESFJs. They admire ESFJs' social skills and their natural compassion and sensitivity to the needs and feelings of others. ESFJs like the even-tempered, practical, hardworking steadiness of ISTJs. They admire their calm, unflappable approach to problem solving.

Because of their differences, ISTJs and ESFJs have the opportunity to help each other grow and develop in important ways. ISTJs help ESFJs slow down to consider some of the less appealing, but nonetheless vital, logical consequences of their actions. ESFJs often credit their partners with helping them develop a thicker skin so they don't take things quite so personally. For their part, ESFJs often help their ISTJ partners become more willing to open up and share their feelings. As a result, ISTJs may become more patient and accepting of the extenuating circumstances that affect others.

The Frustrations

Communication is one of the biggest challenges that face ISTJ and ESFJ couples. ISTJs want and need to consider things carefully before responding or taking action, especially if the subject is of an emotional nature. When ISTJs don't know what to say or aren't really sure how they feel, they often retreat to work it out in silence. And since they don't tend to share their intentions or needs freely, this disappearing act is usually perceived as checking out of the relationship — for hours, days, or in some cases longer. In contrast, ESFJs need and want to talk almost everything out with their partners. They need a close and harmonious connection at all times and become stressed and hurt when there is tension in their relationships. ESFJs need lots of verbal affirmation of their partners' feelings, loving compliments, and credit for their high productivity. ESFJs also want their partners to listen, without judgment, to their feelings, rather than simply pointing out why it is silly to feel as they do or immediately trying to fix the problem. ISTJs are embarrassed by effusive praise and therefore don't usually want to receive or give much of it. They want their partners to be calm and to avoid blowing things out of proportion.

Another challenge comes from this couple's different social needs. ISTJs are very private people, whereas ESFJs are quite outgoing and enjoy greater social stimulation. So conflicts tend to arise when ESFJs don't get enough fun and social interaction and ISTJs don't get enough peace and quiet. ISTJs often rightly accuse their ESFJ partners of not putting them first when they spread themselves too thin with numerous friends and outside commitments. And ESFJs may feel neglected when their ISTJ partners put work ahead of them.

Finally, because both ISTJs and ESFJs like a stable and conventional life together, there can be tension when the need for change arises. ESFJs are usually the initiators, while ISTJs are considerably more cautious. Without enough time to consider, research, and weigh the pros and cons of a proposed change, ISTJs tend to resist or outright refuse to change, citing all the reasons against it. Although they may have reasonable objections, their tendency to focus on the negative is a source of real frustration for ESFJs, who derive so much excitement and energy from making things happen. To be sure, ESFJs often jump into things headfirst without taking the time to do careful research. ISTJs and ESFJs need to set aside regular time to go over their respective lists of concerns, hear each other out, and find reasonable yet compassionate solutions to problems.

How to Reach Your ESFJ Partner

- Don't say no until you've given your partner a chance to tell you the whole idea. Resisting his or her plans will take the wind out of your partner's sails.
- Give verbal (or written) compliments on a regular basis.
- Listen to your partner talk. Support his or her feelings, and don't debate their validity or dismiss them as overreactions.
- Share your feelings and thought process with your partner, rather than keeping them to yourself and assuming your partner knows how you feel.
- Appreciate your partner's hard work and efforts.

How to Reach Your ISTJ Partner

- Don't talk over or for your partner. Let your mate finish his or her thoughts before responding.
- Give your partner plenty of time to make a decision. Remember that even if the first response is no, in time your partner may change his or her mind.

- Get your high social needs met with regular time out with friends, but strive to find a balance between outside activities and quiet time spent at home or participating in some activity your partner enjoys.
- Stay calm and objective during discussions. Make your points clearly, honestly, and as unemotionally as you can.
- Don't put off important discussions too long because you're afraid to rock the boat. Be clear and explicit about what you want your partner to do differently.

ISTJ with ISFJ

The Joys

Relationships between ISTJs and ISFJs are often comfortable and stable, since they share three out of four type preferences and a common temperament. Both tend to be quiet, serious, and cautious people with strong traditional values. They are hardworking and responsible, and they take their commitments very seriously. When it comes to work or home duties, they are utterly dependable and sure to pull their own weight. Typically, both ISTJs and ISFJs are very careful with money and accurate about details such as balancing the checkbook and maintaining their possessions. They tend to like to make and stick with plans, be punctual and reliable, and respect the routines and rituals of their families.

ISTJs' and ISFJs' many similarities are often what initially attracts them to each other. They see in one another a mature and trustworthy mate, someone who will honor traditional family values. Their mutual commitment to fidelity also is unquestionable. But their differences add a spark to the initial attraction. ISTJs are drawn to ISFJs' warmth, genuine concern for others, and their ability to be sympathetic listeners. Most ISFJs are deeply devoted to their families and friends and demonstrate that devotion by going the extra mile for anyone in need. For their part, ISFJs are often attracted to ISTJs because they are so calm, collected, and independent. ISTJs seem to be able to handle any problem or crisis that arises with level-headedness and careful follow-through. ISFJs admire their ISTJ partners' ability to be objective and assertive.

ISTJs' and ISFJs' differences help them to grow and develop in important ways. ISFJs are often able to help their very sensitive partners place less stock in the opinions of others and be more objective in their own decision making. ISFJs often credit their ISTJ partners with helping them become more assertive and independent. ISFJs help their ISTJ partners become more compassionate toward and patient with the feelings of others. ISTJs often say that over time they have become more aware of their own values and that their relationships have assumed a higher priority.

The Frustrations

The most typical frustrations ISTJs and ISFJs experience result from the very different criteria they use to make their decisions. Whereas ISTJs are very logical and often critical, ISFJs are highly sensitive and emotional. ISTJs and ISFJs often miscommunicate when they don't share their very different ways of coming to conclusions. ISTJs think their partners take things too personally and overreact to even minor slights or offenses. For their part, ISFJs often feel that their ISTJ partners are critical of and impatient with their fears and worries. Although both tend to be extraordinarily good listeners, ISFJs often feel that their ISTJ partners are reluctant to share how they really feel. ISFJs want to share their feelings openly and intimately in a supportive and nonjudgmental atmosphere. ISTJs want to talk less about feelings and find it wearying to have to constantly reassure their partners. Such reassurance, they believe, is unnecessary if two people really trust each other.

But when they are ready to share, they too need a nonjudgmental atmosphere in order to feel safe to risk emotional vulnerability.

When ISTJs and ISFJs experience conflict, neither is in a big hurry to discuss it. ISTJs tend to need a lot of time to think through their position and make sense of the issue privately. And ISFJs tend to avoid the disharmony that accompanies discussions of unpleasant subjects. So both partners may initially withdraw and put off a discussion for a few hours or even a few weeks. Eventually, either the tension between them gets to be too much for the ISFJ, or the logical necessity of fixing the problem drives the ISTJ to have a "sit down." The communication styles of ISTJs and ISFJs are also very different. Sometimes the blunt honesty of ISTJs hurts the feelings of ISFJs, while ISTJs may suspect ISFJs of being less than 100 percent candid.

Finally, although both ISTJs and ISFJs tend to be organized and like order and structure in their lives and homes, they may have slightly different standards of neatness. Typically, ISTJs are even more fastidious and concerned with how precisely things are arranged or how quickly they are put away. But ISFJs can be picky about those things as well. And since both like to be in control, this couple is susceptible to power struggles and can accuse one another of being too rigid.

How to Reach Your ISFJ Partner

- Pamper your partner with sensual pleasures and gifts.
- Remember romance. Never underestimate the value of quiet, intimate times together. Offer small, thoughtful expressions of affection (cards, E-mails, and gifts).
- Listen patiently without criticism or judgment, even if your partner is repeating himself or herself.
- Be especially helpful and supportive during stressful or busy times.

- Remember sentimental things and special days such as holidays and anniversaries.
- Don't dismiss your partner's feelings or be critical of his or her reactions.
- Compliment your partner on his or her looks and appreciate the many things he or she does to create and maintain a warm, well-organized, and comfortable home.
- Share your own feelings and personal reactions rather than waiting to be asked.

How to Reach Your ISTJ Partner

- Compliment your partner on tangible achievements and contributions.
- Thank your partner for all that he or she does to keep the house organized and the family safe and secure.
- Respect your partner's need for order and neatness and help maintain his or her routines.
- Be calm and direct. Don't avoid problems, but don't exaggerate their seriousness.
- Gently coax your partner to discuss his or her emotions. Listen respectfully.
- Never question your partner's competence in public.

ESFJ with ESFJ

The Joys

Since two ESFJs have all four type preferences in common and tend to share the same traditional and conservative values, they often experience a very harmonious and loving relationship. They are compassionate, expressive, and caring people who strive to maintain a happy home. Outgoing and talkative, ESFJs tend to know a lot of people and enjoy hosting social events for their many friends, associates, neighbors, and acquaintances. Because they often share similar interests, they can be great companions and playmates, pursuing their many, often physically active, hobbies.

Naturally, ESFJs find it very easy to understand each other, as they are both so literal, practical, and realistic. They share the values of hard work and responsibility, and they are usually unfailingly faithful to all their commitments. ESFJs usually like to make a big deal out of holidays and other special events, making sure everything is organized and planned well in advance. They enjoy talking about and planning for the future, and they tend to appreciate and want nice possessions. ESFJs are generally careful with their money and are willing to make and stick with a budget.

The glue that really holds two ESFJs together is their mutual desire for an intense and meaningful emotional connection. They both want a deep level of emotional intimacy and usually feel comfortable sharing their feelings freely with each other. The sense of having found a soul mate is often the strongest and most enduring attraction for ESFJs. They know that they can fully trust and depend on one another during good times and bad.

Because of their loyalty and mutual trust, many ESFJs are able to help each other grow and develop in important ways. They can learn to slow down and consider their decisions, as well as see more gray areas in what is ordinarily a very black-and-white world. They also tend to encourage each other not to take things so personally and to resist the pressure they feel to always do things that please other people. As they become more direct and honest with each other, they learn to stand up for themselves with other people as well.

The Frustrations

Because ESFJ couples share the same strengths, they often have the same blind spots, which they naturally see more clearly in their partners. Chief among these is their common tendency to take things very personally and to become emotionally upset at even the most constructive criticism. They may have passionate arguments, not really listen to each other, and have a hard time backing down or forgiving each other. They also tend to jump to conclusions and may erroneously assume they know just what their partners are thinking or feeling. Since they tend to avoid honest discussions of small problems, they often let things build up until a blowup occurs. At that point, they know just what to say to hurt their partner and may indeed say things they later regret. A hard lesson for many ESFJs is that true harmony is achieved by taking the time to discuss issues honestly and calmly as they come up.

Another area of frustration for many ESFJ couples is that because both partners tend to like to be in charge, they frequently struggle for control and can be quite inflexible about their own schedules and routines. Creatures of habit, ESFJs may resist any efforts to change their plans, even refusing to take advantage of spontaneous, interesting, or important opportunities. They also can get set in their ways and become very picky about how their homes are set up or their routines carried out. ESFJ couples have difficulty relaxing until all their responsibilities are met and their chores done to their exacting standards. And since they value hard work highly, they can become overtired and neglect their private and fun time together. They need to keep their priorities straight and not get pulled into helping other people or organizing events that take them away from home too often.

Finally, ESFJ couples can face real difficulties if they have strong values that their partners do not share. They can find themselves intractable and unwilling to consider opposing views about what they feel is important. These conflicts can cause deep divisions between otherwise committed and loving partners. ESFJs almost always benefit from outside help in finding ways to accommodate their partners without feeling as if they're compromising their integrity or values.

Advice for ESFJs

• Emphasize the positive. Appreciate and compliment each other frequently, especially expressing gratitude for all the ways your partner makes you happy and keeps life comfortable and running smoothly.
• Be loving and tactful even when you're angry. Don't sacrifice honesty for temporary harmony.
• Think about what would make you happy, then do it for your partner. (For example, do a chore that is your partner's responsibility.)
• Don't bottle things up and then risk blowing up. Try not to keep score.
• Think about what you want to say ahead of time so you can approach your partner calmly, rationally, and not defensively.
• Listen attentively and think before you speak. Don't assume that because you're alike, you know just what your partner wants and feels.
• Let household chores wait sometimes. Schedule downtime just to relax together, and let the outside world wait.

ESFJ with ISFJ

The Joys

With three shared preferences, ESFJs and ISFJs usually have no trouble understanding each other, and they have a tremendous amount in common. These serious, down-to-earth people have traditional values and believe that trust, respect, and emotional openness are the keys to a committed relationship. And because they are so similar, they frequently have common interests and enjoy spending time together doing things such as cooking, gardening, collecting, or enjoying nature. Many ESFJs and ISFJs find the familiarity that comes with sharing so much very comfortable. Both are helpful and considerate of others, and they appreciate being treated that way by their partners.

ESFJs and ISFJs prefer to live in a fairly orderly way. They like the predictability of their routines, and their neat yet comfortable homes reflect their good taste and practicality. ESFJ and ISFJ couples seldom have trouble making decisions, and because they share a strong work ethic, they usually support each other's career decisions.

In addition to their many similarities, ESFJs and ISFJs are often initially attracted to each other because of their different energy levels. ESFJs are often drawn to ISFJs' calm, patience, and loyalty. They especially enjoy being the focus of their partners' loving attention. ISFJs are often attracted to ESFJs' friendliness and social confidence. ESFJs bring a higher level of enthusiasm and excitement to many ISFJs' lives.

Although ESFJs and ISFJs have a lot in common, they can help each other grow and develop in important ways. ESFJs can bring their partners out into the world, exposing them to people and things they might not seek on their own. ISFJs can help their partners focus their energy and "take time to smell the roses."

The Frustrations

Unlike their ISFJ partners, ESFJs are usually very social people. Whereas ISFJs are often content to spend time at home with their partners or families, ESFJs usually want to be out interacting with lots of people. This can cause resentment on both sides. ISFJs may feel neglected and think that their partners consider other people's needs above their own. And ESFJs may feel prevented from doing the things they enjoy. The good news is that once couples of this combination recognize their contrasting needs, they can usually negotiate successful ways to accommodate them.

Another difference that can cause frustration is that ESFJs often need to talk in order to think, and ISFJs prefer to process their thoughts and feelings internally. The result may be that ESFJs feel that they don't know what's going on with their partners or that their partners aren't interested in hearing about what's going on with them. For their part, ISFJs may feel that their privacy is constantly being invaded.

Because ESFJs and ISFJs both place a high value on harmony in their relationships, they are often reluctant to do or say anything that will upset their partners. As a result, they may suppress negative feelings and let issues that could be satisfactorily addressed go unresolved. And when one or both partners' resentments reach a critical level, both are likely to explode in anger and almost always suffer strong feelings of guilt and regret afterward. To compound this problem, both ESFJs and ISFJs tend to have clear expectations of how their partners should behave in most situations. When things go wrong, ESFJs and ISFJs have a tendency to become defensive and blame others, even when it's their own fault.

Finally, because ESFJs and ISFJs both tend to be pretty set in their ways and do not naturally see possibilities, neither may be particularly open to trying new solutions to problems they encounter. They may need to push each other gently to consider new approaches and take on new challenges.

How to Reach Your ISFJ Partner

- Pay attention to your partner. Try not to become so overextended with outside activities that your partner feels neglected.
- Be an attentive, patient, and supportive listener. Recognize your partner's need to think about things before discussing them.
- Resist the urge to try to fix problems immediately or finish your partner's sentences.
- Be patient and recognize that your partner may need a slower, more deliberate pace than you do.
- Don't make promises you can't keep. Give your partner plenty of time to adjust to changes in plans, and recognize that he or she may need more "transition time" than you do.
- Be respectful and considerate. Never share private information about your partner with others without your partner's permission.
- When attending social functions, try to make

your partner comfortable by introducing him or her to people he or she may enjoy talking to.

How to Reach Your ESFJ Partner

• Speak up and let your partner know what is going on and what you need. Don't assume that he or she should automatically know.
• Engage in social events to the extent you feel comfortable. Expect your partner to have stronger social needs than you do. Encourage your mate to participate in social events without you, and don't make him or her feel guilty about doing so.
• Listen to your partner. Understand that he or she needs to think out loud.
• Trust your partner enough to be honest about your feelings.
• Be respectful and considerate.

ISFJ with ISFJ

The Joys

When two people share the same type and are as fundamentally alike as two ISFJs, they tend to feel secure, comfortable, and like family. Two ISFJs, because they know what is expected of them and are happiest with a set schedule, often find it a great relief to know that their favorite routines will be respected and maintained.

Great teammates, partners, and companions, ISFJ couples often experience a mature, emotional connection unlike any either has had before. Both care deeply about the people close to them and are devoted and loyal friends. ISFJs take all their responsibilities, promises, and vows very seriously and love the fact that their partners bring the same degree of commitment to their relationships. Since both have strong values and a clear work ethic, they understand and respect each other's need to live in harmony with their heartfelt convictions. There is rarely a lot of gray area where ISFJs are concerned, and they naturally understand and accept this shared characteristic. They have high standards of personal conduct and appreciate that their partners rarely ask them to compromise on what's important.

It's no surprise, then, that ISFJs are strongly attracted to each other. In addition to their similar styles and attitudes, ISFJs share the same temperaments and tend to be conservative and traditional. Female ISFJs usually like having partners who are gentlemen, and male ISFJs enjoy treating their partners like ladies. Both naturally and comfortably slip into traditional roles. ISFJs pull their own weight and generally work well together, keeping their well-organized homes running smoothly. Utterly accountable and responsible, ISFJs tend to be very careful with money. Most ISFJs like being able to relax around their partners, knowing that they rarely have to wonder where their partners stand on issues or brace themselves for surprises or abrupt changes. Gentle, quiet, and unassuming, ISFJs also appreciate the fact that they are both down-to-earth, sensible people who communicate clearly and thoughtfully. Both partners are eager to please and will do all sorts of practical things to help each other out or to express their appreciation and affection. ISFJs are wonderfully attentive and sympathetic listeners, so they usually consider their partners to be their best friends.

Because of their many similarities, ISFJs have the opportunity to help each other grow and develop in important ways. ISFJ couples help one another become less prone to disappointment and hurt by learning to be a bit more objective in their decision making. By speaking their minds more assertively in the safety of their relationships, they can begin to learn how to avoid being taken advantage of by others. And together ISFJs can gently encourage each other to take some calculated risks and try new things. By asking more questions, they can both make better choices and broaden their horizons.

The Frustrations

Although life flows pretty smoothly for two ISFJs, they do have the potential to get stuck in a rut. If they keep things the same for too long or continually reject new opportunities, over time ISFJs get bored with routines that once felt comfortable. This can be especially painful when just one partner feels the need to change, because it can leave the other feeling abandoned or betrayed. And since both partners tend to avoid confrontation or even discussing unpleasant subjects, they may delay making positive changes much longer than is healthy for either of them.

Another potential area of frustration for ISFJ couples is that because they both prefer a quiet life shared with only a few very close friends, they can find it difficult to initiate social activities. They also may avoid returning phone calls or hosting parties. And because both like things well planned in advance, they may miss opportunities that come up spontaneously. Most ISFJs hold such strong opinions and tend to make such firm and absolute decisions that they sometimes paint themselves into a corner and fail to see alternative solutions to their problems. An ISFJ couple may also face difficulties if they find themselves with conflicting positions on important matters. Differences, and the ensuing disharmony and distance, can feel insurmountable. Spending quiet time alone together generally helps them reestablish their connection and gives them the confidence to overcome obstacles.

Advice for ISFJs

- Encourage each other to pursue separate friends, interests, and activities.
- Be willing to try new things together to keep the spark alive.
- Take turns initiating social activities or answering the phone.
- Beware of your tendency to accept things on face value. Encourage each other to look beyond the known and accepted.
- Make sure you are both pulling your own weight regarding household chores. Thank each other for your efforts.

Chapter 5

Traditionalists with Experiencers: SJs with SPs

ESTJ with ESTP

The Joys

Since ESTJs and ESTPs have three of the four type preferences in common, they often are similar in many ways. Both are active, high-energy, and talkative people who thrive on lots of social interaction. They frequently enjoy being outdoors together, participating in a variety of physical or sporting events, or just running errands. ESTJ and ESTP couples tend to understand each other easily, as they are both literal, realistic, and practical people who focus on details and are constantly aware of the present moment. They are also logical decision makers who take an analytical and objective view of things. Although they are both very friendly and outgoing, they can make the tough calls when they need to and rarely worry about hurting each other's feelings. Matter-of-fact and sometimes direct to the point of bluntness, ESTJs and ESTPs are usually able to receive constructive criticism in the spirit in which it is intended.

ESTJs and ESTPs approach life with different temperamental values, however. ESTJs are much more traditional and conventional than their free-spirited, risk-taking ESTP partners. As ESTPs age, they often find themselves in agreement with their partners' conservative social and political leanings, with a slight variation: ESTJs believe it essen-

tial to follow the rules of society, while ESTPs are strong advocates of taking responsibility for their own actions.

Despite their many similarities, ESTJs and ESTPs are also initially attracted to each other because of their complementary differences. Typically, ESTJs are drawn to ESTPs' playfulness and easygoing natures. ESTJs find ESTPs' irreverence exciting, if occasionally shocking, and admire their responsiveness and adaptability. ESTPs are often attracted to ESTJs because they are ambitious, have a strong work ethic, and possess an ability to set and reach their goals. ESTPs often admire their partners' strength of character, stability, and utter dependability.

Because of their differences, ESTJs and ESTPs have the opportunity to help each other grow and develop in important ways. Typically, ESTJs help their often-distractible ESTP partners focus their considerable energy and stay on track. ESTPs often credit their partners with helping them to follow through and finish more projects successfully and to become more accountable for them. For their part, ESTPs are often able to help their serious and super-responsible ESTJ partners relax a little, have some fun, and learn to laugh at themselves. Many ESTJs say that their partners push them to try new experiences and take more risks. Together, ESTJs and ESTPs often find a middle ground between ESTJs' steadfast respect for authority and ESTPs' casual disregard for it.

The Frustrations

Although ESTJs and ESTPs are compatible in many ways and often enjoy comfortable relationships, they do experience frustrations that stem from their differences. Chief among those are their different needs for order and closure. ESTJs are super-organized people who have strong opinions about the way things should be done. In general, ESTPs are more flexible about how they live, as they are driven by their curiosity and desire to experience as much of life as possible. ESTPs want to keep their options open and constantly gather new information. Sometimes they find their ESTJ partners too opinionated and controlling, whereas ESTJs often think that their ESTP partners don't take things seriously enough. ESTJs also like neat and orderly environments, while ESTPs are typically less bothered by clutter. They find their ESTJ partners' insistence on putting things away exactly where they belong to be excessive. On the other hand, ESTJs tend to do more to organize and clean their households, and given their need for fairness, it's understandable why ESTJs find this inequity irritating. ESTJ and ESTP couples need to be careful that they don't fall into roles that more closely resemble parent and child than two adult partners.

Another area of frustration for many ESTJ and ESTP couples is decision making. ESTJs tend to like everything settled and planned, while ESTPs prefer to stay open to experiences that pop up unexpectedly. ESTPs need plenty of personal freedom, just as ESTJs need predictability. So ESTJs are constantly trying to get their partners to commit to a plan, and ESTPs often feel pressured and crowded. Naturally, the more ESTJs force a decision from their partners, the more likely ESTPs are to find reasons to escape. To be sure, ESTJs do make rather inflexible judgments, and ESTPs are often guilty of procrastinating or changing plans suddenly when something more intriguing comes along.

Finally, since neither ESTJs nor ESTPs are usually very comfortable expressing their true feelings and emotions, they may not take the time to really share their deep and intimate feelings with each other. Although they are great companions and typically understand each other well, they may need to commit themselves to going deeper, discussing their expectations and needs, and risk being emotionally vulnerable in order to establish a strong and enduring relationship.

How to Reach Your ESTP Partner

- Try not to overschedule your partner's spare time. Encourage your mate to enjoy the freedom he or she has without having to account for his or her time.
- Be willing to put off what you're doing to participate in some of the spontaneous suggestions your partner makes.
- Don't force decisions. Respect your partner's need to gather a lot of information, especially from other people, before making a decision or coming to a conclusion.
- Watch your tendency to say no immediately to suggestions or possible purchases. Keep an open mind and really consider the ideas.
- Remember that your way isn't the only way or even the right way. Try to be flexible and accepting of other points of view.
- Be willing to let the small stuff go and experience the moment with your partner. Life is short — enjoy it!

How to Reach Your ESTJ Partner

- Remember to thank your partner for all the many things he or she does to keep your home organized and your life running smoothly.
- Be willing to initiate and complete household chores. Pick up after yourself and put things away.
- Respect your partner's routines and rituals.

Don't interrupt or belittle his or her cherished practices and schedules.

• Watch your tendency to joke and take everything lightly. Be serious when your partner wants to discuss important issues. Maintain eye contact rather than constantly scanning the room.

• Try to be on time or call if you're running late. Follow through on commitments.

• Try not to surprise your partner by bringing home unexpected guests. Check with your partner before you make or accept invitations.

ESTJ with ISTP

The Joys

Although ESTJs and ISTPs have only two preferences in common, they are very important ones. This couple has a similar way of looking at the world and of making decisions. Both partners are generally realistic and practical and accept most things, including their relationships, at face value. ESTJs and ISTPs prefer to operate on a cerebral level and are often equally uncomfortable dealing with too many emotions, either their own or someone else's. At the same time, because neither takes things personally, they can give and receive constructive criticism without hurting each other's feelings. ESTJ and ISTP couples are also quite active and typically enjoy physical activities, especially being outdoors. However, even when they share the same hobbies, they may enjoy them in different ways. ESTJs are more traditional and cautious, while ISTPs like to push themselves and test their limits.

In addition to their similarities, ESTJs and ISTPs are often initially attracted to each other because of their differences. ESTJs are drawn to ISTPs because they are casual, easygoing, and low-key. ESTJs admire ISTPs' relaxed attitude and ability to adapt to life's constant changes. ISTPs are often attracted to ESTJs because they are so friendly, socially confident, and energetic. ISTPs like that ESTJs are ultra responsible and efficient, and they are awed by the sheer number of things ESTJs can accomplish in the course of a day.

Because of their differences, ESTJs and ISTPs have the opportunity to help each other grow and develop in important ways. ESTJs usually help their partners become more focused, accountable, and productive. They can be especially enthusiastic in their support of their partners' efforts to take on additional challenges at work. ISTPs often credit their partners with broadening their social circles and encouraging them to open up and share their thoughts. For their part, ISTPs help their partners slow down and pay closer attention to the process. ESTJs benefit from ISTPs' spontaneity and eagerness to experience and enjoy life.

The Frustrations

One of the areas of frustration for ESTJ and ISTP couples is their different needs for social interaction. Typically, ESTJs are much more outgoing and talkative, and ISTPs are much more private, aloof, and quiet. Although neither type is very comfortable discussing their feelings, ISTPs keep more of their thoughts and reactions to themselves, which can leave their partners feeling shut out. ISTPs sometimes complain that their partners talk too much, crowd them, and don't give them enough time alone. Although ESTJs are more talkative, both partners tend to show their affection through actions rather than words, as neither partner really feels comfortable sharing his or her true feelings. They may avoid or discount the importance of dealing directly with issues at the emotional level. And because they avoid searching for and uncovering the root causes of problems, issues may go unresolved, which can result in deep resentment.

The greatest challenge for ESTJ and ISTP couples may be dealing with their different values. ESTJs are rather serious people who have a strong need to exercise control and be in charge. They are utterly dependable and hardworking, and they believe in pulling their own weight. Generally, they have very strong opinions about right and wrong, and they rarely cut corners or fail to honor their commitments. Because ESTJs are so responsible, they may view their fun-loving ISTP partners as a bit irresponsible and unreliable. For their part, ISTPs crave freedom. They are very independent people who like to immerse themselves in their hobbies or interests. And although they may sometimes enjoy company, they often prefer to be alone. With their adventurous spirit, ISTPs love to respond spontaneously to whatever grabs their attention at the moment. ISTPs may feel neglected when their partners spend more time working than playing with them. It is not unusual for couples with these different temperaments to unwittingly assume the roles of parent and child — a dynamic neither enjoys.

Finally, since ESTJs and ISTPs have such different needs for order and closure, they may butt heads over issues of control and decision making. ESTJs tend to want to make decisions quickly, whereas ISTPs like to gather a lot of information and keep their options open for as long as possible. ESTJs sometimes complain that their partners put things off, and ISTPs often feel nagged and micromanaged by their partners. At the same time, ESTJs may feel let down and resent having to remind their partners to do the things they promised and to reprimand them when they don't.

How to Reach Your ISTP Partner

- Give your partner plenty of space. Don't intrude or crowd him or her.
- Respect your partner's privacy. Patiently encourage your partner to share, but never try to force your mate to reveal more than he or she wants to.
- Learn about your partner's hobbies and interests. Offer to participate, but make sure you also allow him or her to be alone.

- Don't control your partner's time or schedule. Don't make your mate account for every minute of his or her spare time.
- Try to be spontaneous with your partner (plan it, if necessary), especially with regard to having sex under unusual circumstances.
- Be patient with your partner's curiosity. Watch out not to make definitive statements too quickly.
- Don't pressure your partner to participate in social activities if he or she isn't up to it.

How to Reach Your ESTJ Partner

- Follow through on your commitments and do things when you say you will.
- Respect your partner's need for order and neatness, especially in the common areas of your home.
- Try to be more forthcoming with your partner about what is going on with you. Open up and share your thoughts and reactions.
- Do your share of the chores. Surprise your partner by occasionally doing one of his or her chores and giving him or her a break.

ESTJ with ESFP

The Joys

Because of the two type preferences ESTJs and ESFPs have in common, they are typically high-spirited and realistic. Both ESTJs and ESFPs are talkative, friendly, and active people who often enjoy the outdoors and thrive on being around their many friends, neighbors, and associates. They are both sensible and practical, explain things in literal and sequential ways, and are careful with details, so they understand each other very well. They pay close attention to the physical world, are very observant, and have accurate memories of their personal experiences.

In addition to their similarities, ESTJs and ESFPs are often initially attracted to each other because of their differences. ESTJs are drawn to ESFPs' genuine warmth and sensitivity to others. ESFPs are accepting, loyal, and supportive partners, and ESTJs appreciate their gentle, nurturing style. ESTJs also are drawn to ESFPs' affectionate and playful natures and find their irreverence appealing, if sometimes a little outrageous. ESFPs are attracted to ESTJs' strength of character and drive to achieve their goals. ESFPs also admire their partners' calm and honesty. And since ESTJs are so utterly responsible, hardworking, and dependable, they inspire trust and faith in ESFPs.

Because of their differences, ESTJs and ESFPs have the opportunity to help each other grow and develop in important ways. Typically, ESTJs help their fun-loving partners settle down and get serious about finishing projects. ESFPs often credit their partners with helping them become more accountable, consistent, and dependable, as well as encouraging them to be honest and direct. ESFPs find that in time they come to see the value of some traditions and may not be quite so impulsive. For their part, ESFPs help their more serious and straitlaced partners relax and have fun. ESFPs are also great at making ESTJs laugh and encouraging them to express their feelings. ESTJs often say that their partners help them become more sensitive and appreciative of other people and get them to consider other points of view.

The Frustrations

A chief source of frustration for many ESTJ and ESFP couples is their different temperaments. ESTJs are ultraresponsible, traditional, and conservative people who are most comfortable following the rules and maintaining the status quo. In contrast, ESFPs are typically playful and casual people who strive to live and let live and rarely feel the need to control others. So ESTJs are sometimes uncomfortable or even embarrassed by their partners' lack of decorum, while ESFPs feel that their partners are too uptight. ESFPs may fail to understand and respect the rituals ESTJs find so stabilizing while ESTJs may try to rein in their free-spirited partners and impose their values on them.

Frustration among ESTJs and ESFPs also stems from their different needs for order and closure. ESTJs typically believe in the adage of work first and play later, but only if there's still time. ESFPs often find ways of avoiding work or playing as they work to keep life interesting and fun. So ESTJs often end up doing more than their fair share of the household chores or constantly feeling irritated by the amount of clutter and chaos in their homes. Most ESFPs try hard to pick up after themselves and to finish some of the many projects they begin. But even when they have every intention of completing a chore, they are so naturally distractible that they often can't resist their impulses when something more exciting comes along. ESTJs find this maddening, since it often means that their partners fail to show up when or where they promised, or the ESTJs are left doing things that aren't their responsibility. ESFPs also tend to have a harder time budgeting their money, while ESTJs tend to be very careful about money and even frugal.

ESTJs and ESFPs also struggle with decision making. ESTJs quickly gather as much information as they need to make a firm decision, whereas ESFPs want much more information, especially from other people, and wait as long as possible to rule out options. So ESTJs tend to feel frustrated with their partners' lack of commitment or frequently changing mind, while ESFPs feel forced to make hasty decisions. Naturally, the more ESFPs resist deciding, the more their partners push for closure, and the more ESTJs push, the more likely ESFPs are to resist and pull away.

Finally, ESTJs and ESFPs often misunderstand each other because they rely on very different criteria when making decisions. ESTJs trust logic and objective analysis, while ESFPs rely on their personal feelings and values. So ESTJs often think that their partners are overly emotional and inconsistent, while ESFPs feel that their partners are too critical and insensitive to the needs of others. To be sure, ESTJs do tend to dismiss what they don't readily understand, just as ESFPs are prone to being easily swayed by others. ESTJs are naturally quite skeptical of things they haven't proved empirically, while ESFPs tend to take people at their word and are frequently disappointed. ESFPs may need to be more careful to put their partners first rather than getting carried away with their many friends, and ESTJs may need to watch their tendency to be stubborn and to act more like a parent than an equal partner.

How to Reach Your ESFP Partner

- Try not to pin down your partner or restrict his or her freedom. Encourage your partner to enjoy his or her spare time without having to account for it.
- Comment on points of agreement before pointing out errors, flaws, or inconsistencies.
- Be sure to express your appreciation for your partner's efforts and for creating a happy, comfortable home life.
- Be willing to participate in some of the many fun or unusual adventures your partner suggests. Consider the idea fully before saying no.
- Watch your tendency to focus first on the negative. Use thoughtful words and gestures to show and tell your partner that he or she makes you happy.
- Include your partner in your decision making. Resist your tendency to control or insist that things be done your way.

How to Reach Your ESTJ Partner

- Try to follow through on the things you say you'll do. Call if you are running late.
- Give your partner as much warning as possible when you need to change plans. Don't spring surprises on him or her.

- Express your needs and concerns calmly and clearly. Try not to become overly emotional or withdraw.
- Respect your partner's routines, rituals, and schedules, as well as his or her need to keep life somewhat predictable.
- Pick up after yourself, strive to finish projects, and put things back when you're finished using them.

ESTJ with ISFP

The Joys

ESTJs and ISFPs have only one of the four type preferences in common. They share a realistic view of the world and therefore have a source of connection and understanding. Typically practical and down-to-earth, ESTJs and ISFPs live in the present moment and remember the details of what they have personally experienced. Neither partner tends to spend a lot of time worrying about what might happen in the future, and they take most things, including each other, at face value. Therefore, they rarely overanalyze or idealize their relationships.

Frequently, ESTJ and ISFP couples share similar interests, and many enjoy the same recreational activities. For example, both types may derive satisfaction from community service. But ESTJs are motivated to serve and to make tangible, credible contributions, whereas ISFPs are driven to help individuals they love in specific ways. But the value of service can be important common ground. And, as is often the case, it is precisely these differences that initially attract the two. ESTJs find ISFPs gentle, loving, patient, and fun. They admire ISFPs' flexibility and acceptance. ISFPs typically admire how outgoing, energetic, responsible, and decisive their ESTJ partners are. ISFPs love the security of knowing they can count on their partners to follow through and keep their promises.

Because ESTJs and ISFPs are so dissimilar, they have the opportunity to help each other grow and develop in important ways. ESTJs help ISFPs become more logical, organized, and productive. They encourage them to speak up for themselves and be more assertive, which enables them to get more of their needs met. ISFPs help ESTJs become more sensitive to the needs of others and appreciate their relationships. Many ESTJs also credit their ISFP partners with encouraging them to relax and have more fun in life.

The Frustrations

Because of their significant differences, ESTJs and ISFPs face some real challenges in their daily lives. Although ESTJs are logical and objective, they also are often uncomfortable and even impatient when dealing with their own or others' feelings. For ISFPs, how they feel about something is often the most important consideration, but it can blind them to the logical consequences. This dynamic results in frequent miscommunication, as ESTJs inadvertently hurt the sensitive partners' feelings, and ISFPs respond emotionally or illogically to these slights.

Another challenge stems from this couple's different temperaments. Whereas ESTJs are responsible people with a strong work ethic, ISFPs are free-spirited people who value spontaneity and living in the moment. Not surprisingly, ESTJ and ISFP couples frequently experience conflict about money. ESTJs are more conservative about finances and prefer to budget their hard-earned money for high-quality, practical necessities often having to do with their homes. By contrast, many ISFPs like toys and gadgets and tend to spend money impulsively on fun activities and vacations. Similarly, ESTJs take a conservative approach to investing, while ISFPs are often more comfortable taking some risks.

In their desire to make things happen and be efficient, the super-organized ESTJs can be bossy and controlling. In contrast, ISFPs, in their desire to enjoy as much of life as they can, can be unreliable, making promises they may not be able to keep. ESTJs always seem to have a list of jobs that need to be done around the home. Although ISFPs want to please their partners, they seldom feel the same drive to be productive. Not surprisingly, ESTJs and ISFPs often have very different standards of neatness. ESTJs want things organized and free of clutter. ISFPs tend to be casual and more concerned about comfort and aesthetic appeal.

When problems or conflicts arise, ESTJs want to address them head-on, unless it's a very emotional issue, in which case they may try to avoid it. Instinctively, ESTJs like to talk about and fix problems immediately. By contrast, ISFPs are very often uncomfortable confronting their partners, and since their feelings are so important and private, they may need time to decide how they feel. The bottom line is that ISFPs generally want more sharing, understanding, and support, while ESTJs typically want more direct, honest discussions that eliminate problems and restore order and calm.

Finally, ESTJs tend to need much more social stimulation than ISFPs, so they tend to be active in groups or committees that take them out of the house or keep them on the phone in the evening. ISFPs are usually more selective about social involvement and typically have a few very trusted friends with whom they like to spend their free time. ISFPs often prefer to relax at home with their partners, while ESTJs are usually eager to get together with a group of friends. As a couple, they need to be sure to strike a balance to maintain a close connection.

How to Reach Your ESTJ Partner

- Surprise your partner by taking over some domestic tasks.
- Be particularly respectful of your partner's desire for order and neatness in common living areas.

• Strive to do what you say you will and when you say you will.

• If you need to change plans, give your partner a sound, logical reason and time to adjust to the new plan.

• Initiate conversation. Agree to times when you will discuss things together.

• Acknowledge, out loud, how much you appreciate the little things your partner does to maintain your home.

• Try to frame your suggestions or arguments using logic rather than emotion.

• Encourage your partner to share his or her feelings about important matters with you.

How to Reach Your ISFP Partner

• Surprise your partner with events or presents.

• Don't expect or demand that your partner be as neat as you are.

• Try not to impose too many rules or be too bossy. Realize that you may have to do many of the things you really want done yourself.

• Realize that sometimes plans have to change. Try to plan for spontaneity.

• Give your partner plenty of private time. Set aside times when your mate is not to be disturbed, and encourage him or her to enjoy the freedom not to respond during those times.

• Give your partner plenty of hugs, show affection, and say "I love you" a lot.

• Ask about the things that really matter to your partner, and really listen without telling your partner how to fix any problems. Be gentle and watch your tendency to be painfully honest and insensitive to your partner's feelings.

• Don't dismiss your partner's feelings. Watch your tendency to be overbearing or intimidating.

ISTJ with ESTP

The Joys

ISTJs and ESTPs have two important type preferences in common, giving them similar outlooks and compatible decision-making styles. Matter-of-fact, realistic, and practical, ISTJs and ESTPs pay close attention to the details of the world around them and usually have accurate memories. They are down-to-earth people who trust their own experiences to guide their choices and help form their beliefs. As a couple, they understand each other and communicate in clear, direct, literal ways. ISTJs and ESTPs also base most of their decisions on logical analysis rather than emotional appeals. They can give and receive constructive criticism without taking it personally or having their feelings hurt. Rarely clingy or highly sentimental, ISTJs and ESTPs usually enjoy and appreciate a high degree of honesty and straightforwardness in their relationships.

In addition to their similarities, ISTJs and ESTPs are often initially attracted to each other because of their differences. ISTJs are drawn to ESTPs because of their enormous energy, charm, and self-confidence. ESTPs' ability to adapt to change gracefully and to respond enthusiastically to the moment is impressive to most ISTJs. ISTJs also admire ESTPs' fun-loving and playful natures. ESTPs are often attracted to ISTJs because of their steadiness, stability, and calm, even in a crisis. ESTPs admire how capable, responsible, and accountable ISTJs are and how they inspire trust and respect in others.

Because of their differences, ISTJs and ESTPs have the opportunity to help each other grow and develop in important ways. In general, ISTJs help ESTPs slow down, calm down, and settle down so that they take their commitments more seriously. ESTPs credit their partners with encouraging them to think before they act and to follow through on projects they start. For their part, ESTPs help their partners relax, learn to laugh at themselves, and generally have more fun. ISTJs say that their partners also get them to participate in a wider range of social and physical adventures. And ISTJs find that as they learn to keep their options open longer, they make fewer snap decisions.

The Frustrations

Despite the many complementary aspects of their relationship, ISTJs and ESTPs experience frustration that stems from their different attitudes toward order and closure. ISTJs like their environments to be very organized and their lives planned. They are comfortable with the regularity of their routines and like to know what to expect. ESTPs are much less predictable and enjoy the excitement of the unexpected. ESTPs pride themselves on their ability to turn on a dime and to follow their curiosity and impulses wherever they lead them. ISTJs often think that their partners bring about too much chaos, while ESTPs find that their partners try too hard to pin them down. ISTJs commonly fall into the role of a parent — constantly reminding their partners to pull their own weight, not spend money impulsively, and follow through on commitments. ESTPs, by contrast, tend to act like perpetual children — forgetting or neglecting their responsibilities, then apologizing but never changing their ways. To be sure, ISTJs may have to be willing to relax some of their standards regarding neatness, organization, and frugality, and ESTPs need to be more conscientious and considerate about their plans and actions.

ISTJs and ESTPs also experience frustration when it comes to making decisions. ISTJs generally take in very little information before they make a firm decision and come to an ironclad judgment. In contrast, ESTPs are very inquisitive and need much more information before they feel comfortable eliminating options and coming to a conclusion. So ISTJs often think that their partners

are too noncommittal, and many ESTPs find their partners bossy and controlling.

Another area of frustration for ISTJ and ESTP couples is their different needs for social stimulation and conversation. ISTJs tend to have a small group of close friends but also need plenty of time alone. ESTPs are very social and public. They love to be around a lot of people and thrive on the stimulation they get from talking, laughing, and doing things with others. ESTPs tend to talk a lot and get bored and restless when they have to sit still or be quiet for any length of time. ISTJs generally feel crowded and pressured to entertain, while ESTPs sometimes feel frustrated by their partners' lack of initiative and their resistance to having people around. ISTJs also need time to consider their reactions and feelings before talking about them, while ESTPs tend to blurt out whatever pops into their heads. When ISTJs are upset, they usually withdraw, sometimes for extended periods of time, leaving their partners confused and frustrated by the lack of information or participation. By contrast, when ESTPs are upset, they often have brief, explosive reactions and then quickly return to a calm, casual demeanor.

Finally, since neither ISTJs nor ESTPs are comfortable discussing their deep feelings or risking vulnerability, they may have to work hard to establish and maintain close emotional connections. Because ISTJs are rather detached and ESTPs tend to avoid serious issues by making jokes, they can both put off discussions of important issues, to the detriment of their relationships.

How to Reach Your ESTP Partner

- Be willing to occasionally let the little things go. Watch your tendency to be picky about order and precision.
- Trust your partner. Encourage your mate to enjoy his or her spare time without having to account for every minute.
- Try to participate in as many social activities as

you can with your partner. Encourage him or her to go alone when you're not up to it.

• Participate in some of the adventures your partner suggests. Don't automatically say no.

• Be willing to stop what you're doing. Occasionally leave things unfinished to enjoy the moment and have fun with your partner.

How to Reach Your ISTJ Partner

• Respect your partner's routines and rituals. Don't disrupt his or her schedules.

• Give your partner as much warning as possible when you change plans. Don't spring things on your partner and expect a positive reaction.

• Be patient with your partner's longer adjustment time. Listen supportively if he or she complains a bit while making a transition.

• Strive to be prompt and not to leave your partner waiting or wondering where you are.

• Watch your tendency to be impulsive and insensitive to your partner's genuine fears for your safety and security.

• Don't put your partner on the spot publicly. Watch your own flamboyancy and irreverence around your partner.

ISTJ with ISTP

The Joys

Because ISTJs and ISTPs share three type preferences, they are similar in several important ways. Both are realistic and down-to-earth people who are tuned in to the present moment. They also are thoughtful and practical, and they tend to take things at face value. They feel comfortable spending time alone, with each other, or with a small group of close friends. They often enjoy hobbies that allow them to use their bodies in some way — such as sports, woodworking, or making crafts. Because ISTJs and ISTPs share the same decision-making style, they communicate in an honest,

direct, and sometimes blunt way. But since they both appreciate the value of constructive criticism and are fairly thick-skinned, they rarely take offense. ISTJs and ISTPs are quite literal, and they don't spend a lot of time looking for hidden meanings or agendas. Rather, they accept people and each other for who they are.

Although their similarities make ISTJs and ISTPs comfortable with each other, it is often their differences that are the source of their initial attraction. ISTJs are drawn to ISTPs' adventurousness, spontaneity, and spirited nature. ISTJs admire how ISTPs are ever ready to drop what they're doing to pursue some exciting new adventure. ISTPs are often attracted to ISTJs because they are so utterly reliable and trustworthy. Most ISTPs admire how seriously ISTJs take their responsibilities and how hardworking and committed they are.

Because of their different temperaments, ISTJs and ISTPs have the opportunity to help each other grow and develop in important ways. ISTJs are often able to help ISTPs resist some of their impulses so they are better able to follow through on the projects they start. ISTPs often say that their partners help them become more accountable and successful. For their part, ISTPs help their partners relax and enjoy the moment. Many ISTJs credit their partners with encouraging them to question some of their rather rigid judgments so they become more accepting and adaptable.

The Frustrations

Although ISTJs and ISTPs are different on only one type preference, it is this difference of organizational style that causes most of their frustrations. ISTJs are extremely responsible people who are driven to do the right thing. But to ISTPs, being free to experience as much of life as possible is equally important. These opposing values come to light in myriad ways on a daily basis. Because of their clear work ethic, most ISTJs need to complete their work before they can relax, so they push hard to do what is expected of them and to honor their commitments. Because of ISTPs' play ethic, they rarely feel compelled to finish something they are working on when a more enjoyable alternative presents itself. As a result, ISTJs are often cast in the parent role — the stern disciplinarian who enforces the rules and cracks the whip. ISTPs are cast as the errant child, having to be reminded to pick up their clothes, get to appointments on time, and finish the jobs they start. Although neither partner wants it to be this way, ISTJ and ISTP couples may have trouble breaking this dynamic.

ISTJs and ISTPs also often have very different opinions about how their households should be run. Predictably, organized ISTJs want "a place for everything and everything in its place." Naturally, they take it as a sign of disrespect when their partners fail to do their share of the chores. Most ISTPs think that their partners are a little obsessive and generally dislike their partners' attempts to control them. The more ISTPs feel restricted, the more likely they are to leave the room in search of some peace and quiet. And the more ISTPs disengage, the more resentful ISTJs become.

ISTJs and ISTPs also hold conflicting views on money management. True to their conservative natures, ISTJs tend to be cautious and sometimes frugal. They like to plan ahead, know what to expect, and budget and spend their money on essential purchases. But true to their more spontaneous natures, ISTPs tend to be impulsive spenders, often buying things they haven't budgeted for and sometimes can't afford, such as expensive cars, clothes, or toys. Again, control issues plague this couple, and they may need to keep their finances separate or find a way of accommodating each other's needs. Although most ISTJs and ISTPs are direct and honest and can usually come up with practical solutions to concrete problems, neither are very comfortable or good at dealing with the more vague and vulnerable realm of feelings. Both

tend to retreat from discussions of feelings, and neither are especially skilled at imagining alternatives that aren't readily apparent. When they reach an impasse, one party is likely to withdraw to think things through — but also to mistakenly hope that if they leave it alone, the issue will somehow resolve itself. There is a real danger that when these two independent-minded and self-contained people are faced with conflicts, they will dig in their heels and retreat to their respective corners. They need to make an effort to be better listeners and to use compromise as the best way to reconcile differences.

How to Reach Your ISTP Partner

- Don't fence your partner in! Accept that your mate needs lots of space and the freedom to pursue his or her interests.
- Try to participate in some of the activities that interest your partner, such as watching a baseball game on TV, even if you're not a big fan.
- Make yourself available to do some things with your partner spontaneously. Agree either to leave what you're doing or to plan for free time.
- Watch your tendency to impose rules and structure on your partner.
- Make sure to provide your partner with plenty of sensory stimulation, including back rubs, hugs, and lovemaking.
- Surprise your partner with tickets to an event he or she likes. Plan the details for this unexpected evening out.

How to Reach Your ISTJ Partner

- Do what you say you will, when you say you will. Be prompt or call when you're running late.
- Strive to finish more of the projects you start.
- Help your partner with chores without being asked. Lighten your partner's load.
- Share your thoughts and reactions. Open up

and let your partner know what's going on with you.

- Avoid springing surprises on your partner. When you have to change plans, give your partner plenty of time to adjust.
- Respect your partner's rituals, routines, and schedules.
- Plan ahead so you're prepared for important holidays and celebrations. Participate in the events your partner plans.

ISTJ with ESFP

The Joys

With only one type preference in common, ISTJs and ESFPs face some considerable challenges, but they do share a very practical view of the world. Both are down-to-earth, realistic, literal, and sensible people who trust the lessons of their own pasts and learn best through hands-on experience. They often enjoy the outdoors, music, and time spent with family. The bottom line for many ISTJ and ESFP couples is mutual trust and a willingness to have very explicit and concrete discussions about their needs and what ought to be changed.

Often it is their many differences that initially attract ISTJs and ESFPs to each other. ISTJs enjoy ESFPs' playful, loving, free-spirited energy. ESFPs make everyday experiences fun, and they have a social ease and expressiveness ISTJs admire. ESFPs are often attracted to ISTJs because of their unquestionable sense of responsibility, integrity, and strong beliefs. ESFPs admire and respect ISTJs' commitment to their work and families, as well as their calm, quiet confidence.

As a result of their many differences, ISTJs and ESFPs have the opportunity to help each other grow and develop in important ways. ISTJs help their partners become better organized, plan ahead, and be more apt to follow through and finish some of the many projects they begin. ESFPs

often credit their ISTJ partners with helping them learn to remain objective and not take so many things to heart. For their part, ESFPs can help their ISTJ partners be more open, comfortable, and expressive of their feelings. ESFPs encourage ISTJs to try new adventures and generally relax and enjoy themselves more.

The Frustrations

It's understandable that two people with so many differences may frequently find themselves at odds. Typically, ISTJs and ESFPs approach life with different philosophies: ISTJs are careful and cautious, while ESFPs are impulsive and free-spirited. Conflict arises when ISTJs want to follow a more conservative path and ESFPs wish to take chances and explore the unknown. ISTJs tend to try to control, order, and plan ahead, while ESFPs fly by the seat of their pants, adapting as they go and taking as many opportunities as possible. ISTJs often feel frustrated when their partners are not concerned about being accountable or are frequently changing directions. And ESFPs often feel that their partners take the fun out of experiences by insisting that they carefully research and plan, allowing for little, if any, spontaneity.

Another area of common frustration is this couple's different needs for order. ISTJs work toward maintaining organization and structure within their homes. They like their houses to be clean and tidy and their routines to be respected and followed. ESFPs are much less interested in structure and want to be free to take advantage of spontaneous opportunities. So ESFPs often feel that their partners are too demanding and picky, while ISTJs often think their homes are too chaotic and become upset when the house rules are inadvertently ignored. ISTJs also like plenty of advance notice when plans must change, whereas ESFPs love surprises and are usually unfazed by changes, even sudden ones. While ISTJs are decisive and efficient, if sometimes brusque, ESFPs often struggle with making decisions and tend to need a lot more information before they feel confident that they've made the right choice.

ISTJs and ESFPs also have very different social needs. ISTJs like and need a lot of uninterrupted time alone to pursue their interests in depth, while ESFPs are social butterflies and like lots of friends and activities to keep them busy. ISTJs are often irritated by the ways their partners intrude on their privacy and constantly pressure them to participate in activities. In contrast, ESFPs often feel a bit lonely and isolated. ISTJ and ESFP couples do well to maintain some separateness in their activities while still protecting their time together.

Finally, ISTJs and ESFPs base their decisions on different criteria, which can result in serious challenges. ISTJs tend to be rather critical in their observations and judgments and often think that their emotional partners are overreacting to small concerns. ESFPs tend to take what their partners intend as constructive suggestions very personally and get their feelings hurt easily. ESFPs are so accepting that they can be gullible, while ISTJs are so detached that they sometimes appear judgmental and cold. And since both ISTJs and ESFPs tend to keep their feelings inside, one partner may be quite upset without the other one knowing it. To strengthen the relationship, ISTJs generally need to be more diplomatic and appreciative, while ESFPs need to be more direct and honest.

How to Reach Your ESFP Partner

- Try to surprise your partner with thoughtful little gifts or expressions of affection.
- Listen patiently, without criticism or judgment.
- When you need time alone or time to think, let your partner know so that he or she doesn't take it personally. Never give your partner the silent treatment.
- Watch your tendency to be inflexible, judgmental, and negative. Don't prevent your

partner from experiencing the kind of social life he or she wants.
- Appreciate and recognize your partner's efforts to get things accomplished and the fun and laughter he or she brings to life.

How to Reach Your ISTJ Partner

- Be prompt; finish your chores; have dinner ready on time. Keep the house tidy.
- Don't spend money impulsively. Be more thorough with tasks such as keeping track of checks and balancing the checkbook.
- If you're running late, try to call to let your partner know.
- Hold your tongue occasionally. Speak your mind after your partner has had a chance to cool down.
- Leave your partner alone when he or she is busy or stressed. Don't interrupt or invade your partner's privacy or insist that he or she participate in every social activity.
- Don't procrastinate. Stick to plans and decisions after they are made.

ISTJ with ISFP

The Joys

ISTJs and ISFPs have two of the four type preferences in common. Both are quiet, private people who like lots of time alone and understand and respect their partners' need for solitude. They often have a small group of close friends whom they have known for a long time, but they usually prefer the peace and quiet of an evening at home to the bustle of a big night out. ISTJs and ISFPs are very practical and realistic people with good common sense. Both pay close attention to facts and details and tend to be most comfortable with those things, people, and experiences they already know and trust.

ISTJs and ISFPs tend to be initially attracted to each other because of their differences. ISTJs are often drawn to ISFPs' genuine warmth, caring, sincerity, and lack of pretense. ISFPs are loving, affectionate, and nurturing people who possess a cheerful outlook and well-developed people skills. For their part, ISFPs are often attracted to ISTJs because of their stability, maturity, and steadfastness. ISFPs like that they can depend fully on ISTJs to follow through and to ensure a secure life together. Even though ISFPs are free-spirited and fun loving, most quickly adapt to the more traditional lifestyle that ISTJs follow and don't mind a clear division of household labor.

Because of their differences, ISTJs and ISFPs have the opportunity to help each other grow and develop in important ways. Typically, ISTJs help ISFPs get better organized, so they are less overwhelmed by complicated tasks. ISFPs often credit their ISTP partners with helping them not take things so personally and become more assertive about their needs. ISFPs help their ISTJ partners develop a deeper level of sensitivity to the needs and problems of others. ISTJs often find that their relationships with other people improve as they become more appreciative and gentle. And many ISTJs say that their partners help them be less rigid so they can relax and have more fun.

The Frustrations

Perhaps the most common frustrations ISTJs and ISFPs experience stem from the different ways they come to conclusions and make decisions. ISTJs are logical, detached, and objective, while ISFPs are emotional, sensitive, and personally affected by everything. ISTJs can be insensitive and not consider how their actions or comments will affect other people. They are often surprised by the extent to which their partners take things personally and are confused when even constructive criticism is rarely taken as it was intended. Because

ISTJs strive to make life more efficient and orderly, they first notice things out of order and projects that need completing. Only later do they acknowledge accomplishments or effort. In contrast, ISFPs tend to hear any criticism as a personal attack, even if the comment is not directed at them. ISFPs often complain that their partners don't really listen supportively to their problems and feelings and that they place more importance on what is logical than what is meaningful. When ISFPs accuse their partners of not caring, they are usually wrong. But to be sure, ISTJs don't always express their concern verbally. When ISFPs feel judged or that their feelings are dismissed, they usually withdraw and hold on to their hurt for a long time, especially if they don't feel that their partners are genuinely apologetic. A healthy airing of problems is important to the long-term health of their relationships. ISFPs need to resist their inclination to avoid conflict, just as ISTJs need to make sure the atmosphere remains accepting and free of criticism.

Another area of frustration for ISTJs and ISFPs is their different needs for order and closure. ISTJs like things settled and decided, so they tend to make quick decisions and hold strong and sometimes unyielding opinions. ISFPs are very curious and flexible people who prefer to keep their options open so they can follow their impulses and explore life. So ISTJs often think that their partners are too indecisive and equivocal, while ISFPs feel that their partners are too controlling and rigid. Most ISTJs want their homes neat and orderly and are irritated by clutter or unfinished projects around the house. They want things put away and routines maintained. They often feel that their need for order isn't respected, but ISFPs often feel that their partners are always on the lookout to find some task they have failed to do according to their partners' strict standards. ISTJ and ISFP couples need to examine both the standards and whose responsibility it is to maintain them. It's not fair for ISTJs, regardless of their gender, to have to do more than their fair share of household tasks. Nor is it reasonable for ISFPs, regardless of their gender, to always accommodate their partners' sometimes excessive desire for order. The need to have things done a certain way, while reasonable in moderation, needs to be balanced with the happiness and comfort of both partners.

How to Reach Your ISFP Partner

- Focus on the positive; express your appreciation and affection.
- Resist the urge to point out mistakes or errors all the time.
- Remember to soften your words; avoid criticism; smile.
- Be willing to leave some things unfinished occasionally and respond spontaneously to the many opportunities for fun that come up.
- Try to go with the flow and not be so concerned about getting things done. Participate in some of the adventures your partner suggests.
- Express your feelings and ask for your partner's advice about how best to manage difficulties with other people.
- Compliment your partner's efforts, especially those tasks that he or she does only to please you.

How to Reach Your ISTJ Partner

- Try to pick up after yourself and keep the common areas of your home neat and tidy.
- Work at staying organized and not letting important deadlines or projects slip.
- Listen for the constructive suggestions in your partner's criticism. Remember that your partner is only trying to help.
- Calmly and directly express your needs and feelings. Don't exaggerate for effect or overreact.
- Ask for your partner's advice about how to organize or manage complicated projects or how to deal objectively with conflicts.

ESFJ with ESTP

The Joys

ESFJs and ESTPs share two of the four type preferences and tend to be talkative, outgoing, and friendly people who like to be busy with their many friends. Physically active, enthusiastic, and high-spirited, they often enjoy participating in or watching sporting events, having fun together in practical ways, and sharing their mutual love of the outdoors, animals, and action. Sensible and realistic, ESFJs and ESTPs generally find it easy to understand each other because they are both explicit, clear, and focused primarily on relevant details and the facts at hand. Both are rather matter-of-fact and often have well-developed common sense.

In addition to their shared interests and commonality, ESFJs and ESTPs are often drawn to each other because of their differences. ESFJs are attracted to ESTPs' fun-loving and playful natures. Many ESTPs are very flirtatious, romantic, and charming. ESTPs also are so spontaneous that they sometimes sweep ESFJs off their feet with generous surprises. ESFJs find their partners' calm and casual attitude appealing and are impressed by their pragmatism. For their part, ESTPs are often drawn to ESFJs' genuine warmth, deep concern for others, and strong personal values. ESTPs like the fact that ESFJs are totally committed to their relationships and respect their direction, diligence, and ambition.

Because of their differences, ESFJs and ESTPs have the opportunity to help each other grow in important ways. Typically, ESFJs help ESTPs become a bit more time conscious, learn to make and stick with plans, and become more reliable. ESTPs say that because their partners insist on a heartfelt connection, they become more willing and able to deepen their commitments. ESFJs also encourage ESTPs to assess their personal values and become more sensitive to and appreciative of others. ESFJs often credit their partners with helping them lighten up and have more fun. Many ESFJs find that they are less likely to take things so seriously, become more objective and pragmatic, and become better able to relax their compulsion to do things just to please others. ESTPs also encourage ESFJs to ask more questions, so they make fewer hasty or poorly informed decisions.

The Frustrations

Two main areas of frustration for most ESFJ and ESTP couples stem from their different ways of making decisions and their different needs for closure and order. ESFJs tend to make almost all their decisions based on their personal values and how they feel about the issues and the people involved. Although ESTPs may be charming, fun, and congenial, they nevertheless make decisions in a cooler, more logical way. So ESFJs often come to conclusions that ESTPs think are irrational or overly emotional, while ESTPs tend to be so pragmatic that they appear to pay little attention to how their decisions will affect others. ESFJs often think that their partners are being insensitive and impatient with their intense feelings and sometimes explosive reactions. ESFJs also have a much greater need to talk about how they feel, often in great detail. The more action-oriented ESTPs prefer to quickly solve the problem at hand. Once they think they've covered an issue, they may become irritated and restless with the redundancy.

ESFJs need a deep and emotional connection with their partners and often push for more intimacy and sharing than their partners are comfortable with. And when ESTPs inevitably (though inadvertently) hurt their ESFJ partners' feelings, ESFJs respond emotionally or else they withdraw. ESTPs may apologize quickly, but if ESFJs don't feel that their partners are being totally sincere, they tend to act in ways that punish their partners. This dynamic is exacerbated when the ESFJ is a woman and the ESTP is a man, since gender roles tend to conspire with their types to intensify their reactions. What ESTPs intend as constructive criticism or consider merely an observation is often taken personally by ESFJs. And if something doesn't affect them personally, ESTPs tend to be so casual that they appear indifferent.

The other main source of frustration for ESFJs and ESTPs is their different needs for closure and order. Most ESFJs have very strong values and rarely consider compromising on issues in which they believe strongly. But for ESTPs practically everything is negotiable. Interestingly, ESTPs often become much more conservative as they age, but they are usually always kids at heart and continue to challenge authority and any situation that limits their personal freedom. Frequently, ESFJs feel that their partners ignore the rules or disregard the routines and rituals that ESFJs cherish, while ESTPs feel restricted and controlled by their ESFJ partners. ESFJs also make decisions very quickly and can be inflexible, especially about important issues. In contrast, most ESTPs need much more information before they are comfortable committing themselves. So ESTPs often feel that their partners not only pressure them to make decisions but also hold them to their choices, even when something new or better comes along. For ESFJs, ESTPs' style of making last-minute plans, and their tendency to change plans in midstream, is unnerving and inconsiderate.

Finally, ESFJs and ESTPs often experience conflicts about how neat and organized their homes should be. ESFJs notice messes and want to put everything quickly in its place, especially if other people are going to see it. Casual and comfort-minded ESTPs rarely mind disorder and often think that their partners are too concerned about what other people think. So ESFJs do more of the household chores and resent it, while ESTPs may be willing to help but may not initiate or finish chores. Rather than working as a respectful team, this dynamic tends to deteriorate until the ESFJ partner acts like the disapproving parent and the ESTP the irresponsible child. ESFJ and ESTP couples need to stop and honestly, yet lovingly, discuss ways of compromising and bringing parity back to their relationships.

How to Reach Your ESTP Partner

• Give your partner plenty of personal freedom and the opportunity to have unstructured time.
• Encourage your partner to socialize with friends, stop in for spontaneous visits, and cultivate a variety of friendships.
• Compliment your partner on his or her looks. Thank your mate for the things he or she does impulsively to help brighten your day.
• Be calm and direct. Try not to exaggerate or overreact.
• Don't avoid conflict or sugarcoat things. Be direct and honest.
• Try to be more spontaneous and to try some of the adventurous suggestions your partner makes.

How to Reach Your ESFJ Partner

• Never dismiss your partner's feelings, even if you don't understand them; listen sympathetically.
• Volunteer to help out around the house, even if the chore isn't yours to do. Ask what you can do that would be most useful — then do it!
• Respect your partner's need for order. Keep common areas clean and tidy, especially when other people are visiting.
• Try to be on time and follow through on projects you start.
• Be gentle, appreciative, and concerned. Share your feelings.
• Compliment your partner on his or her looks and accomplishments.
• Focus on the positive before discussing anything negative.

ESFJ with ISTP

The Joys

ESFJs and ISTPs share one of the four type preferences — the one that gives them a similar and realistic view of the world. They both tend to pay close attention to facts and details and are generally sensible and practical people. They often enjoy the physical world, sports, and being in nature. Down-to-earth ESFJs and ISTPs tend to be most trusting of their own experiences and a bit skeptical of new or unproven ideas. Interestingly, although ESFJs and ISTPs do not have the same temperament, they often share very conservative personal values, which is often a source of great commonality and connection.

In addition to their similarities, ESFJs and ISTPs are frequently attracted to each other because of their many differences. ESFJs often appreciate ISTPs because of their independence, lack of pretense, unshakable calm, and curious, easygoing natures. ESFJs often admire ISTPs because they seem to be good at so many things and are adaptable and responsive to the moment. For their part, ISTPs are often drawn to ESFJs because of their warmth, outgoing and enthusiastic spirit, and strong values of self-discipline and commitment. ISTPs admire ESFJs' social skills and their ability to understand other people's feelings and motivations.

It is precisely these differences that give ESFJs and ISTPs the opportunity to help each other grow and develop in important ways. Typically, ESFJs are able to help their ISTP partners become gentler, more compassionate, and more connected to the important people in their lives. ISTPs often say that their partners help them learn to trust people and to articulate their own needs and feelings better. By contrast, ISTPs are often able to help ESFJs become more objective and independent of the opinions and needs of others. ESFJs credit their partners with helping them slow down and live without a rigid plan of action.

The Frustrations

Significant differences between ESFJs and ISTPs account for many of their most common frustrations. One is their different need for order, structure, and planning. ESFJs like things very neat and orderly and tend to want to plan everything in advance. They like to be on time (or early) and rarely put off doing a chore to the last minute. In fact, they often have trouble relaxing or playing when there's still work to be done. Conversely, ISTPs have much more playful natures than ESFJs and find any unnecessary structure or agenda limiting. They prefer to experience life as they find it, without any expectations or the desire to control anyone or anything. Therefore, ESFJs often feel that they are assuming more of the everyday responsibilities and feel frustrated with their partners' apparent lack of concern for their heavy burdens. ISTPs often feel that ESFJs impose a sense of urgency on them. ESFJs are usually in a hurry to get things finished — a drive rarely shared or really even understood by the more relaxed, casual, and easygoing ISTPs. Naturally, the more frantic and demanding ESFJs become, the more ISTPs pull away. And ESFJs' resistance to any suggestion or adventurous impulse that doesn't fit into their daily plan often irritates ISTPs.

Another area of difference between ESFJs and ISTPs is that ESFJs like to talk and want to discuss everything in minute detail, whereas ISTPs tend to be people of action and few words. So ESFJs are often hungry for conversation, while ISTPs frequently feel that their privacy is being violated. ESFJs also need much more social stimulation than do most ISTPs and tend to spend lots of time out with friends or talking on the telephone. ISTPs need much more time alone to pursue their own projects and interests without interruption.

But the most serious conflict for ESFJs and ISTPs arises from their radically different ways of making decisions. ESFJs base almost every decision on how they feel about an issue, which they often express as a black-and-white value judgment. ESFJs take almost everything personally and are easily hurt by insensitivity or criticism. Conversely, ISTPs are driven to understand the underlying issues and are often unaffected by how other people feel about their actions. As a result, ISTPs can be very critical and appear rather cold and detached. Satisfaction for ESFJs lies in deep emotional connections to the people they love, and they almost always desire a closeness based on sharing that their ISTP partners may not feel comfortable with. Because ISTPs avoid anything too pressured or contrived, they will generally participate in this sharing only to the extent that it feels genuine and natural.

In their zeal to reduce tension and restore harmony, ESFJs may avoid issues of contention or put such a diplomatic spin on things that they create mistrust in their ultrahonest ISTP partners. ESFJs are also prone to very emotional responses, which their ever-calm ISTP partners may dismiss as overreactions. Meanwhile, ESFJs struggle with feelings of loneliness as their private and removed partners fail to share their feelings. Ironically, the less needy and demanding ESFJs behave, the more appealing and attractive they are to ISTPs. And the more gentle and open ISTPs are, the calmer and more relaxed their ESFJ partners become. For both partners sharing is an interesting but difficult process of letting go.

How to Reach Your ISTP Partner

- Never betray your partner's confidence by sharing intimate information with others.
- Give your partner plenty of time to think about important matters and feelings before having to discuss them. Respect his or her privacy.
- Listen carefully and attentively. Stop whatever you're doing, because you may miss what your

partner is saying and he or she probably won't repeat it. Ask questions and wait patiently for answers.

- Try to be flexible with your schedule and willing to participate in some of the adventures your partner suggests. Plan to be spontaneous.
- Encourage your partner to spend time alone working on projects or interests. Allow him or her to opt out of some of the social events you wish to attend.
- Enjoy quiet time together. Don't automatically assume something's wrong when your partner is silent.

How to Reach Your ESFJ Partner

- Share your thoughts and feelings, especially your feelings and needs regarding the relationship.
- Express your happiness and satisfaction. Tell your partner what you like.
- Appreciate the many ways your partner keeps things running smoothly. Say thank you and ask what you can do to help.
- Observe important dates and holidays. Try to plan ahead so you'll be prepared with a thoughtful and appropriate gift.
- Try to participate in as many social activities as you can. Tell your partner when you're genuinely too tired to go so he or she won't take it personally.
- Focus on the positive. Be sure you give critical feedback gently and lovingly.

ESFJ with ESFP

The Joys

Since ESFJs and ESFPs share three of the four type preferences, they often have a lot in common and are fairly compatible. They are both high-energy, active, and talkative people who have lots of friends and acquaintances and thrive on the stimu-lation they get from being around others. ESFJs and ESFPs also are utterly practical and understand each other's literal and down-to-earth sensibility. As a couple, they are expressive and affectionate and enjoy taking care of each other. They usually place a high value on being kind and thoughtful and are especially sensitive to the needs and feelings of others. Sympathetic, warm, friendly, and appreciative, they pour a lot of their energy into their many relationships.

In addition to their many similarities, ESFJs and ESFPs are often initially attracted to each other because of their differences. ESFJs are drawn to ESFPs because of their free-spirited, fun-loving, happy-go-lucky attitudes. ESFPs are great fun to be around and have a relaxed and accommodating style. ESFJs also appreciate that their partners are so generous and accepting. ESFPs are often attracted to ESFJs because they admire how responsible and mature they are and how hard they work to make a stable life for themselves and their families. ESFJs also are typically very expressive of their feelings and free with their compliments and expressions of appreciation.

ESFJs and ESFPs also have some differences that help them both develop in important ways. Typically, ESFJs help ESFPs become better organized and able to complete more of their projects. ESFPs often credit their partners with helping them settle down, take things more seriously, and become more dependable and accountable. For their part, ESFPs help their partners lighten up and enjoy the fun in ordinary moments. ESFJs often say that their partners help them worry less about what other people think of them, which in turn helps them let go of their often frantic need to please others.

The Frustrations

Despite their many shared beliefs and characteristics, ESFJs and ESFPs often experience frustrations that stem from their different temperaments. ESFJs are traditional and conservative people, while ESFPs are free-spirited, unconventional, and at times even irreverent. Most ESFJs feel that it is important to work first and, if there's still time, play later. But their ESFP partners think that play is important because life is meant to be enjoyed. So ESFJs sometimes perceive their partners as irresponsible and careless, while ESFPs feel that their partners are demanding. And since ESFJs have such strong, value-based opinions, they often try to impose them on others and risk being controlling. ESFPs embrace a "live and let live" philosophy and don't like to be controlled, so instead of forcing confrontations, they may just ignore or neglect their partners' agendas.

Another area of frequent frustrations is ESFJs' and ESFPs' different needs for order and closure. ESFJs like a lot of structure and are happiest when issues are settled. Leaving things up in the air makes them uncomfortable, so they sometimes push hard for closure and may make hasty decisions. In contrast, ESFPs like to have almost unlimited options and need to follow their curiosity wherever it leads. They dislike making decisions because having to do so makes them feel trapped. ESFJs are continually pressing their partners to make choices, agree to purchases, or commit to plans before their partners feel ready. ESFJs have a sense of urgency about them that their partners rarely share and can find annoying and unnecessary. For their part, ESFJs are often left finishing projects, putting things away, and generally managing more of the household responsibilities than is fair, while their playful and impulsive partners are off on their latest adventures. The situation is compounded by the fact that neither ESFJs nor ESFPs are comfortable discussing unpleasant subjects, as doing so creates the disharmony they both loathe. A healthy airing of differences is vital, however, since both types tend to take everything personally and become emotional when they feel hurt, taken advantage of, or neglected. Learning

how to address issues immediately, honestly, and lovingly is an especially important skill for ESFJ and ESFP couples to acquire.

How to Reach Your ESFP Partner

- Plan a surprise party for your partner. Do all the planning and organizing, but make it a purely fun and spontaneous event for your partner.
- Try not to press or pressure your partner for answers or decisions. Be patient with his or her need to gather a lot of information.
- Be willing to adjust your plans or postpone what you're doing to accompany your partner on the adventures he or she suggests.
- Encourage your partner to spend time with friends or pursuing interests that you don't share. Don't make him or her feel guilty.
- Don't immediately say no. Wait and consider the many suggestions that your partner makes, even if they may at first seem irresponsible or far-fetched.

How to Reach Your ESFJ Partner

- Try to be where you say you will, when you say you will be.
- Help out with chores. Pitch in and do extra chores when your partner is especially tired, stressed, or busy at work.
- Try to maintain some semblance of a predictable pattern and not to disrupt your partner's important routines or rituals.
- Express your gratitude and appreciation for all the things your partner does to keep your home and life organized and running smoothly.
- Try to finish some of the projects you start. Put things away when you're finished with them, and don't leave clutter around.
- Respect your partner's need to be prepared. Try not to surprise him or her with unexpected guests.

ESFJ with ISFP

The Joys

Because of the two type preferences ESFJs and ISFPs share, they tend to be realistic, down-to-earth, and practical people who see the world in much the same way. They often feel instantly comfortable with each other, and the most important link between them is their shared need for a deep emotional connection. Both have a strong desire for peace and harmony and a great sensitivity to the needs of others. Because they are such physically oriented people, touch is very important to them, and they often express their affection by holding hands, giving each other back rubs, or making love. ESFJs and ISFPs much prefer to be physically engaged than sitting around talking about theoretical subjects. And they often enjoy many of the same recreational activities, such as hands-on hobbies and crafts, participating in or watching sports, or simply experiencing nature. Because they both have a strong aesthetic sense, they want their homes to be comfortable and beautiful.

In addition to their many shared characteristics, ESFJs and ISFPs are often initially attracted to each other because of their differences. Naturally outgoing, but serious and responsible, ESFJs are often drawn to the more playful and spontaneous ISFPs. They like ISFPs' gentleness, easygoing nature, and enjoyment of the moment. ISFPs often marvel at how organized and productive ESFJs are, and they admire how comfortable and skillful they are in social situations.

When recognized for the complementary strengths they are, these natural differences can present a wonderful opportunity to help both partners grow and develop in important ways. ESFJs can help ISFPs learn to be more comfortable about making decisions, and ISFPs often credit their partners with helping them finish some of the projects they start. Through the loving assistance of their ISFP partners, ESFJs can learn to relax more, enjoy the process, and ask more questions, instead of always rushing off to do something else. ESFJs often say that their partners encourage them to have more fun and not to take things so seriously.

The Frustrations

One of the primary sources of frustration for ESFJ and ISFP couples is their different values. ESFJs are very traditional and conservative people who have a strong work ethic. ISFPs are generally much more playful and risk-taking people who value living in the moment. So conflicts tend to arise over exactly when some necessary task or chore will be done because ESFJs want it done immediately. As a result, ESFJs often feel that they are responsible for an unfair share of the chores. Because ISFPs would usually rather put off work in favor of play or relaxation, they often neglect to follow through on their commitments, making their ESFJ partners feel that they are unreliable. Whereas ESFJs often feel overworked, ISFPs often feel pressured and bossed around by their partners.

Another area of potential conflict, although usually a much more manageable one, is their different social needs. Typically, ESFJs need a lot of stimulation from other people, while ISFPs prefer to be with a few close friends or alone with their partners. ESFJs and ISFPs who learn to identify this potential conflict early in their relationships tend to find ways to balance the time each has to be with their own friends and the time they spend together. A potential danger that ESFJs and ISFPs face as a couple is their mutual discomfort with conflict. To avoid any disharmony or risk hurting their partners' feelings, they have the tendency to put off confrontations and avoid open, honest discussions. ESFJs are typically quicker to confront their partners — especially if they are operating under stress — and ISFPs are more likely to suffer in silence. This pattern can cause little problems to escalate into larger ones unless there are regular opportunities to share their feelings honestly and calmly. Airing disagreements is ultimately the only way to create true harmony and maintain a close, intimate emotional connection.

How to Reach Your ISFP Partner

• Accommodate your partner's need for freedom to respond to the moment. Whenever possible, encourage his or her spontaneity.
• Try not to place unnecessary restrictions on your partner's activities, overschedule, or make your partner account for all his or her time.
• Provide plenty of physical stimulation, such as touching and back rubs. Encourage your partner's desire for spontaneous lovemaking.
• Give your partner time to process his or her feelings before talking about problems. Don't interrupt or finish your partner's sentences.
• Try to deal with conflicts immediately, but always positively and gently.
• Express your appreciation of your partner's efforts to be helpful.
• Be sensitive to your different social needs. Don't drag your partner to social engagements too often (be sure to introduce him or her to compatible people when you do).
• Surprise your partner.

How to Reach Your ESFJ Partner

• Try to accommodate your partner's need to have things settled and decided. Don't postpone decisions or keep things up in the air for too long.
• Honor the commitments you make. If you have to change plans, give your partner time to adjust and accept the change.
• Let your partner know if you need time to think about your feelings before discussing them. Then agree on a time to discuss them and make sure to be available when you say you will be.
• Tell your partner often how much you

appreciate all the little things he or she does to keep your household running smoothly.
• Respect your partner's need for order and tidiness, especially in the common areas of the house.
• Surprise your partner with flowers, treats, or the kinds of practical gifts he or she likes (tools, clothes, appliances, and the like).
• Remember and celebrate formal holidays such as Mother's or Father's Day, anniversaries, and birthdays.
• Try to let your partner know when you want physical intimacy so he or she can mentally prepare for it.

ISFJ with ESTP

The Joys

The one type preference ISFJs and ESTPs have in common gives them both a realistic and practical approach to life. They are very observant and pay attention to the way things actually are rather than spending a lot of time wondering how they might be. They tend to communicate literally and sequentially and often are blessed with good common sense. Although ISFJs are more traditional and ESTPs are much more free-spirited, as a couple they often share conservative personal, social, and political values.

Often the greatest source of the initial attraction between ISFJs and ESTPs is their many differences. ISFJs are drawn to ESTPs' charm, confidence, and playfulness. ISFJs also like how gracefully ESTPs are able to turn on a dime, adapt to life, and emerge from any jam smiling. ISFJs admire ESTPs' flexibility and willingness to take risks and have fun. ESTPs are attracted to ISFJs because of their gentleness, warmth, and sincerity. ESTPs know they can completely trust their loyal ISFJ partners, and they usually admire how sensitive and responsible their partners are in regard to all their commitments.

Because of their differences, ISFJs and ESTPs are able to help each other grow and develop in important ways. Typically, ISFJs help ESTPs settle down and become more careful with commitments, more organized, and more productive. By encouraging ESTPs to resist some of their impulses, ISFJs help them become more accountable and responsible people. Most ESTPs also say that their partners help them become more genuine and sensitive to the people they love. For their part, ESTPs expose ISFJs to a wider range of experiences, encourage them to take some calculated risks, and generally get them to laugh and enjoy life more. ISFJs also credit their partners with helping them not to take everything so seriously and with learning to speak their minds honestly and directly.

The Frustrations

Because of their many differences, ISFJ and ESTP couples can experience frequent frustrations. Chief among these is their different ways of making decisions. ISFJs have strong and somewhat inflexible opinions about proper behavior and the right way to treat others. They are very sensitive and sympathetic and strive to help the people they care about, so they always consider the effects their decision will have on others. Naturally, they want their partners to be as considerate, thoughtful, and loving as they are. However, ESTPs are more objective in their decision making. Ever logical and pragmatic, ESTPs make rational judgments regardless of how other people feel about them. So ESTPs sometimes think that their partners are inconsistent and too easily swayed by others' opinions, and ISFJs may feel that their partners are insensitive and tough. ISFJs react emotionally to many experiences — even those that don't directly affect them — while ESTPs are not as deeply affected by others' hardships or emotions.

ISFJs and ESTPs may have to work hard to communicate well. ISFJs are easily offended and

may withdraw when they are upset, and they avoid confrontations and do what they can to restore harmony quickly. ESTPs are very direct, honest, and outspoken, but they can also be critical and a bit selfish. Because ESTPs are seldom comfortable discussing their vulnerabilities, they may avoid the emotional intimacy their ISFJ partners crave. Emotional distance usually is an obstacle to physical intimacy for ISFJs, although it rarely has the same effect on ESTPs.

Another area of frustration for ISFJ and ESTP couples is their different needs for order and closure. ISFJs like their homes to be neat and presentable, but ESTPs are much more concerned with comfort. Many ISFJs have trouble relaxing when there are chores to be done, so they often pressure their partners to help out. And though most ESTPs find their partners' strong work ethic admirable, they rarely share the same sense of urgency to finish projects. ESTPs like to keep as many options as possible open and often feel hemmed in by their partners. They sometimes think that their partners force premature decisions and account for their time unnecessarily. For their part, ISFJs are often frustrated by the number of issues left unresolved and the amount of work left for them to do while their partners are relaxing or out having fun. ISFJs' strong need for stability can sometimes be in direct conflict with ESTPs' need for freedom. ISFJs' concerns for safety and security are rarely shared by their more risk-taking and free-spirited ESTP partners.

Finally, ISFJs and ESTPs sometimes experience frustrations about their differing preferences for talk versus action. ISFJs are reflective, selective, and private, while ESTPs are usually gregarious, talkative, and even flirtatious. ISFJs generally need time alone to think things through, whereas ESTPs are often at their best acting extemporaneously. ISFJs sometimes feel overwhelmed and exhausted by their partners, and regularly feel that their partners don't listen attentively to them. ESTPs get restless and bored when they don't have a lot of people to play with or when it takes a while for their partners to speak their minds. Patience and plenty of quality private time together are important to maintain a close connection.

How to Reach Your ESTP Partner

- Try not to put too many demands or restrictions on your partner. Remember that freedom is very important to him or her.
- Be willing to stop what you're doing and spontaneously participate in some of the activities your partner suggests.
- Watch your tendency to be rigid about your opinions and values. Consider letting the small things go.
- When you're upset, try to be calm, clear, and direct. Tell your partner explicitly what you need and want. Try not to overreact or exaggerate.
- Don't force your partner to make decisions before he or she is ready. Respect your mate's curiosity and need to gather a lot of information first.

How to Reach Your ISFJ Partner

- Respect your partner's need for order. Pick up after yourself and initiate household chores.
- Respect your partner's routines and rituals.
- Strive to be prompt and dependable. Always keep your promises.
- Try not to change plans suddenly. Give your partner as much warning about changes as you can.
- Be patient, gentle, and sympathetic. Listen supportively and encourage your partner to share his or her frustrations with you. Don't try to fix your partner's problems.
- Give your partner plenty of time to be alone. Don't pressure your mate to accompany you to every social event, and be sure to introduce him

or her to compatible people when he or she does go with you.
- Watch your tendency to be flirtatious. Be careful not to embarrass your partner in public.

ISFJ with ISTP

The Joys

ISFJs and ISTPs have two of the four type preferences in common and typically understand each other well. They are naturally realistic and down-to-earth, and because they tend to communicate literally, they find it easy to follow each other's train of thought. ISFJ and ISTP couples usually share fairly conservative values, even though ISTPs are more rebellious and free-spirited. They both have good common sense and trust their own experiences to guide them. ISFJs and ISTPs also have a similar need for time to reflect before taking action, so they respect each other's privacy and desire to spend time alone. They typically prefer small groups of close friends to large social gatherings.

In addition to their similarities, ISFJs and ISTPs are often initially attracted to each other because of their differences. ISFJs are drawn to ISTPs because they're quietly confident, adventurous, and fun to be with. ISFJs find ISTPs to be playful, exciting, and a bit mysterious, and they admire the fact that ISTPs are so accepting and spontaneous. Many ISTPs are attracted to ISFJs because of their natural warmth, gentleness, and sensitivity. ISFJs like to nurture the people they care about, and ISTPs enjoy the pampering. ISTPs also admire how hardworking and dependable ISFJs are in their every endeavor.

Because of their differences, ISFJs and ISTPs have the opportunity to help each other grow and develop in important ways. Typically, ISFJs encourage ISTPs be more sensitive, which helps them understand others and deepen their emotional connections to their partners, families, and friends. Many ISTPs credit their partners with helping them become more accountable, more willing to resist temptation, and more likely to finish the projects they start. For their part, ISTPs help ISFJs lighten up and not take life so seriously. ISTPs make patient coaches, and they encourage their hesitant partners to try new experiences and take modest risks. ISFJs also say that their partners help them be less judgmental about other people's choices. By encouraging their partners to temper their natural urge to please others, ISTPs also can help them become more honest and assertive.

The Frustrations

ISFJs and ISTPs certainly experience their share of frustrations, many of which stem from the different ways they make decisions and their different needs for structure and order. ISFJs make very personal and even emotional choices, while ISTPs are almost always logical and objective. ISFJs sometimes feel that their partners are insensitive and harsh, whereas ISTPs think that their partners are too emotional and dramatic. ISFJs are easily offended, and frequently their partners' brusque and critical style hurts their feelings.

ISTPs find their partners' tendency to worry excessively both annoying and unnecessary. ISTPs also feel frustrated when their ISFJ partners aren't direct with them and wait so long to speak their minds that small issues become big ones. For their part, ISTPs have a tendency to become impatient with their partners' reactions when they don't understand or share them. And rather than admit they are out of their element, ISTPs avoid the discussion and retreat. ISTPs usually want clear, honest, and direct feedback, while ISFJs need their partners to be gentle, complimentary, and diplomatic. Neither approach comes easily to the other. When conflicts arise, ISFJs and ISTPs both need time to think about things before discussing them.

But ISTPs are more naturally aloof and private about their feelings and are less affected by tension, so they can leave issues unresolved longer. In fact, most ISTPs will rarely risk being vulnerable, even with their partners. By contrast, ISFJs are driven to restore harmony, and they not only want to be loved and appreciated, but they also want to be needed. So when ISTPs retreat into silence, ISFJs feel alone and upset.

Another big source of frustration for ISFJs and ISTPs is their different needs for order and closure. Most ISFJs want a neat, well-organized home that is always presentable to other people. They find clutter distracting and feel a need to finish all their chores before they can relax. ISTPs seldom care a lot about what other people think and have little need to keep their homes neat. Although they generally take care of their prized possessions, they are less bothered by disorder and rarely feel the urgency to straighten up, especially according to someone else's timetable. Whereas ISTPs are more relaxed about everything and think that their partners are sometimes too bossy, ISFJs often feel that their partners are lazy and even irresponsible when it comes to household chores. To be sure, ISFJs can be overly concerned about appearance, and ISTPs can find any number of reasons to avoid chores — often by just leaving the house to do something more interesting.

For ISFJs, accountability and trust are inextricably linked, so they perceive a fulfilled promise as an expression of devotion. But for ISTPs, encouraging one's freedom is tantamount to expressing one's trust. ISFJ and ISTP couples who find ways of accommodating each other's differences in this area find they experience far fewer conflicts.

How to Reach Your ISTP Partner

- Try not to become overly emotional or to blow things out of proportion. Stay calm and be clear and direct.
- Encourage your partner's freedom to be alone or

to pursue his or her interests without having to account for the time.

- Ask your partner to listen carefully when you have something important to say. Be sure you do the same, because your partner might not repeat himself or herself.
- Compliment your partner on tangible things such as looks, achievements, and financial contributions. Appreciate the thoughtful little nonverbal things your partner does to demonstrate his or her devotion.
- Be willing to occasionally stop what you're doing and leave things unfinished to enjoy the spontaneous adventures your partner suggests.
- Watch your tendency to try to control, boss, or force decisions on your partner.

How to Reach Your ISFJ Partner

- Express your feelings. Tell your partner how much you care and how happy he or she makes you.
- Appreciate the many ways your partner makes your home comfortable and safe and takes good care of you.
- Respect your partner's rituals and routines. Don't change plans suddenly or disregard your partner's schedule.
- Be willing to make a special effort to be supportive when your partner is especially busy or stressed. Pitch in and help without being asked.
- Make a big deal out of holidays and celebrations. Plan ahead so you have thoughtful gifts and cards for your partner.
- Keep your promises.

ISFJ with ESFP

The Joys

Because ISFJs and ESFPs have two important preferences in common, they often share strong values

of caring, loyalty, and trust. Both tend to be very realistic, practical, and down-to-earth, and they live fully in the moment and pay close attention to the details of everyday life. ISFJs and ESFPs are typically warm, compassionate, and kind to one another and to others. Both strive to please their partners, families, and friends in tangible ways and often express their deep feelings in thoughtful cards and notes. Great companions, ISFJs and ESFPs usually share similar interests, such as being active outdoors, and they may have similar tastes in friends.

But the differences between ISFJs and ESFPs are often the source of their initial attraction. ISFJs are often drawn to the happy-go-lucky playfulness of ESFPs, who are usually very loving and affectionate and have the ability to bring energy and joy to the simplest activity. Their natural irreverence and zest for living are a source of inspiration to many ISFJs. For their part, ESFPs are often drawn to ISFJs' sincerity and devotion. ESFPs love that they can totally depend on their steady, responsible, and unpretentious partners to bring a sense of calm and grounding to their lives.

Because of their differences, ISFJs and ESFPs have the opportunity to help each other grow and develop in important ways. Typically, ISFJs help ESFPs learn to plan things out ahead of time, be more careful with money, and generally become better organized by sticking to some of the systems their ISFJ partners devise. ESFPs often credit their partners with adding a measure of depth, focus, and greater meaning to their lives by helping them rein in some of their impetuousness. For their part, ESFPs often help their serious and hardworking ISFJ partners relax, not take everything quite so seriously, and enjoy life more. They also encourage their ISFJ partners to be more spontaneous and adventurous.

The Frustrations

The primary source of frustration for many ISFJ and ESFP couples stems from their different temperamental values and work ethics. ISFJs are very hardworking, responsible, and serious, and sometimes they put work ahead of all other activities. ISFJs rarely leave things unfinished or shirk their responsibilities. By contrast, ESFPs place a high value on enjoying each experience fully, so their partners' seriousness and cautiousness sometimes frustrate them. They accurately accuse ISFJs of exhausting themselves with work, being inflexible, and refusing opportunities to socialize. ISFJs are sometimes unnerved and irritated by ESFPs' carelessness with important deadlines, their relaxed attitude about time, and their general lack of follow-through. And whereas ISFJs like to have their homes tidy and efficiently run, ESFPs are far less concerned about neatness or following house rules. ESFPs can be quite impulsive and may unintentionally disrupt the routines and rituals their partners find so comforting. This imbalance may provoke ISFJs to act like parents and ESFPs like children rather than two equal adults compromising and working together.

In addition to their different needs for order and social simulation, ISFJs and ESFPs may have communication problems. Because ESFPs say whatever pops into their heads, they sometimes speak out of turn or put their foot in their mouth. ISFJs prefer to think things through carefully ahead of time but may not share what they're thinking or feeling, leaving their partners wondering where they stand. Neither ISFJs nor ESFPs deal well with conflict. Eager to please and naturally sensitive, neither wants to discuss unpleasant subjects for fear of hurting the other's feelings, so issues sometimes go unresolved longer than they should. When this couple has uncomfortable discussions, they both take criticism very personally and may withdraw with hurt feelings. But ultimately their mutual desire for harmony and their emotional connection is strong enough to bring them back to equilibrium and closeness.

How to Reach Your ESFP Partner

- Be willing to try some of the adventures your partner suggests.
- Don't force your partner to make decisions too quickly or discourage him or her from collecting as much information as he or she needs.
- Be patient with your partner's need to think out loud and discuss options with you.
- Encourage your partner to go out with friends and spend time pursuing his or her interests even if you don't always go along.
- Surprise your partner. Do something impetuous and romantic.
- Watch your tendency to try to control your partner's schedule or force him or her constantly to account for his or her time.

How to Reach Your ISFJ Partner

- Respect your partner's need for order and routine. Don't change things without his or her input and approval.
- Try to be where you say you will be. Wear a watch and be on time. Minimize the number of interruptions and surprises in your partner's routine.
- Don't disclose personal information about your partner to others.
- Try to keep better track of things. For instance, balance the checkbook and pay bills on time.
- Respect and honor your partner's values and beliefs. Try to remember and observe important holidays and celebrate special occasions.
- Be sure to give your partner plenty of quiet time alone, especially after a busy or stressful day.
- Don't put your partner on the spot in public.

ISFJ with ISFP

The Joys

Because ISFJs and ISFPs share three type preferences, they often experience a close emotional connection and understand each other's needs and feelings. They are quiet, gentle, and down-to-earth people who generally prefer to keep their lives simple and their interactions genuine and one-on-one. ISFJs and ISFPs are very realistic and communicate in literal and sequential ways, something they both readily understand. Sensitive and sympathetic, they care deeply about others and prefer the company of sincere and earnest people. They are often cautious about new things, especially new social experiences. As a couple, ISFJs and ISFPs protect each other's need for time alone and often enjoy spending time together outdoors.

In addition to their many similarities, ISFJs and ISFPs are also initially attracted to each other because of their differences. ISFJs often are drawn to ISFPs because of their free-spirited and accommodating style. ISFPs care deeply about their partners' happiness and are almost always ready to adapt to what their partners need or want in order to please them. ISFPs are often attracted to ISFJs because they admire how organized and productive they are. ISFPs often like ISFJs' loyalty and dependability, as well as their sense of commitment, strong values, and willingness to work hard for the people they love.

Because of their differences, ISFJs and ISFPs have the opportunity to help each other grow and develop in important ways. Typically, ISFJs help ISFPs commit themselves to finishing the projects they start and generally become more productive. ISFPs may credit their partners with helping them become more accountable and organized. For their part, ISFPs help ISFJs learn to relax and enjoy themselves. ISFJs say that their partners lovingly encourage them not to be so serious or fearful of new experiences. ISFPs remind ISFJs that life is short and a gift to be enjoyed.

The Frustrations

Despite their many similarities, the frustrations many ISFJs and ISFPs experience often stem from their different temperaments. ISFJs are usually very careful, traditional, and conservative people who trust and are comfortable with routine and convention. By contrast, ISFPs are naturally free-spirited, carefree, and somewhat nonconforming people. Whereas ISFJs pride themselves on their diligence, ISFPs are more impulsive and playful and have a "live and let live" attitude. ISFJs are respectful of authority and impressed with status, while ISFPs are somewhat irreverent. ISFJs often feel that their partners are too casual, while ISFPs feel that their partners are too serious and overly concerned with what other people think.

ISFJs and ISFPs also differ in their need for order and structure. ISFJs generally want their homes to be well organized and tidy, while ISFPs are not bothered by clutter and want things comfortable and low-key. Most ISFJs have a hard time relaxing until all their work is done and things are where they belong. Often they are still bustling around long after their partners have sat down to relax or read, and they may feel resentful when their partners don't initiate household chores. ISFPs are generally willing to do what's asked of them, but ISFJs often feel frustrated that they always need to request help. On the other hand, ISFPs often feel that their partners have a heightened sense of urgency about getting things accomplished that they rarely share. They find their partners' artificial deadlines annoying and unnecessary and don't like it when their partners try to control them. Naturally, whenever ISFPs feel controlled, they tend to resist or quietly move away from the situation, which causes their ISFJ partners to feel even more alone and hurt.

Another area of frustration for ISFJ and ISFP

couples revolves around their different needs for closure. ISFJs like things settled, decided, and predictable. They don't like surprises and often resist or complain about changes in plans. ISFPs are much more easygoing and adaptable. They like to leave their options open for as long as possible, and they don't want to be forced into a decision before they're ready. ISFPs tend to need a lot of information before coming to a conclusion. The more decisive ISFJs sometimes feel irritated when their partners won't commit to a course of action, and ISFPs feel trapped by the inflexibility of their partners' decisions.

Finally, since ISFJs and ISFPs are both very sensitive and tend to take most things personally, they may withdraw when they are upset or confused instead of discussing what's wrong. Although both are easily offended, ISFJs tend to be a bit more so, and while both have trouble speaking up for themselves, ISFPs can be even less assertive. Both need plenty of time to process their thoughts and reactions, and they need to agree to speak truthfully as well as diplomatically to each other about problems when they arise. Rather than stay on the surface of subjects, they need to work together to dig deeper and express themselves fully so that they can resolve conflicts.

How to Reach Your ISFP Partner

- Be willing to stop what you're doing and listen attentively to your partner.
- Participate in some of the spontaneous adventures your partner suggests.

- Encourage your partner's interests and activities even if you don't share them. Don't try to make him or her feel guilty for doing things without you.
- Respect your partner's need to gather a lot of information and keep his or her options open. Don't pressure your partner to make a decision before he or she feels ready.
- Avoid nagging. Be explicit about tasks with which you want help and when you really need them to be done, then leave your partner to do them.
- Try suggesting that you work on chores cooperatively.

How to Reach Your ISFJ Partner

- Try to be where you say you will, when you say you will.
- Make an effort to put things away, pick up after yourself, and finish some of the projects you begin.
- Respect your partner's need for order, and don't be careless about taking care of the possessions you share.
- Try not to change plans suddenly or change directions after you have agreed on a course of action.
- Try to come to conclusions a bit faster or to tell your partner when you need more time or information before you are ready to decide. Avoid procrastinating.
- Respect your partner's routines and rituals. Try not to disrupt his or her plans.

Chapter 6

Traditionalists with Conceptualizers: SJs with NTs

ESTJ with ENTJ

The Joys

ESTJs and ENTJs share three of the four type preferences, so they usually understand each other and get along quite well. Since they both have high energy and are friendly, outgoing, and talkative, they have lots of friends and enjoy the stimulation they get from being around others. Active and involved people, ESTJs and ENTJs tend to join organizations and volunteer their time for a host of activities at work and in their communities. They are also organized and hardworking and generally have great enthusiasm for being productive. ESTJs and ENTJs tend to hold strong opinions and like to make decisions, even tough ones. They both want their environments to be orderly and structured, so they typically contribute equally to maintaining a well-kept home. Finally, they are calm, honest, and direct people who speak their minds and can give and receive constructive criticism without taking it personally. They tend to enjoy regular, lively, and even heated debates and respect each other's sound reasoning.

Given their many similarities, it's no surprise that ESTJs and ENTJs are often attracted to each other. But they are also drawn to each other because of their differences. ESTJs are often initially attracted to ENTJs because they are ambitious, have a clear plan for the future, and really seem to be going somewhere. ESTJs admire

ENTJs' creativity and originality, as well as their confidence and ability to lead and inspire others. ENTJs are often drawn to ESTJs because they are utterly dependable and steady people. ESTJs earn the trust of ENTJs through their diligence and faithful follow-through.

Because of their differences, ESTJs and ENTJs have the opportunity to help each other grow and develop in important ways. Typically, ESTJs help ENTJs pay closer attention to important details, so they make fewer mistakes, create more workable projects, and increase their personal and professional competence. Many ENTJs credit their partners with encouraging them to participate in more physical activities and to communicate more clearly and simply. For their part, ENTJs are often able to help their ESTJ partners see alternatives and solve problems in new ways. ESTJs say that their partners help them see patterns and connections they would otherwise miss and inspire more confidence in the future.

The Frustrations

Despite their many shared characteristics, ESTJs and ENTJs do experience frustrations that often stem from their differences. Specifically, because of their temperamental differences, they sometimes have conflicting values. ESTJs are very traditional and conservative people who trust their past experiences and strive to maintain the status quo. Most ESTJs find change stressful and difficult to manage. However, ENTJs are so independent that they often see conventions as limiting and find change exciting and even vital to their ability to stay engaged. ESTJs sometimes believe that their partners shake things up unnecessarily, while ENTJs think that their partners resist positive changes. ENTJs can be know-it-alls, be condescending, and make things much more complicated than they need to be. ESTJs can resist even good ideas, but often they come around, so getting them to consider a new approach takes some effort and patience.

Another significant source of frustration for ESTJs and ENTJs stems from their different ways of noticing the world. ESTJs are very realistic and practical, whereas ENTJs are highly imaginative and focus on possibilities. So ESTJs tend to communicate sequentially, carefully working through information, reading and following directions, and trusting their experiences to guide their actions. ENTJs are usually curious about theories and love to think about and discuss the big picture. They tend to think and speak in leaps and bounds, skip around from one subject to another, and make big transitions quickly. ESTJs are sometimes frustrated by their partners' abstract and complex explanations, while ENTJs find that their partners are too plodding and slow. ESTJs need their partners to respect their need for accuracy and careful management of facts, details, and money, just as ENTJs need their partners to encourage their pursuit of new challenges and creative ideas.

Finally, ESTJs and ENTJs sometimes experience frustration that results from their similarities. Because they are both so verbal and talkative, they sometimes interrupt each other and may not listen well. Their mutual tendency to be critical and demanding can become hurtful, so they may need to consciously and actively practice expressing appreciation for each other rather than always picking at each other's flaws. And because neither is especially comfortable with emotions, ESTJ and

ENTJ couples may have to force themselves to really share their feelings and vulnerabilities in order to strengthen the depth and intimacy of their emotional connection.

How to Reach Your ENTJ Partner

- Encourage your partner's efforts to take on increasing challenges. Don't resist his or her need for change and professional growth.
- Be patient with your partner's long-winded, complicated, or ambiguous stories.
- Consider your partner's new ideas and suggestions for change. Watch your tendency to say no before giving your mate a fair hearing.
- Listen respectfully and appreciatively to your partner's theories and vision for the future. Resist the urge to point out factual errors or be negative and critical.
- Try not to become fixated on details, especially negative ones.

How to Reach Your ESTJ Partner

- Thank your partner for all the little things he or she does to make your home comfortable and well run. Express your appreciation of the chores your partner does every day.
- Respect your partner's need for routines and predictability. Honor the rituals and holidays that are important to him or her.
- Try to tell stories or give explanations in a step-by-step manner, and don't leave out important details.
- Be careful with facts and money. Balance the joint checkbook and watch your tendency to spend money on less-than-practical things.
- Watch your tone and avoid sounding arrogant or refusing to admit you may not always be right.

ESTJ with INTJ

The Joys

ESTJs and INTJs share two of the four type preferences, and they both make decisions based on logic rather than emotion. Therefore, issues that might potentially cause conflict are typically discussed dispassionately, and the partner who has the most airtight argument usually convinces the other of the correctness of his or her position. Since both partners often have a rather tough hide, neither is likely to be offended by this process. ESTJs and INTJs also share a desire to live in an orderly, structured way, where plans are made and kept and each partner knows what is expected. Couples tend to follow the rules they establish for their relationships. Decisions are usually made quickly, the couples' homes are neat and tidy, and both partners are very productive.

In addition to the important similarities that give this couple daily comfort, they are usually attracted to each other because of their differences. ESTJs are often drawn to INTJs for their intellectual acuity, competence, and independence. INTJs are often attracted to the outgoing energy, productivity, and traditional sensibilities of ESTJs.

ESTJs and INTJs are able to help each other grow and develop in important ways. ESTJs often provide their partners with a realistic and practical perspective on important ideas. They also can supply the energy and savvy it takes to help INTJs convert their ideas into workable plans. For their part, INTJs expand their ESTJ partners' intellectual and artistic horizons, show them the connections they might otherwise miss, and help them slow down and reflect on things before acting.

The Frustrations

One of the most important differences between ESTJs and INTJs is their different ways of noticing the world. ESTJs are extremely realistic, practical people who are careful with details and pay close attention to facts. INTJs usually love ideas and live a large part of their lives mulling them over. So ESTJs are sometimes too concrete and specific for INTJs' tastes, and INTJs are too abstract, complex, and general for ESTJs to understand.

ESTJs and INTJs also have very different social needs. Typically, ESTJs want and enjoy more social interaction than their INTJ partners. When this is the case, ESTJs may resent having to push their partners into accompanying them to social occasions, and INTJs may be just as resentful at being pressured to go. And even in nonsocial contexts, ESTJs often lament that they can't get their INTJ partners to talk about things to the extent they would like — and accuse them of retreating from conversations that don't interest them. INTJs, on the other hand, often feel pressured to converse, especially about superficial subjects, even when they feel they have nothing to say.

Temperamental differences between ESTJs and INTJs can also be a source of conflict. ESTJs tend to have very traditional values, especially with regard to home and hearth. Although also very work-oriented, ESTJs are more likely to put their family lives ahead of career success. This is particularly true of female ESTJs. INTJs, however, are often very career-driven and prone to make family a lower priority than their mates believe they should. They may want to take full advantage of career opportunities, even if they have to inconvenience their families to do so. Because ESTJs tend to be cautious and conservative, they can discourage their partners from taking on new challenges or risks, especially when their financial security may be affected.

Finally, ESTJs and INTJs are both strong-willed, determined people who are usually not reticent about making their wants and desires known. When their objectives clash, both partners can become stubborn and inflexible. And since neither partner tends to be especially good at dealing with emotions — their partner's or their own — they may not share their vulnerabilities. When one gets upset, the result may be an angry outburst, which is likely to trigger a similar response. Since neither is naturally skilled or comfortable in this area, conflict resolution can be a messy and painful process. Similarly, ESTJs and INTJs may have trouble uncovering and addressing underlying emotional issues, so they may feel unable to solve certain problems permanently.

How to Reach Your INTJ Partner

• Respect and compliment your partner on his or her good ideas and accomplishments.
• Recognize that your partner needs time to think about things before responding.
• Resist the urge to push your partner into doing the things you want to do, when you want to do them (even if you think it's for his or her own good).
• Respect your partner's need to spend time alone. Don't drag him or her to social events or activities that he or she doesn't want to attend.
• Support and encourage your partner's career aspirations and decisions.
• Consider learning something — a language or skill — together.

How to Reach Your ESTJ Partner

• Recognize and appreciate all the little things your partner does to maintain the house and make your life easier.
• Try to accommodate your partner's need to talk things through.
• Make time to do things together.
• Try to let your partner know what's going on in your life and include him or her in as much decision making as you can.
• Resist the urge to critique your partner and offer

suggestions as to how he or she could improve his or her life.
• Try not to impose your own high standards on your partner.
• Try to be flexible and realize that compromising now and then won't jeopardize your independence.

ESTJ with ENTP

The Joys

ESTJs and ENTPs share two of the four type preferences, giving them similar social needs and decision-making styles. Both are high-energy people who enjoy lots of interaction with others and usually like to juggle several projects at once. They are great conversationalists and tend to think out loud. They are also naturally logical and objective about most things, including their relationships, so they can often critique each other constructively without feeling attacked. Since both types are motivated by achievement, they take great pride in their own and each other's accomplishments.

In addition to their similarities, ESTJs and ENTPs are often initially attracted to each other because of their differences. ESTJs are drawn to ENTPs' creativity and quick thinking. They admire ENTPs' originality, flexibility, and optimism, even when confronted with formidable obstacles. ENTPs are attracted to ESTJs because they seem so stable and in control of their lives. ENTPs also respect ESTJs' decisiveness and ability to organize and complete projects efficiently.

Because of their differences, ESTJs and ENTPs have the opportunity to help each other grow and develop in important ways. ESTJs help ENTPs get and stay organized, so they experience the benefits of actually finishing their inventive projects. ENTPs credit their partners with helping them pay closer attention to details and do necessary reality checks. For their part, ENTPs encourage ESTJs to take the long view and focus on future implications rather than paying so much attention to the moment. Many ESTJs admit that their partners help them stay open to new ideas and possibilities and encourage them to be more spontaneous, so they enjoy life more.

The Frustrations

One of the most common sources of frustration for ESTJ and ENTP couples is their differences in temperament. ESTJs tend to be cautious, responsible, traditional people. They find comfort in structure and rules and like others to do the same. They tend to see things in terms of black and white, good and bad. By contrast, ENTPs tend to be very independent, creative people who shun convention and established ways of doing things. Conflicts occur when ESTJs voice concern rather than support for ENTPs' newest, greatest idea. Because creativity and innovation are the lifeblood of ENTPs, when ESTJs insist on pointing out the flaws instead of the benefits of an idea, ENTPs feel undermined and discouraged. Likewise, when ENTPs act impulsively, especially with regard to safety or finances, ESTJs tend to react angrily at what they see as irresponsible behavior.

ENTPs are often very ambitious and drawn to exciting possibilities and entrepreneurial ventures. They also change careers or jobs frequently because they get bored easily. This can cause anxiety for ESTJs, who are much more conservative and believe the adage that "a bird in the hand is worth two in the bush." Because ENTPs are generally very confident, they can sometimes communicate an air of superiority or even arrogance. On the other hand, because ESTJs are such responsible, take-charge people, they can come across as being bossy and controlling.

Perhaps the greatest source of conflict comes from ESTJs' and ENTPs' different needs for closure. ESTJs tend to make quick decisions, which means they stop gathering information much sooner than ENTPs do. ESTJs complain that their partners are indecisive, don't always keep their promises, and change plans at the last minute. As a result, ENTPs often feel pressured to make a decision before they are ready. ESTJs also prefer their homes to be neat and well organized, whereas ENTPs prefer a more fluid lifestyle, fewer rules, and more opportunities to experiment.

ESTJs and ENTPs are likely to struggle with control issues. Ironically, both types often feel that their partners are trying to control them, though in different ways. ENTPs complain that ESTJs set too many rules and limit their freedom. ESTJs complain that their partners bring too much chaos into their lives.

Finally, since both partners are so naturally logical and objective, neither is especially sensitive to, or comfortable dealing with, the emotions of others. While they are direct and honest, they may avoid becoming vulnerable and taking the time to really explore the root causes of problems. ENTPs are generally more comfortable expressing their feelings than ESTJs, who tend to be very private about them. This can create tension for both partners.

How to Reach Your ENTP Partner

- Listen with an open mind and try to be supportive of your partner's creative suggestions or ideas.
- Try not to impose more rules or structure than is absolutely necessary.
- Plan to be spontaneous. Spend time with your partner just being free to go with the flow.
- Recognize your partner's many creative solutions to problems and compliment him or her on them.
- Relax and let your partner show you a good time. Be willing to leave chores undone.
- Surprise your partner. Plan a getaway or party.

How to Reach Your ESTJ Partner

- Demonstrate your appreciation for all the little ways your partner makes your life and home run smoothly.
- Pitch in and do extra chores. Be sure to follow through with precision on all your commitments.
- Respect your partner's need for order and neatness. Be careful to keep common areas of the house tidy.
- Watch your tendency to be too critical and arrogant with your suggestions. Remember, you could be wrong.
- Make sure to consult your partner before acting on things or making large purchases.

ESTJ with INTP

The Joys

Because they share the one type preference, ESTJs and INTPs have in common an analytical and objective style of making decisions. Their similar approach to solving problems helps them communicate directly and honestly, and neither is afraid of or is hurt by healthy conflict. Instead, they are able to bring up issues for discussion, share their frank opinions about them, and move toward a fair resolution. As long as they curb their impatience and avoid sarcasm, they can usually solve problems equitably.

But it's the differences between ESTJs and INTPs that are often the source of attraction. Both appreciate and respect the other's honesty and no-nonsense style, but ESTJs also are drawn to INTPs' irreverence, individuality, and unusual sense of humor. ESTJs admire INTPs' unique and creative minds as well. INTPs are often attracted to ESTJs' high energy, social ease, and friendliness. INTPs also find ESTJs reasonable, responsible, and very steady partners.

Because of their many differences, ESTJs and INTPs have the opportunity to help each other develop in important ways. ESTJs are often able to help INTPs pay more attention to details and make fewer factual mistakes. INTPs often credit their partners with encouraging them to get out in the world, meet new people, and simplify their ideas so others can understand them. For their part, INTPs are often able to help ESTJs slow down and look beyond the obvious to better understand underlying meanings or implications. Many ESTJs find that their partners broaden their horizons by encouraging them to consider new ideas and keep their options open longer. Over time, and with consistent levels of trust, ESTJs often come to experience and express deeper feelings of connection, and INTPs begin to enjoy and participate in some of the everyday sensory pleasures of life.

The Frustrations

The most fundamental difference between ESTJs and INTPs is their different temperaments. ESTJs are traditional, conservative, and careful people who trust their experiences and are comfortable keeping things the way they are. INTPs are imaginative and independent thinkers, curious about the future and interested in growth and change. ESTJs are, for the most part, happy with the status quo and skeptical of new ideas, whereas INTPs are energized by shaking things up. Therein lies the potential for conflicts when ESTJs unintentionally dismiss INTPs' innovative ideas because they don't see the immediate or practical benefits of them. Whereas ESTJs like routines and find them comforting, INTPs rarely have a sustained interest in observing or maintaining them. INTPs sometimes create unnecessary stress for ESTJs by leaving many projects unfinished or neglecting their chores because they've lost track of time. Because ESTJs crave order and structure, they try to control their environments (and the people in them) to the point where their partners feel crowded and manipulated. INTPs are fiercely independent, and this is perhaps the greatest source of dissatisfaction for these couples. INTPs also are nonconformists and are likely to ignore the traditions ESTJs have cherished since childhood. ESTJs perceive this disregard as disrespectful and insensitive.

Since ESTJs have such a strong work ethic, they often do more than their fair share of the work around the house. Most ESTJs simply can't relax and enjoy the moment when there are still chores left undone. This dynamic is especially common when the ESTJ is female and feels societal pressure to manage the home efficiently. For their part, INTPs often feel nagged about the mess they create and about their lack of initiative in helping out. ESTJ and INTP couples need to use their mutual sense of fairness to find a solution that doesn't compromise either of their needs.

Finally, ESTJs are typically quite talkative and like to think things through out loud. But they can also be strongly opinionated and overbearing. INTPs are very private people and do most of their processing internally, so although it may look as though they are sitting idly by, much activity is going on inside their heads. INTPs are reticent or even unwilling to discuss things they have not considered fully, especially emotional issues. They need a lot of information before making a decision. By contrast, ESTJs make very quick decisions and move ahead with determination. ESTJs tend to be frustrated by the lack of input or reaction from their partners, while INTPs feel irritated by the invasion of their privacy. By pursuing their individual interests and friendships, while still finding plenty of quality time together, ESTJs and INTPs can maintain a balance that is comfortable for them both.

How to Reach Your INTP Partner

- Admit that you are simply processing information out loud, while respecting your partner's strong need for time and privacy.
- Avoid the tendency to criticize new ideas out of hand. Make yourself listen completely to your partner's views before offering constructive criticism.
- Try not to be too rigid about your schedules and routines. Allow for the possibility that an interruption might be good.
- Appreciate the unique perspective your partner brings to discussions. Compliment him or her on good ideas.
- Let your partner take you off the beaten path. Try his or her innovative ideas and indulge in fantasies.
- Slow down and ask more questions. Make time for your partner to share things that are important or interesting to him or her.

How to Reach Your ESTJ Partner

- Realize that your partner cannot read your mind and wants to know what you are thinking. Explain that you are processing information internally and simply need more time.
- Watch your tendency to be cynical and avoid sarcastic comments.
- Respect the routines that are most important to your partner and do your best not to upset them.
- Compliment your partner on all that he or she does to make your life comfortable and safe. Appreciate your mate's efforts and tangible accomplishments.
- Tell other people how great your partner is. ESTJs may receive third-party compliments with more credibility than direct ones.
- Work toward being on time and following through on projects. Do your share of the household chores.

• Avoid the tendency to overanalyze everything, looking for flaws and faults. Try to just enjoy the moment.

ISTJ with ENTJ

The Joys

ISTJs and ENTJs share two of the four type preferences, giving them an analytical decision-making style and a clear preference for order and closure. They tend to be very direct and honest, sometimes to the point of bluntness. They are logical and objective in their decision making and are outwardly calm and unemotional. ISTJs and ENTJs tend to appreciate constructive criticism and are usually willing to help each other solve problems quickly and efficiently. They tend to be supportive and interested in each other's work, and both are hardworking and serious about their responsibilities.

Since they both like structure in their lives, ISTJs and ENTJs tend to plan ahead, maintain a fairly predictable routine, and keep their homes well organized and efficiently run. However, their definitions of *neat* may differ. ISTJs tend to like things meticulously organized, more so than most ENTJs have the patience for (especially if the ENTJs have to maintain them). But they tend to respect each other's habits and rituals even if they don't agree with them. ISTJs and ENTJs often enjoy working as a team to set and meet their goals, and they usually derive satisfaction from finishing projects. They both tend to have strong opinions and can engage in heated debates without either person becoming upset or offended. Their discussions are intellectually stimulating and often have a markedly competitive edge.

Despite their similarities, ISTJs and ENTJs are often attracted to each other because of their differences. ISTJs are often attracted to ENTJs' ambi-

tion, energy, and intensity. ENTJs are confident and appear to handle everything effortlessly. For their part, ENTJs are often attracted to ISTJs' calm, independence, and down-to-earth attitude. ISTJs are unflappable, dignified, and self-contained, all qualities ENTJs find appealing. Because of their differences, ISTJs and ENTJs are able to help each other grow and develop in important ways. ISTJs help ENTJs become more practical, especially regarding money and the timely use of resources. ENTJs say that their partners help them to become more selective, particularly when airing their many ideas and thoughts, and to learn to respect other people's need for quiet and privacy. For their part, ENTJs are often able to help their ISTJ partners relax some of their strong need to have things stay the way they've always been. ISTJs credit their partners with helping them consider new ideas and be more optimistic about the future. ISTJs also become more responsive and socially comfortable with their partners' support.

The Frustrations

A common source of frustration for many ISTJ and ENTJ couples is their different temperaments. ISTJs are very traditional and cautious, whereas ENTJs are more adventurous and innovative. ISTJs often believe that their partners are changing things too much and too quickly, while ENTJs think ISTJs are too resistant to new ideas. Uncertainties, especially financial ones, are typically much harder on ISTJs than on ENTJs. And since both are particularly strong-willed and even stubborn, they can become intractable, sarcastic, and unwilling to compromise. When ENTJs are especially keen on some idea or principle, they can get quite intense and even combative. This tends to repel their more reserved and conservative ISTJ partners. Naturally, this is frustrating to ENTJs, until they understand that ISTJs respond this way to avoid feeling drained. This couple also tends to be so driven and hardworking that they may not take the downtime they each really need to be together or to rest. And since neither is naturally very spontaneous, they may not take advantage of the opportunities for relaxation that come up unexpectedly.

Another significant difference is that ISTJs are very realistic, while ENTJs are creative and theoretical. Their communication is hampered when ENTJs are confusing and vague and ISTJs are too measured and specific. In addition, subjects that excite one partner often don't interest the other. ENTJs live for creative challenges and need a good deal of variation in their professional lives. Because these constant changes are stressful to most ISTJs, they are not always as supportive as their partners might wish. Their resistance and pessimism about unproven ideas runs in sharp contrast to ENTJs' confidence and optimism. ENTJs also are insulted whenever their partners question their competence.

Finally, since neither ISTJs nor ENTJs share their feelings easily, especially those of fear or vulnerability, they may ignore issues and problems longer than they should, neglecting the important emotional dimensions of their relationships. They can be unintentionally insensitive to other people, and recognizing their own shortcomings in their partners is often very annoying to them.

How to Reach Your ENTJ Partner

- Try to understand your partner's need to talk about, circulate, and create new ideas. Listen with interest and patience as he or she works them out aloud.
- Recognize and appreciate your partner's individuality and uniqueness.
- Try to express your appreciation in words. Write it out if that's easier for you.
- Be patient with the length of time some of your partner's ideas take to become real. Support his

or her investment of time and energy, especially for really big or complicated ideas.
- Try to trust your partner's innovation and hunches even when they seem far-fetched or too far in the future. Avoid pointing out errors in fact right away.
- Compliment your partner's great ideas and verbal skills.
- Brag about your partner to other people, knowing it will get back to him or her.

How to Reach Your ISTJ Partner

- Remember to give your partner plenty of time to think things through before expecting or requiring an answer. Allow your partner to share his or her thoughts when he or she is ready.
- Demonstrate your appreciation by pitching in and doing extra chores. Be sure to follow through with precision on the things you are supposed to do.
- Don't skip important steps or leave out vital facts.
- Be sure to give your partner extra time, quiet, and space when things are particularly busy or stressful.
- Compliment your partner on his or her looks and express appreciation of the many things he or she does to keep things running smoothly.

ISTJ with INTJ

The Joys

ISTJ and INTJ couples share three of the four type preferences, which often leads to a stable, comfortable, and compatible relationship. They often understand each other's need for a quiet and private life. Specifically, ISTJs and INTJs both like a household that is neat, organized, and orderly, as well as the opportunity to pursue their own interests and enjoy plenty of time alone. ISTJs (and INTJs, to a lesser degree) like their lives to be predictable and measured.

Perhaps the greatest area of satisfaction for this combination is their shared desire for honest and direct communication. Neither ISTJs nor INTJs are emotional people, and they discuss most things in a rational and calm manner. Since neither tends to exaggerate or overreact, they are usually forthright as they talk through problems or plan projects. They especially enjoy discussing issues objectively and in great depth and are good at listening to each other's perspectives and opinions. Many ISTJs and INTJs are relieved by the absence of hidden agendas and emotional ambush tactics, and they feel safe and accepted as individuals.

But ISTJs and INTJs are also attracted to each other because of their differences. ISTJs are impressed with INTJs' freethinking style and willingness to take risks, especially intellectual ones. INTJs are often drawn to the unpretentiousness and down-to-earth quality of ISTJs. They are especially appreciative of all the little things ISTJs do to make life run more efficiently. Since neither partner tends to be easily offended, they use patience and good-natured humor to help each other grow and develop in important ways. ISTJs help INTJs become a bit more realistic, enabling them to create better, more workable ideas. Many INTJs say that their ISTJ partners help them notice important details and find enjoyment in the simple things in everyday life. For their part, INTJs help their ISTJ partners become more open to and accepting of new ideas, and they help their partners see the patterns and meanings of their experiences. ISTJs often credit their INTJ partners with broadening their horizons and helping them take calculated risks.

The Frustrations

The chief sourse of frustration for most ISTJ and INTJ couples stems from their different ways of noticing the world around them. ISTJs focus most intently on facts, realities, and details, so they frequently feel a little confused by their INTJ partners' intuitive leaps in thinking. To understand a concept, ISTJs need details to be presented in a step-by-step manner. With experience, they begin to see patterns more easily. In contrast, INTJs focus primarily on the possibilities and implications and find it tedious and overwhelming when their partners bombard them with facts and details. INTJs need a mental framework on which they can hang all the details for them to be relevant and useful.

INTJs also tend to make assumptions about the way things could be, which can conflict with ISTJs' desire to keep things as they are. Change for change's sake makes ISTJs very nervous, while too much of the same thing makes INTJs antsy. Also, ISTJs say that their INTJ partners' many inventive ideas often fail to take into account hard facts such as available time and money. Since both ISTJs and INTJs need to feel in control, they find confusion frustrating and even threatening. ISTJs push for decisions and closure, while INTJs engage in a more complex process of thinking through their options. INTJs sometimes feel pressured to make choices, and ISTJs feel frustrated by the lack of participation of a partner who has drifted away into his or her own world.

Since neither type is especially flexible, the couple can, without plenty of honest discussion and willingness to compromise, find themselves at loggerheads on a regular basis. ISTJs and INTJs also tend to avoid emotional risks and are inclined to try to work out problems privately. Allowing issues to "go underground" can be dangerous, as it keeps couples from developing the bond that comes from discussing and working out difficulties together. ISTJs and INTJs may need to pay special attention to the emotional side of their relationships, and help each other risk vulnerability to deepen their connection.

How to Reach Your INTJ Partner

- Go slowly when offering a lot of details about things that need to be done. Focus on the big picture first.
- Respect your partner's opinions and compliment him or her on the inventiveness and originality he or she brings to life.
- Be specific about what you want and need in the way of assistance with household chores.
- Understand that your partner is fundamentally a very independent person. Make sure there is plenty of opportunity for your mate to follow his or her inspirations and satisfy his or her intellectual curiosity.
- When your partner is under stress, be sure to give him or her plenty of privacy, and don't overwhelm your partner with too many details.

How to Reach Your ISTJ Partner

- Watch your tendency to close yourself off. Be sure to tell your partner when you need more time to consider things.
- Don't be condescending or arrogant. Never criticize your partner or question his or her knowledge in public.
- Avoid becoming so engrossed in your own projects that you become oblivious to what's going on with your partner.
- Tell others how much you appreciate your partner, knowing that he or she will hear this compliment from an objective third party.
- Don't assume that your partner knows what you want. Be specific and direct.
- Especially when your partner is under stress, don't ask him or her to make any unnecessary changes.
- Try to include all the steps or important facts your partner needs to make a decision.

ISTJ with ENTP

The Joys

Because ISTJs and ENTPs have one type preference in common, they typically share a strong desire for honesty, directness, and sound logical reasoning. They tend to understand and respect each other's well-conceived opinions and enjoy engaging in cerebral discussions and even heated debates. Since both partners are relatively thick-skinned, they rarely take things personally and are able to receive constructive criticism in the spirit in which it is intended. ISTJs and ENTPs enjoy communication that is clear and direct, and both feel free to speak their minds.

Although ISTJs and ENTPs have in common an analytical decision-making style, they frequently are initially attracted to each other because of their differences. ISTJs are often drawn to ENTPs because they are so energetic and charming, and they have great social poise. ENTPs exude confidence in almost any situation, and ISTJs find them clever and entertaining. ISTJs also admire ENTPs' creativity, spirit, and ability to improvise. ENTPs are often attracted to ISTJs because of their stability, calm, and independence. ENTPs admire how practical and down-to-earth most ISTJs are and like that they are so trustworthy, responsible, and reliable.

Because of their differences, ISTJs and ENTPs have many opportunities to help each other grow and develop in important ways. Typically, ISTJs help ENTPs focus some of their enormous energy and talent so they are better able to commit themselves to the projects they start. ENTPs often credit their partners with encouraging them to pay closer attention to important details, which helps them make their ideas more practical and workable. For their part, ENTPs often help broaden the horizons of ISTJs by encouraging them to try new ways of doing things and looking for possibilities they never considered before. ISTJs often report that their partners help them relax, become more flexible, and have more fun.

The Frustrations

Since ISTJs and ENTPs have many fundamental differences, they often experience frustration resulting from the ways they communicate. ISTJs are very · literal, realistic, and methodical, while ENTPs tend to jump from topic to topic and use more figurative, even vague, language. ISTJs want a firm grasp on the specifics, while ENTPs want to discuss the possibilities and implications. ISTJs sometimes find their partners' chaotic thought processes dizzying and confusing, and ENTPs become bored with the plodding, methodical explanations their ISTJ partners provide.

Another source of frustration for many ISTJ and ENTP couples is their different needs for order and closure. ISTJs like their homes neat and organized, with a place for everything and everything in its place. ENTPs are much more casual, and since they often start far more projects than they can finish, they tend to leave clutter and piles everywhere. Because ENTPs get bored quickly, they rarely have the energy to perform routine maintenance chores and assume their share of household responsibilities.

ISTJs and ENTPs also conflict over making decisions, since ISTJs like to have things settled, and ENTPs usually want to put off decisions until they can gather more information. ENTPs routinely feel that their partners force decisions, while ISTJs feel that their partners won't make and stick to a plan of action. Naturally, the more trapped ENTPs feel, the less likely they are to make genuine commitments, and the more things are left up in the air, the more prone ISTJs are to exert some kind of control.

Finally, ISTJs and ENTPs usually have very different social needs. Most ISTJs need much more time alone than ENTPs, who need to be around a variety of people on a regular basis. ISTJs and ENTPs also may clash temperamentally, since ISTJs are very traditional and conservative, and ENTPs are essentially nonconformists. ISTJs typically like to maintain the status quo, while ENTPs find it exciting and interesting to rock the boat and question authority. ISTJs must remember that their partners thrive on constant challenge and discovery, and ENTPs need to respect their partners' need for the comfort that comes with a fairly predictable and stable life.

How to Reach Your ENTP Partner

- Encourage your partner to socialize and spend time with friends and colleagues, even if you don't wish to join in. Participate as much as you can.
- Watch your tendency to be negative and try not to say no immediately to a new idea.
- Avoid pointing out factual errors in your partner's ideas. Be enthusiastic and supportive.
- Be willing to consider alternatives, even seemingly outlandish ones. Try to be flexible and willing to experiment.
- Compliment your partner on his or her intelligence and creativity. Appreciate the fun, energy, and excitement he or she brings to the relationship.
- Surprise your partner.

How to Reach Your ISTJ Partner

- Don't invite people home without checking with your partner, and give your mate as much warning as possible.
- Slow down and try not to go in too many directions at once. Focus your energy and attention, and listen carefully when your partner is speaking.
- Don't skip steps, leave out vital details, or neglect to tell your partner important information.
- Respect your partner's need for routines and

predictability. Don't change plans suddenly or ignore rituals that he or she finds comforting.

• Encourage your partner to spend time alone. Don't pressure him or her to join you in every social activity.

• Be clear when you're changing the subject or making an abrupt transition.

• Compliment your partner on tangible things. Express your appreciation of the stability and calm your mate brings to the relationship.

ISTJ with INTP

The Joys

With two type preferences in common, ISTJs and INTPs both tend to be serious, quiet, and independent people who understand and respect each other's need for privacy and time alone. ISTJs and INTPs are typically pensive and reserved people who generally like to think things through before talking about them. Both are somewhat hesitant about social situations and prefer to spend time with a small group of trusted friends. ISTJs and INTPs are also very calm, logical people who base their judgments on objective analysis. They are usually able to offer and receive constructive criticism as helpful suggestions, and they rarely take things personally.

In addition to their areas of commonality, ISTJs and INTPs are often attracted to each other because of their differences. ISTJs are very traditional and conservative, and INTPs are often drawn to their commonsense approach to life. Most INTPs admire ISTJs' responsibility and maturity, as well as the fact that they need little hand-holding. ISTJs are often attracted to INTPs because of their originality, offbeat sense of humor, and intellectual curiosity. ISTJs also admire INTPs' irreverence, flexibility, and spontaneity.

Because of their differences, ISTJs and INTPs have the opportunity to help each other grow and develop in important ways. Typically, ISTJs encourage INTPs to finish some of the projects they start and help them pay closer attention to important, though mundane, details. INTPs often credit their partners with helping them become more accountable, dependable, and trustworthy. For their part, INTPs help their partners ignore some of their need to be productive so they can enjoy themselves more. Many ISTJs say that their partners help them develop curiosity and openness to new things and generally become less fearful of the unknown. INTPs encourage ISTJs to question the status quo, which helps them become more flexible, while ISTJs demonstrate the benefits of discipline and sensual pleasures. Together they can help each other become more aware of their feelings and more willing to share their emotions.

The Frustrations

The most common frustrations for ISTJs and INTPs stem from their different needs for order and closure. Most ISTJs prefer life to move along at a predictable pace. They don't welcome sudden changes and may become upset when their favorite routines are disrupted or disregarded. ISTJs usually have very firm plans and can be inflexible and resistant to new ways of doing things. In contrast, INTPs tend to resist routines because they get bored easily and are energized by the challenge of the unexpected. So INTPs often feel a bit stifled by the rules ISTJs impose, and ISTJs often feel unnerved and thrown off balance by INTPs' unpredictability and general disregard for structure. Since they are both strong-willed people, they frequently come to an impasse, which they then ignore, hoping the storm will blow over.

Another source of conflict for many ISTJ and INTP couples is the way they make decisions. ISTJs tend to take in just enough information to make a decision quickly and absolutely. INTPs are very inquisitive people and like lots of time to gather information before ruling out options.

Whereas ISTJs rarely change their minds, INTPs seem never to close the door on new possibilities, sometimes switching directions at the last minute. ISTJs also like to plan and hate to be rushed or be late. INTPs often run behind schedule, since they easily get lost in their projects and are much less concerned about clocks, calendars, and other people's schedules. ISTJs want INTPs to be more accountable, and INTPs want ISTJs to stop trying to control them.

ISTJs and INTPs may also fail to communicate clearly because of their different perspectives. ISTJs are very literal and linear thinkers and often find INTPs too vague, abstract, and unrealistic. INTPs tend to get bored with things they've already considered or discussed and sometimes find their partners too methodical and predictable. ISTJs and INTPs need to state their positions carefully and respectfully and listen to each other without assuming they know how the other feels.

Finally, ISTJs and INTPs need to work together to create an open, safe atmosphere in which they can explore and deepen their emotional connection. Since both partners find talking about feelings difficult, they need to encourage each other to articulate their emotions without fear of judgment or dismissal. By consciously cultivating this side of themselves, they can strengthen their connection.

How to Reach Your INTP Partner

- Respect your partner's independence, and don't demand that he or she participate in all the activities in which you are interested.
- Try not to control your partner's schedule or impose too many rules or expectations on him or her.
- Honestly consider some of your partner's ideas before saying no or pointing out why they don't make sense.
- Compliment your partner on his or her innovation and fresh ideas.

- Be patient with your partner's sometimes complicated way of describing things. Listen patiently and ask questions so you better understand your partner's perspective.
- Never question your partner's competence or put him or her on the spot in front of others.

How to Reach Your ISTJ Partner

- Beware of your tendency to be vague or abstract. Try to stick to the subject at hand and present your points in a step-by-step fashion.
- Respect your partner's need for order and predictability. Try to give him or her as much advance notice as possible when you need to change plans.
- Don't put your partner on the spot publicly or question his or her authority or competence in front of others.
- Try to finish projects you start in a timely manner. Keep common areas of your home free of clutter, piles, and mess.
- Thank your partner for all the things he or she does to keep your life moving along smoothly and efficiently.

ESFJ with ENTJ

The Joys

ESFJs and ENTJs have two preferences in common, which makes them similar and different in important ways. They are both big talkers who like discussing current events, their various activities, and their reactions with others. They also are very active, energetic people who often have similar needs to be around others. And since they are both planners and doers, they make quick decisions and typically have several projects going at once. Because they are naturally organized and productive, they get great satisfaction from all that they accomplish.

In addition to their similarities, ESFJs and ENTJs are often initially attracted to each other because of their differences. ESFJs are often drawn to ENTJs because they are so confident and independent. ESFJs often admire ENTJs' strength, intelligence, and ambition. ENTJs are often attracted to ESFJs' warmth, friendliness, sensitivity, and desire to take care of others. While ESFJs are good at paying close attention to the present and seeing clearly what needs to be done, ENTJs are good at looking ahead, anticipating future needs, and developing plans to meet them. ESFJs appreciate ENTJs' creative problem-solving skills, just as ENTJs often admire ESFJs' nurturing of relationships and their ability to support the emotional and social aspects of life.

As a result of their differences, ESFJs and ENTJs have the opportunity to help each other grow and develop in important ways. ESFJs can help ENTJs develop more sensitivity to others, improve their communication skills, assess their personal values, and express their feelings. ENTJs often say that their partners help them appreciate their lives and the people in them. For their part, ENTJs help ESFJs remain more objective so they can make choices that are right for them, regardless of other people's opinions. ESFJs also credit their partners with helping them be more honest and assertive about their needs.

The Frustrations

Probably the greatest challenges for ESFJ and ENTJ couples stem from their different ways of making decisions. ESFJs consider their personal values first, while ENTJs use objective analysis to come to conclusions. The most important criterion for superlogical ENTJs is whether a decision makes good sense. Sometimes they may fail to consider how their partners are likely to feel about or be affected by their actions, and they act insensitively. In sharp contrast, most ESFJs are highly sensitive. The more outspoken, thick-skinned, and direct ENTJs often feel that they have to "walk on eggs" and be less than 100 percent honest to avoid hurting their partners' feelings. For most ESFJs, maintaining a harmonious relationship is their top priority, so they will usually go to great lengths to avoid conflict. But if they put off honest discussions of real problems too long, hurt and resentment fester, and they may engage in passive-aggressive behavior or explode in emotional outbursts. When ENTJs aren't made aware of their offensive behavior, it's easy for them to perceive their partners' outbursts as irrational overreactions. To compound the problem, most ENTJs are not very comfortable with or skilled at dealing with emotions, so they also may have trouble controlling their tempers when under stress.

Not only are ESFJs extremely sensitive, but they can also be quite judgmental. They tend to see things as either black or white, right or wrong, and they often try to impose their values on their partners. This rarely works because ENTJs are very independent and opinionated as well.

Another complaint of many ESFJs is that their partners put career opportunities ahead of family obligations. Ironically, as committed as ESFJs are to their relationships, they sometimes put other people's needs ahead of their partners' when they become so involved in other people's lives that they take on their burdens. And although most ESFJs take great pleasure in making their homes warm and welcoming places, they often get stuck performing more than their fair share of the maintenance, which can make them feel overloaded, unappreciated, and resentful.

Temperament differences also can contribute to stress and result in discord. By nature, ENTJs are excited by new challenges, while ESFJs prefer predictability. ENTJs are compulsive learners who are stimulated by analyzing big ideas and controversial issues. To them, a spirited debate is both fun and energizing, while to most ESFJs such a debate feels like an argument. Since both ENTJs and ESFJs tend to be strong-willed, driven people, they may experience power struggles over whose agenda will win out.

How to Reach Your ENTJ Partner

- Respect and appreciate your partner's many good ideas and superior creative problem-solving skills.
- Recognize and support your partner's career and work. Compliment your partner on his or her achievements and accomplishments.
- Try not to take your partner's comments or critiques too personally. Step back and remember that your partner's motivation is to help you.
- Learn about some of the issues or activities that interest your partner so you can discuss them with him or her.
- Never question your partner's competence in public.
- Resist the urge to point out factual errors in your partner's ideas or to insist on seeing evidence that an idea will work.
- Be honest and direct when your partner does something that hurts or offends you.

How to Reach Your ESFJ Partner

- Pay close attention to the relationship. Put your partner and family ahead of your work.
- Try not to be critical. Appreciate the positive and be gentle with constructive criticism.
- Don't dismiss your partner's feelings. Resist the urge to try to fix problems before your partner has a chance to vent his or her feelings.
- Respect your partner's need to maintain traditions and have things remain the same. Acknowledge and celebrate formal occasions such as birthdays and anniversaries.
- Express your love and appreciation of all the things your partner does to nurture you.

- Recognize your partner's need for emotional as well as physical intimacy.

ESFJ with INTJ

The Joys

ESFJs and INTJs share one of the four type preferences, so they have in common a desire for life to be fairly orderly, planned, and structured. Respectful of each other's routines, they generally like their homes to be organized and neat and are happiest without too many unexpected upheavals. They are decisive and opinionated, even if their judgments are based on different values or beliefs. ESFJs and INTJs characteristically make quick and unwavering decisions and are most comfortable when things are settled.

But it is their many differences that often attract ESFJs and INTJs to each other. ESFJs appreciate INTJs' calm objectivity and ability to understand complex issues. They also admire INTJs' wit, intellect, creativity, and independence. INTJs are often drawn to ESFJs' warmth, nurturing, and social ease — they seem to be loved by everyone. INTJs also admire ESFJs' strong work ethic, dependability, and eagerness to please and help others.

Because of their significant temperament and type differences, INTJs and ESFJs have the opportunity to help each other grow and develop in important ways. ESFJs help INTJs better understand other people by learning to pay closer attention to the details that are important to others. INTJs often credit their partners with helping them develop more compassion for others and encouraging them to take notice of the beauty found in the moment. INTJs help ESFJs make more balanced choices by learning to be less concerned about the opinions of others. Intellectually curious, INTJs also broaden their partners' horizons by exposing them to new ideas and experiences.

The Frustrations

Since they are so different in some important ways, ESFJs and INTJs have their share of conflicts and frustrations. ESFJs are very social people who easily and often overextend themselves. As a result, they may have little energy left for their partners. INTJs, for their part, spend so much time wrapped up in their own ideas and projects that they frequently opt out of activities with their partners or families. Also, ESFJs and INTJs may misunderstand each other because they routinely focus on very different things. ESFJs are so realistic and practical that they may not be interested in their partners' more abstract and future-oriented projects. Global and theoretical INTJs can be dismissive of the more down-to-earth activities of ESFJs. The most successful ESFJ and INTJ couples encourage each other to pursue their own interests while making sure they take time to listen to and support each other.

The most common source of frustration for ESFJs and INTJs is their different communication styles. ESFJs want to talk everything out — at length and extemporaneously. But INTJs prefer to think things through carefully and share only ideas that are fully and perfectly formed in their minds. So ESFJs feel as if they have to pull information out of their partners, and INTJs feel pressured to share their thoughts prematurely. ESFJs are very sensitive and sympathetic and get their feelings hurt easily and often. Even the most innocuous or constructive suggestion can be perceived as a personal criticism. INTJs are frequently confused and annoyed by ESFJs' hypersensitivity, as well as by their tendency to hold grudges or sulk rather than deal with problems. But to be sure, INTJs can be very critical and impatient with their partners' feelings, making it difficult for ESFJs to feel safe to share their emotions with them. Instead, ESFJs may avoid dealing directly with problems rather than risk confrontation. Of course, this habit backfires when resentments left unresolved grow into larger, more upsetting disputes. The solution is to balance ESFJs' need for harmony with INTJs' need for honesty, a process that is complicated by gender role expectations. INTJ women may be seen as cold and heartless, while ESFJ men may be seen as wishy-washy and too easily swayed by others' opinions. ESFJs and INTJs need to be willing to allow each other the freedom to pursue their own interests, in their own styles, while supporting and respecting their natural differences.

The ultimate challenge for this couple is to balance ESFJs' conservatism and need to fit in with INTJs' independence and desire for originality. ESFJs and INTJs often have different social and political values and may simply agree to disagree. ESFJs are naturally suspicious of new ideas and don't like things to change. They'd rather deal with a known quantity, even if it's less than ideal, than experience the stress and chaos of disruption. INTJs are so interested in seeking truth and new challenges that they may force change to stay energized.

How to Reach Your INTJ Partner

• Never publicly question your partner's competence or knowledge.
• Discuss small problems immediately, but give your partner time to think about his or her response.
• Encourage your partner's individual interests and pursuits. Don't interrupt or distract your mate from getting to the satisfying depth he or she needs.
• Be willing to consider your partner's original ideas. Resist the urge to point out factual errors immediately.
• Don't accuse your partner of being unfeeling. Share your feelings, but don't demand that your partner share his or hers, especially before he or she is ready.
• Be calm, rational, and logical in your

arguments. Try not to repeat yourself, become emotional, or exaggerate.

How to Reach Your ESFJ Partner

• Begin with the positive; be appreciative and complimentary.
• Smile, maintain eye contact, and stop what you're doing to look into your partner's eyes when he or she is speaking.
• Thank your partner for all the tangible ways he or she makes life more comfortable and happy.
• Remember to observe the important holidays and rituals your partner loves. Make a special effort to celebrate anniversaries and birthdays.
• Be gentle with constructive criticism.
• Don't become impatient with your partner's emotional reactions, and never attempt to talk your mate out of the way he or she feels.

ESFJ with ENTP

The Joys

Although ESFJs and ENTPs share only one of the four type preferences, they often have similar social needs. Both like to entertain and be around a variety of people. They also are likely to lead active, busy lives and to be involved in many projects at the same time. Although they often see things differently, their mutual desire to talk about things helps them stay connected.

Although they are both friendly, talkative, and outgoing, ESFJs and ENTPs are often initially attracted to each other because of their differences. ESFJs often find ENTPs to be utterly charming, confident, and exciting. ENTPs' quick, clever minds are a source of delight to many ESFJs, who admire their unique sense of humor and ability to improve and adapt. ENTPs are often drawn to ESFJs because they are warm, sincere, and sensitive. ENTPs find that ESFJs' devotion and strong

sense of responsibility make them totally trustworthy.

Because ESFJs and ENTPs have many complimentary strengths, they have the opportunity to help each other grow and develop in important ways. ESFJs help their partners enjoy the present moment and follow through on their commitments. ESFJs also offer ENTPs a healthy dose of realism, which makes their ideas eminently more workable. And most ENTPs say that their partners help them become more sensitive to how their actions may affect others. For their part, ENTPs infuse ESFJs' lives with optimism. They encourage ESFJs to look down the road, see the big picture, and dream up creative ways of making positive things happen. Many ESFJs credit their partners with giving them more confidence and the courage to speak their minds, even in the face of skepticism.

The Frustrations

ESFJs and ENTPs are different in some fundamental ways, so it's not surprising that they often have trouble communicating. The literal ESFJs, who listen to each word for meaning, sometimes have trouble following the more global-thinking ENTPs, who quickly move from one thought to the next and often start thoughts in mid-sentence. ESFJs frustrate ENTPs, who feel slowed and overburdened by unnecessary specifics. ENTPs live for possibilities, so they're constantly dreaming up new schemes. Although their ideas are usually inventive, they make ESFJs nervous because the ideas require so much adaptation and are generally based on instinct rather than experience. In their efforts to be helpful, ESFJs take the wind out of their partners' sails by pointing out errors of fact or reminding them of practical concerns such as available time and money. When it comes to making decisions about finances, this difference can create conflict.

Another source of frustration for ESFJ and

ENTP couples is their different tolerances for conflict. ESFJs are extremely sensitive but also easily offended. ENTPs can be very charming, but they can also be glib and critical and can get so wrapped up in themselves that they act insensitively toward others. Because dealing with conflict is especially uncomfortable for ESFJs, who crave harmonious relationships, they may be reluctant to confront their partners with their dissatisfaction or to discuss problems between them. ENTPs don't find conflict nearly so stressful and, in fact, find a lively argument to be intellectually stimulating.

The differences in ESFJs' and ENTPs' temperaments are also responsible for some of the frustrations they experience. ESFJs are among the most traditional of all people. They find change difficult and instead love familiar routines and habits, working hard to keep things as they are. ENTPs are perpetual learners and experimenters. By nature, they seek out the new and the different, the exciting, and, to some extent, the dangerous, and they quickly tire of anything too familiar. ESFJs often wish that their partners would shift their priorities from advancing their careers to spending more quality time with them and their families. By contrast, ENTPs sometimes wish that their partners would push themselves intellectually or be more willing to experiment sexually. Some ENTPs may have to work to keep their zest for life in check, especially those who are in committed relationships. They typically like to flirt, and even when they don't act on their impulses, they often make their very observant and loyal ESFJ partners feel insecure and resentful.

Finally, a perpetual source of frustration for people of this type combination is the issue of control. ESFJs are most comfortable when things are decided and plans are made and kept. They want to be prepared and to do things right. ENTPs usually prefer to improvise and are energized by responding to opportunities as they unfold, even if that means changing plans abruptly. This difference is a perpetual sore spot for both partners. ESFJs are likely to interpret their partners' desire to back out of a commitment as a personal betrayal, while ENTPs don't see this as a big deal and therefore feel resentful and controlled.

How to Reach Your ENTP Partner

- Laugh at your partner's jokes and enjoy his or her witticisms. Appreciate your mate's problem-solving skills.
- Encourage and support your partner's career decisions.
- Try not to force your partner into eliminating options prematurely. Be patient with his or her boundless curiosity.
- Don't fence your partner in. Encourage him or her to cultivate other friendships, and don't ask your mate to account for every minute of his or her time.
- Resist the urge to make value judgments about your partner's behavior or friends.
- Recognize your partner's need for spontaneity and accommodate it whenever you can. Plan for unstructured time.
- Try to be flexible and choose your battles carefully. Share control.
- Try to roll with the punches and not be offended by things your partner says that inadvertently hurt your feelings.

How to Reach Your ESFJ Partner

- Don't dismiss your partner's feelings as insignificant, unimportant, or overreactions.
- Patiently give your partner as much time as he or she needs to express his or her feelings fully. Listen without trying to fix the problem.
- Try not to change plans. Give your partner as much time as possible to adjust.
- Ask about what is happening in your partner's life. Listen with empathy and support.

- Follow through on commitments. Finish the projects you start.
- Express your appreciation of all that your partner does for you and to make your home a comfortable, warm place.
- Try to schedule spontaneous time (such as on vacations) to make it easier for your partner not to follow a plan.
- Plan ahead to acknowledge birthdays, anniversaries, and other events that are important to your partner.

ESFJ with INTP

The Joys

Because ESFJs and INTPs are completely opposite types, they often have interesting and challenging relationships, and their many differences are frequently the source of their initial attraction to each other. ESFJs are drawn to INTPs' calm and self-contained style and to their creativity, complexity, and unusual sense of humor. Because INTPs are a bit mysterious to ESFJs, they feel compelled to figure them out. INTPs are often attracted to ESFJs' vivaciousness and warmth. ESFJs are naturally affectionate, expressive, and eager to do thoughtful things for others. They love to nurture and take care of their partners, which many INTPs find very appealing. When INTPs and ESFJs share similar values or interests, they can create a deep and enduring connection.

Because ESFJs and INTPs tend to see and interact with the world in such fundamentally different ways, they can help each other grow and develop in important ways. ESFJs help INTPs create and maintain some order around them so they can be more organized and disciplined and get more accomplished. INTPs also credit their partners with helping them become more sensitive to their families' needs and feelings. For their part, INTPs

are often able to help ESFJs let go of some of their need for control and enjoy more spontaneity and adventure. Many ESFJs say that they become more assertive, more willing to make decisions others may not like, and more objective, so they get their feelings hurt less frequently.

The Frustrations

ESFJs and INTPs often experience conflict and frustration that stem from their different communication styles. ESFJs need to discuss issues to understand them fully, while INTPs find it frustrating to try to make sense of things before they have processed their thoughts internally. ESFJs frequently keep talking after INTPs think the issue is resolved, or they want to rehash details or engage in what INTPs consider gossip. ESFJs and INTPs also respond differently to conflict: ESFJs need plenty of verbal encouragement and can become volatile and emotional, while INTPs usually become quiet and withdrawn. ESFJs are also much more social and want to spend lots of time with friends or talking on the phone. INTPs almost always have a small group of close friends and prefer to spend time pursuing their own interests, such as reading, working on the computer, or quietly thinking their own thoughts.

ESFJs tend to be very realistic and conservative. They respect traditions and love observing rituals and holidays with great sentiment and fanfare. INTPs are much less conforming, sentimental, and willing to participate in rituals for which they don't have a genuine affinity. Whereas ESFJs like to keep things the same and derive great comfort from maintaining their routines, INTPs like to shake things up and invite change and innovation. They find too many rules or too much repetition boring and restrictive. Ideas and possibilities that INTPs find fascinating, however, are often met with resistance when ESFJs can't see any immediate practical benefits. Most ESFJs feel that change creates too much chaos, but INTPs find change interesting and invigorating.

ESFJs have great energy for completing projects. They often move with lightning speed and want everyone around them to pitch in and work cooperatively and efficiently. In their zeal, they can be bossy and make snap decisions, which INTPs find frustrating and insulting. By contrast, INTPs prefer to think about projects beforehand and figure out the smartest and most interesting ways of doing them. They start with great intentions, but their energy often drains away after the creative aspects of a project are over. Many INTPs leave projects almost finished, which drives their ESFJ partners crazy.

Varying concepts of order and closure also create conflict for this couple, because most ESFJs demand a neat and organized home. They want to please others and are very aware of what's appropriate. They often end up doing a greater portion of the household chores and complain that their partners either don't notice what needs to be done or aren't willing to help out. If ESFJs don't feel appreciated for their efforts, they feel hurt and resentful. INTPs generally care more about their own personal standards than other people's. They are also more relaxed and casual about appearances, so they find ESFJs' fussing annoying and unnecessary. Naturally, the more ESFJs nag and complain, the more INTPs tune them out emotionally or physically leave the room.

Perhaps the greatest source of frustration for both ESFJs and INTPs is their very different ways of making decisions. ESFJs are driven to maintain harmony and are upset and stressed by unresolved problems. But they also tend to avoid healthy confrontations and may pretend things are better than they are because they have trouble being direct and honest, especially about unpleasant subjects. On the other hand, INTPs are very direct, even to the point of bluntness. Yet they avoid discussions

that require them to be vulnerable or to share their fears, especially when they don't feel able to articulate their feelings accurately. Since ESFJs tend to take everything personally and INTPs tend to be unintentionally insensitive, there is a great risk of mutual frustration if they don't learn to hear each other out and compromise.

How to Reach Your INTP Partner

- Respect your partner's need for time alone and uninterrupted quiet. Encourage your mate's independence, and don't pressure him or her into going places with you.
- Educate yourself about your partner's work and take a genuine interest in his or her projects.
- Be calm, direct, and honest in your communication. Try not to repeat yourself or become overly emotional.
- Give your partner the time and opportunity to think things through fully before expecting an answer or a reaction.
- Don't talk too much or finish your partner's sentences.
- Don't bring up old hurts or resurrect previously settled issues.
- Compliment your partner on his or her innovative ideas and unique approach to problems.
- Solicit your partner's advice about logical consequences or future implications of ideas.

How to Reach Your ESFJ Partner

- Be gentle and diplomatic, especially when discussing unpleasant subjects or problems.
- Share specific details about your day, especially the people involved.
- Demonstrate that you're listening by making comments. Maintain eye contact and stay physically close.
- Express your feelings and appreciation in words. Compliment your partner on the many

things he or she does to make your home happy and comfortable.

- Initiate and then follow through on chores and projects. Don't leave things unfinished, and always pick up after yourself.
- Be willing to discuss issues even after you think they're settled. Indulge your partner's need to figure things out aloud.
- Never dismiss your partner's feelings, even if they don't seem logical.

ISFJ with ENTJ

The Joys

ISFJs and ENTJs have only one of the four type preferences in common, but they can still have a very complementary relationship. Their shared desire for closure and order focuses their efforts on finishing projects in a timely matter, maintaining a neat and well-organized home, and can help them enjoy working together as a team. They both have pretty definite opinions, and when these coincide, they share a powerful bond.

These two types bring a host of different perspectives and styles to the table, but their differences are often the source of their initial attraction. ISFJs are typically drawn to ENTJs' intellectual prowess, quick and creative minds, dry wit, and sometimes unusual sense of humor. ISFJs admire how ENTJs see everyday things in unusual ways and bring a fresh perspective to life. ISFJs respect ENTJs' natural objectivity, ambition, and independence. For their part, ENTJs are frequently attracted to ISFJs (especially male ISFJs) for their warmth, sincerity, and gentleness. ENTJs also admire ISFJs' unpretentious style and conscientiousness. ISFJs make their partners feel nurtured, appreciated, and admired.

Because of their many differences, ISFJs and ENTJs can help each other grow and develop in important ways. Learning to understand each other better teaches them how to be more effective with other people as well. Specifically, ISFJs help their ENTJ partners slow down and appreciate the world. ENTJs learn how to accurately express their feelings and become more sensitive to other people. They find that they can let go of some of their competitiveness and their need to rush full speed toward the finish line. In turn, ENTJs often help their ISFJ partners take more initiative and become less resistant to trying new things. Many ISFJs credit their partners with helping them handle disharmony and thus build stronger and deeper relationships. Finally, ENTJs often support their ISFJ partners' efforts to be more assertive, which makes them less apt to be taken advantage of.

The Frustrations

Since ISFJs and ENTJs have such different styles, they have plenty of opportunities for conflict. Temperamentally, ISFJs are much more conservative and traditional than their independent and highly driven ENTJ partners. Whereas ISFJs like routines and rituals, ENTJs are more concerned with constantly improving themselves (and their partners!) and seeking new challenges. ISFJs are frustrated by their partners' tendency to always think about the future, rather than simply enjoy what they have at present. For their part, ENTJs may find ISFJs too hesitant to take action and too resistant to their many innovative ideas. Change is exciting to ENTJs, but it can be scary or stressful to many ISFJs.

Another common source of frustration for ISFJs and ENTJs is that during discussions, ENTJs tend to focus on more global and interrelated concepts, while ISFJs tend to stay on point, moving step-by-step through their thought processes. ISFJs also need more time to process their thoughts before talking about them, which may be irritating to the quick-thinking and very verbal ENTJs. ENTJs can be abrupt and impatient and may overpower the more gentle ISFJs. When ISFJs feel hurt or offended, they tend to withdraw, sometimes holding on to grudges for a long time. ENTJs find this very frustrating, since they prefer others to point out offensive behavior so they can quickly make it right and move on. Since ISFJs take most things personally, especially comments intended as constructive criticism, ENTJs need to be especially gentle and choose their words carefully.

ISFJs and ENTJs perceive arguments in very different ways. To ISFJs, any disagreement means disharmony, and they want to end it as quickly as possible. To postpone confrontations, ISFJs may avoid speaking up about issues that make them unhappy. To ENTJs, discussions, even heated ones, are beneficial and even enjoyable. They like the stimulation and rarely feel threatened or worried by debates. Whereas ISFJs may agree to a solution quickly simply to get it over with, ENTJs are likely to keep the discussion going until they reach an effective and logical solution. But their partners may be too exhausted or upset at that point to want anything but time alone to pull themselves together.

Finally, even though most ISFJs and ENTJs enjoy a shared commitment to getting things done, they each want to be the one who makes the decisions and can sometimes struggle with issues of control. So they need to establish a fair division of power. And although both tend to like a neat and orderly home, ISFJs typically take on more of the routine and mundane chores because they don't mind the repetition as much and want to please their ENTJ partners. Receiving some help and feeling appreciated for all they do helps ISFJs feel much better about this inequity. ENTJs are wise to make sure their hardworking partners never feel taken for granted.

How to Reach Your ENTJ Partner

- Congratulate your partner on and celebrate his or her professional achievements.
- Stay with the discussion, even if it's

uncomfortable, so you can reach what your partner sees as an effective solution.
- Be patient with your partner's tendency to bring in seemingly unrelated issues. Ask for clarification if you need it.
- Don't close down or withdraw. Rather than sulking in silence, explain what you're feeling and why.
- Be sincere and even selective in your expressions of affection. Make sure they are authentic.

How to Reach Your ISFJ Partner

- Allow your partner plenty of private time before expecting a discussion about how to resolve a problem. Never divulge personal information about your partner to others.
- Begin by appreciating the positive. Be encouraging, gentle, and complimentary.
- Watch your tendency for perfectionism and your desire to constantly play the devil's advocate. Never criticize as a way of helping your partner become more effective.
- Be generous in your expressions of affection. Offer thoughtful notes, cards, and small gifts as tokens of your affection.
- Compliment and thank your partner for all the little things he or she does to make your home comfortable, harmonious, and well run. Express your appreciation of the amount of time your mate spent on each task (at the time it is finished).
- Share your feelings and let your partner help you better understand your reactions and those of other people.

ISFJ with INTJ

The Joys

ISFJs and INTJs have two of the four type preferences in common and often share a need for quiet time alone and an organized lifestyle. Naturally private, serious people, ISFJs and INTJs prefer substantive interactions on a one-on-one basis and tend to most enjoy the company of each other and a small group of close friends. When they work on professional or home-based projects, they like to be able to focus and concentrate for long stretches of time without interruption. Since they also share a desire for order and closure, ISFJs and INTJs tend to respect and accommodate each other's rituals, routines, and schedules. Both like to make decisions and to make and then stick with a plan of action. And both like to be prepared for their responsibilities, to follow through on commitments, and to avoid unexpected changes if at all possible. Since INTJs and ISFJs like order, both are generally willing to do their fair share to keep their homes neat and efficiently run.

But it is often their many differences that are the source of the initial attraction for ISFJs and INTJs. Typically, ISFJs are attracted to INTJs' intellectual intensity, depth, and their creative and unique way of looking at the world. INTJs are independent, calm, and logical, and ISFJs admire their ability to make sense of complex and sometimes confusing experiences. INTJs often are drawn to ISFJs because of their genuine warmth and loyalty to others. INTJs admire the gentleness and compassion of ISFJs, as well as their habit of being nurturing, loyal, and loving partners. ISFJs possess a great understanding of the confusing needs and feelings of others and are skillful at dealing with those feelings.

It is precisely their many differences that give ISFJs and INTJs the opportunity to help each other grow and develop in important ways. Typically, ISFJs help INTJs become more sensitive and patient with other people, and INTJs often say that their partners help them express their feelings and connect more deeply with others. For their part, INTJs are generally able to help ISFJs develop a thicker skin so they don't take things so personally or get their feelings hurt as often. Also,

INTJs help ISFJs look ahead and gain optimism about the future and confidence in their ability to manage new challenges.

The Frustrations

In addition to the complementary aspects of their relationships, ISFJs and INTJs have temperamental differences that are the source of much frustration. ISFJs are conservative people who are cautious and comfortable with convention, whereas INTJs are very independent people who are more interested in learning new things and constantly expanding their range of competence. Whereas ISFJs often want to keep things as they are, observe revered traditions, and repeat satisfying habits, INTJs are highly skeptical of and uncomfortable with anything that feels contrived. INTJs tend to question everything and like to discuss and debate issues with passion and depth. Most ISFJs find nearly all change — even proposed change — unnerving, and they are often upset by their partners' lack of respect for the status quo.

Another area of frustration for ISFJs and INTJs stems from their different communication styles. ISFJs are extremely realistic, literal, and down-to-earth. They usually say exactly what they mean — in diplomatic and careful terms — and mean what they say with heartfelt earnestness. By contrast, INTJs are among the most abstract and global thinkers of all the types. They tend to communicate in very complex and analytical ways, so ISFJs often feel frustrated by their partners' vague and confusing leaps. For their part, INTJs feel frustrated by their partners' slower, more methodical pace. ISFJs prefer to discuss the present and the past, while INTJs are more interested in thinking about the future. And ISFJs rely heavily on their personal and subjective values to guide their decisions, while INTJs rely on logical, objective reasoning. ISFJs often feel that their partners don't give enough consideration to the needs and feelings of others. Conversely, INTJs think that ISFJs are far too concerned about and restricted by what other people think.

ISFJs and INTJs have very different needs when it comes to expressing their feelings. ISFJs like to feel a strong emotional connection at all times, so they tend to press their partners for more emotional disclosure than they feel comfortable with. And since INTJs are very private people, they often, though inadvertently, shut their partners out. INTJs are especially loath to share their fears or vulnerabilities with anyone. And although INTJs are otherwise very honest and direct, they can also be overly blunt, critical, and demanding. For their part, ISFJs tend to take a very personal view of almost everything and often have trouble hearing the constructive suggestions their partners offer. When ISFJs are hurt, they tend to withdraw, and they seldom speak up and address conflict head-on. Usually, after an important cooling-off and private processing period, ISFJs and INTJs find that they can hear each other's positions and reach a loving compromise that clears the air.

How to Reach Your INTJ Partner

- Maintain constant and genuine interest in your partner's career and professional strivings. Ask about your partner's work and listen attentively.
- Never publicly question your partner's knowledge or competence.
- Seek your partner's advice, especially about future implications or alternative solutions to problems.
- Compliment your partner on his or her creativity and on the uniqueness of his or her innovations. Always be genuine.
- Remain calm and try to stay unemotional when discussing issues or problems with your partner. Try not to repeat yourself.
- Strive to stay open to new ways of doing things. Avoid responding negatively to changes or refusing to consider unusual alternatives.

How to Reach Your ISFJ Partner

- Smile and look lovingly at your partner, especially when you first see him or her.
- Slow down and be patient, particularly when you are discussing new topics or suggesting a new way of looking at old problems.
- Begin by commenting on points of agreement. Emphasize the positive, and don't dwell on the negative.
- Watch your tendency to be critical, arrogant, or condescending.
- Compliment your partner on tangible things. Thank your mate for all the little things he or she does to keep your life running smoothly.
- Make an effort to share your feelings, thoughts, and reactions with your partner. Don't shut him or her out.

ISFJ with ENTP

The Joys

Like other couples whose types are opposite on all four preferences, ENTPs and ISFJs have much to offer each other and great opportunities to help each other grow and develop. But they also face some serious challenges. ISFJs and ENTPs are often attracted to each other because of their many differences. ENTPs are drawn to the calming energy, nurturing, and natural compassion typical of the steady and responsible ISFJs. And ISFJs find ENTPs' high-energy, fun-loving, "anything's possible" approach to life exciting.

Because of their many differences, they can help each other grow and develop in important ways. ENTPs often broaden ISFJs' horizons by exposing them to ideas and people they might not otherwise experience. They can also challenge their partners to improve themselves and become more self-confident. ENTPs are good at helping the more serious and traditional ISFJs to lighten up. They bring excitement and fun into their relationships and make their partners laugh. For their part, ISFJs bring stability, loyalty, and good old-fashioned common sense to their relationships. They provide loving, comfortable homes, are stalwart supporters of their partners, and are very attentive to their partners' needs. They often love preparing for and celebrating traditional holidays. And being realistic and down-to-earth, ISFJs provide their more future-oriented, theoretical mates with an important sense of grounding.

The Frustrations

Their many differences do create substantial obstacles for ISFJs and ENTPs. One difference is that ENTPs are naturally drawn to and energized by new and exciting adventures. They thrive on overcoming unexpected challenges and want to be out in the world meeting new people, talking about new possibilities, and making things happen. In contrast, ISFJs prefer to spend their time on more traditional family- or home-centered activities, working hard, or having fun with people they know well and trust implicitly.

The fact that ENTPs and ISFJs often have very different interests can further pull them in different directions. ENTPs enjoy a good argument. To them, debating an issue is an intellectual exercise and a source of great fun. And although the discussion may get heated, they seldom take things personally. ISFJs feel just the opposite. They don't like having to think on their feet, defend their positions, or engage in activities that create disharmony. They feel frustrated when ENTPs are unable to support their theories with solid facts. Similarly, when faced with conflict in their relationships, ENTPs are likely to want to confront the issue head-on, while ISFJs are more likely to want to delay the process, at least until they've had adequate time to think through their position. Then they want to lovingly and diplomatically discuss ways of getting past the unpleasant experience.

Most ISFJs find great comfort in structure and routine. They like things settled, agreements adhered to, and their environments neat and orderly. Regardless of their gender, the bulk of major responsibilities like keeping the house, managing the finances, and raising the children tend to fall on their shoulders. While ENTPs are appreciative of all their partners do, they often act in ways that undermine ISFJs' efforts, such as not putting things away, being sloppy with bank deposit receipts and other paperwork, and not upholding rules with their children.

The social needs of ENTPs and ISFJs are often at odds. ENTPs are quick to drop whatever they're doing if an intriguing or fun opportunity presents itself, especially if lots of people are involved. ISFJs prefer to plan their time and are most comfortable alone with their partners or in small gatherings of close friends. Since both ISFJs and ENTPs usually choose like-minded friends, they may find each other's friends unappealing. ISFJs are born with a desire to please and will go to great lengths to accommodate their partners' needs, but their self-sacrificing behavior can also cause resentment. And ISFJs can be somewhat controlling and unwilling to try some of their partners' more adventurous suggestions. For their part, ENTPs are great at starting things but can frequently fail to follow through. This causes significant frustration for ISFJs, who don't feel comfortable until a job is finished and can become so obsessed with the end product that they take the fun out of the process.

How to Reach Your ISFJ Partner

- Spend quiet time with your partner doing things he or she enjoys. Give your partner your undivided attention.
- Agree to finish a project that is important to

your partner, then actually do it when you say you will!

• Share power. Don't dominate or intimidate to win an argument or get your way.

• Let your partner know in advance that you want physical intimacy so he or she can prepare for it. Anticipate your partner's needs and watch for signs that he or she needs to reconnect emotionally.

• Share the household chores and respect your partner's need for your home to be clean and uncluttered.

• Try not to be critical. Be gentle in discussing issues and start with something positive.

• Let your partner know — in words and actions — how much you appreciate all the little things he or she does to make your home and life comfortable.

• Don't dismiss your partner's tendency to worry and fret about things, especially when he or she is under stress. That is the time for gentle reassurance.

How to Reach Your ENTP Partner

• Try not to nitpick or nag about small annoyances. Pick your battles and be specific about what you want done and when.

• Support your partner's wide range of friends and activities. Try to develop an interest in one of his or her interests or hobbies.

• Give your partner space. Try not to control or use guilt to get him or her to do things according to your timetable.

• Let your partner brainstorm without interruption. Compliment your mate's innovation, even if you see some realities or details that make his or her ideas impractical or unworkable.

• Try to be open to sexual experimentation and to accommodate your partner's desire for spontaneity and variety.

• Express your love and appreciation verbally. Speak up immediately and calmly when you have a problem.

ISFJ with INTP

The Joys

While ISFJs and INTPs have only one of the four type preferences in common, they do share a common need for quiet, a respect for each other's privacy, and a preference for a small, close circle of friends. This is often a connection that helps them overcome some formidable obstacles.

In addition to their shared characteristics, ISFJs and INTPs are often initially attracted to each other because of their differences. ISFJs are generally drawn to INTPs' wit, creativity, intelligence, and uniqueness. They are often the most interesting person the ISFJ has ever met. INTPs present a constant challenge, since they are so individualistic and nonconforming. They often provoke ISFJs to think in new ways and reconsider things they never questioned before. INTPs are often drawn to ISFJs' gentleness, genuine consideration, and sensitivity. ISFJs typically work hard to maintain a warm and secure home and generally make INTPs feel very nurtured and loved. Whereas INTPs offer ISFJs challenge and fun, ISFJs offer their partners stable, calm, and affectionate environments.

But because of their many differences, ISFJs and INTPs can help each other grow and develop in important ways. ISFJs help INTPs focus more of their attention on important relationships, deepening their connection to their families and helping them become more patient and affectionate. INTPs often say that their partners encourage them to notice more important details, which helps them make their impressive ideas more workable. For their part, INTPs often help their ISFJ partners see patterns and deeper meaning. ISFJs say that they become more objective, making them less apt to get their feelings hurt and more able to let go of their strong need to please other people. Many ISFJs find that with their partners' influence, they become more flexible and curious, which helps them make better decisions.

The Frustrations

ISFJs and INTPs have some big differences, not the least of which is their different temperaments. ISFJs are very cautious, traditional, and responsible people with strong conservative values. They place home and hearth about all else and are deeply upset by change or disruption in their routines. INTPs, in contrast, value their personal competence and independence above all else. They are often quite irreverent and rarely care much about what other people think of their actions or lifestyles. They are innovators, always thirsty for learning and new challenges. Whereas ISFJs work hard to maintain a neat, attractive, and orderly home, INTPs rarely even notice the disorder because they are focused on possibilities and the future. INTPs have little interest in anything remotely routine, while ISFJs find routines comforting. ISFJs are concerned about practical ways in which they can help others, while INTPs are energized by thinking about new ways to solve complex problems.

Conflict generally arises when ISFJs don't respect or appreciate the importance INTPs place on learning, work, and professional growth, or when INTPs dismiss how important family, tradition, and service to others are to ISFJs. Since ISFJs and INTPs often have very diverse interests, they frequently have different tastes in people and may not appreciate their partners' choice of friends. Their social lives can be challenging and require that they find ways to balance time alone, time with mutual friends, and time among their own friends.

Finally, ISFJs and INTPs must work hard to develop a means of communicating with each other that meets their different needs. ISFJs want

their partners to be patient, open, and gentle. Above all, they want to feel a close connection based on shared feelings and unquestioned faithfulness. INTPs want their partners to be direct, unemotional, and consistent. They want to feel free to be themselves instead of being forced to comply with someone else's expectations of how they're supposed to feel or behave. This may be especially true for female INTPs. INTPs should take heed not to dismiss ISFJs' feelings or act condescending when they think their partners are overreacting.

How to Reach Your INTP Partner

- Be willing to listen and learn about your partner's interests and pursuits. Try to understand enough to share his or her passions.
- Try to be more adventurous inside and outside of the bedroom. Let your partner show you some unexpected pleasures and experiences.
- Discuss your concerns and needs clearly, directly, honestly, and calmly.
- Try to relax and occasionally put off what you could do today but can wait until tomorrow so you can play with your partner.
- Always be open and truthful about how you feel. Avoid games.
- Compliment your partner on his or her achievements and competencies.
- Don't force intimate conversations, but do tell your partner how much you appreciate it when he or she opens up and shares.
- Try to let go of some social or external expectations. Trust that important things will get done — but perhaps not exactly when or how you planned.

How to Reach Your ISFJ Partner

- Make an effort to get to know the people your partner cares about. Listen carefully for details about co-workers, family, and friends, and respond to discussions about them.

- Express your appreciation for the myriad ways your partner takes good care of you, your home, and your family.
- Be patient with your partner's sensitivity and need for harmony in all his or her relationships.
- Respect your partner by accommodating his or her need for structure and routine.

- Initiate discussions about feelings and values. If you need time to think things through before sharing, tell your partner — don't just clam up.
- Try to pick up after yourself, pull your own weight regarding chores, and finish projects you start.
- Watch your tendency to be dismissive and superior.

Chapter 7

Traditionalists with Idealists: SJs with NFs

ESTJ with ENFJ

The Joys

ESTJs and ENFJs share two of the four type preferences and often enjoy an energetic and respectful relationship. Since both are talkers, they like to share details and stories about their days with each other. Expressive, friendly, and outgoing, ESTJs and ENFJs often have a wide social circle and usually enjoy entertaining and being out with friends. They are active people who love to work as a team to get projects finished and share a sense of accomplishment. ESTJs and ENFJs like issues to be settled, and both enjoy making decisions. Very responsible and productive, they generally keep their homes orderly, respect each other's routines and rituals, and like to maintain predictability in their lives.

In addition to their similarities, ESTJs and ENFJs are often initially attracted to each other because of their differences. ESTJs are drawn to ENFJs' warmth, generosity, and accurate insights about other people. ESTJs admire ENFJs' creativity, vivid imagination, and boundless optimism, as well as their charm and unusual sense of humor. ENFJs are attracted to ESTJs because their calm, objective, and mature reactions inspire great trust and confidence, especially in times of crisis. Most ENFJs also admire ESTJs because they are so hardworking, dependable, and sensible. ENFJs

often think of their partners as people they can always lean on.

Because of their many differences, ESTJs and ENFJs have the opportunity to help each other grow and develop in important ways. ESTJs help ENFJs develop more objectivity so they don't take things personally and get hurt or disappointed so easily. ENFJs often credit their partners with helping them pay more attention to the realities of life and see the logical consequences of their actions. For their part, ENFJs often help their partners increase their sensitivity to other people and become more appreciative and less demanding and critical. ESTJs often say that their partners encourage them to seek more emotion and meaning in their relationships, as well as to be open to unusual ideas.

The Frustrations

Because ESTJs and ENFJs have different temperaments, they often have disparate values and beliefs. ESTJs are very traditional and conservative, while ENFJs are less interested in convention and more curious about change and growth. ENFJs place harmonious relationships above almost everything else, while ESTJs are more businesslike and nononsense. ESTJs often complain that their partners are too concerned about pleasing other people, while ENFJs feel that their partners' natural brusqueness is sometimes offensive or embarrassing.

Another source of frustration for many ESTJ and ENFJ couples is their different ways of seeing the world. Whereas ESTJs are super-realistic and pay close attention to the details of their experiences, ENFJs notice patterns and are much more interested in possibilities and future implications. So ESTJs sometimes think that their partners are too vague and abstract and find it particularly maddening when ENFJs are careless with facts. For their part, ENFJs are bored and frustrated by their partners' insistence on carefully going over every detail, since they naturally anticipate where their partners are going. ESTJs are also naturally skeptical of unusual approaches or unproven theories, so they unintentionally take the wind out of their partners' sails when they immediately point out why their ideas won't work.

But perhaps the biggest frustration for ESTJ and ENFJ couples stems from the different ways they make decisions. ESTJs rely first and foremost on an analysis of the facts and are rarely convinced of anything that doesn't make sound logical sense. ENFJs are compelled by the potential impact of their decisions on others and rely on their strong personal values to make choices and form opinions. ESTJs sometimes think that their partners are being irrational, emotional, and inconsistent, while ENFJs frequently feel that their partners are insensitive, critical, and demanding.

When communicating, ESTJs think it's imperative to be direct and truthful, even if doing so requires being blunt. ENFJs are superdiplomatic and may avoid direct confrontations in order to spare their partners' feelings or restore harmony. ESTJs are sometimes impatient with the depth and extent to which ENFJs react, since ENFJs may respond emotionally rather than tell their partners clearly why they are upset. What ESTJs intend as constructive suggestions usually feel like personal attacks to ENFJs. In addition, ENFJs almost always want more romance, tenderness, and emotional sharing than their partners are comfortable with. So ESTJs feel pressured to share feelings they

aren't sure of, and ENFJs feel lonely and suffer from a lack of intimacy they crave. In the midst of conflict, ESTJ and ENFJ couples sometimes need a brief period apart so the ENFJ partner can calm down and the ESTJ partner can collect his or her thoughts and prepare to share his or her feelings.

How to Reach Your ENFJ Partner

- Talk about the relationship and how you feel it is progressing and changing. Express your feelings and tell your partner you love him or her. ENFJs need to hear the words.
- Be willing to consider other points of view. Support your partner's feelings even if you don't share or completely understand them.
- Encourage your partner's quest for more personal meaning and professional growth.
- Compliment your partner on his or her insights and creativity.
- Watch your tendency to dismiss or discount new ideas or approaches before considering them.
- Focus on the positive. Appreciate your partner's many contributions and efforts.
- Watch your tendency to sound critical and demanding. Soften your tone of voice, smile, and emphasize the positive.

How to Reach Your ESTJ Partner

- Thank your partner for all the detailed work and household chores he or she does.
- Compliment your partner on tangible things such as looks, projects accomplished, and financial contributions.
- Do thoughtful things to make life run more smoothly. Remember to pick up the dry cleaning, make a nice meal, or clean out a closet.
- Be prepared to offer accurate details and facts and to present your ideas logically. Don't skip steps.
- Don't assume that you know where your

partner is going and interrupt or finish his or her sentences.

ESTJ with INFJ

The Joys

ESTJs and INFJs have one type preference in common, sharing a desire to have things settled and decided. Many ESTJ and INFJ couples value the fact that they can count on each other to do what they say they will do. They take all their commitments seriously and are equally dependable in good times and in bad. Since they are usually well organized, daily routines make sense and are comfortable for both of them. In fact, many ESTJ and INFJ couples say that they are a great team when cleaning the house or putting on an event together. And because they both like order, they tend to be neat and organized and are fairly thrifty with their money. ESTJs and INFJs also have strong opinions, and regardless of whether or not they agree, they usually respect each other's deeply held convictions.

It is usually their differences that are the initial source of attraction between ESTJs and INFJs. ESTJs are drawn to INFJs' warmth, compassion, creativity, and integrity. INFJs bring a texture and depth to life that many ESTJs find fascinating. INFJs are frequently attracted to ESTJs' steadiness, responsibility, politeness, and willingness to talk about things. ESTJs' high energy level helps bring INFJs out of their own worlds and exposes them to experiences — especially active physical ones — they might ordinarily avoid.

Because of their many differences, ESTJs and INFJs can help each other grow and develop in important ways. ESTJs help INFJs live more fully in their bodies and in the moment. With time and support, INFJs become more objective and critical of their many ideas so they can ultimately make them more workable. INFJs say that their ESTJ partners help them become less idealistic so they experience fewer disappointments. For their part, INFJs help ESTJs become more patient, forgiving, and compassionate with others. ESTJs often say that their partners teach them to look at issues more deeply and see more subtleties than they normally would.

The Frustrations

Since ESTJs and INFJs are so different, they often have to work hard at their relationships. ESTJs are very realistic and down-to-earth, while INFJs are quite idealistic and theoretical. Most ESTJs see life in fairly simple, clear, even black-and-white terms. INFJs see the complexities of life and focus on all the possibilities. ESTJs are sometimes confused by their partners' circuitous thought processes and bored with their abstractions. INFJs may get annoyed or embarrassed that their partners miss subtle clues and plow ahead without regard for others' feelings. INFJs also usually aren't interested in many of their partners' more physical or competitive interests, such as sports. Instead, INFJs love to think about and discuss important issues as they strive to understand their unique purpose in life and contribution to making the world a better place. ESTJs typically have more realistic objectives, but they also have plenty of energy for serving their families and communities in tangible ways.

The primary area of frustration for ESTJ and INFJ couples is communication. ESTJs are supremely logical and decisive, so they sometimes inadvertently offend or intimidate their partners or dismiss their partners' feelings as overreactions. Many ESTJs are unaware of how other people feel and may be intolerant of differences or weaknesses in others. Because INFJs are so sensitive and empathetic, they may become upset with how coolly their partners treat others. When they do become upset, INFJs want to go off by themselves and think about things, then discuss them later. By contrast, most ESTJs would rather deal with issues and problems calmly and immediately. ESTJs are very literal and direct, so they don't appreciate their partners' more vague or complicated style. When they discover a problem, INFJs are likely to want to brainstorm alternatives, while ESTJs typically want to stick with approaches that have worked in the past. And since both partners want to do things in their own ways, they can be a bit rigid. ESTJs might insist that theirs is the smarter or more expedient way, while INFJs might assert that theirs is the morally correct way.

How to Reach Your INFJ Partner

- Be patient with your partner's more complicated thought process. Give him or her time to think things through before talking about them.
- Listen carefully and fully to your partner's ideas. Be willing to consider things that may seem impractical at first.
- Wait before saying no or refusing to try a new approach. Give yourself time to think about it.
- Express your feelings. Be willing to share your full range of emotions, including your fears and vulnerabilities. Express appreciation for your partner's thoughtfulness.
- Don't demand that your partner accompany you to every social event. Respect his or her need for privacy and time to reflect.
- Demonstrate an interest in your partner's projects. Listen respectfully and ask questions so that you better understand your mate's passions.

How to Reach Your ESTJ Partner

- Ask for the time you need to think about issues or problems before discussing them. Don't just disappear without giving your partner warning.
- Do thoughtful, tangible things to show your affection for your partner, such as cooking a nice meal, cleaning the house, or remembering to pick up the dry cleaning.
- Ask your partner for his or her opinion, then listen respectfully to it.

- Never criticize or undermine your partner's competence in public.
- Encourage your partner to get together with friends. Make sure he or she feels free to socialize without you when you're not in the mood.
- Tell your partner, as well as other people, how proud you are of his or her achievements. (Third-party compliments are great.)

ESTJ with ENFP

The Joys

Although ESTJs and ENFPs are different in many significant ways, they do share one of the four type preferences, which makes them both high-energy, social, and expressive people. Some of their best times are spent discussing things and laughing together. They tend to have a wide circle of friends and acquaintances, and they enjoy hosting and participating in all kinds of gatherings. But it is often their many differences that are the source of their initial attraction. ESTJs are drawn to ENFPs' warmth, sensitivity, zest for living, and sense of adventure. Many ESTJs report that life with an ENFP is great fun, even if it's also a bit chaotic. ENFPs are attracted to ESTJs for their steadiness, dependability, and hardworking nature. ENFPs seem to know intuitively that their ESTJ partners will always be there for them, and they love the sense of stability and trust that evokes.

Because ESTJs and ENFPs have so many natural differences, they have many opportunities to help each other grow and develop in important ways. ESTJs help ENFPs develop a thicker skin so they are less vulnerable to criticism and better able to make decisions that are in their best interests. ENFPs also credit their partners with helping them become more organized and more apt to pay attention to the facts and details they ordinarily miss. For their part, ENFPs help their ESTJ partners pay closer attention to feelings (their own and others') and become less stubborn and demanding. ENFPs also may help their partners gain an appreciation for trying new things.

The Frustrations

With so many differences, ESTJs and ENFPs must work hard to establish and maintain a high degree of closeness in their relationships. One common source of frustration is their different ways of seeing the world and making decisions. ESTJs are practical and realistic people. They are often frustrated, and sometimes annoyed, by their ENFP partners' inquisitiveness and irresistible desire to explore all the possibilities — even those that seem irrelevant — and by their penchant for skipping over steps they don't find interesting. On the other hand, ENFPs are often frustrated by their partners' insistence on having the facts ahead of time and in order before being ready to act. Because ENFPs want to go where their inspirations lead them and have utter confidence in their hunches, they can feel restricted or undermined by their more deliberate partners.

ESTJs and ENFPs also tend to struggle with communication, since ESTJs are logical and critical and ENFPs are emotional and sensitive. ESTJs often accuse ENFPs of overreacting and taking things too personally. In a genuine effort to be helpful, ESTJs may point out why they think their partners are having a problem and how they ought to fix it. But what ENFPs really want is for their partners to listen and provide support and encouragement. ENFPs also want their partners to express their appreciation and affection and to avoid being impatient. But many ESTJs are uncomfortable expressing their deep feelings and fear being vulnerable. And they sometimes feel pressured to share with their partners. ESTJs and ENFPs also deal with conflict in different ways. ESTJs tend to address issues head-on, immediately and decisively. By contrast, ENFPs generally avoid conflict as long as possible, and then they are very diplomatic, gentle, and eager to reestablish harmony quickly. ESTJs are especially irritated when their partners are unhappy yet won't be honest or clear about what they want done differently.

Another major source of frustration for ESTJs and ENFPs involves the amount of order and neatness each needs. ESTJs like a clean, well-organized home and are often frustrated by their partners' casual attitude about putting things away, keeping bank accounts balanced, or planning ahead. ENFPs often feel that their partners are too controlling, demanding, and unwilling to respond to spontaneous opportunities. In addition, whereas ESTJs usually want to make very quick decisions, ENFPs need much more information before they are willing to forgo their options. Regardless of gender, ESTJs often end up doing an unfair share of the household chores, since they need to have projects completed before they can relax. This often becomes a source of resentment for ESTJs, who may respond with hurtful criticism. Although ENFPs generally feel guilty about making their partners unhappy, when they feel criticized, they tend to withdraw inside themselves.

How to Reach Your ENFP Partner

- Wait before you criticize or point out flaws in your partners' ideas.
- Listen with an open mind, especially regarding new ideas or possibilities.
- Don't nag about housework or chores that are left undone. Instead, help out even if it's not your turn or your chore.
- Express your feelings, including your fears and sadness. Let your partner be a resource for you.
- Try not to tell your partner how to do things. Offer opinions if asked, but remember that there's usually more than one way to do something.
- Try to relax about the little things, especially timetables and schedules. Don't force your part-

ner always to do things according to your timetable.

- Tell your partner how much you appreciate him or her. Compliment your partner on his or her great ideas and the fun he or she brings to the relationship.

How to Reach Your ESTJ Partner

- Try to be on time, say what you mean, and mean what you say. Don't break dates.
- Don't neglect or ignore the traditions or rituals your partner wants to follow.
- Try to get your facts straight or let your partner do the research, especially regarding big purchases, travel plans, and the like.
- Be calm and clear when discussing a problem. Try not to exaggerate or get overly emotional.
- Listen for the constructive elements in your partner's suggestions. Remember that he or she is trying to help.
- When your partner's first reaction is negative, give him or her a little time and the opportunity to change his or her mind.
- Compliment your partner on the many ways he or she makes life more comfortable. Thank your mate for the tangible things he or she does to show you love.

ESTJ with INFP

The Joys

Because ESTJs and INFPs have no type preferences in common, they face significant challenges, but they also have the opportunity to create a very complementary relationship. With mutual respect and appreciation, they can balance each other's styles, perspectives, and parenting philosophies. In fact, most ESTJ and INFP couples are drawn to each other because of their many differences. ESTJs are often attracted to INFPs for their warmth, gentleness, curiosity, and uniqueness. INFPs are sensi-

tive and nurturing to those close to them, and ESTJs find themselves cared for in ways they have never experienced before. This is especially true for ESTJ women who often have never met a man so interested in creating a deep and truly personal connection. For their part, INFPs are typically attracted to ESTJs because they are strong, dependable, and outgoing. ESTJs tend to exude a social confidence and clear sense of purpose that INFPs find appealing.

The differences between ESTJs and INFPs often provide each of them with a strong counterbalance and the opportunity to grow and develop in important ways. ESTJs help their INFP partners become more outspoken and assertive. INFPs often say that their partners help them become more organized, more attentive to important details, and better able to follow through on their projects. By learning to be more objective and not to take things quite so personally, INFPs also experience fewer disappointments. For their part, INFPs help their ESTJ partners gain increased self-awareness that helps them better understand themselves and others. ESTJs say that their partners help them become more compassionate, patient, and accommodating of other people and especially of their weaknesses.

The Frustrations

Because of the fundamental differences in their natures, ESTJ and INFP couples have frequent misunderstandings. Traditional and conservative ESTJs are happiest with a set plan and no sudden changes. Philosophical and unconventional INFPs are on a perpetual quest for self-discovery and strive to understand themselves and others better. ESTJs are often frustrated by the extreme sensitivity of INFPs, while INFPs are often hurt and frustrated by their partners' critical and often blunt reactions. When ESTJs see something that needs improvement, they tend to immediately point out what's wrong, while INFPs tend to look for areas of agreement and harmony. ESTJs express strong, sometimes harsh, opinions, and INFPs tend to be personally offended by negativity, even if it's not directed at them.

Another area of recurring conflict for many ESTJs and INFPs is their different needs for order and closure. ESTJs like their routines to be maintained and their rituals to be respected. For example, many ESTJs like to have dinner at a specific time. By contrast, their INFP partners may prefer to eat when they're hungry, even if it's at a different time each night. Whereas ESTJs are ruled by clocks and calendars, INFPs rely on inspiration to move them forward. ESTJs also like to finish projects right away and to keep their homes clean, orderly, and neat. INFPs usually find maintenance exhausting and boring, and they are rarely able to keep it up for an extended period of time. They are comfortable with change, are energized by it, and generally see it as an opportunity to experience another aspect of life. ESTJs tend to make quick decisions and absolute judgments, and they find it unnerving to leave things hanging any longer than is necessary. INFPs, by contrast, usually have a harder time making decisions and like to explore as many options as possible. ESTJs tend to feel frustrated by the length of time it takes their partners to decide or to finish projects, and INFPs often feel pushed into things before they're ready.

ESTJs and INFPs also have very different communication styles. Because ESTJs are so outspoken, they may frequently interrupt or even intimidate their partners. They like to talk about things directly and honestly, with no holds barred, and then take immediate action. INFPs tend to need more time to think about things and like to spend much more time alone. They may not be completely sure how they feel unless they have private time to process their thoughts. And seldom do they enjoy the same amount of socializing that their ESTJ partners do.

By far the greatest impediment to good communication for ESTJs and INFPs is their different needs for emotional connection. Supremely logical and matter-of-fact, ESTJs are frequently impatient with the complexity and intensity of their partners' feelings. They need to figure out what's wrong and fix the problem immediately. Although they are usually very honest, they can also be blunt and insensitive. Most ESTJs are uncomfortable being vulnerable, even with their partners. In contrast, INFPs take almost everything personally. The measure of a satisfying relationship for most INFPs is a deep and intimate emotional connection that allows them to feel safe to be totally open with their partners. INFPs want partners who are eager and willing to have a harmonious relationship, while ESTJs want a partner who is willing to be honest even when things are unpleasant.

How to Reach Your INFP Partner

- Be gentle, patient, and supportive. Understand that it may take a while for your partner to be ready to talk about what's upsetting him or her.
- Listen, listen, and listen some more! Be attentive and understanding of your partner's emotions, even if you don't understand them.
- Watch your tendency to be critical. Accentuate the positive rather than first commenting on what needs to be fixed.
- Don't dismiss your partner's feelings, even if you don't understand or share them.
- Slow down and enjoy the moment. Give yourself time to think about options and gather information.
- Express your appreciation of your partner's efforts in completing a task. Compliment your partner on his or her good ideas and unique perspective.

How to Reach Your ESTJ Partner

- Clean or organize something. Initiate chores around the house.
- Finish projects you start or pack them up out of sight.
- Respect your partner's desire to have a regular routine. Don't disrupt important rituals.
- Thank your partner for all that he or she does to make your home comfortable and orderly. Appreciate your mate's tangible contributions.
- Try to be direct and calm, especially when you are upset. Get right to the point and try not to overreact.
- Tell your partner when you need time alone to recharge or to think about what's wrong. Don't disappear and withdraw when there are problems to be discussed.

ISTJ with ENFJ

The Joys

ISTJs and ENFJs are very different kinds of people, with only one type preference in common. They do share a preference for being organized, productive, and decisive. In fact, when they work together as a team — whether it's cleaning the house, preparing for a party, or getting ready for a vacation — they often experience a real sense of pleasure. The many differences between ISTJs and ENFJs account for much of their initial attraction. ISTJs are often attracted to the spirit, charm, and enthusiasm for life that ENFJs display in abundance. They find their partners' confidence, optimism, and emotional availability invigorating and exciting to be around. ENFJs bring a joy and richness to everyday life that ISTJs admire. ENFJs often are drawn to ISTJs because of their calm, steadiness, and dependability. ENFJs respect how responsible, conscientious, and hardworking their

partners are and appreciate the order and stability they bring to their lives.

Because of their many differences, ISTJs and ENFJs have the opportunity to help each other grow and develop in important ways, as long as the relationship includes mutual respect and patience with each other's growth. ENFJs often help their partners share their feelings and become more open to opposing viewpoints. Many ISTJs credit their partners with helping them be more appreciative and patient with other people and with new ideas. For their part, ISTJs often help ENFJs develop a thicker skin and learn to take things less personally. ENFJs say that their partners' influence makes them more careful with important details and more likely to think through a project before diving into it.

The Frustrations

The biggest source of frustration and dissatisfaction for most ISTJ and ENFJ couples lies in the quality and quantity of their communication. ISTJs, naturally logical and matter-of-fact, tend to be reluctant to share their inner thoughts and feelings. Many ISTJs simply do not know, especially on the spur of the moment, how they feel. They need time, privacy, and the chance to think things through before responding, or they risk feeling foolish. ISTJs naturally want to be in control. If they don't understand their partners' feelings, they sometimes feel vulnerable or inept, which again causes them to retreat so they can get the perspective they need to process their reactions. The more they are pushed to share, the more likely they are to become silent and angry.

But that response runs completely counter to ENFJs' need for connection. ENFJs live for emotional and spiritual closeness and intimacy. They respond emotionally to almost everything and want to talk about their reactions and concerns right away in order to reestablish harmony and equilibrium. ENFJs will even risk not being completely honest or rushing to forgive their partners. ENFJs are typically quite dramatic and may exaggerate to make a point or to get their partners' attention, a habit many ISTJs find very annoying. Rather than making the impression they want, they tend to crowd and overwhelm their private ISTJ partners. For most ENFJs, physical intimacy can come only after a close emotional connection is made through talking and sharing. For ISTJs, however, physical intimacy is often a prerequisite to sharing emotionally.

ISTJs and ENFJs also have very different approaches to solving problems. ISTJs trust their sense of what's real and logical and are usually quick to discount possibilities that seem far-fetched or impractical. Hence when ENFJs eagerly share their new ideas with their partners, ISTJs may unwittingly shoot them down. For ISTJs, it doesn't make sense to waste a lot of energy on something that's not realistic. But for ENFJs, possibilities are exciting, and closing them off before they have been explored is frustrating. Above all, ENFJs need their ISTJ partners not to dismiss their feelings and inspirations, and ISTJs need their ENFJ partners not to be so quick to jump on the emotional roller coaster of each new experience or someone else's trauma.

How to Reach Your ENFJ Partner

- Listen without criticizing or dismissing your partner's feelings. Don't be too controlling or bossy.
- Initiate anything social.
- Express your feelings (write letters if it's easier than communicating verbally).
- Comment on the joy and enthusiasm your partner brings to life. Compliment your partner on his or her good ideas and people skills.
- Be positive; look for the good stuff. Smile and touch your partner.
- Recognize your partner's strong social needs.

Don't make him or her feel bad about going out without you.
- Be patient with your partner's long-winded and dramatic stories.
- Offer to spend time just being with your partner. Take a walk or go out for coffee.
- Ask for time to think about your response to a situation if you need it — but don't take too long.

How to Reach Your ISTJ Partner

- Do chores your partner really wants done. Bring more order to the house and take care of your partner's possessions.
- Give your partner plenty of time alone to think things through.
- Don't exaggerate. Be clear and precise, and use real examples. Stay calm and keep small issues small.
- Be specific about what you want your partner to do. Don't be vague; show, don't tell.
- Give plenty of physical contact. Look for evidence of your partner's feelings in a loving look or a compliment you hear from someone else.
- Try not to take things so personally. Accept your partner's constructive criticism in the spirit in which it is intended.
- Initiate a regular routine that you both enjoy (going out to breakfast, hiking, playing golf together) to create the closeness you desire.

ISTJ with INFJ

The Joys

Because of the two type preferences ISTJs and INFJs have in common, they often share a need for quiet, solitude, and reflection, as well as a desire for order and closure. Both are typically serious and private people, so they tend to respect each other's needs for time alone. Naturally careful and cautious, they are hesitant to jump into social situations or change plans abruptly without advance notice. ISTJs and INFJs also tend to like matters settled and enjoy a well-organized home.

In addition to these similarities, the differences between ISTJs and INFJs often attract them initially. ISTJs are drawn to INFJs' warmth, imagination, tenderness, and genuine concern for the welfare of others. ISTJs admire the spiritual dimension and deep faith many INFJs possess. INFJs are often attracted to ISTJs' utter dependability and responsibility, as well as to their natural directness and honesty. ISTJs usually provide a levelheaded, analytical approach to problem solving that is a good balance to INFJs' more global and compassionate view.

Because of their differences, ISTJs and INFJs have the opportunity to help each other grow and develop in important ways. ISTJs help their partners become more logical and objective so they learn to take fewer things personally. INFJs often credit their partners with helping them pay closer attention to details so they make fewer mistakes, which helps increase their overall competence. For their part, INFJs are often able to help their partners become more sensitive to the needs, feelings, and problems of others. ISTJs often say that their partners help them to be more patient and appreciative of other people and more willing and able to speak from their hearts.

The Frustrations

Despite the complementary aspects of their relationships, ISTJs and INFJs often feel that their communication is out of sync. ISTJs are utterly matter-of-fact, so they are often mystified by INFJs' more imprecise sense of things. INFJs often admit that they have trouble adequately describing their perceptions and ideas in terms ISTJs can understand. INFJs are often frustrated by ISTJs' lack of imagination or enthusiasm for their many unusual ideas. They also tend to jump from thought to thought, motivated by inspiration and possibilities, while ISTJs are much more linear and concrete in their thinking.

In addition to seeing the world quite differently, ISTJs and INFJs typically have different values. ISTJs are very traditional and conservative and have faith in things they have personally experienced. In contrast, INFJs are less conventional and more concerned with exploration, personal growth, and self-expression. INFJs love theories and ideas about which ISTJs are naturally skeptical. ISTJs like things to remain constant and find repetition satisfying, while INFJs are drawn to the new and the different and quickly become bored by routine. Although ISTJs and INFJs are both to some extent creatures of habit, ISTJs tend to resist change much more strongly than do INFJs. When things change suddenly or when ISTJs are forced to consider extremely novel approaches, their first inclination is to dig in their heels and resist.

Another source of frustration for ISTJs and INFJs is that ISTJs respond in logical and objective ways, while INFJs have much more personal reactions. ISTJs generally think that their partners overreact and exaggerate, while INFJs typically feel that their partners are insensitive and even cold. ISTJs are honest and direct, but they can also be blunt and insensitive, especially if they are caught off guard. Whereas ISTJs characteristically take a hard line on issues, INFJs naturally look for extenuating circumstances and are profoundly moved by the feelings of others. Ultimately, the most common concern INFJs express is that they are often hurt by their partners' apparent lack of caring, but they will put off confronting their partners for the sake of harmony. Also, since ISTJ and INFJ couples often enjoy different activities and friends, they need to be careful not to spend so much time away from each other that they lose emotional contact.

How to Reach Your INFJ Partner

- Try to anticipate your partner's needs. Step in and help out with big projects or mundane tasks without being asked.
- Support your partner's visions and dreams. Avoid squelching your mate's enthusiasm by endlessly pointing out why his or her ideas aren't practical.
- Listen enthusiastically to your partner's ideas. Resist the urge to say no immediately to suggestions for change.
- Never dismiss your partner's feelings or beliefs, even if you don't understand or share them.
- Share your thoughts, feelings, and reactions. Talk, talk, and talk some more!
- Initiate discussions rather than always waiting for your partner to drag things out of you.
- Resolve conflicts and work to restore harmony. Never resort to silence.

How to Reach Your ISTJ Partner

- Initiate physical affection and contact, including back rubs and other sensual pleasures.
- Write letters and notes to express yourself, giving your partner a chance to think about what you've written and respond in kind.
- Thank your partner for all the tangible things he or she does around the house to keep things running smoothly and efficiently.
- Cook your partner's favorite foods, remember to pick up the dry cleaning, and keep the house neat and tidy.
- Avoid changing plans abruptly or being insensitive to your partner's routines.
- Go slowly when suggesting change. Plant the seed and give your partner time to get used to the idea.
- Be direct, calm, and explicit. Don't exaggerate or overreact.
- Listen respectfully even if you think you can

anticipate where your partner is going. Don't interrupt or put words in your partner's mouth.

ISTJ with ENFP

The Joys

Since ISTJs and ENFPs have no type preferences in common, they often seem like polar opposites. But many couples experience a strong attraction, as each has what the other lacks. ISTJs are often attracted to ENFPs' high energy, enthusiasm, optimism, and creativity. ENFPs bring a fun and adventurous element to everyday living, often saying and doing things that are irreverent, clever, and original. ENFPs have a warmth and emotional availability that brings a new, more intense dimension to ISTJs' lives. ENFPs often are drawn to ISTJs' steadiness, responsibility, and calm. ISTJs have a focus and maturity that ENFPs long to have themselves, and ISTJs are generally down-to-earth, unflappable, and superdependable.

Because of these differences, ENFPs and ISTJs have a great opportunity to help each other grow and develop in important ways. ISTJs help their partners focus more carefully on the facts, details, and individual steps of their projects so they make fewer mistakes. ENFPs often credit their partners with helping them be more direct, assertive, and willing to confront conflicts head-on. ENFPs also say that their ISTJ partners help them become more organized, accountable, and realistic. For their part, ENFPs often help their serious and hardworking partners relax, have fun, and take occasional risks. ISTJs credit their partners with cultivating their gentler and more patient sides and with helping them be more flexible and open to new ideas.

The Frustrations

Their many differences give most ISTJ and ENFP couples sizable hurdles to clear on a daily basis, especially in the area of communication. Typically, ENFPs want much more talk and sharing, especially about feelings and possibilities, than do ISTJs. ISTJs crave structure and predictability in their daily lives and are more traditional than the nonconforming and liberal-minded ENFPs. Whereas ISTJs are not bothered by, and are perhaps even stimulated by, the tug of a good argument, ENFPs generally avoid anything too contentious or confrontational. Otherwise, ENFPs typically like lots of stimulation and are always eager to meet new people and explore new areas of work and play. Meanwhile, ISTJs are often exhausted by the high level of interaction their partners stir up and prefer to stick with established routines or to spend quiet time with their partners pursuing an interest they share.

Generally, one of the most difficult challenges for this couple stems from their views of change. ENFPs like and need to talk about limitless possibilities, and they love to think creatively. Because most ISTJs find constant change unsettling and stressful, their natural reaction is to resist it. ENFPs often feel that their enthusiasm for possibilities is being squelched by the realism of their ISTJ partners. For their part, ISTJs find the endless chatter about things that might never actually happen and the repeated leaps in logic frustrating and even threatening to the calm they prefer.

During conflict, ISTJs tend to withdraw into silence so they can carefully think through their positions, opinions, and feelings before sharing them. By contrast, most ENFPs want to work things out spontaneously in an effort to reestablish harmony immediately. The end result is that both partners feel misunderstood and unappreciated. Rather than talking through issues with respect and compromise, couples tend to fall into a pat-tern of arguing and blaming, followed by periods of silence and distance. To maintain trust and connection, it is imperative that ENFPs stay calm and focused and ISTJs commit to sharing their emotions while remaining open and supportive.

How to Reach Your ISTJ Partner

- Try not to get overinvolved in activities and commitments outside the home.
- Ask your partner's advice, then listen to him or her attentively and respectfully.
- Offer physical affection and intimacy in the form of back rubs and sexual contact.
- Don't pressure your partner to speak before he or she has time to think. Don't talk over your partner, try to remain calm, and don't exaggerate.
- Compliment your partner on tangible things such as his or her looks, achievements, or financial contributions.
- When it comes to change, be patient and give your partner time to adjust. Respect your partner's rituals and routines.

How to Reach Your ENFP Partner

- Compliment your partner on his or her good ideas, imagination, originality, and insights.
- Ask for time to think things through rather than shutting down. Don't resort to the silent treatment.
- Watch your tendency to react negatively to new ideas or approaches your partner proposes.
- Avoid making judgments about what your partner says. Resist the urge to point out factual mistakes.
- Focus on the positive. Be patient and gentle, especially when your partner is upset or confused.
- Trust your partner and encourage him or her to explore many different interests and friendships.
- Avoid nit-picking and obsessing about details.

ISTJ with INFP

The Joys

Since ISTJs and INFPs share only one of the four type preferences, their relationships are often challenging and interesting, but they also entail a lot of conflict. Over time, many couples learn to appreciate each other's points of view and complementary decision-making styles. Since both types are usually quiet, pensive, and reserved, they understand and respect each other's needs for time alone and for the opportunity to concentrate on their interests without interruption. They tend to maintain a small group of close friends and enjoy spending quiet time together.

ISTJs and INFPs are often initially attracted to each other because they are so different. ISTJs tend to be drawn to INFPs because of their warmth, compassion, and creative minds. ISTJs are often impressed with their partners' creativity and depth, as well as their personal, unique, and compassionate perspective on life. For their part, INFPs are often attracted to ISTJs because they are so calm, stable, and steady. They also admire ISTJs' ability to plan ahead and respect their sense of responsibility and their unshakable commitment to the things in which they believe.

Their many differences give ISTJs and INFPs the opportunity to help each other grow and develop in important ways. Typically, ISTJs help INFPs become more realistic and logical in their dealings with people, which may result in fewer disappointments. INFPs say that their partners help them finish some of the many interesting projects they start and generally to become more organized. INFPs are often able to help their ISTJ partners open up to new experiences and become less resistant to change and innovation. ISTJs also credit their partners with helping them become more sensitive to and less critical of others.

The Frustrations

The frustrations for ISTJs and INFPs often stem from their different temperaments, communication styles, and ways of making decisions. ISTJs are conservative and cautious people who are most comfortable when their routines are maintained and life proceeds at a predictable pace. INFPs are curious seekers of meaning, forever questioning the status quo and often agitating for change. ISTJs often feel that their partners don't respect their rituals and schedules, while INFPs frequently feel that their partners don't understand or appreciate the importance of their inspirations and ideas.

ISTJs and INFPs also misunderstand each other because ISTJs are specific, linear, and literal, and INFPs tend to think and speak in leaps and bounds. ISTJs get confused and irritated when their partners are vague, don't finish their sentences, leave out important facts, or talk endlessly about abstractions or theories. By contrast, INFPs sometimes become dispirited by their partners' lack of enthusiasm for their global interests and creative ideas, and they feel frustrated by their partners' inability to follow the intuitive leaps INFPs make so effortlessly.

Another area of frustration for ISTJs and INFPs revolves around their different decision-making styles. ISTJs are very cool and objective and are rarely convinced by anything but sound logical reasoning. INFPs are emotional, passionate, and most easily persuaded by the impact their choices may have on others. ISTJs often think that INFPs are too illogical and inconsistent and that they don't make sense. What ISTJs don't understand, they tend to discount as irrelevant. Since INFPs are so sensitive, their feelings get hurt easily and often, and they frequently feel that their partners are cold and insensitive. What ISTJs intend as merely an objective observation may be perceived by their partners as a personal insult. And since INFPs' feelings run so deep, they often won't admit that they're hurt and instead withdraw, sometimes for an extended period of time. Most INFPs want harmony so badly that they will cling to their idealistic views of their relationships rather than accept things as they are. Interestingly, although ISTJs tend to be very matter-of-fact, direct, and honest, they also have the tendency to retreat into silence when they feel angry or hurt. So this couple needs to be careful to truthfully but tactfully tell each other what's troubling them, even if they need time to process the issue privately before discussing it together.

Finally, ISTJs and INFPs have very different needs for order and closure. ISTJs like to be in control and to make as many decisions as they can. They like their homes to be neat and well organized, and they are often frustrated by the amount of clutter INFPs leave behind. INFPs are less concerned about tidiness and more interested in enjoying and learning from their experiences, so they tend to have several projects going at once. Because ISTJs have such a strong work ethic, they often feel compelled to remind their partners to finish chores and put things away. ISTJs also tend to do more than their fair share of the household chores, in part because they can't relax until everything is done.

How to Reach Your INFP Partner

- Compliment your partner on his or her many fresh and original ideas. Ask for advice about how to approach problems in a new way.
- Give your partner plenty of time to gather the amount of information he or she needs to make good choices.
- Respect how passionately your partner feels about his or her beliefs. Be careful not to discount or dismiss them.
- Don't press for decisions until your partner

has an opportunity to sort things through internally.
- Stay open and consider the new experiences your partner wants to check out. Beware of your tendency to resist change.
- Use a gentle and appreciative tone of voice. Avoid criticizing or being condescending.

How to Reach Your ISTJ Partner

- Try to be on time and accountable so your partner doesn't worry about you or isn't inconvenienced.
- Do what you say you will. Follow through on your commitments.
- Finish the projects you start. Put things away when you're finished using them.
- Compliment your partner on tangible things. Thank your mate for all the little things he or she does to keep your life on an even keel.
- Be careful with money. Remember to record checks in the register and balance the checkbook.
- Once you agree on a course of action, try not to change or abandon plans in midstream. If your plans change, give your partner as much warning as possible.

ESFJ with ENFJ

The Joys

Because ESFJs and ENFJs share three of the four preferences, they are similar in many ways. Both tend to be energetic, enthusiastic, and eager to please. They are blessed with great organizational skills and generally like to work hard to make things happen. Sensitive, sympathetic, and helpful, they are naturally aware of the needs and wishes of others and derive great satisfaction from making people happy. They are devoted, supportive, and loyal friends and responsible, contributing members of their communities. ESFJs and ENFJs are also highly verbal and are always talking about one thing or another with their partners. And as very social people, they are energized by being with others and love to entertain.

ESFJs and ENFJs tend to be decisive and most comfortable when they make and follow a plan. They like their homes to be neat and organized, and since both are extremely hard workers — sometimes to the point of being obsessive — they seldom experience conflicts about following through with household chores. They can make a highly productive team when they work together on a project. Often, but not always, ENFJs' talents lie in imagining possibilities, and ESFJs' in the physical execution of the plan.

In addition to their shared qualities of sensitivity, compassion, and responsibility, ESFJs and ENFJs are often attracted to each other because of their different ways of seeing the world around them. ESFJs are often drawn to ENFJs because of their creativity, vivid imagination, and ability to express themselves with eloquence and grace. ESFJs also admire the original and accurate insights ENFJs have, especially about their relationships and other people. ENFJs are often attracted to ESFJs' down-to-earth sensibility. ENFJs also respect their partners' traditional values and steadfast commitment to the things and people they care about.

Because of their differences, ESFJs and ENFJs have the opportunity to help each other grow and develop in important ways. ESFJs help their ENFJ partners live more in the moment and pay attention to and appreciate life's little pleasures. For their part, ENFJs help ESFJs see possibilities they might ordinarily miss and become more optimistic about the future. Together, they can help each other relax and have fun.

The Frustrations

Although ESFJs and ENFJs have many of the same strengths, they also share the same weaknesses.

For example, both like to talk and are very expressive and friendly. But they may sometimes compete for airtime, finish each other's sentences, and interrupt rather than be the patient and attentive listeners they want their partners to be. Also, because they are both organized, decisive, and driven to accomplish their agendas, they can work so hard that they don't take time to rest unless they are sick. And if they disagree about how or when something needs to be done, they can be stubborn and inflexible. This is especially painful when they are on opposite sides of important issues.

Perhaps the greatest challenge for ESFJ and ENFJ couples is dealing effectively with conflict. Because harmony is so important to them, they avoid unpleasantness. And since they are both so careful to avoid hurting their sensitive partners' feelings, they are sometimes less than direct and truthful. Rather than addressing problems as they come up, they tend to ignore them or put an optimistic spin on them, all the while hoping they'll go away. Growing tension can be almost unbearable for these harmony seekers, and an emotional eruption is almost inevitable. Because neither one is particularly objective, especially in the heat of an emotional episode, they may become increasingly negative and hurtful. Although these outbursts often clear the air, they are painful for both partners.

Another potential frustration for ESFJ and ENFJ couples is that as caring and responsible people, they may become so involved in other people's problems, either at work or with friends and family, that they neglect their partners. Both have trouble saying no to requests for help, so it's easy for them to become overextended and not have enough energy for their spouses and families.

Finally, although ESFJs and ENFJs generally understand and appreciate each other, they may sometimes see things from different perspectives. ESFJs are very literal and specific, and sometimes they find ENFJs' more global and vague explanations confusing. For their part, ENFJs are sometimes frustrated by ESFJs' insistence on keeping things the way they've always been. ESFJs sometimes feel nervous and impatient with ENFJs' wanderlust, since they see it as a sign of dissatisfaction with life, which ESFJs naturally take personally. ENFJs are more idealistic and future-oriented, and they can't help imagining how things could be different. ENFJs also rely on their gut instincts, while ESFJs are much more tuned in to what is happening at the moment and are more comfortable trusting their own experiences.

How to Reach Your ENFJ Partner

- Appreciate your partner's ability to imagine possibilities. Support his or her ideas whenever you can.
- Engage in "dream planning" — making wish lists of desired careers, trips, and the like — even though your dreams may never become reality.
- Resist your urge to point out the factual errors in your partner's ideas or constantly correct inaccuracies.
- Prioritize your time. Make sure you devote enough time to your partner and family.
- Be willing to give and receive honest feedback. Share your feelings, even though doing so may temporarily upset your partner.
- Try not to get upset when your partner talks about changes. Allow him or her to fantasize without limits.

How to Reach Your ESFJ Partner

- Recognize and appreciate all the thoughtful things your partner does to keep your life, home, and family running smoothly.
- Be willing to give and receive honest feedback. Share your feelings; don't gloss over them.
- Be clear, specific, and direct in communicating with your partner. Offer plenty of real-life examples to make your point.

- Let your partner know when you're about to change subjects. Don't skip steps.
- Be careful to keep your promises.
- Be patient with your partner's need to adjust to the idea of changes.
- Reassure your partner by reminding him or her of past experiences where the unknown worked out well.
- Respect your partner's need to maintain routines and keep things the same. Avoid making a lot of changes, especially big ones, without consulting your partner.

ESFJ with INFJ

The Joys

ESFJs and INFJs share two of the four type preferences. They have in common a value-based decision-making style, which often results in a strong and meaningful emotional connection. Caring, sensitive, and warm, ESFJs and INFJs are usually concerned about other people and eager to please. They strive for harmony in their relationships and are generally willing to discuss important personal issues to keep their emotional connections strong. Women often find this a big change from past relationships since male INFJs and ESFJs are generally so much warmer and more expressive than men of some other types. ESFJs and INFJs also share a mutual desire to keep their lives organized and their homes neat. Although ESFJs tend to be more concerned about precision and details, they both like things planned and settled, make fairly quick decisions, and pride themselves on their productivity, dependability, and responsibility.

In addition to their areas of commonality, ESFJs and INFJs are often initially attracted to each other because of their differences. ESFJs are drawn to INFJs because of their individuality, unshakable integrity, and strong personal beliefs. INFJs often possess vivid imaginations and a unique vision for how the world might and should be, which ESFJs find inspiring and exciting. INFJs are attracted to ESFJs because of their vivaciousness, high energy, and willingness to help other people. ESFJs usually possess a level of common sense that INFJs admire, as well as a genuine and natural friendliness that INFJs find appealing and sometimes enviable.

Because of their differences, ESFJs and INFJs have the opportunity to help each other grow and develop in important ways. ESFJs help INFJs make their visions more workable by paying closer attention to the important steps in a process, noticing the details of a project, and considering the potential implications. INFJs often say that their partners help them participate more fully in the world and become more optimistic about the future. For their part, INFJs help ESFJs think about the far-reaching implications of their actions and become more open to new approaches to old problems. ESFJs also credit their partners with helping them slow down so they make better choices.

The Frustrations

Despite their many shared qualities and attitudes, ESFJs and INFJs have fundamentally different temperaments. Most ESFJs are much more traditional and conservative than their partners, and most INFJs are more introspective and philosophical. So ESFJs sometimes feel frustrated that their partners don't seem to be satisfied with their lives and endlessly question how things might be better or more meaningful. ESFJs don't like change and find it unsettling when their partners fantasize about lifestyles ESFJs don't think are realistic or practical. ESFJs prefer to maintain the status quo, and since they feel strongly about almost everything, they can be a bit rigid about the right way to do things. INFJs also tend to hold strong beliefs and often take a moral position about the way things ought to be. These two highly opinionated types may find themselves at odds, especially if

their strongly held values are in conflict, and they may find themselves pushing their individual agendas to the detriment of their relationships.

Frustration also stems from their different ways of seeing the world. ESFJs are very practical, sensible people, while INFJs are very imaginative, idealistic, and always interested in new possibilities. INFJs need and want their partners to listen to their ideas and encourage their innovative projects. ESFJs are most interested and enthusiastic about setting and realizing achievable goals. In an effort to be helpful, they are often quick to point out the practical flaws in their partners' ideas. Naturally, INFJs find this very insensitive and deflating, and they can allow it to undermine their confidence. When INFJs feel hurt, they often withdraw. For their part, ESFJs often feel frustrated when their partners are careless about essential details or skip over important steps. They feel insulted by INFJs' tendency to act superior and impatient when they don't immediately grasp an abstract concept.

Finally, ESFJs and INFJs often have different needs for social stimulation. ESFJs are very active, busy people who tend to have lots of friends and to get involved in a variety of outside activities. INFJs need much more time alone and prefer to maintain a smaller group of close, trusted friends. ESFJs are sometimes frustrated when they feel that their partners are resisting their efforts to participate in social activities, and INFJs often feel overwhelmed and exhausted by the whirlwind of activity. INFJs prefer more intimate, one-on-one interactions and like to discuss things in depth. By contrast, ESFJs change the subject often and may become bored with their partners' desire for focus and concentration. ESFJs also tend to have a hard time saying no to the requests of friends and neighbors, and they may put other people ahead of their partners. INFJs tend to consider their own needs and plans first and may appear a bit selfish and self-involved to their ESFJ partners.

How to Reach Your INFJ Partner

- Respect your partner's need to think things through, especially important issues, before discussing them.
- Encourage your partner to pursue his or her interests, projects, and friendships independently without worrying that it will hurt your feelings.
- Listen enthusiastically and respectfully to your partner's ideas and visions. Ask questions to demonstrate your interest.
- Don't interrupt or rush your partner into another topic. Be patient with his or her desire to discuss ideas in depth.
- Resist the urge to immediately point out why an idea may not be practical or workable.
- Don't try to make your partner feel guilty for not participating in as many social activities as you do.

How to Reach Your ESFJ Partner

- Participate in as many activities and experiences as you can. When you need to opt out, reassure your partner that it's not personal and encourage him or her to attend anyway.
- Try to include all the facts and steps in a story or project. Don't start in the middle of a sentence assuming that your partner is with you.
- Keep track of details such as money. Remember to record checks in the register and keep other records.
- Compliment your partner on tangible things. Express your appreciation of all the little things your mate does to keep life organized and operating efficiently.
- Don't lose yourself so completely in your work that you neglect your share of the household chores and responsibilities.
- Try to avoid moralizing, and don't analyze your partner.

ESFJ with ENFP

The Joys

With two of the four type preferences in common, ESFJs and ENFPs often have a nice balance of similarities and differences. Perhaps their most important similarity is their strong desire for an emotional connection and a harmonious relationship. When ESFJs and ENFPs share priorities and morals, they almost always experience a high degree of satisfaction because both tend to make decisions based on their personal values. They love to feel like a team, united in their beliefs and commitment to the things they care about. They typically work hard to ensure good communication, and since both are big talkers, communication isn't usually a problem. As long as they remain courteous and listen as much as they speak, they tend to find it rewarding to share their concerns and experiences. They are almost always diplomatic, empathetic, and loving, and unless they are especially tired, they are eager to know what's happening in their partners' lives and ready to provide unwavering support.

Great companions, ESFJs and ENFPs are usually high-energy, active, and social couples. They tend to have busy calendars and enjoy participating in a variety of activities. Many times what sparks the initial attraction between ESFJs and ENFPs is their gregarious, outgoing natures. In addition, ESFJs are often attracted to ENFPs' originality, gentleness, easygoing spirit, and optimism. ENFPs are often drawn to ESFJs' organizational ability, eagerness to please, and down-to-earth common sense.

Despite these similarities, ESFJs and ENFPs have differences that help them grow and develop in important ways. ESFJs help their partners notice more details, which makes their innovative ideas more workable. ENFPs frequently credit their ESFJ partners with helping them become more realistic, organized, and productive. ENFPs help ESFJs become more optimistic about the future, open to new ideas, and willing to take more risks. ESFJs often credit their ENFP partners with helping them become more assertive and less dependent on others to feel validated.

The Frustrations

Perhaps the greatest source of conflict for ESFJs and ENFPs is the difference in their temperaments. ESFJs are very conservative and traditional people, often skeptical of new ideas and irritated by sudden disruptions of their cherished routines. ESFJs tend to be speedy decision makers and opt to keep things the way they are rather than invite the chaos that inevitably accompanies even positive changes. By contrast, ENFPs are more curious, nonconforming, and idealistic people who love new possibilities and experiences. They find restrictions suffocating and almost any repetition boring. ESFJs often unwittingly throw cold water on ENFPs' enthusiasm and ideas when they immediately point out the practical concerns that ENFPs rarely notice. Although ESFJs' intentions are always good, ENFPs can feel unsupported, dispirited, and frustrated. ESFJs also tend to feel passionately that their ways are the best ways and to force their partners into following their plans. For their part, ENFPs may unintentionally create stress and insecurity for their partners because they routinely ignore the importance of order to ESFJs. ESFJs find it nerve-racking when ENFPs run late or don't keep promises. Since ESFJs take most things personally, they tend to misinterpret these actions as deliberate slights.

Another area of potential danger is that both ESFJs and ENFPs try so hard not to hurt each other's feelings that they are often less than completely honest and direct. Both tend to avoid confrontation, but when they do have a conflict, ESFJs are likely to explode with great emotion, while ENFPs are more likely to keep their deep feelings to themselves. ESFJs may hold grudges and punish their partners by not forgiving them. ENFPs tend to feel guilty and apologize first, but they often feel that their partners take things too seriously and ought to lighten up. Saying this only makes their partners feel more hurt and criticized, however.

ESFJs and ENFPs also regard time and order very differently. ESFJs want their homes to be neat and organized, especially when they are expecting company. ENFPs are much less concerned about clutter and are more spontaneous and casual about entertaining. Housework is often a bone of contention between these two types, as ESFJs feel that they do an unfair share of the chores, while ENFPs feel constantly hounded to finish projects according to their partners' schedules. ESFJs are more conservative and careful with money and investments than ENFPs, and they want to make and stick with a budget. ENFPs often are more likely to make financial decisions based on their needs at the moment. Unless these couples keep their finances separate or budget discretionary funds for both partners, they may clash frequently over money.

Finally, because ESFJs and ENFPs generally have many work and social commitments, they can run into trouble when both partners direct too much time and energy outside the home and the relationship. ESFJs and ENFPs need to guard against fatigue and maintain good communication by protecting their private time.

How to Reach Your ENFP Partner

- Don't immediately shoot holes in your partner's ideas, pointing out why they won't work. Be an enthusiastic listener and encourage your mate's imagination.
- Try to relax a bit about deadlines and schedules. Be willing to let things go occasionally.
- Don't overschedule your time as an individual and as a couple. Try to plan for free time.
- Try to focus on the positive.
- Encourage your partner to have some free time

and pocket money that he or she doesn't need to account for.

- Compliment your partner on his or her good ideas, imagination, and creativity.
- Try not to resist your partner's unusual suggestions. Give them a try and see how they might broaden your horizons.

How to Reach Your ESFJ Partner

- Pitch in and complete chores without being asked (especially chores that are yours to do anyway).
- Offer some factual background when suggesting a new approach. Patiently explain the potential benefits you and your partner will derive.
- Try not to start talking in the middle of a thought. Clearly identify transitions or changes of subject.
- Compliment your partner and express your appreciation for all that he or she does to make your home comfortable and warm. Give credit where credit is due.
- Try to keep track of money and receipts and to record expenses. Make an effort to stick to a budget.
- Give your partner some warning if you change plans or invite guests home. Allow him or her to adjust to these changes in plans.

ESFJ with INFP

The Joys

ESFJs and INFPs share only one of the four type preferences, but they typically experience a strong emotional connection if they share common values. ESFJs and INFPs have a naturally well-developed sense of empathy, a deep need for harmony, and a willingness to accept the extenuating circumstances of life. Since they work hard to understand their partners and take great care to communicate their love and appreciation, they want and expect the same kindness and consideration in return. ESFJs and INFPs often seek to deepen their understanding of each other and to figure out what it takes to make their partners happy. Typically, both value relationships and good communication highly, and they consider their partners to be their best friends.

ESFJs and INFPs are often attracted to each other in part because they sense a real soul mate but also because of their differences. ESFJs may find the calm, introspection, and loyalty of INFPs appealing, while INFPs are often drawn to the enthusiasm, productivity, and warmth of ESFJs. Because of their many type differences, these couples can help each other grow and develop in important ways. ESFJs help their INFP partners become more organized so they can make more of their creative ideas become reality. For their part, INFPs help ESFJs slow down and look beyond the obvious, find deeper meaning, and be less rigid about their plans and agendas.

The Frustrations

Because ESFJs and INFPs are quite different, it's understandable that they usually experience a variety of frustrations. The practical and traditional ESFJs are usually leery of change, whereas the idealistic and imaginative INFPs are curious about possibilities and new ways of doing things. Typically, ESFJs want to talk things through immediately, while INFPs want to think about them first. Many ESFJs find their partners mysterious because their calm exteriors belie intense internal processes. INFPs have passionate beliefs but are less likely to share them. This can be confusing to their ESFJ partners, who are quite comfortable expressing their emotions, even in public. Without some kind of status report, ESFJs often feel left out of their partners' private worlds.

The natural energy levels of ESFJs and INFPs are also very different, as is the amount of conversation they prefer. And since both ESFJs and

INFPs take things personally and may resort to blaming each other for being insensitive, they need to work hard to carefully, honestly, and clearly articulate their concerns. As they practice maintaining their objectivity, they find it easier to hear, and not be threatened by, their partners' feelings.

Another difference between ESFJs and INFPs is their conflicting decision-making styles. ESFJs usually form instant and firm opinions about almost everything, which they like to express or act on immediately. Their rapid-fire judgments may eliminate any chance for deliberation. INFPs typically have a far more contemplative style and usually require more time to ponder their thoughts. ESFJs' ultrapractical nature makes them skeptical of ideas that seem, at least on the surface, unrealistic or unworkable. This sometimes leaves INFPs feeling that their innovation and creativity are not supported. While ESFJs tend to get caught up in the details of everyday life, INFPs are often interested in the big picture but may ignore details they find boring or repetitive.

The decisive, take-charge-and-finish-what-you-start attitude of ESFJs sometimes feels a bit overbearing to INFPs, and the easygoing, dreamy style of INFPs may appear lazy and undependable to ESFJs. ESFJs resent feeling overworked because they constantly have to clean up or organize the house. INFPs feel criticized, controlled, and nagged into helping out with mundane chores that could just as easily wait until another time. This dynamic is intensified by the fact that ESFJs are often busy with volunteer commitments, so it may appear to INFPs that their partners place other people's needs ahead of theirs. For their part, INFPs can be rather self-absorbed and distracted by their own needs for solitude and inner reflection. Ironically, the busier and more frantic ESFJs become, the more silent and withdrawn INFPs become. This is a red flag that it's time to stop everything and talk to each other.

Finally, since neither type tends to have well-developed logic and critical thinking skills, they may both make decisions, especially financial ones, that don't serve them well. These couples often find that hiring a financial adviser is a great investment.

How to Reach Your INFP Partner

- Before insisting that your partner help you with something, step back to determine whether the project really needs to be finished now.
- Allow your partner to show you the joys of a lazy afternoon or the delights of diversions found off the beaten path.
- Remember to ask your partner's opinion, then allow plenty of time for him or her to think about the issue before answering.
- Don't interrupt or finish your partner's sentences. Listen to his or her dreams and allow yourself a flight of fancy.
- Enjoy spending time together in silence.
- Beware that your strong emotional reactions may cause your partner not to share his or her feelings. Calm down and use a softer voice to draw your partner to you.

How to Reach Your ESFJ Partner

- Look for things that need to be done around the house, then do them. Pitch in and share household chores so your partner will be finished sooner and can relax.
- Share your thoughts and feelings. Express yourself verbally.
- Be sure to tell your partner (in words) that you appreciate all the effort he or she puts into making your life run smoothly.
- If you need more time to think something through, let your partner know so that he or she won't think you either don't care or have no opinion.
- Initiate discussions, intimacy, and projects. Act on your impulses.

• Agree to get out and do social things with your partner from time to time.

ISFJ with ENFJ

The Joys

ISFJs and ENFJs share two important type preferences and typically have a very strong, loving connection and a common need for harmony. Both like to live their lives in ways that are in sync with their personal values. They are usually very supportive of each other and place a high value on cooperation. They know they can totally depend on each other to follow through on their commitments and be where and when they say they will be.

ISFJs and ENFJs usually enjoy a comfortable partnership, but it's the differences between them that are the source of their initial attraction. ENFJs are drawn to ISFJs' gentleness, calm, and genuine warmth. ISFJs tend to win ENFJs over with their loyalty, thoughtfulness, and earnestness. They make their partners feel so utterly nurtured and accepted. ISFJs often are attracted to ENFJs' confidence, energy, charisma, and the level of excitement that surrounds them. They greatly admire ENFJs' articulateness and their ability to take an idea and run with it. They are impressed, if also a bit exhausted, by the breathtaking pace that ENFJs maintain.

Because of their differences, ISFJ and ENFJ couples can help each other grow and develop in important ways. ENFJs often broaden the horizons of their more cautious and unassuming partners, helping them stretch their imaginations, try new things, and look beyond the obvious and the routine. ISFJs tend to bring stability and security to the idealistic ENFJs, helping them to become more grounded and realistic and to slow down so they can appreciate the simple things in life.

The Frustrations

Because ISFJs and ENFJs tend to make decisions based almost exclusively on their feelings and personal values, they both see things in rather absolute terms. They have a propensity to take firm positions on issues of morality. Since neither partner is likely to back down or compromise their values, their need to be right can conflict with their need to be united as a couple. Their mutual desire for control surfaces when they are deciding how and when to spend money and how flexible they should be as parents. When both people want to be in charge and also tend to avoid direct confrontation, they may resort to passive-aggressive behavior until the conflict mushrooms into a full-scale argument. Typically, ENFJs will finally initiate a discussion, an act they don't relish but are more willing to perform than are their quieter, more private ISFJ partners. Whenever one person is solely responsible for an unpleasant but important aspect of a relationship, however, resentment can build. The challenge for these couples is to find ways of calmly, honestly, and regularly bringing up small irritations and hurts before they threaten the health of the relationship.

ENFJs and ISFJs also share a desire for order and neatness in their homes. But since both partners take their commitments very seriously and drive themselves to finish the tasks they start, they may make hasty decisions because neither is comfortable leaving things open. They also can be too exhausted for each other at the end of a long, busy day.

Another potential area of frustration is their different perspectives on change. ISFJs are very realistic and practical people who primarily trust their own experiences. They are careful, conservative, and traditional and tend to resist new approaches. ENFJs love new ideas, even if nothing ever comes of them. They are much more nonconventional that their ISFJ partners, are more interested in the big picture, and enjoy fantasizing about the future. ENFJs are energized by projects that promote personal growth and development and are constantly searching for deeper meaning. To ENFJs change represents possibilities for growth, while to ISFJs it may signal stress and chaos. ISFJs are happiest when they are steadily and quietly maintaining traditions and the comforts of home. The trick for this couple is to broaden each other's perspectives without causing too much conflict in the process.

Most ENFJs have a great need for social stimulation and get involved in many different activities outside the home, whereas ISFJs tend to put family first and are more selective about their outside commitments. While ENFJs and ISFJs tend to pursue very different interests, they also value a close connection, so they sometimes have trouble allowing for healthy separation.

Finally, most ENFJs and ISFJs express themselves differently. ISFJs are very private and reflective people. They want to think things through carefully before speaking, then be clear and precise, especially about important matters. ISFJs often feel that ENFJs are not really listening but instead waiting impatiently to jump in to make a point. When ISFJs feel pressured to hurry up and finish their sentences, they tend to become anxious and close up. ENFJs are often frustrated by ISFJs' slow and deliberate pace, their lack of sharing, and by having to draw their partners out. They need to be patient and supportive while still working hard to discuss unpleasant but important subjects.

How to Reach Your ENFJ Partner

- Share your worries and frustrations before they become big issues.
- Don't suppress feelings and concerns. Trust your partner to help you sort out your feelings.
- Be sure to take your turn initiating activity and

discussion rather than always waiting for your partner to do it.
- Wait until your ENFJ partner has given you the entire picture before resisting a new or unusual idea.
- Be honest rather than resorting to criticism or silence.
- Be willing to participate in as many social activities with your partner as you can. Encourage him or her to go without you when you're not up to it.

How to Reach Your ISFJ Partner

- Be patient in all interactions, especially if you want something different or are suggesting change.
- Watch your tendency to assume. Do reality checks with your partner.
- Listen carefully, giving your partner your full attention, and don't jump to conclusions before you've heard your partner's full story. Don't finish his or her sentences.
- Take the time to draw out your partner, listening for meaning and patterns.
- Patiently accommodate your partner's need for a predictable schedule. Respect his or her routines and rituals.
- Never disclose personal information about your partner to others.

ISFJ with INFJ

The Joys

ISFJs and INFJs share three of the four type preferences, giving them very similar styles, energy, and attitudes. Many ISFJ and INFJ couples describe their relationships as complementary and comfortable because they easily understand and accommodate each other. They are both quiet, serious, conscientious people who like to spend time alone, together, or with their families or a few close friends. ISFJs and INFJs are both gentle, caring, and sensitive to the feelings and needs of others. They have high personal standards of conduct based on their strong values; chief among these are integrity, honor, and trustworthiness. ISFJs and INFJs also enjoy a predictable lifestyle, take their commitments seriously, and respect each other's rituals and routines. They like a neat and well-organized home and like to plan things out and make decisions together.

With so many important qualities in common, it's no surprise that ISFJs and INFJs enjoy being together. But in addition to their similarities, ISFJs and INFJs are often attracted to each other because of their differences. In general, ISFJs are more practical, and INFJs are more imaginative. ISFJs are often initially attracted to INFJs because of their originality, creativity, and unique take on things. INFJs see the unusual in everyday events, and their sense of humor is often dry and surprising. ISFJs also admire INFJs' articulateness and their ability to help their partners express themselves more accurately and eloquently. Most of all, ISFJs love feeling totally understood by their naturally intuitive partners. INFJs are often drawn to ISFJs' unpretentious demeanor and genuine warmth. ISFJs' steadiness and dependability make INFJs feel secure. Above all, INFJs feel accepted and loved by their earnest and devoted partners.

Because of their differences, ISFJs and INFJs have the opportunity to help each other grow and develop in important ways. Typically, ISFJs help INFJs learn to pay closer attention to some of the important details of life. They also help their partners develop better habits with money, time, and other resources and take better care of their homes and possessions. INFJs often credit their ISFJ partners with helping them enjoy simple pleasures by being more patient and growing more appreciative of everyday events. For their part, INFJs often help

ISFJs stay open and look beyond what is apparent or expected. ISFJs often find that they become less fearful of the unknown and can become more optimistic and confident about the future. ISFJs also say that their INFJ partners help them better understand and articulate their feelings.

The Frustrations

Since ISFJs and INFJs are so alike, they are sometimes irritated by each other's lack of initiative, need to carefully and methodically plan things out in advance, and general resistance to change. They sometimes struggle over who's in charge, and they may find it difficult to balance their need for time alone with the demands of busy professional and social lives. When they become fatigued, they may be short and cross with each other.

The more fundamental frustrations for ISFJ and INFJ couples tend to stem from their different temperaments. ISFJs are very conservative and traditional people, and they tend to be especially careful regarding anything unproven. The more naturally nonconforming INFJs sometimes find their partners too slow and overly cautious about new experiences. INFJs also feel a bit alone when their partners don't immediately grasp the significance of events or experiences they find profound. For their part, ISFJs often don't realize how important the brainstorming and dreaming process is to INFJs. ISFJs are sometimes hurt by INFJs' focus on tomorrow and how things could be, which to them implies that their partners are dissatisfied with the way things are now. And when INFJs are impatient or condescending about ISFJs' more careful and realistic views, ISFJs feel belittled and criticized. ISFJs sometimes become irritated with their partners' disregard for their important rituals and their general carelessness concerning important facts, steps, and details. When ISFJs are always responsible for the tedious tasks of daily life, they begin to feel taken for granted.

Since ISFJs and INFJs are both very sensitive, their feelings get hurt easily. An innocuous comment, misconstrued as a dismissal, can cause pain and lead to feelings of isolation. And since neither type is especially eager to talk about unpleasant things, they tend to withdraw and hold on to their grievances longer than is healthy. When confrontations do occur, INFJs are typically the ones to initiate the discussion after noticing familiar patterns and sensing something brewing. At that point, INFJs need to try to stay on the topic and not bring in unrelated issues, just as ISFJs need to try not to become too defensive or discouraged by the temporary conflict. Usually, when both have time to gather their thoughts and then discuss issues calmly and honestly, they can regain their equilibrium and reestablish the harmony they both want.

How to Reach Your INFJ Partner

- Try to articulate your thoughts and feelings rather than assuming your partner knows how and what you feel.
- Be patient with your partner's desire to uncover the hidden or subtle meanings of things.
- Focus on the positive, especially in everyday matters such as money and maintaining your home and possessions.
- Compliment your partner on his or her many fresh ideas, unique mode of expression, and ability to see the big picture.
- Be patient with your partner's sometimes vague or convoluted stories.
- Thank your partner for encouraging you to plan for the future.

How to Reach Your ISFJ Partner

- Appreciate all the tangible and thoughtful things your partner does to take care of you, your home, and your family.
- Participate in some the physical activities your partner enjoys, especially those that get you out of the house and into the natural world.

- Be specific about your requests, concerns, and complaints.
- Don't gloss over important steps or leave out key information. Carefully keep track of money.
- Try not to make or even suggest too many changes too quickly.
- Respect your partner's routines and honor the practices that bring him or her comfort.

ISFJ with ENFP

The Joys

ISFJs and ENFPs have only one preference in common, but it is an important one that often gives them a strong emotional connection. Sympathetic, caring, and sensitive to each other's needs, ISFJs and ENFPs value harmony and mutual support. They tend to care deeply about other people and enjoy being of service to them.

Their differences often are the source of the initial attraction between ISFJs and ENFPs. ISFJs find ENFPs outgoing, enthusiastic, charming, and clever, if somewhat unpredictable. ENFPs are often attracted to ISFJs' gentleness, quiet energy, and thoughtfulness. They admire their partners' thoroughness and integrity and find their stability a calming influence. ISFJs like working quietly behind the scenes to make sure people get what they need, while ENFPs love dreaming up new and creative activities and getting people excited about them.

Because of their differences, ISFJs and ENFPs have a great opportunity to complement each other and help each other grow and develop in important ways. ISFJs help their partners become more successful by making them aware of important issues that need to be considered and by helping them complete tasks. ENFPs help their partners see possibilities, experience new people and things, challenge themselves, and enjoy life more. When these couples are able to harness their different strengths while working together on a project, they can be very effective.

The Frustrations

Since these couples are different on three type preferences, they face some formidable challenges. ISFJs are by nature very traditional and take comfort in established routines, especially ones in regard to the home. By contrast, ENFPs are individualists who march to the beat of their own drummers. They are not very good at following rules and enjoy doing things in unconventional ways. ISFJs don't always express excitement or faith in their partners' frequent innovations because they often see them as unrealistic, which leaves ENFPs feeling unsupported and misunderstood. Likewise, ENFPs sometimes fail to appreciate the multitude of mundane yet important things their partners do to make their lives run smoothly. This typically causes ISFJs to feel overworked and taken for granted.

ISFJs and ENFPs also have very different social needs. Whereas ISFJs often prefer to spend time alone with their partners or with a small group of close friends, ENFPs usually have a large and varied group of associates (playmates, really) with whom they enjoy spending as much time as possible. These two types also have very different communication styles. ENFPs are big talkers who think out loud, while ISFJs need to think things through before they're ready to discuss them. ENFPs often feel that their partners don't share enough, while ISFJs often feel rushed or interrupted.

The greatest source of friction between ISFJs and ENFPs is their different ways of approaching the day-to-day activities of life. ENFPs are interested in the process and are comfortable leaving issues unresolved, drawers open, and clean clothes in the laundry basket. ISFJs like and want issues decided and tasks (especially ones such as cleaning up after dinner, making the bed, or balancing the checkbook) completed. ISFJs are quite conser-

vative people who love the comfort of traditions and enjoy predictability in their lives. ENFPs are usually unconventional and find repetition, even of a pleasant experience, unimaginative and boring. So it follows that ENFPs love to be spontaneous, to drop in on friends, go out to dinner at the last minute, or even to change long-standing plans if a more exciting opportunity presents itself. This type of behavior frustrates ISFJs, who much prefer knowing what to expect, planning things out in advance, and always following through with commitments.

How to Reach Your ENFP Partner

- Support your partner's social life by entertaining as often as possible or encouraging your partner to spend time with friends.
- Plan some spontaneous time. Make yourself available to do whatever strikes your partner's fancy.
- Be willing to experiment sexually, including what you do, and when and where you do it.
- Be sure your partner doesn't feel pressured to leave parties before he or she wants to. Agree to take two cars so you can leave early if you wish.
- Be patient when your partner presents a new brainstorm or idea. Try to be enthusiastic and diplomatic when giving solicited feedback.
- Don't immediately shoot down ideas, even though you may see practical details your partner has overlooked.
- If possible, make sure your partner has his or her own space (home office or workroom, for example) to decorate and keep as messy as he or she likes.

How to Reach Your ISFJ Partner

- Before going to a social function together, give your partner as much specific information as possible about who will be there and what he or she can expect. Make sure to introduce your partner to people before you wander away.

- Try to keep the house, especially common areas, tidy. Put things away.
- Honor the commitments you make, especially engagements or activities that are important to your partner.
- Acknowledge the considerate things your partner does to make your home a safe, comfortable place.
- Remember special dates: anniversaries, birthdays, and holidays. Give presents that are aesthetically pleasing but also practical and useful.
- Give your partner plenty of time to prepare for discussions, especially those that concern feelings. Don't expect your mate to respond immediately.
- Try to spend some time together without talking, such as reading in bed, watching TV, or taking a walk.
- Respect your partner's routines and rituals.

ISFJ with INFP

The Joys

ISFJs and INFPs share two preferences, so they are usually fairly independent and have well-defined interests. They tend to have similar needs for privacy and intimate friendships, and they are content to spend time alone. Some of their most pleasurable moments are spent together doing something quiet, like reading, that doesn't call for much talking. ISFJs and INFPs are very sensitive to each other's needs and supportive of each other's projects. Their homes tend to be calm, peaceful places where loud arguments and confrontations rarely occur.

Although their different ways of looking at the world sometimes present a challenge, ISFJs and INFPs provide a necessary balance to each other. ISFJs are good fact finders and researchers, collecting all the necessary information in a thorough and methodical way. INFPs are usually dreamers and enjoy thoughtful and creative brainstorming. The combination of the two styles often produces a better end result than either could produce on their own.

In addition to their emotional connections, ISFJs and INFPs are often initially attracted to each other because of their differences. ISFJs are often drawn to INFPs because of their creativity, empathy, and originality. ISFJs admire INFPs' more casual and unconventional approach to life. INFPs are often attracted to ISFJs because of their kindness, quiet strength, and stable, mature attitudes. Most INFPs respect the traditional values ISFJs hold dear, although they don't always share them.

Because of their differences, ISFJs and INFPs have the opportunity to help each other grow and develop in important ways. ISFJs are often able to help INFPs pay closer attention to facts and details, which makes their ideas more workable. Many INFPs credit their partners with helping them follow through on their commitments and accept life the way it is rather than only fantasizing about how it might be. For their part, INFPs are often able to help ISFJs consider original or unusual approaches to problems and have more faith in the future. ISFJs say that their partners help them relax, enjoy the moment, and not work so hard to please other people.

The Frustrations

One common source of frustration for ISFJs and INFPs is that ISFJs prefer to discuss things they have some direct knowledge of while INFPs usually enjoy philosophical discussions about big ideas or important issues of the day. Most INFPs love possibilities and often come up with novel ideas or solutions to problems. They rely on their gut instincts rather than on facts or personal experience. But ISFJs often are uncomfortable operating without some evidence that an idea is workable, and when they look for some proof or try to provide some fact-based feedback, INFPs can feel undermined and criticized.

ISFJs and INFPs also approach time and work differently. ISFJs generally pay attention to the present and have a serious work ethic. By contrast, INFPs usually are focused on the future and have a more casual play ethic. This difference sometimes results in a low-grade but ongoing conflict. ISFJs take on projects with characteristic caution, but once they are committed, they work tirelessly to see them through to completion. INFPs are usually enthusiastic about new projects, but they are unrealistic about how long they will take and tend to get bored once the creative part has been done. They may then leave things half-finished. ISFJs find it very frustrating when INFPs bail out or don't pull their own weight.

ISFJs and INFPs are very sensitive and caring people, and they sometimes want harmony so much that they tiptoe around problems rather than deal with them head-on. Without a constructive plan for dealing with conflict, some couples actually stop talking to each other for hours or days at a time, which undermines their emotional connections.

Finally, perhaps the most frequent source of frustration for ISFJ and INFP couples is their different needs for order and closure. ISFJs like to live in an orderly, purposeful manner. They want things to be decided and to remain constant, and they usually take great comfort in being able to maintain their routines and habits. On the other hand, INFPs prefer to be spontaneous and enjoy adapting to new experiences that arise unexpectedly. INFPs complain that their partners are too focused on getting the job done rather than enjoying the process, while ISFJs feel that their partners don't follow through and finish chores. INFPs sometimes feel that they are being pushed into doing things they don't want to do, but ISFJs counter that if they didn't provide the motivation, nothing

would get done. ISFJs do well to choose their battles, and INFPs may need to work at being more consistent in order to reduce some of these conflicts. Open, honest, and loving discussions usually lead to a renewed sense of connection and harmony.

How to Reach Your ISFJ Partner

- Be specific, especially when discussing things that bother you.
- Respect your partner's traditions, rituals, and routines. Don't disrupt your partner's schedule.
- Try not to change plans without plenty of warning.
- Respect your partner's need for a neat and tidy environment. Be especially careful to maintain order in the common areas of your home.
- Express your appreciation of the day-to-day things your partner does, such as paying bills, keeping things in working order, and preparing for holidays.
- Find time to enjoy the physical activities you both enjoy.

How to Reach Your INFP Partner

- Respect your partner's need to be involved in activities that take advantage of his or her creativity, even when this means your partner must spend large amounts of time outside the home.
- Try to be open to new experiences and to explore new things.
- Plan time to be spontaneous. Be willing to leave things unfinished to participate in the spur-of-the-moment suggestions your partner makes.
- Try to learn more about the projects and issues that interest your partner. Make time to discuss them.
- Respect and appreciate the alternative perspective your partner brings to your relationship.
- Try to engage in "dream planning" about the future.

Chapter 8

The Experiencers²: SPs with SPs

ESTP with ESTP

The Joys

As with all couples who share all four type preferences, ESTP couples tend to understand each other and get along easily. Active, fun loving, and spontaneous, ESTPs can raise having a good time to an art form. Talkative, friendly, and energetic, they like to be around people and usually prefer outdoor physical activities such as sports to more passive, intellectual activities such as discussing politics or current events. More than many of the other type combinations, they are great playmates. ESTPs are among the most flexible and adaptable types. They have the capacity to be fully engaged in whatever they're doing at the moment and seldom think about what came before or what will come later. Comfortable being spontaneous, they can shift gears quickly to take advantage of exciting new opportunities.

Not surprisingly, ESTPs are often initially attracted to each other because they're so easygoing, relaxed, and fun. Because they tend to be realistic and down-to-earth, they take their relationships at face value, seldom imposing unreasonable expectations or trying to control their partners. Since they share many of the same blind spots and strengths, they have the opportunity to help each other grow and develop in important ways. They can encourage each other to be more compassionate and gentle with other people and

consider the effects of their actions on others. They may help each other resist temptations and follow through on their responsibilities, making them more organized and accountable.

The Frustrations

Like most couples of the same type, ESTPs may both avoid the tasks neither partner likes or does well. For these couples, those tasks are usually regimented, routine maintenance chores such as balancing the checkbook, paying bills, and making or confirming appointments. While it's hardly fair, these tasks typically fall on the shoulders of the partner who dislikes them less, the one who has more free time, or the woman. And because both partners value their freedom so highly, the more responsible partner often resents the fact that his or her freedom is curtailed and that they are left holding the bag.

"Don't worry, be happy" could be this couple's theme song, and ESTPs' propensity for ignoring unpleasantness, coupled with their general lack of awareness and concern about tension, can be both a blessing and a curse. On the plus side, they don't let minor problems or conflicts bother them, which leads to an easy day-to-day compatibility. But they also may not be particularly perceptive about which issues are important and deserve their attention. As a result, they tend to avoid conflicts simply to keep things low-key and on an even keel. Constantly staying on the surface of issues can ultimately undermine the health of the relationship, however, and allow resentment and dissatisfaction to brew.

Finally, since ESTP couples, especially young ones, are so focused on the present and on having a good time, they run the risk of making decisions that are not in their best interests. For example, rather than make and stick with a budget and create a long-term investment plan, they may impulsively spend money on temporary pleasures such as vacations. Inevitably, one of the partners is more fiscally conservative than the other and becomes unnerved by the other's carefree spending habits. Another concern for many ESTP couples is that out of necessity, one partner almost always has to assume the more responsible role. Since both partners are naturally free-spirited and dislike anyone attempting to control them, this is likely to create frustration for the one being reined in as well as for the one trying to impose some structure. They may need to agree to some reasonable limits so they can return to their more equal and fun-loving relationship.

Advice for ESTPs

- Enjoy the ride!
- Figure out ways to share responsibilities so that one partner doesn't feel overwhelmed and resentful.
- Seek outside help for doing things that neither partner may enjoy or be good at doing, such as financial planning.
- Try to look down the road and imagine how your lives may be different so you can anticipate future needs.
- Be willing to be vulnerable to each other. Consider getting outside help if you have problems you can't solve yourselves.
- Take turns being the "grown-up." Pull your own weight so the division of labor is fair.

ESTP with ISTP

The Joys

Because ESTPs and ISTPs share three type preferences and many temperamental values, they often have a very easygoing and complementary relationship. They are casual, adaptable people who take life as it comes. Both are playful free spirits who are happiest enjoying the moment, not looking for trouble or worrying about the future. Observant, curious, and impulsive, ESTPs and ISTPs are total realists, ever practical and pragmatic. Since they both communicate in a very direct, literal, and no-nonsense way, they tend to understand each other well. Objective and logical in their decision making, they are rarely given to exaggeration or emotional reactions.

With so many fundamental characteristics in common, it's no surprise that ESTPs and ISTPs enjoy being together. But in addition to their similarities, ESTPs and ISTPs are often initially attracted to each other because of their different energy levels. ESTPs are drawn to ISTPs because they are so calm and unflappable. ISTPs tend to exude a quiet confidence that ESTPs find appealing, while ISTPs are attracted to ESTPs' enthusiasm and social ease. Usually everyone likes ESTPs because they are fun and entertaining.

This difference gives ESTPs and ISTPs the opportunity to help each other grow and develop in important ways. ESTPs get their partners out of isolation and into society, which widens their social circle. ISTPs say that their partners encourage them to open up and share their private thoughts and reactions. For their part, ISTPs calm their partners down, encourage them to think before they act, and help them focus their considerable energy on fewer projects. They can each help the other follow through on their commitments and do the important planning both tend to avoid.

The Frustrations

Although they have much in common, ESTPs and ISTPs experience frustration stemming primarily from their different needs for social interaction and quiet. ESTPs are very active people who find it almost impossible to sit still for any length of time. They quickly grow restless without the opportunity to talk with other people. They tend to say whatever pops into their heads and rarely know what they're going to say before they say it. In contrast, ISTPs are much more private and reflective people who need a lot of time alone. They are easily drained by superficial chitchat and won't participate in a conversation unless the subject is something they're really interested in. ESTPs sometimes find it difficult to engage their partners in conversation and often feel they have to drag information out of them. And ISTPs often feel intruded on and pressured to talk about things they either have no interest in or haven't had time to consider carefully.

ESTPs also tend to leap before they look and sometimes find themselves in hot water they could have avoided. Even more risky, they have been known to share private information about their partners with other people. For their part, ISTPs can be neglectful of their partners because they inhabit their own worlds, and they can miss out on interesting opportunities because they aren't ready to participate. Rare is the ISTP who can be hurried, and rarer still is the ESTP who can be idle for very long. ESTPs may need to let some social activities go, just as ISTPs may need to be willing to entertain occasionally. And together they may need to find ways to accommodate each other's desires to be with friends, to be alone, or to spend time quietly enjoying each other's company.

ESTP and ISTP couples may also struggle with a fair distribution of household labor. Although neither partner is especially concerned with order or organization, tasks such as paying bills, balancing the checkbook, and arranging schedules must be done, and these couples may run into trouble if both partners avoid those chores for too long. ESTPs and ISTPs also are not inclined to delve into problems in search of underlying causes. They take things at face value and can miss important implications and connections. It's important that they take the time to look beyond the obvious and be willing to try alternative approaches to solving problems. Also, since neither partner is comfortable being vulnerable, they may avoid sharing their deepest feelings with each other. When thing are going smoothly, this isn't a big problem, but when they inevitably run into difficult times, they will need that emotional connection to manage conflicts without losing touch with each other. Taking the time to be quiet, serious, and genuine with each other will strengthen these couples' bond and fortify them against life's challenges.

How to Reach Your ISTP Partner

- Ask fewer questions, then wait patiently for your partner's answer.
- Never interrupt or finish your partner's sentences.
- Respect your partner's need for privacy. Give him or her plenty of time alone.
- Never share personal information about your partner with other people.
- Be willing to pass on social activities and enjoy quiet time with your partner.
- Tell your partner you appreciate how attentive he or she is when you're together.

How to Reach Your ESTP Partner

- Try to participate in as many social events as you can. Encourage your partner to go without you if you're not up to it.
- Share your thoughts, reactions, and feelings with your partner.
- If you need time to think about something

before discussing it, tell your partner. Don't just disappear.

- Reach out to your partner and make an effort to start some discussions.
- Thank your partner for all the thoughtful things he or she does to help you.

ESTP with ESFP

The Joys

ESTPs and ESFPs have a lot in common: three of the four type preferences and shared temperamental values. The hallmark of ESTP and ESFP relationships is fun. These couples often desire similar lifestyles and are easygoing, relaxed, and always eager and able to respond to the moment. Playful and fun loving, ESTPs and ESFPs constantly search everyday events for amusing or exciting opportunities. They love to laugh and are usually able to tease and be teased in equal measure.

In addition to their shared love of a good time, ESTPs and ESFPs are generally outgoing, talkative, and active people who often share an interest in the outdoors and sports and may love to experience physical thrills and risks. Realistic, practical, and hands-on, ESTPs and ESFPs usually understand each other well, since they are both so literal and down-to-earth. Casual and free-spirited, neither likes to be restricted, so they rarely worry about rules or structure, nor do they like to plan too far ahead.

It's not surprising that people with so much in common find each other attractive. But in addition to their similarities, ESTPs and ESFPs are often drawn to each other because of their differences. Typically, ESTPs are attracted to ESFPs because of their genuine warmth and sensitivity. ESTPs admire how well ESFPs understand other people and make those they care about feel nurtured and pampered by their constant devotion and affection. For their part, ESFPs are often attracted to

ESTPs' calm and pragmatic style. ESTPs often exude confidence and can be very charming and exciting.

Because of their differences, ESTPs and ESFPs have the opportunity to help each other grow and develop in important ways. ESFPs credit their partners with helping them become more direct, straightforward, and honest. ESTPs often help ESFPs detach themselves a bit in their dealings with other people so they don't get their feelings hurt as easily. Conversely, ESFPs help ESTPs become more sensitive to the needs and feelings of others. ESTPs often say that their partners bring a depth and meaning to their relationships by helping them become less superficial and more willing to express their true emotions.

The Frustrations

The primary source of conflict and frustration for ESTPs and ESFPs is their different ways of making decisions and judgments. ESTPs are so logical about their decisions that they rarely stop to consider how their actions may affect others. They are usually able to remain objective and calm, even during a crisis, while ESFPs tend to take almost everything to heart and have very emotional reactions. When ESFPs learn of a sad event affecting someone, even a stranger or an animal, they feel great sympathy, which ESTPs don't usually understand or share. ESTPs often think that their partners overreact, while ESFPs sometimes feel that their partners are impatient and dismissive of their feelings.

When dealing with conflict, ESTPs tend to have brief but intensely angry reactions, which they get over quickly once they've vented. But they may not apologize as quickly or genuinely as their partners want. In contrast, ESFPs are harder to provoke, but they hold on to hurts and disappointments much longer and may withdraw when they're upset. ESFPs will even avoid healthy confrontations in order to maintain harmony or risk rocking the boat. Naturally, the more ESFPs withdraw, the less patient ESTPs become. Conversely, the more direct and calm ESFPs are, the more willing and able ESTPs are to resolve issues.

Both partners are playful and easygoing, but ESFPs usually want to have deeper, more intimate discussions than their ESTP partners do. The compromise lies in ESFPs being more discriminating about the subjects that are really important and worthy of deep discussions and ESTPs being willing to be serious and to move beyond a superficial treatment of issues.

Finally, like many other couples with similar strengths, ESTPs and ESFPs tend to share the same blind spots. In this case, neither partner wants to be in charge, but they also don't like being controlled. And since neither partner is especially interested in handling the more mundane or repetitious chores, one person generally ends up doing more of the planning and organizing necessary to meet important deadlines. This is especially true regarding money. Both ESTPs and ESFPs tend to enjoy spending money impulsively on toys and fun activities. But when neither is especially good at budgeting and neither cares a lot about saving, one person ends up having to act like a parent rather than an equal partner. This naturally causes conflict, which can be reduced when the partners either take turns being responsible for the checkbook or devise some fair, reasonable, and flexible way of staying on top of their finances while still enjoying life.

How to Reach Your ESFP Partner

- Be genuine and gentle. Compliment your partner's looks and his or her efforts to make you happy.
- Be tactful and positive. Start a discussion by mentioning points of agreement or expressing your appreciation of the good things before pointing out what needs fixing.

- Surprise your partner with thoughtful gifts or cards to demonstrate your devotion.
- Apologize when you hurt your partner's feelings. Take responsibility and "fess up" when your actions cause problems.
- Be patient with the depth and intensity of your partner's feelings. Never dismiss your partner simply because you don't share his or her reactions.

How to Reach Your ESTP Partner

- Be calm and logical when discussing problems or things you wish were different.
- Try not to overreact or exaggerate.
- Don't withdraw and become silent. Explain why you are upset and let your partner know you need time alone.
- Respect your partner's competence. Never undermine your partner in public.
- Try to explain the logical reasons for your reactions. Don't assume that your partner is unfeeling simply because he or she doesn't feel as you do.

ESTP with ISFP

The Joys

Because ESTPs and ISFPs share two type preferences and the same temperament, their relationships are typically easygoing and flexible. They are fun-loving, spontaneous people who enjoy being physically active and following their impulses to explore as much of life as possible. They are rarely concerned about rules, structure, or order, and they have a gift for finding fun and excitement in everyday experiences. Typically blessed with good common sense, ESTPs and ISFPs also share a realistic and practical approach to life. They are very observant, pay close attention to facts and details, and are straightforward, literal, and down-to-earth.

In addition to their shared characteristics, ESTPs and ISFPs are often initially attracted to each other because of their differences. ESTPs are often drawn to ISFPs because of their genuine warmth, unwavering loyalty, and strong desire to nurture and please. ESTPs like the fact that their partners are so affectionate and sensitive to the needs and feelings of others. ISFPs have a depth that most ESTPs find calming and appealing. ISFPs are often attracted to ESTPs' enthusiasm, playfulness, and sense of humor. ESTPs sometimes sweep ISFPs off their feet with their irresistible charm, energy, and self-confidence. ISFPs also admire ESTPs' ability to be objective and honest about themselves.

Because of their differences, ESTPs and ISFPs have the opportunity to help each other grow and develop in important ways. ESTPs generally encourage ISFPs to speak their minds and become more assertive. ISFPs credit their partners with toughening them up a bit so they don't take as many things to heart or get their feelings hurt as often. For their part, ISFPs encourage ESTPs to slow down and be more thoughtful and considerate. When ESTPs allow themselves to be serious, their partners help them understand other people better and learn to express their feelings.

The Frustrations

Despite their many similarities, ESTPs and ISFPs experience frustrations that stem from their different ways of coming to conclusions and making decisions. ESTPs are the ultimate pragmatists, always able to find the most expedient ways to get things done. But in their efficiency, they are sometimes unaware of how their actions affect the people close to them. ISFPs, by contrast, are very sensitive and make most decisions based on their personal values. They are supremely diplomatic and sometimes feel that their ESTP partners are too harsh when they make off-the-cuff remarks that unintentionally offend others. In their desire to avoid hurting people's feelings, ISFPs can be meek and indirect, a quality many ESTPs find irritating. To be sure, ESTPs can be blunt and tactless, while ISFPs avoid even healthy conflict and have a hard time being totally honest.

When conflicts do occur, ESTPs generally prefer to deal with them quickly and to avoid rehashing old issues or delving too deeply into their private feelings. Because they're so uncomfortable revealing their fears or insecurities, they tend to stay on the surface instead of delving into underlying problems. Although ISFPs are more comfortable dealing with emotions, they are reflective people who usually need time to consider how they feel and to put their thoughts together before talking about them. ISFPs need to watch their tendency to push their partners toward intimacy, just as ESTPs need to be more sensitive and patient.

Many ESTP and ISFP couples have very different needs for social interaction and time alone. ESTPs are very outgoing and like to stay busy throughout the day. ISFPs typically have a smaller group of close friends with whom they like to play and share, and they tend to become exhausted and overwhelmed by too much activity or too many pressures. ESTPs sometimes feel frustrated by their partners' lack of initiative and resistance to entertaining. Conversely, ISFPs feel pressured to go out when they'd rather relax at home. ESTPs also tend to think out loud and may be frustrated when they can't engage their partners in conversation. ISFPs sometimes wish that their partners would stop talking and spend more quiet time with them.

Finally, since neither ESTPs nor ISFPs are predisposed to plan ahead or are comfortable with structure, they may find themselves unprepared or racing to meet deadlines. While most ESTPs and ISFPs are very generous, they may struggle to hold on to and budget their money. And since neither partner likes to be the boss or to be controlled, they may resist each other's attempts to stay on top of things. They usually need to agree on some flexible spending guidelines that allow both partners to have some discretionary funds to use as they wish.

How to Reach Your ISFP Partner

- Be gentle and sympathetic. Slow down and use a soft voice.
- Compliment your partner on his or her looks. Recognize the effort your partner makes to show you his or her love.
- Give your partner time to think things through before expecting an answer or response. Respect your partner's privacy and need to spend time alone.
- Don't pressure your partner into doing things socially or put him or her on the spot in public.
- Listen attentively and sympathetically when your partner is sharing his or her concerns and feelings. Don't interrupt or try to fix problems right away.
- Be willing to forgo social opportunities to spend quiet time alone with your partner doing something you both enjoy.
- Share your feelings. Be willing to be serious and not make everything into a joke.

How to Reach Your ESTP Partner

- Surprise your partner. Do something outrageous and fun.
- Speak your mind. Be direct, honest, and to the point. Don't expect your partner to read your mind or heart.
- Try to stay calm and unemotional. Don't exaggerate or blow things out of proportion.
- Participate in as many social activities as you can. Be sure to encourage your partner to go without you, and don't use guilt to keep him or her home.
- Encourage your partner to think out loud. Be an attentive and supportive listener.

- Don't pressure your partner to express his or her feelings until he or she has had time to think about them.

ISTP with ISTP

The Joys

With all four type preferences and the same temperament in common, ISTPs generally have easy-going and relaxed relationships based in great part on similar interests, styles, and mutual respect. They are calm and casual people who face life realistically and adapt to change with ease and a matter-of-fact style. Free-spirited ISTPs are perhaps the most emotionally self-contained of all the types and embrace the credo "Live and let live." They like a lot of independence in their relationships and respect their partners' separate friendships and interests. Utterly in the moment, ISTPs rarely plan ahead, since doing so inhibits their ability to take advantage of spontaneous opportunities.

ISTPs respect each other's needs for privacy and time alone to work on projects or just relax. Rarely do ISTP couples demand a lot of attention or participation from each other. Although they like to have fun together exploring nature or being physically active, they also like to keep their own company as well. Most ISTPs have a small group of equally realistic and low-key friends who enjoy the same activities. Naturally observant, curious, and impulsive, ISTPs tend to conserve their energy for when it is really needed, then spring gracefully into action. As a couple, ISTPs usually understand each other well and communicate honestly, unemotionally, and literally. They are usually able to stay relaxed, logical, and calm even under stress.

Because they are so alike, most ISTPs find it very comfortable and easy to be together. But their shared blind spots mean they can help each other become more aware of the needs and feelings of others and encourage each other to be more understanding and sensitive. They also can help each other open up and share their private thoughts, which keeps them from becoming too removed and isolated. But ISTPs need to work together to become more accountable as they strive to follow through on their commitments and do the important planning they'd both rather avoid. While most ISTPs have no trouble giving in to the temptation of the moment, they sometimes have to work toward incorporating moderation into their lives.

The Frustrations

Most of the frustration ISTP couples experience stems from their common shortcomings. Neither has an especially urgent need to socialize or be with a lot of people, so they sometimes cut themselves off from the outside world. And since they are reluctant to commit themselves to plans too far in advance, they may miss out on fun or interesting experiences. Although ISTPs share all the same natural preferences, they are still individuals and often have different strengths of preference. So, one partner may actually want more involvement with friends or have a greater need for planning than the other.

Another area of frustration for many ISTP couples is that neither needs a lot of external structure or order, so they may not have much energy for routine or repetitive household chores. They also may not be very good at keeping track of their finances, making and keeping medical appointments, returning phone calls, and following up on things. They may both avoid these unpleasant tasks for so long that they have to scramble to meet important deadlines. In addition, although ISTPs are curious, they also are indecisive, so they often postpone decisions or delay making purchases until the last minute. Both are impulsive

spenders and often buy toys and adventures rather than essentials. They are so utterly focused on the moment that they have to be careful to plan for their future financial security.

But the most potentially serious concern for many ISTP couples is that because they are both so private and emotionally self-contained, they often avoid sharing their feelings and allowing themselves to be vulnerable to each other. They typically need a lot of time to think through what they wish to share. And when ISTPs don't know how they feel, they may not be willing to risk admitting that fact. If they stay on the surface of issues for too long and put off having important, though difficult, discussions about their feelings and needs, they may jeopardize the long-term health of their relationships. Rather than remaining distant and detached, they need to be willing to take emotional risks to create the kind of strong and close connections that will sustain them through difficulties in the future.

Advice for ISTPs

- Keep each other's counsel. Never share personal information about each other with friends or family members.
- Listen attentively. Encourage your partner to share freely without fear of criticism or dismissal.
- Open yourselves up to each other and share your true feelings. Be patient with each other as you try to articulate your fears and insecurities.
- Get professional advice regarding financial planning, budgeting, or developing good communication skills.
- Look ahead. Think about where you want to be professionally and personally five and ten years from now. Set up firm strategies to get you there.
- Don't use your similarities as an excuse to avoid doing the things you need to do but don't enjoy doing.

- Commit to regular times to check in and talk about the status of your relationship and what each of you wishes to change about the relationship.
- Be appreciative and positive and watch your tendency to be critical.
- Consider creating a contract for household responsibilities. Keep it flexible, but be willing to follow through on it.

ISTP with ESFP

The Joys

ISTPs and ESFPs share two of the four type preferences and the same temperamental values, which means they feel free to respond to as much of life as they can. They tend to be relaxed, easygoing, and casual people who prefer not to have too many restrictions or too much structure imposed on them. Realistic, practical, and down-to-earth, ISTPs and ESFPs possess common sense and are very attentive to detail. Since they focus on the facts and realities around them, they typically communicate in a straightforward and literal way and understand each other's points of view even if they don't always agree with each other. They are observant, aware of the moment, unpretentious, and fun loving. Both ISTPs and ESFPs are accommodating and generally accepting of individual differences.

In addition to their similarities, ISTPs and ESFPs are often initially attracted to each other because of their differences. ISTPs are often drawn to ESFPs because they are so warm, loving, and outgoing. Because everyone seems to like ESFPs, they tend to have a wide circle of friends. ISTPs feel very nurtured and cared for by their sympathetic and eager-to-please partners. ISTPs also admire ESFPs' genuine compassion and their effective communication skills. ESFPs are often drawn to ISTPs because they are so cool, calm, independent, and self-contained.

ISTPs are the ultimate pragmatists and very logical people. ESFPs admire how adventurous and unflappable ISTPs are, especially during times of stress or crisis.

Because of their differences, ISTPs and ESFPs are often able to help each other grow and develop in important ways. Typically, ISTPs help ESFPs stop and think more objectively so they don't take things quite so personally or get their feelings hurt as often. ESFPs say that their partners encourage them to reflect before they speak, to slow down, and not to feel compelled to please others so much of the time. For their part, ESFPs help ISTPs become more aware of and able to express their feelings. ISTPs often credit their partners with helping them become gentler, more appreciative of their blessings, and generally more engaged with the people they care about.

The Frustrations

The chief source of frustration for many ISTP and ESFP couples stems from their different criteria for making decisions. ESFPs are very sensitive and concerned about the needs and feelings of others, which they factor in to every decision. They often feel that their partners are impatient with the intensity of these feelings and the lengths to which they are willing to go to maintain harmony. ISTPs are much more logical and detached in their dealings, so they are less likely to understand or relate to their partners' involvement in others' problems. ISTPs don't see any logical rationale for emotional reactions and often wish that their partners would calm down. This can make them a bit dismissive and impatient, however. ESFPs often complain that their partners are too private and remote and won't share their feelings, while ISTPs sometimes complain that their partners are too clingy and needy.

ISTPs and ESFPs naturally express themselves in very different ways. ESFPs are warm and diplomatic, while ISTPs are people of very few words and rarely say anything they don't really mean. What appears to ESFPs as a cold or unfeeling reaction from their partners is often simply an honest and matter-of-fact observation. ESFPs usually have difficulty receiving constructive criticism, something their partners don't fully understand. And ESFPs are not especially assertive people who feel things very deeply but also hold on to hurts for a long time. ISTPs can be unintentionally insensitive and critical of their partners and other people.

Another source of frustration for many ISTP and ESFP couples is their different needs for social interaction. ESFPs love to be around a lot of people throughout the day, while ISTPs are much more private. Most ESFPs are very active, busy people who sometimes put the needs of others ahead of their own partners'. ISTPs often have such a strong need for quiet and solitude that they may cut themselves off from family activities, especially after a busy day at work.

ESFPs and ISFPs both like to gather a lot of information before coming to a final conclusion or decision, so they frequently run out of time before they're ready to commit themselves. And both are so relaxed and easygoing that neither is inclined to impose much structure or order on their lives. They may inadvertently overlook chores, miss deadlines, and put off decisions. Their homes are usually very relaxed and comfortable, but they may have to wrestle over household chores neither wants to do. Like many other couples, it is typically the woman, regardless of her type, who does more than her fair share of picking up after people and organizing the home. If she's an ESFP, this will make her feel unappreciated, and if she's an ISTP, she will be angered by the blatant unfairness.

How to Reach Your ESFP Partner

- Be patient and supportive, especially when your partner is upset or overwhelmed.
- Don't dismiss your partner's feelings simply because you don't share or understand them.

- Participate in as many social events and activities as you can. Encourage your partner to go without you when you don't want to join in.
- Be gentle and affectionate. Try to express your feelings in words as well as actions.
- Ask about your partner's day. Listen and try to remember stories concerning people your partner cares about.
- Appreciate all the thoughtful ways your partner cares for you and attends to your needs.

How to Reach Your ISTP Partner

- Acknowledge and appreciate the tangible things your partner does to contribute to the quality of your life.
- Respect your partner's need to be alone.
- Encourage your partner to have unstructured time to pursue his or her own interests. Don't require your partner to account for his or her free time.
- Listen attentively when your partner is talking or sharing. Stop what you're doing and give him or her your full attention. Don't interrupt or ask too many questions.
- Be calm and clear about your needs and feelings. Be direct and honest about problems and concerns.
- Watch for the many small things your partner does to demonstrate his or her affection and devotion.
- Curb your tendency to become overly involved in other people or things outside your home and relationship.

ISTP with ISFP

The Joys

ISTPs and ISFPs share three of the four type preferences and the same temperament. They typically have very relaxed and compatible relationships because they respect each other's independence and privacy. Most ISTP and ISFP couples prefer to keep things simple and don't like a lot of rules or structure that keeps them from following their impulses. They tend to be curious and enjoy being out in nature exploring the physical world around them. ISTPs and ISFPs are low-key, quiet people who need plenty of time away from the distractions and clamor of others. They often enjoy being with a handful of close, trusted, and similarly down-to-earth friends. Sensible, practical, and realistic, ISTPs and ISFPs are both literal and unpretentious, and they usually understand each other quite well. Spontaneous and free-spirited, they rarely have any interest in trying to control other people and want lots of freedom.

In addition to their many similarities, ISTPs and ISFPs are often attracted to each other because of their differences. ISTPs are drawn to the genuine warmth and generosity of ISFPs, who express their devotion and affection in so many verbal and nonverbal ways that ISTPs often feel very loved and nurtured. By contrast, ISFPs are attracted to ISTPs because they are so calm, capable, and quietly confident. ISFPs admire how ISTPs seem to be utterly comfortable in their own skins and able to adapt easily to almost any surrounding.

Because of their differences, ISTPs and ISFPs have the opportunity to help each other grow and develop in important ways. Typically, ISTPs help ISFPs learn not to take everything so personally, which protects them from getting their feelings hurt so often. Many ISFPs say that their partners also help them become more assertive about their needs and less likely to be taken advantage of. For their part, ISFPs help ISTPs understand other people and be more patient and sensitive to their feelings. ISTPs also credit their partners with helping them express themselves and connect on a deeper emotional level.

The Frustrations

The chief source of frustration for most ISTPs and ISFPs stems from their different decision-making styles. ISTPs are very logical, analytical, and objective people who can be quite detached at times. But ISFPs have very personal and oftentimes emotional responses to most things, so ISTPs are sometimes confused and irritated by what they perceive as their partners' high drama and overreactions. ISFPs just as often feel criticized and hurt by their partners' impatience with the depth of their feelings. ISTPs generally aren't comfortable expressing their feelings, fears, or concerns, and when they do demonstrate their affection, it is through actions rather than words. Because ISFPs love to hear how much their partners appreciate them, they often feel left out or hurt when their partners refuse to verbalize. Most ISTPs think that their love is self-evident. They're physically there, they say, and that ought to communicate their commitment. ISFPs, however, take this lack of effusiveness personally, but pressuring their partners to share before they feel genuinely moved to do so is a waste of time and only tends to push them farther away. When ISTPs and ISFPs have an argument or conflict, both tend to withdraw to think things through. ISTPs benefit from the time to consider how they feel, and ISFPs generally find that the solitude helps them calm down and respond more clearly.

Finally, since neither ISTPs nor ISFPs enjoy or do a lot of planning, budgeting, or organizing, they may run late, miss important deadlines, or find themselves struggling with their finances. They don't spend a lot of time anticipating the future or considering alternatives, and they may sometimes be caught unprepared for events. Rather than insist that either of them manage these difficult chores, these couples may benefit from the expertise of qualified professionals.

How to Reach Your ISFP Partner

- Respect your partner's feelings, even if you don't understand them. Never discount these feelings or accuse your partner of overreacting.
- Try to share what you're thinking and feeling. Don't shut your partner out.
- Tell your partner when you need time alone so he or she won't take it personally.
- Be gentle and complimentary. Smile and be affectionate.
- Recognize all the things your partner does to make you happy, and tell your partner when you are happy.
- Do thoughtful things to show your partner you are thinking of him or her. Occasionally bring home treats and romantic surprises.

How to Reach Your ISTP Partner

- Respect your partner's privacy, strong need for freedom, and desire to spend time alone.
- Try not to pressure your partner to share his or her feelings or reactions before he or she is ready.
- Compliment your partner on his or her many skills and talents. Express your appreciation of the ways your partner demonstrates his or her devotion and commitment.
- Resist the urge to nag your partner. Be clear and explicit about things you wish were different, then be quiet and wait for them to change.
- Encourage your partner to pursue his or her interests without you. Give your explicit permission and express your trust in your partner.
- Listen carefully and attentively to your partner. Try to remember that his or her constructive criticism or logical analysis is meant to help you.

ESFP with ESFP

The Joys

Because ESFP couples have all four type preferences in common, they usually enjoy a very easy and fun-filled relationship. ESFPs are generous, supportive, and affectionate people. Like two puppies, ESFPs love to have a good time and are playful, eager to please, and casual. ESFP partners typically understand each other well, since they are both realistic, down-to-earth, and unpretentious. They are also sensitive and sentimental, and they make sympathetic listeners. They are very spontaneous, even impulsive, people who are generally ready and eager at a moment's notice to help each other or a friend.

With so many qualities in common, it's no wonder that ESFPs are often attracted to each other. But ESFP couples usually also have similar blind spots, so they can help each other grow and develop in important ways. For instance, they can help each other slow down and focus more and also follow through on promises and commitments. As they learn to think through the potential implications of their actions together, they may foresee outcomes and avoid mistakes they would ordinarily make. Also, by planning ahead together, they can better manage their money and prepare for the future. In the safety of their relationships, they can practice speaking their minds and dealing more directly with the kinds of problems both prefer to avoid.

The Frustrations

ESFPs have a mutual desire for freedom and as a couple tend to be impulsive and even a bit reckless. Neither likes rules, nor are they particularly impressed by authority. While they are both very fun loving, free-spirited, and spontaneous, they may sometimes get so caught up in the excitement of the moment that they neglect or unintentionally abandon plans and commitments. It is so hard for ESFPs to pin themselves down and eliminate options that they may find themselves over-extended or leaving people they care about hanging. When it comes to making decisions, ESFPs may take so much time to gather information that they miss opportunities or deadlines or have to rush to make decisions at the last minute.

ESFPs also tend to be somewhat skeptical of ideas or approaches with which they have no experience. As a result, they may become pessimistic, have trouble seeing ways to overcome difficulties, or keep making the same mistakes over and over again. They may become frustrated with the fact that they have so much trouble holding on to or budgeting their money, since they both rarely look ahead. When one of the partners is more fiscally conservative than the other, they may struggle over control. In general, ESFPs have little interest in trying to control other people and have even less desire to be controlled. Unless they are both willing to share the responsibility for making and sticking with a budget, they may have arguments about spending.

Another source of frustration for many ESFP couples is that neither partner especially likes to plan ahead or maintain order. They may accuse each other of being sloppy or not taking the initiative in performing household chores. Someone ultimately has to load the dishwasher or fold the laundry, and although one partner may have a stronger desire for neatness than the other, they need to work together to complete these chores without placing an unfair burden on one of them. Instead of always opting for the fun and easy way out, ESFP couples may have to push themselves to work hard and advance their careers.

Far and away the most serious source of frustration for ESFP couples is that neither partner is willing to bring up and honestly discuss problems. ESFPs are very sensitive and eager to please, but they also prefer to tiptoe around conflicts and to avoid discussing the tough topics. Neither partner likes to give or receive criticism, and as a result they may neglect to mention their dissatisfaction and inadvertently threaten the health of their relationships. ESFPs tend to enjoy a very close emotional connection, but they need to be careful not to become too dependent on each other. By doing the hard work of communicating honestly, they can advance as a couple and strengthen their commitment.

Advice for ESFPs

- Support each other in striving for professional development and growth.
- Encourage each other to be independent. Make allowances for each partner to have time alone and personal space.
- Slow down, focus your attention, and be willing to be serious when your partner needs you to be.
- Take time on a regular basis to discuss the status of your relationship. Be honest and direct.
- Admit your insecurities but be willing to take steps to become more independent as individuals.
- Figure out a system to divide up household chores and stick with it.
- Consider hiring a professional financial planner to help you develop a budget and invest for the future.

ESFP with ISFP

The Joys

With three out of four type preferences in common, ESFPs and ISFPs are often great companions and friends. Whatever they are doing captures their full attention, and they throw themselves into life with joyful abandon. For most ESFP and ISFP couples, similar interests give them an important connection, since they value having fun together. Luckily, that's pretty easy to do with two playful, easygoing, and free-spirited people.

ESFPs and ISFPs have much in common besides their temperamental natures. They are relaxed, flexible, and accommodating, and they are happiest when they can respond to the moment rather than plan ahead or lock themselves into something that might preclude a better opportunity. Realistic, sensible, and usually blessed with great common sense, ESFPs and ISFPs pay close attention to details and trust their experiences to guide their actions. Both are naturally warm, gentle, and affectionate and genuinely enjoy making their partners happy. They love being outside and often enjoy many of the same outdoor activities and hobbies. Utterly loyal, ESFPs and ISFPs are very generous and are almost always willing to drop whatever they're doing to help others.

In addition to their shared tendency to be up for anything and their other similarities, ESFPs and ISFPs often are initially attracted to each other because of their one significant difference. ESFPs are drawn to ISFPs because of their calm demeanor. ISFPs are thoughtful, modest, and very sensitive people in whom ESFPs feel they can place their full faith and trust. ISFPs are often attracted to ESFPs because of their charm, high energy, responsiveness, and humor. ISFPs usually like the adventurousness of ESFPs and find themselves easily caught up in the excitement that surrounds them.

ESFPs and ISFPs have the opportunity to help each other grow and develop in important ways. ESFPs are often able to expand ISFPs' horizons and encourage them to become more active and engaged in life. ISFPs often say that their partners make wonderfully patient and enthusiastic teachers. For their part, ISFPs help ESFPs slow down, center themselves, and learn to be more gentle and accepting in their dealings with others. ESFPs credit their partners with helping them to focus and to invest themselves fully in their relationships.

The Frustrations

ESFPs and ISFPs are so casual and easygoing that they sometimes neglect to take deadlines seriously or be as responsible with their commitments as they ought to be. ESFPs, and to a lesser degree ISFPs, are quite impulsive, especially concerning money. They often buy things just to make themselves feel better or to liven things up when life gets too routine or dull. Neither ESFPs nor ISFPs excel at managing finances, so one partner generally takes on the chore of saving and budgeting — and ultimately limiting the spending of the other. Since neither partner likes to be controlled, this can breed resentment in both.

Another frustration ESFP and ISFP couples experience develops because both are prone to putting off in-depth discussions of unpleasant subjects in an effort to avoid hurting each other's feelings. They may hold on to grievances for a long time and may not be as honest or assertive as they need to be with each other and with other people. While they are both very agreeable, they may allow other people to intimidate them. Naturally sensitive, ESFPs and especially ISFPs take criticism or rejection personally and may withdraw rather than speak up and risk confrontation.

Both ESFPs and ISFPs often put off decisions for as long as possible so they can stay open to other options. As a result, they may run late, miss important deadlines, and unintentionally let friends down by failing to commit to plans ahead of time. And as a couple, they sometimes find themselves unprepared due to a lack of planning. Happily, this rarely causes them great stress unless one partner is saddled with an unfair amount of the organizing and winds up feeling unappreciated.

Finally, ESFPs and ISFPs tend to have different needs for social interaction and stimulation. Most ESFPs are happiest when socializing with lots of people. They love meeting new people and have a wide variety of friends and acquaintances. ISFPs have deep and loving friendships, but they tend to have fewer of them and are most comfortable with a smaller group of very close friends. ISFPs also enjoy spending more time alone or quietly with their partners. ESFPs get bored and restless with too much inactivity, while ISFPs are generally content to stay home. This tends to cause friction between them only when one or both partners insist that they do everything together. These playmates are wise to allow for some separation in their relationship.

How to Reach Your ISFP Partner

• Offer physical contact and affection. Express your feelings in words and actions.
• Slow down and really listen to your partner. Don't talk over him or her, and don't interrupt.
• Pay close attention when your partner is talking. Beware of your tendency to be easily distracted.
• Encourage your partner to take the time he or she needs to be alone to process his or her thoughts and feelings. Don't pressure or rush your partner to share before he or she is ready.
• Recognize and praise your partner's efforts to get things done or accomplish a number of tasks.
• Be sure to pull your own weight, and don't neglect your chores.
• Don't pressure your partner into socializing when he or she isn't up to it.

How to Reach Your ESFP Partner

• Try to join your partner in as many social activities as possible. Encourage your partner to attend events without you when you are too tired or not interested.
• Pull your own weight and do your chores willingly and regularly. Actions speak louder than words.
• Speak up for yourself. Don't keep things to yourself for too long.

• Be an enthusiastic listener and supporter of your partner's need to think out loud.
• Surprise your partner. Invite a group of his or her friends over for a spontaneous get-together.

ISFP with ISFP

The Joys

Since ISFPs share all four type preferences, they typically have an easygoing, affectionate, and fun-filled relationship. They find in each other a playmate, lover, and trusted confidant. Although they appear quiet, gentle, and unassuming, they have passionate feelings for their loved ones. ISFPs are sensitive and bighearted people who will do whatever it takes to please and nurture their partners. As a rule, they take life at face value, are adaptable and accepting, and rarely try to pressure or control anyone. Free-spirited and cheerful, most ISFPs enjoy being together, being in nature, and being around animals. They are curious and impulsive, so they enjoy the present moment without a lot of planning or structure.

With so much in common, it's no surprise that ISFPs are often attracted to each other. After all, it feels very comfortable to be so understood, appreciated, and loved. Because they share many of the same blind spots, they have the opportunity to help each other grow and develop in important ways. ISFPs encourage each other to speak their minds, so they aren't as likely to be intimidated or taken for granted by others. They help each other pay more attention to deadlines and generally become more accountable. In the safety of their relationships, they may be better able to offer constructive criticism and to hear it without taking it personally.

The Frustrations

The primary frustration for many ISFP couples is that both are usually so unassertive and want harmony so much that they ignore problems and avoid confrontations for fear of causing their partners pain. They are deeply sensitive and offended by any perceived cruelty or by harsh words. ISFPs get their feelings hurt very easily and are reluctant to speak up or defend themselves or their positions. Both partners tend to retreat and take a long time to get over things that upset them. Without open and frequent communication, one or the other partner may feel confused and isolated. And since both are so disturbed by tension, they may become physically ill if conflicts go on for too long without a peaceful resolution. ISFP couples need to agree to discuss problems frankly and immediately so small issues don't fester and threaten the health of their relationships.

Another frustration for many ISFP couples is that since they both live so completely in the present, they rarely plan ahead or anticipate the future. Although this means they can fully and unabashedly enjoy themselves and find pleasure in everyday experiences, they also can get caught up in the moment and lose track of time. When they suddenly find themselves unprepared or in a crisis, they may become frightened and upset with each other. Since they are prone to indulging in whatever captures their attention or appeals to their immediate desire, they can sometimes have trouble resisting their impulses. For instance, ISFPs are very generous people and are happy to spend their money on fun experiences or spontaneous treats for each other. But they can sometimes undermine each other's attempts to eat more healthfully or exercise more moderation. They may benefit from

the services of a qualified financial adviser to help them make and stick to a household budget.

Finally, ISFPs may experience conflict when one partner strives for more personal or professional growth. ISFPs are, generally, accepting people who choose the path of least resistance, which means they may get in a rut or end up in a dead-end job. Inevitably, someone needs to take a chance, save for the future, or plan for their retirement. Yet when only one partner is responsible for all or most of the planning and follow-through, the balance in the relationship can shift, and this may lead to resentment. ISFPs need to share responsibilities and resolve to revisit plans for the future together so they stay in sync. By staying honest and loving with each other, they can usually manage the transitions of life.

Advice for ISFPs

- Don't compare your relationship to anyone else's or to society's model of what an ideal relationship is.
- Take turns handling the chores neither of you enjoys, such as calling people, following through, and making decisions.
- Encourage each other to participate in activities independently. Allow for some separation.
- Try to plan ahead and stick to your budget so you don't end up unprepared or in financial trouble.
- Be willing to speak honestly and directly about problems as they come up. Don't sacrifice the long-term health of your relationship for temporary peace and harmony.

Chapter 9

Experiencers with Conceptualizers: SPs with NTs

ESTP with ENTJ

The Joys

ESTPs and ENTJs share two type preferences and tend to be energetic, talkative, and active people. They enjoy being out in the world doing things together or socializing with others. ESTPs and ENTJs often are great companions but also are comfortable being apart. Since they are both quite verbal, they enjoy sharing the events of their days and give both compliments and criticism freely. Many ESTP and ENTJ couples find that these regular discussions keep them feeling connected to each other. ESTPs and ENTJs also are logical decision makers who are rarely convinced by anything but sound reasoning, and both are able to make tough decisions when necessary. Many of these couples enjoy the stimulation of debating and the competitive aspect of their relationships. Although ESTPs are more playful, both partners tease and criticize each other without becoming defensive or hurt. Unless they are very stressed, they tend to remain calm, unemotional, and objective even during heated discussions.

In addition to their areas of similarity, ESTPs and ENTJs are often attracted to each other because of their differences. ESTPs often admire the ambition and high standards of ENTJs. They are attracted to ENTJs' quick and creative minds, their independence and leadership, and their confidence and social sophistication. For their part,

ENTJs are drawn to the spontaneity and easygoing, free-spirited attitude of ESTPs. ESTPs seem to be able to transform even mundane, everyday events into adventures. ESTPs draw ENTJs out into the physical world and help them to appreciate its pleasures.

Because of their differences, ESTPs and ENTJs have the opportunity to help each other grow and develop in important ways. Many ESTPs say that their partners help them focus some of their energy, making them less distractible and better able to finish some of the projects they start. ENTJs help ESTPs raise their personal standards and look beyond the moment to the potential implications of their actions. In addition to helping their partners have more fun, ESTPs encourage ENTJs to back up their ideas and opinions with accurate facts and make them more practical. For both ESTPs and ENTJs, developing tact and genuine sensitivity to other people's needs and feelings is an area that requires mutual effort.

The Frustrations

Since neither ESTPs nor ENTJs are especially eager to share their fears or vulnerabilities, they may need to devote serious effort to cultivating a deep and interdependent commitment. When these couples have recurrent issues that cause discontent, ENTJs frequently see patterns more quickly and initiate discussions. The most common source of frustration for ESTPs and ENTJs is their different needs for closure and order. ESTPs are very casual and easygoing people who are generally not bothered by disorder or mess. They take life as it is and rarely sweat the small stuff. By contrast, ENTJs usually need lots of order and neatness and find piles of clean clothes or unwashed dishes irritating. Not that ENTJs actually enjoy housework — they find it boring and repetitious — but they will do it to satisfy their exacting standards and to maintain order. ENTJs tend to bustle around straightening up, while ESTPs may view their resulting stress with amusement.

Another area of frustration is that ENTJs like to plan things out well in advance and generally stick with a chosen strategy. In contrast, ESTPs are very curious and adaptive people and rarely like feeling locked into anything, because they might miss out on whatever interesting options come up. ESTPs often feel that their partners impose too much structure, while ENTJs often feel frustrated by their partners' lack of accountability and commitment.

Another source of frustration for many ESTPs and ENTJs is that while ESTPs are extremely realistic, practical, and pragmatic, ENTJs are focused on the future, love theories, and can be quite inventive. But ESTPs sometimes think that their partners are too abstract and vague, make extravagant claims, or base their opinions on false data. And ENTJs sometimes find ESTPs unimaginative and unwilling to accept anything that can't be proved by experience and facts. Both are naturally competitive and critical, and both enjoy a spirited debate. But if a discussion becomes too intense, they may become more annoyed than amused.

Finally, ESTPs and ENTJs tend to use their free time differently. ESTPs are usually more active and physical, often enjoying sports or outdoor activities. ENTJs often choose more intellectual or challenging professionally related activities. But since both are curious about new experiences, they may enjoy sampling each other's hobbies or interests while still maintaining the freedom to do their own thing.

How to Reach Your ENTJ Partner

- Compliment your partner on his or her professional accomplishments and the many large and daunting projects he or she takes on with skill and confidence.
- Ask your partner's opinion and advice. Never question his or her competence in public.
- Pay attention when your partner is talking about something of interest to him or her. Maintain eye contact rather than scanning the room.
- Don't count on your partner to keep you on schedule, then complain about too many reminders and too much nagging.
- Work at being punctual and accountable. Finish some of the projects you start.

How to Reach Your ESTP Partner

- Respect your partner's need for freedom and encourage him or her to go off and explore at will.
- Be willing to leave tasks unfinished from time to time to take advantage of your partner's adventurous impulses.
- Watch your tendency to have a secret agenda for your partner — things you want accomplished but you may not be clear and explicit about asking for.
- Beware of your tendency to overplan and add too much structure to experiences. Don't nag about messes or unfinished projects.

ESTP with INTJ

The Joys

Because of the one type preference ESTPs and INTJs have in common, they share a preference for objective analysis. Both make decisions that are generally fair and logical, and both tend to be direct, honest, and naturally thick-skinned. They are curious and concerned about underlying principles, respect each other's competence, and are independent. The women in these couples, regardless of their type, feel burdened by social pressures to be nurturing, which may not come naturally or easily to them. If their partners understand and accept this about them, these couples are usually able to devise a fairly egalitarian distribution of labor.

ESTPs and INTJs are most often initially attracted to each other because of their many differences. ESTPs are drawn to INTJs because of their calm, independence, maturity, and intellectual prowess. ESTPs admire INTJs' creativity and their vision to see beyond the moment to forecast future trends. For their part, INTJs are attracted to ESTPs because they are so friendly, outgoing, and energetic. ESTPs bring the party with them wherever they go, and their partners often admire their social ease and wide circle of friends. Life is certainly more fun and exciting with an ESTP around!

Because of their many fundamental differences, ESTPs and INTJs have plenty of opportunities to help each other grow and develop in important ways. ESTPs help their partners relax some of their impossibly high standards by offering them regular doses of reality. ESTPs encourage INTJs to pay more attention to the moment, take some risks, and develop patience for details. As INTJs gain more common sense, their great ideas become more workable. Most INTJs also say that their partners bring laughter and adventure to their lives. For their part, INTJs help their partners focus their considerable energy and become better organized and more accountable. ESTPs credit their INTJ partners with helping them see past the obvious and take an interest in the big picture so they better understand the connections between things. Together, as ESTPs and INTJs become more motivated to improve and deepen their rela-

tionships, they naturally become more sensitive, appreciative, and understanding of each other and other people.

The Frustrations

Since ESTPs and INTJs are so different, there are plenty of potential frustrations. ESTPs have a much stronger need for action and interaction, adventure and fun. But they typically exhaust their more private, reserved, and solitary INTJ partners with their need to be on the go all the time. The sheer amount of talk, activity, and chaos can be difficult for INTJs to take. INTJs are very private, independent, and strong-willed people, but ESTPs sometimes find them stubborn, too serious, and unwilling to have fun. Temperamentally, ESTPs live for and in the moment and usually respond to life at full throttle, often with a "fly by the seat of your pants" attitude. They're easygoing, unflappable, and superadaptive. In contrast, INTJs like to plan things in advance and consider all the possible implications and outcomes, then rarely deviate from their well-considered path. ESTPs often think that INTJs are too stuck inside their own heads, while INTJs may find ESTPs superficial and reckless. So decision making can often create friction for ESTP and INTJ couples. ESTPs need to ask far more questions and gather much more information before making decisions than do their decisive INTJ partners. And INTJs want to think things through carefully before taking action, unlike their more impulsive ESTP partners.

Another source of potential frustration for ESTP and INTJ couples is that while ESTPs are the ultimate realists, INTJs are not. ESTPs are usually interested in tangible things that have practical utility while INTJs are much more interested in theories and abstract concepts. Therefore, ESTP and INTJ couples often find that they don't share a lot of interests. ESTPs rarely have the patience for the depth of INTJs' intellectual pursuits, and most INTJs don't enjoy the highly physical or social activities ESTPs favor. These couples usually find that it makes more sense for them to pursue their own interests while making sure they spend time together participating in activities they both enjoy.

Another common source of frustration is their different needs for neatness. INTJs want order around them, since they find it distracting and irritating to stumble over clutter in their homes. They generally like dinner at a certain time each day and typically want their homes to be clean and presentable. ESTPs are much less concerned about clocks, calendars, deadlines, and neatness. They are among the most distractible of all types, and they often think more is better. ESTPs can easily get carried away with whatever project they are doing and fail to notice the mess they've created or the lateness of the hour. ESTP and INTJ couples also experience conflict over promptness, since ESTPs often run late and INTJs like to be early. So ESTPs feel nagged and controlled, and INTJs feel exasperated and inconvenienced by this conflict. Fortunately, they can apply their shared sense of fairness to come up with a compromise that is comfortable for them both.

Finally, since they often experience difficulty understanding each other and are generally uncomfortable discussing their emotions, they may have trouble communicating in satisfying ways. They need to share their fears and vulnerabilities with each other so they can develop an intimate and lasting connection.

How to Reach Your INTJ Partner

- Respect your partner's need for quiet time alone to think things through in depth.
- Ask for your partner's views on conflicts. Seek out his or her perspective to better understand the causes and dynamics of conflicts.
- Respect your partner's need for predictability, order, and ritual, especially after a busy and taxing day.

- Don't spring things, especially social events, on your partner.
- Be careful not to get overextended by activities outside the home. Protect the quiet time you share with your partner.
- Avoid being critical or flippant. Be sure to take your partner's concerns seriously.
- Try to educate yourself about some of your partner's interests and passions.

How to Reach Your ESTP Partner

- Encourage your partner to get his or her social needs met. Try to participate as much as possible and make sure you encourage your mate to go places without you.
- Make an effort to switch gears. Suggest that you do something spontaneous or surprise your partner.
- Trust and encourage your partner to pursue his or her own interests.
- Share your reactions and thoughts freely. Explain when you need time alone.
- Watch your tendency to be critical and demanding. Don't be condescending and impatient.
- Try to simplify rather than complicate your communication style.

ESTP with ENTP

The Joys

Since ESTPs and ENTPs share three of the four preferences, they have a lot in common. Both are outgoing, friendly, and highly verbal people who like to be around others. They tend to think out loud and maintain a running commentary on what they observe and experience. ESTPs and ENTPs are active people, seldom content to sit on the sidelines and watch the action. These are people who jump in, make things happen, and have fun in the process.

ESTPs and ENTPs enjoy improvising and

responding rather than making and sticking to plans. Impulsive by nature, one of the things they appreciate most about each other is their shared penchant for spontaneity — they're likely to drop whatever they're doing and act on impulse. ESTP and ENTP couples are also rather competitive and enjoy good-natured teasing, since they both see it as entertainment and neither takes it personally. Their competitive spirit can surface in activities such as sports or in their careers. ESTPs and ENTPs are good negotiators, able to make compelling arguments and usually able to see, even if they don't always agree with, their partners' points of view. They are flexible and able to modify their positions when their partners present logical reasons to do so.

ESTPs and ENTPs feel comfortable with each other because of their similarities, but they are often attracted to each other because of their differences. ESTPs are often drawn to ENTPs because of their intellectual perspective, creativity, and ambition. ENTPs are often most attracted to their partners' free-spiritedness, earthiness, and ability to enjoy physical pleasure fully. Because of their differences, ESTPs and ENTPs have the opportunity to help each other grow and develop in important ways. ESTPs can help ENTPs bring realism and practicality to their original ideas. ESTPs also encourage their partners to get out in the real world and enjoy the moment. For their part, ENTPs help their partners look beyond the obvious and the expected to consider alternative solutions to problems.

The Frustrations

Despite their many similarities, there are also some significant differences between these two types, which cause frequent frustrations. While ESTPs live very much in the moment, carefully observing and responding to whatever they are experiencing, ENTPs are more strategic thinkers who contemplate how their experiences relate to other, some-

times future, events. ENTPs love to create alternative ways of doing things and are talented innovators driven by their inspiration. But the more practical, down-to-earth ESTPs may not always see the possibilities and need convincing — in the form of empirical evidence — that these ideas are going to work. When their inspiration is questioned, ENTPs can feel undermined and become resentful. And because ENTPs have such confidence in their ideas and insights, they may be dismissive of their partners' more realistic, though pedestrian, ideas or suggestions. Naturally, this can create resentment in ESTPs. ENTPs also are more adventurous about trying new experiences, especially with regard to travel, whereas ESTPs like physical risks and are more comfortable doing things and visiting places they know.

Both ESTPs and ENTPs are generally willing to raise issues that need discussing. However, neither are particularly good listeners, and they are often less skilled at understanding and dealing with the underlying causes of problems. As a result, discussions may escalate into loud arguments. Both ESTPs and ENTPs can be quite competitive, and when a conflict arises, it is easy for them to slip into an adversarial mode. But once they have vented their feelings, the intensity often subsides quickly, and they can calmly try to solve the problem.

Another frustration for ESTPs and ENTPs is that neither likes to plan ahead or follow through on mundane chores. But in reality, someone has to be responsible for paying the bills, registering the car, and preparing the taxes. Typically, these tasks fall on the one who dislikes them less or on the female partner. In addition, because ESTPs and ENTPs are both drawn to the outside world they run the risk of neglecting each other and their relationships. Being the social and fun-loving people they are, many ESTPs and ENTPs are natural flirts, and although their flirtations are generally harmless, too much of it can inspire jealousy and hurt feelings in their partners. Both need to be careful to rein in their impulsiveness and protect the long-term health of the relationship by putting it first.

How to Reach Your ENTP Partner

• Appreciate and encourage your partner's innovative ideas. Don't undermine them by requiring proof that they'll work.
• Don't respond too quickly. Be willing to give even far-fetched ideas a fair hearing.
• Make an effort to learn about the projects your partner finds fascinating.
• Ask your partner's advice on the implications of actions or how he or she sees the future unfolding.
• Be willing to discuss theories and implications from time to time.

How to Reach Your ESTP Partner

• Respect your partner's high physical needs and offer plenty of tactile stimulation, such as massages, back rubs, and lovemaking.
• Don't be condescending or act superior, and don't dismiss your partner's ideas or suggestions as too simplistic.
• Give your partner plenty of facts and specifics. Show him or her how your suggestions are workable.
• Resist the urge to analyze your partner, tell your partner what's wrong with him or her or tell your partner how he or she can improve.
• Practice listening attentively. Don't immediately suggest ways for your partner to fix his or her problems.
• Try to participate in activities your partner enjoys.

ESTP with INTP

The Joys

ESTPs and INTPs share two of the four type preferences, so they typically have an easygoing and flexible relationship. ESTPs and INTPs are both very adaptable and enjoy responding to life and pursuing whatever piques their curiosity. Neither is especially concerned about structure or driven to make decisions, but ESTPs and INTPs do share a preference for deciding in a logical and objective way. They both speak their minds honestly and can usually receive constructive criticism in the spirit in which it is intended. They also understand each other's essentially autonomous natures and respect each other's core values: for ESTPs it's freedom, and for INTPs it's independence. They are rarely clingy or dependent, they often have different interests and friendships, and they are typically not threatened by spending time apart.

In addition to their similarities, ESTPs' and INTPs' differences are often the source of their initial attraction. ESTPs are drawn to INTPs because of their intellectual intensity, creativity, and offbeat sense of humor. Many ESTPs admire INTPs' original ideas, calm self-assurance and fierce independence. INTPs are often attracted to ESTPs because of their charm, enthusiasm, and social confidence. ESTPs impress INTPs with their adventurousness, good humor, friendliness, and lack of pretense. And INTPs also appreciate ESTPs' realism and down-to-earth attitude.

Because of their differences, ESTPs and INTPs have the opportunity to help each other grow and develop in important ways. ESTPs help INTPs live more in the moment and encourage them to pay closer attention to important details, which helps them be more accurate and less prone to make mistakes. ESTPs encourage INTPs to get out among people and be more physically active. Many INTPs credit their partners with introducing them to experiences they might never have had. For their part, INTPs have a calming and centering effect on ESTPs, who tend to flit from one social activity or project to the next. INTPs help ESTPs see beyond the moment, trust in the viability of possibilities, and fantasize about the future. Many ESTPs say that their partners help them slow down, think before they act, and become a bit less scattered and distracted.

The Frustrations

Despite their many shared characteristics, ESTPs and INTPs also experience common frustrations. One fundamental difference between the two is that the ever-practical ESTPs tend to trust only their own experiences and are skeptical about anything speculative. By contrast, INTPs are most energized by original possibilities and become bored very quickly with anything ordinary or repetitive. It seems to ESTPs that INTPs ignore or refuse to participate in anything that doesn't involve an intellectual challenge, while INTPs think that their partners are unwilling to try unconventional approaches. This difference reveals itself in their communication as well. ESTPs tend to be very literal and specific. They want and give all the details, in the exact order they experienced them. But INTPs focus on the big picture and leap from topic to topic; they may not finish their sentences and can be very abstract and complex. So ESTPs are sometimes frustrated by how vague their partners are, and INTPs are often bored and impatient with how concrete their partners are. And both can be impatient, but INTPs are more often guilty of being condescending. To be sure, INTPs feel frustrated when their partners don't "get it" quickly enough, just as ESTPs are dismissive when they don't immediately see the value of INTPs' sometimes far-fetched ideas.

Another source of frustration for ESTP and INTP couples is their different needs for discus-sion. ESTPs are very expressive and talkative, while INTPs are more private and reflective. ESTPs need a lot of people around them on a daily basis, while INTPs need more time alone and are considerably more selective about their interactions. ESTPs also generally discuss things as they come up, but INTPs often want to think things through first. So ESTPs sometimes feel shut out when INTPs won't share, and INTPs feel that their partners often invade their privacy and force premature discussions.

Because ESTPs and INTPs are so casual and relaxed about rules and order, they may struggle over responsibility for household chores and routine maintenance. Neither likes to feel limited by routine and both tend to procrastinate and leave projects half-finished — ESTPs because they are so easily distracted, and INTPs because they get bored with anything remotely repetitive. They may need to engage their shared sense of fairness to divide chores equitably.

Finally, since neither ESTPs nor INTPs are comfortable sharing their feelings and aren't naturally aware of how other people feel, they can both act insensitively. When their friendly debates become too frequent or continue past the point of fun for either partner, they can turn hurtful. And since neither ESTPs nor INTPs like to feel vulnerable, they may not share their feelings or take the risks necessary to achieve a deep emotional connection.

How to Reach Your INTP Partner

- Respect and protect your partner's privacy and independence. Don't be possessive or constantly question your partner's activities.
- Don't intrude on your partner when he or she needs time alone to think or work on his or her ideas or projects.
- Appreciate and compliment your partner on his or her many great ideas and original innovations.

- Don't pressure your partner to accompany you to social events. Check with your partner before inviting people home.
- Listen carefully and attentively when your partner is talking. Don't interrupt or finish his or her sentences. (A brief period of silence doesn't always mean your partner is really finished.)
- Never publicly question your partner's competence or put your partner on the spot.
- Slow down and spend quiet time with your partner.

How to Reach Your ESTP Partner

- Participate in as many social activities with your partner as you can. When you aren't in the mood, encourage your partner to go without you.
- Share your thoughts and ideas. Discuss the events of your day, include your partner in your projects, and invite your partner to tell you about his or her day.
- Watch your tendency to get lost in your work or inside your head. Take a break and go have some fun with your partner.
- Compliment your partner on tangible things such as looks and the many things he or she does to make your home more comfortable or your life more fun.
- Be specific and clear. Let your partner know when you are changing subjects. Try not to skip over important details.

ISTP with ENTJ

The Joys

ISTPs and ENTJs have one of the four type preferences in common, giving them a shared desire for logic and a need to understand the principles at work around them. ISTPs and ENTJs connect best on an intellectual level, and both are direct, honest, and emotionally self-contained. They like to analyze issues objectively and rarely get their feelings hurt from the free give-and-take of constructive criticism. They appreciate and respect each other's drive for competence and are supportive of one another's need for independence.

In addition to their shared approach to decision making, ISTPs and ENTJs are often initially attracted because of their many differences. ISTPs are drawn to ENTJs because of their great confidence, energy, and enthusiasm. ENTJs often dazzle ISTPs with their quick minds, brilliant ideas, and ability to convince other people to participate in their plans. ISTPs admire ENTJs' ability to get big projects started and their decisive and organized ways of getting things done. ENTJs are often attracted to ISTPs' easygoing, calm, and casual natures and their down-to-earth realism. ENTJs also admire ISTPs' natural understanding of the physical world and their ability to have fun without a lot of planning or fuss.

Because of their many differences, ISTPs and ENTJs have the opportunity to help each other grow and develop in important ways. ISTPs are able to help ENTJs pay closer attention to important details, facts, and steps so they can make their many ideas more workable. ISTPs also help ENTJs slow down and enjoy the present moment instead of always planning for or dreaming about the future. Many ENTJs say that their ISTP partners encourage them to ask more questions, release some of their control over their surroundings, and make their standards more realistic. For their part, ENTJs are often able to help ISTPs follow through on projects and commitments, raise their personal standards, and become more accountable. Many ISTPs credit their partners with helping them try unconventional approaches, be more open to possibilities, and be more willing to share some of their reactions and thoughts with other people.

The Frustrations

While most ISTP and ENTJ couples have many opportunities for growth, they nonetheless experience frequent frustrations that stem from their differences. ISTPs are very private and independent, while ENTJs are very verbal and social. ISTPs often feel intruded on or pressured to participate in social experiences, while ENTJs often feel cut off from their partners and in need of an infusion of energy from other people. Many ISTP and ENTJ couples enjoy outdoor experiences together, since these activities provide opportunities to be both active and quiet.

Another area of frustration for ISTPs and ENTJs is their different ways of noticing the world around them. ISTPs are generally very observant and attuned to details, while ENTJs notice things that are out of the ordinary and the connections between them. Communication can be a challenge, since ISTPs tend to be literal and sequential, going step-by-step and being accurate with facts, while ENTJs focus on the big picture, leap from idea to idea, and can be complex and abstract. So, ISTPs often find ENTJs vague and confusing, and ENTJs think that ISTPs are too concrete and unimaginative. ISTPs also consider ENTJs' fantasies about the future a waste of time, while ENTJs are frustrated by ISTPs' skepticism and mistrust of anything unproved or novel.

The biggest source of conflict for most ISTP and ENTJ couples is their different needs for order and closure. ISTPs are very casual and relaxed people who resist too much structure because it limits their ability to be spontaneous. ENTJs, on the other hand, like to impose order when there is none because it gives them a sense of calm and predictability. ENTJs like working first and playing later, if there's time, while ISTPs find fun in everyday experiences and are much less serious about deadlines, clocks, and calendars. So ISTPs sometimes think that their partners are too bossy and control-ling, just as ENTJs consider their partners too irresponsible and impulsive. ISTP and ENTJ couples often struggle to achieve a fair distribution of household tasks and to establish a standard for how much each person should be contributing to the relationship.

These couples also have different drives to make decisions, which can cause frustration. ISTPs are very curious people who like to gather a lot of information before making decisions while ENTJs are usually very decisive and uncomfortable leaving things up in the air for any length of time.

Finally, because neither ISTPs nor ENTJs are especially eager or comfortable sharing their feelings, fears, or vulnerabilities, they may not spend the time needed to build a strong emotional connection. Neither likes to be needy or dependent, so they may have to work hard to foster the closeness they may want but are afraid to risk asking for.

How to Reach Your ENTJ Partner

- Use words; your partner really needs to hear verbally how much you appreciate and love him or her.
- Compliment your partner on his or her achievements and competence.
- Share your thoughts and reactions freely. If you need time to mull something over, say so instead of sitting silently and not responding.
- Try to finish projects you start. Strive to be prompt.
- Respect your partner's schedules, rituals, and routines, and try not to disrupt them.

How to reach your ISTP Partner

- Respect your partner's need for privacy and solitude. Don't interrupt or talk too much.
- Try to allow for unstructured time with your partner to relax and enjoy each other's company without an agenda or timetable.
- Be willing to let the small stuff go and not nag

your partner to complete chores or account for his or her spare time.

- Encourage your partner to spend time alone and not feel pressured to accompany you to every social function. When your partner does participate, make sure to introduce him or her to interesting people.

- Give your partner time to think about important issues or concerns before expecting to discuss them. Write notes.

ISTP with INTJ

The Joys

ISTPs and INTJs share two of the four type preferences, so they frequently have a similar need for privacy and a common analytical decision-making style. ISTPs and INTJs tend to be quiet, self-contained people who share a desire for personal freedom and autonomy. As a couple, they understand and encourage each other to explore their individual interests without the pressure many other couples experience to do things together. ISTPs and INTJs are also logical, analytical, and curious about the underlying principles at work in the world. They tend to be able to give and receive constructive criticism and because they're so naturally objective, they rarely get their feelings hurt or succumb to emotional outbursts.

In addition to their similarities, ISTPs and INTJs often are initially attracted to each other because of their differences. ISTPs are drawn to INTJs because of their originality and nonconformist thinking. ISTPs also admire INTJs' creativity and ability to see possibilities, as well as their high personal and professional standards. ISTPs have great respect for INTJs' focused energy, ambition, and confidence. INTJs are often drawn to ISTPs because of their adventurousness, flexibility, and amazing ability to adapt to almost any situation. INTJs admire ISTPs' easygoing style

and ability to have fun, and they see their partners as their connection to the world.

Because of their differences, ISTPs and INTJs have the opportunity to help each other grow and develop in important ways. ISTPs keep INTJs from becoming too preoccupied or single-minded and instead get out and participate in society. INTJs say that their partners help them see the realities of life around them and get them to relax and enjoy the present moment. For their part, INTJs help ISTPs see the big picture, understand the connections between things, and explore issues in greater depth. Many ISTPs credit their partners with encouraging them to raise their standards, become more ambitious, and follow through on more of the projects they start.

The Frustrations

Despite their areas of similarity, ISTPs and INTJs sometimes experience frustrations that stem from their differences. They frequently have misunderstandings because they communicate in different ways and focus on very different kinds of information. ISTPs are extremely realistic, practical, and pragmatic, while INTJs are imaginative, conceptual, and focused on creative possibilities. So ISTPs sometimes find INTJs too vague and abstract, and INTJs find ISTPs too literal and specific. ISTPs rarely trust things with which they have no experience and instead prefer a hands-on approach to life. They are often skeptical about INTJs' many theories and ideas. Most INTJs also are skeptical, but once a concept is proved to be logically sound, they tend to embrace it even if it has no practical utility. As a result, ISTPs sometimes think that their partners are too focused on the future and find many of their ideas outlandish or implausible. INTJs are dispirited by their partners' need to immediately point out the factual errors in their visions or dismiss their potential.

Another common area of frustration for many ISTP and INTJ couples is their clearly different needs for order and closure. ISTPs usually view the clutter around them as resources — something they may never use but like to have around just in case. Most INTJs have a characteristically strong need for order and are happiest when things are settled and decided and their environments are free of distracting clutter. ISTPs think that their partners are obsessive about throwing things away and are constantly nagging them to tidy up, and INTJs often feel frustrated by the chaos their partners generate and their inability to pick up after themselves.

ISTPs and INTJs also have different needs for making plans in advance. ISTPs essentially take life as it comes, rolling with the inevitable punches. They are very adaptable and ready at a moment's notice to take advantage of any opportunity that piques their curiosity. They try to keep their options open for as long as possible and avoid getting locked into plans that prevent them from following their impulses. By contrast, INTJs are very deliberate and don't want their rituals and routines disrupted. INTJs often push ISTPs for decisions and are maddened by their partners' tendency to procrastinate, change their minds, or fail to follow through on their commitments. When pressed, many ISTPs will agree to a plan but will ultimately do whatever they want anyway. These irrepressible free spirits are rarely controlled or limited for very long.

Finally, both ISTPs and INTJs may need to consciously work at communicating their feelings to each other. Since neither is comfortable sharing their fears, worries, or vulnerabilities, they may have trouble establishing intimacy with their partners. Taking the time to express their affection, leave notes, or do thoughtful things for each other will reinforce their commitment and strengthen their emotional connection.

How to Reach Your INTJ Partner

- Listen attentively to your partner's theories and ideas. Be patient with his or her sometimes convoluted or complex explanations.
- Try to be prompt and follow through on the projects you start.
- Avoid changing plans abruptly or changing your mind after you and your partner have agreed on a course of action.
- Respect your partner's need for order and routine. Try not to disrupt your mate's schedule or dismiss his or her need for predictability.
- Compliment your partner's creativity and innovative solutions. Never question your partner's competence publicly.

How to Reach Your ISTP Partner

- Respect your partner's need for physical adventure and the opportunity to take risks.
- Provide the facts in a step-by-step way. Don't skip around or leave out important details.
- Try not to lecture or give intellectual dissertations. Be clear and direct.
- Be willing to experiment and try some of the physical experiences your partner suggests. Accompany your mate in as many activities as possible or encourage him or her to go without you.
- Don't fence your partner in. Relax and try to have fun in the moment.
- Watch your insistence on always being right. Be willing to admit when you're wrong or don't know the answer. Apologize when you make a mistake.

ISTP with ENTP

The Joys

The two type preferences ISTPs and ENTPs share give them a relaxed and casual attitude about life as well as a similar way of making decisions. Both are naturally spontaneous and adaptable people who enjoy following their impulses to experience as much of the world as they can. ISTPs and ENTPs tend to have fun at every opportunity and rarely stand on ceremony or worry too much about what others think of them. Easygoing, playful, and irreverent, they respect each other's independence and have little need to control or pressure their partners to do anything they don't want to do. ISTPs and ENTPs are also analytical people who value directness, honesty, and sound logical reasoning. They can and do tease each other and offer constructive criticism without either partner taking offense or getting their feelings hurt.

In addition to their similarities, ISTPs and ENTPs are often initially attracted to each other because of their differences. ISTPs typically find ENTPs to be very clever, funny, and charming. Many ISTPs admire how at ease and confident their partners are in almost any setting and are impressed with their quick minds and almost limitless creative energy. ENTPs are attracted to ISTPs because they're so down-to-earth and unpretentious. ISTPs exude a quiet confidence and often possess impressive technical know-how. ENTPs also like ISTPs' utter calm and unflappability, especially under pressure or in a crisis.

Because of their differences, ISTPs and ENTPs have the opportunity to help each other grow and develop in important ways. ISTPs help ENTPs slow down and focus some of their energy so they can become more selective about where they apply their many talents. ENTPs credit their partners with helping them pay closer attention to important details and realities so their ideas will ultimately be more workable. For their part, ENTPs help ISTPs look beyond the obvious and broaden their horizons. ISTPs say that their partners encourage them to make connections and look for underlying meaning. ENTPs also get ISTPs out in the world socially and infuse their lives with energy and intellectual stimulation.

The Frustrations

Despite their many similarities, ISTPs and ENTPs have some significant and fundamental differences. For instance, their temperaments are quite different. ISTPs are free spirits, while ENTPs tend to be more curious intellectuals. ISTPs subscribe to a "live and let live" philosophy and are curious about the physical world, while ENTPs constantly strive for increased mastery and are much more fascinated by the cerebral world of psychology and personal politics. ENTPs enjoy talking about possibilities and concepts, while ISTPs often become bored and restless when the subject is less than practical or concrete. ISTPs are sometimes frustrated by the theoretical discussions ENTPs love, and ENTPs sometimes feel that the subjects ISTPs prefer are too literal and pedestrian to interest them. Because the different ways they notice the world are in direct opposition to each other, the two types seldom see issues or events the same way. ISTPs tend to hold conservative views and are expressly concerned about people taking personal responsibility for themselves, while ENTPs typically have more liberal social views when they are young and often become more politically conservative with age. Regardless, politics in general is endlessly fascinating to most ENTPs but rarely holds much interest for ISTPs.

Another common source of frustration for ISTP and ENTP couples stems from their different social needs. ISTPs are very private people who need and want lots of time alone. They like to have plenty of opportunities to engage their bodies or pursue their active projects without interruption or input from other people. In contrast, ENTPs are very social and typically have a wide and varied circle of friends and associates. ENTPs become bored and distracted if required to spend any extended period alone and are almost always eager for some spontaneous social interaction. ENTPs tend to think out loud and love a spirited conversation, while ISTPs tend to be people of action but few words. ISTPs are sometimes frustrated by their partners' incessant chatter and questions, just as ENTPs tend to wither when they don't get enough interaction or are shut out of their partners' lives. Since ISTPs speak quietly and usually say things only once, ENTPs who are busy or distracted may miss important information. Although both ISTPs and ENTPs respect each other's autonomy, they may need to work hard to establish and maintain a close emotional connection. It may be difficult for them to admit their fears or vulnerabilities, but they may have to make that a priority if they are to create a deep and lasting commitment.

How to Reach Your ENTP Partner

- Listen with enthusiasm and interest to your partner's stories and express support for his or her many ideas.
- Compliment your partner on his or her quick thinking and clever connections.
- Resist the urge to point out factual errors in your partner's inspirations or throw cold water on them.
- Express yourself in words. Make an attempt to tell your partner what you're thinking or what happened during your day.
- Be willing to participate in some of your partner's many social events. Encourage your partner to go anyway when you're too tired or not interested.
- Consider some of the more unusual suggestions your partner makes. Be willing to trust your partner's hunches and instincts.

How to Reach Your ISTP Partner

- Slow down and explain your ideas and plans clearly. Go step-by-step, and don't skip important facts.

- Try to identify when you are changing subjects or making a big transition.
- Strive to get your facts straight and be accurate.
- Don't pressure your partner to accompany you to all the social events you wish to attend. When your mate does accompany you, be sure to introduce him or her to people with similar interests.
- Make it easy for your partner to opt out of social activities when he or she is too tired. Be willing to stay home and spend quiet time with your partner.
- Respect your partner's private nature. Don't share personal information about your partner or your relationship with others unless your mate gives you permission.
- Compliment your partner on his or her great common sense. Look for the thoughtful actions and gestures he or she makes to demonstrate his or her affection.
- Try to develop an interest in your partner's hobbies and participate whenever he or she wants you to, even if it's just watching a TV program together.

ISTP with INTP

The Joys

Since ISTPs and INTPs share three of the four type preferences, they tend to have a very comfortable and easygoing relationship. Typically quiet, casual, and private people, they usually give each other plenty of space and time alone to pursue their own interests, friendships, and projects. Calm and independent, ISTPs and INTPs often understand each other easily and describe their relationships as egalitarian and low-key. Since both partners are relatively thick-skinned, they don't take criticism personally. Neither needs a lot of social stimulation, and both are happiest when they are able to follow their own impulses and inspirations without a lot of fuss, planning, or hurry.

Not surprisingly, ISTPs and INTPs are often initially attracted to each other because of their many similarities. But they also are drawn to each other because of their different ways of noticing the world around them. ISTPs often find INTPs' intellectual curiosity, quirky sense of humor, and quick thinking appealing. They also admire INTPs' originality, creativity, and frequently brilliant minds. INTPs are often attracted to ISTPs because of their common sense, levelheadedness, and pragmatism. Many INTPs find the adventurousness of ISTPs exciting and stimulating.

Because of their differences, ISTPs and INTPs have the opportunity to help each other grow and develop in important ways. ISTPs help INTPs try some new physical or outdoor activities. INTPs credit their ISTP partners with helping them be more in the present moment, pay closer attention to some of the important and relevant details of life, and generally have more fun. For their part, INTPs are often able to help ISTPs look beyond the obvious and notice the greater, more far-reaching implications of their actions. ISTPs say that their partners bring added depth to and understanding of the subtleties of events. Both ISTPs and INTPs can, through time and a willingness to deepen their relationships, gain more sensitivity to their own needs and feelings as well as those of others.

The Frustrations

Although ISTPs and INTPs often make great companions, they sometimes get so self-involved that they fail to connect emotionally or spend much quality time sharing their thoughts and feelings with each other. Neither ISTPs nor INTPs are outwardly warm or affectionate people, and since neither partner tends to need or want a lot of emotional intimacy, they can become more like roommates than lovers. They need to be sure they don't get so focused on their own interests that they fail to take the time to become actively involved in their partners' lives. ISTPs and INTPs also tend to be somewhat oblivious to the needs and feelings of others. They may need to consciously work at expressing appreciation and find ways of regularly demonstrating their affection for their partners. Although the tacit understanding between them may be sufficient most of the time, their relationship will be enriched by the efforts they make to understand each other better and connect emotionally.

Since ISTPs and INTPs tend not to be especially tactful or expressive, they can be somewhat abrupt or curt. Likewise, their tendency to be ultracasual about almost everything can seem to be a lack of concern or caring. And although they can appreciate constructive criticism, when it becomes too frequent or negative, it makes both partners feel unappreciated. Rather than discussing irritations or frustrations as they come up, both partners tend to keep their feelings and reactions private. As a result, they may stew in silence and later explode in anger.

Another potential frustration for ISTPs and INTPs is that neither partner is inclined to plan things in advance or impose a lot of external order, so they may find their lives becoming chaotic and their homes inundated with clutter. Also, they both like to gather lots of information before making decisions, but they may procrastinate about making big purchases or decisions or find themselves under great pressure when important deadlines loom. They often run late, neglect to finish the projects they begin, and criticize each other for things left undone.

Finally, ISTPs and INTPs may not completely understand or be enthusiastic about their partners' projects. For the most part, ISTPs get involved with experiences that are too repetitious to engage INTPs' imaginations, and INTPs are fascinated by topics that are too abstract or theoretical for most

ISTPs. Both partners tend to grow restless when trying to listen to or participate in each other's activities. It is very important that they strike a balance between doing their own things and being actively involved in each other's lives.

How to Reach Your INTP Partner

- Be willing to learn about your partner's projects so you can share that important part of his or her life.
- Compliment your partner on his or her innovative ideas and original take on things.
- Tell your partner you appreciate the ways he or she brings new meaning or variety to your life.
- Don't assume your partner knows how you feel or what you think. Try to express yourself verbally or in writing.
- Let your partner help you apply his or her creativity to solving your problems.

How to Reach Your ISTP Partner

- Encourage your partner's physical pursuits and interests. Try to participate in as many of them as you can.
- Try to focus on the here and now and pay attention to the experiences of the moment. Listen fully and completely when your partner is telling you something important.
- Compliment your partner on his or her ability to bring fun and adventure to your life.
- Show your partner that you appreciate him or her by doing thoughtful things to make life easier. Make a nice meal or surprise your partner with a special treat.
- Watch your tendency to act superior or condescending.
- Be physically available to your partner. Offer back rubs and spontaneous lovemaking.

ESFP with ENTJ

The Joys

Because ESFPs and ENTJs share one of the four type preferences, they are typically high-energy, active, sociable people who enjoy the company of others. Many ESFP and ENTJ couples have very busy lives with full professional and personal schedules. Both are friendly and talkative people who think out loud and enjoy discussing their days and sharing both important and trivial events.

As with many couples, their differences are often the source of their initial attraction. ESFPs are drawn to the calm, capable confidence of ENTJs. They admire ENTJs' willingness to take on big challenges and their ability to organize complicated projects and come up with creative solutions to almost any problem. ENTJs are usually staunch supporters of their ESFP partners' efforts and professional accomplishments. ENTJs are drawn to ESFPs' great warmth, generosity, and fun-loving nature. They appreciate ESFPs' zest for life and are comforted by their capacity for nurturing. ESFPs are eager to please their partners and often find lots of small, thoughtful ways to demonstrate their affection.

Because of their many differences, ESFPs and ENTJs have the opportunity to help each other grow and develop in important ways. ESFPs help their driven and career-focused partners to slow down and take time to enjoy the moment. This enables ENTJs to be better listeners and pay more attention to their families and personal relationships. ESFPs also help ENTJs become more aware of their own feelings and better articulate their fears and vulnerabilities. For their part, ENTJs help their ESFP partners be more assertive and articulate when speaking their minds. ESFPs say that their partners help them to become more organized and productive and to see the big picture rather than getting lost in the details.

The Frustrations

Because ESFPs and ENTJs are different in so many ways, they may experience frustration and conflict. ESFPs tend to put their personal lives ahead of their professional ones. They are always ready and eager to drop what they're doing to help a friend or participate in some fun activity. ENTJs, by contrast, have a very strong work ethic and take a dim view of what they consider to be the frivolous activities of their partners. ENTJs work first and play later, and they expect everyone else to do the same. ESFPs' naturally casual attitude toward just about everything can be a source of irritation for their partners. For their part, ESFPs may consider their partners' high standards both excessively demanding and unrealistic. And since many ENTJs place such a high value on their professional achievements, their partners and families may feel neglected and resentful.

ESFPs and ENTJs also have very different ways of expressing their feelings and making decisions. ESFPs react emotionally and have a strong need for harmony and intimacy in their relationships. They want their partners to listen supportively and be willing to share themselves fully. ENTJs are more detached and logical. They rarely have much patience for other people's feelings and want to solve problems quickly. ESFPs tend to be very sensitive, so what their partners intend as constructive suggestions often feels like personal criticism. ENTJs may inadvertently hurt their partners' feelings or dismiss them as overreactions, and ESFPs may hold on to disappointments or hurt feelings and become moody.

Another area of frustration for these couples stems from their different needs for order and planning. ESFPs live in the present moment, rarely consider the future, and like to be free to respond to the opportunities of the day. They love surprises and are usually delighted by unexpected guests. In contrast, ENTJs like to have a plan for the day, the month, and even the year. They enjoy their own rituals and routines and usually don't like interruptions or sudden changes. ENTJs also like order, so they find clutter and disorganization in their homes very distracting and irritating. While ESFPs like their homes to be clean, they are generally more interested in making sure they are warm, comfortable places to be and are less bothered by messes.

ESFPs are very curious people who need a lot of information before making decisions, especially important ones. ENTJs are superdecisive, take-charge people, so they tend to make speedy and absolute decisions. So ESFPs often feel that they are being controlled or rushed, while ENTJs feel exasperated by the number of loose ends and the agonizing their partners go through before making even small decisions. ESFP and ENTJ couples need to strike a fair balance and find a loving compromise to avoid unending struggles.

How to Reach Your ENTJ Partner

- Try to be prompt and where you say you will be. Keep promises or call when you're going to be late.
- Give your partner as much notice as you can before changing plans or inviting people over.
- Ask for your partner's advice, then listen respectfully.
- Appreciate your partner's professional endeavors and compliment him or her on his or her achievements.
- Be calm and clear in your communication. Try not to overreact or repeat yourself.
- Strive to follow through on projects and finish things you start.

How to Reach Your ESFP Partner

- Listen, listen, and listen some more! Resist the urge to point out reasons for problems or try to fix things immediately.
- Be patient and gentle. Accentuate the positive and express your feelings.

- Appreciate the many ways your partner nurtures you and makes your life easier and more fun.
- Be physically attentive to your partner. Pay close attention when he or she is talking.
- Try to adapt to and participate in some of the adventures your partner suggests.
- Surprise your partner by doing something spontaneous and fun.

ESFP with INTJ

The Joys

Because ESFPs and INTJs have no type preferences in common, they are often intrigued by their differences and have interesting and exciting relationships. But they also face significant challenges and may have to work hard to understand each other. ESFPs are often initially attracted to INTJs because of their independence, creativity, and calm and logical reactions. INTJs tend to be ambitious and have a clear plan for the future. ESFPs admire how organized and self-disciplined their partners are and how they pour themselves into their chosen fields of study or work. ESFPs also respect and admire INTJs' intellect and ability to make creative and unexpected connections. INTJs are often attracted to ESFPs' warmth, energy, and love of life. ESFPs are generous, nurturing, and eager to please, and INTJs often feel loved and cared for in a way they never have before. INTJs also admire the way ESFPs are loved by so many people, and they appreciate how down-to-earth, unpretentious, and naturally sensitive they are to others.

Because ESFPs and INTJs are so different, they have many opportunities to help each other grow and develop in important ways. Specifically, ESFPs help INTJs pay closer attention to the joys and beauty of the world around them and appreciate the gifts of other people and nature. Serious and focused, INTJs say that their partners pull them out of the worlds inside their heads to participate in fun activities or exciting adventures. INTJs often credit their partners with encouraging them to express their feelings and let other people help them rather than trying to solve all their problems themselves. For their part, INTJs help ESFPs focus some of their energy and attention so they are more likely to follow through on commitments. INTJs also help ESFPs slow down, be more objective, and anticipate future needs instead of just diving headlong into things. And ESFPs often say that their partners provide them with stability, calm, and a plan for the future.

The Frustrations

Despite their many opportunities for mutual growth, ESFPs and INTJs have some significant differences, which result in frequent frustrations. ESFPs are essentially easygoing, adaptive, playful, and freedom-loving people who like to live fully in the present moment. In contrast, INTJs are quiet, ambitious, and intellectual people who strive to find, meet, and exceed ever-increasing challenges. Therefore, ESFPs and INTJs often have different interests and goals. ESFPs are very social people who have lots of friends and want to spend most of their time having fun with the people they care about. INTJs are considerably more private and maintain a smaller group of companions who usually share their professional interests. ESFPs are very verbal, while INTJs carefully think through their ideas and reactions before discussing them. So ESFPs sometimes feel lonely and shut out of their partners' lives, and INTJs often feel crowded and interrupted by small talk. ESFPs often complain that their partners spend too much time working, and INTJs think that their partners spend too much time with other people and projects outside the home.

Another area of difference is that ESFPs focus on the present, the facts, and the realities of life, while INTJs focus on the future, its possibilities and implications. In conversations, ESFPs tend to overwhelm INTJs with too many details, especially when discussing other people, and INTJs for their part are often vague, abstract, or too complicated to understand. ESFPs ask a lot of questions but may not wait for their partners to answer before interrupting and asking more questions. INTJs tend to become particularly impatient when their partners don't instantly make the cognitive connections apparent to them.

But typically, the most profound frustration for ESFPs and INTJs stems from their different ways of making decisions. ESFPs are guided by their strong personal values and desire to please others. They usually have emotional reactions and are very sensitive to criticism and rejection. INTJs are objective, logical, and analytical in their decision making. They have very high standards, tend to be critical and demanding, and are so thick-skinned that they rarely understand their partners' reactions. To be sure, INTJs can be dismissive or impatient when their partners are greatly affected by the stresses and disappointments of everyday life. While INTJs are sometimes blunt and tactless, they are nonetheless truthful and direct. ESFPs are so careful not to hurt other people's feelings that they may avoid frank and truthful discussions or don't speak up about their needs. In their desire to accommodate and restore harmony, ESFPs may be less than totally honest or make promises and commitments they can't fulfill.

Finally, ESFPs and INTJs tend to struggle with issues of control, order, and decision making. ESFPs like to leave their options open, while INTJs like a predictable plan and an efficiently run home. ESFPs often begin projects they don't finish and may have trouble making decisions. While ESFPs are prone to procrastination, INTJs tend to make snap judgments and can be stubborn and inflexible. ESFPs don't like their partners' tendency to

pressure them into making decisions, and INTJs don't like to leave things up in the air or to have plans change suddenly. ESFPs and INTJs often need to find a compromise between these two extremes so they aren't constantly clashing and don't lead entirely separate lives.

How to Reach Your INTJ Partner

- Give your partner time alone to relax and unwind, especially after a busy day.
- Don't pressure your partner to participate in social activities more than he or she wants to.
- Respect your partner's routines and rituals. Don't disrupt or interfere with them.
- Be willing to commit to a plan of action and not make sudden changes or back out at the last minute because something more fun comes up. Follow through on your promises.
- Never tease your partner or question his or her knowledge or competence in public.
- Listen respectfully and attentively when your partner talks. Don't interrupt or finish his or her sentences.
- Explain when you really need your partner to listen supportively. Tell your mate that the issue is important to you and ask him or her to wait before criticizing or finding flaws in your thinking.
- Try to be calm and clear in your arguments. Present your thoughts logically, don't repeat yourself, and try not to give an excessive amount of detail.

How to Reach Your ESFP Partner

- Listen attentively and supportively when your partner is sharing his or her feelings with you. Focus on the details and remember important information about people.
- Watch your tendency to be impatient, dismissive, and critical. Don't say that your partner's feelings don't make sense.

- Be willing to stop what you're doing and participate in some of the social or spontaneous activities your partner enjoys. Encourage your partner to attend events without you if you can't accompany him or her.
- Share your feelings with your partner. Resist your tendency to work everything out privately without your partner's help or input.
- Express your appreciation of and devotion to your partner. Tell your mate that he or she makes you happy.
- Make a clear distinction between your partner's behavior (which you may not like) and how much you care about your partner as a person.
- Make sure your partner feels free to enjoy his or her friends and social activities even if you don't wish to participate. Don't limit your partner's freedom.

ESFP with ENTP

The Joys

ESFPs and ENTPs share two of the four type preferences and tend to have easygoing and energetic relationships. They are active, outgoing people who have a lot of friends and acquaintances and who thrive on the stimulation they derive from being around other people. ESFPs and ENTPs also are flexible, are able to adapt to life's ups and downs, and usually get along well even when under stress. Good companions and friends, they are somewhat impulsive, ready to respond to fun or exciting opportunities that present themselves spontaneously.

In addition to their areas of commonality, ESFPs and ENTPs are often attracted to each other because of their differences. ESFPs are drawn to ENTPs because of their wit, charm, creativity, and stunning personal confidence. ESFPs are impressed with ENTPs' quick thinking and ability to improvise and see beyond what other people think is possible. ENTPs are often attracted to ESFPs because of their genuine warmth and deep concern for others, their relaxed style, and their naturally adventurous spirit. ENTPs like that their ESFP partners are perpetually ready and willing to help other people and nurture their partners in many thoughtful and sensual ways.

Because of their many differences, ESFPs and ENTPs have the opportunity to help each other grow and develop in important ways. ESFPs are able to help ENTPs better understand the needs and feelings of others. ENTPs often credit their partners with helping them become more compassionate and less competitive. As they focus more of their attention on the details of the present, they may find they make fewer mistakes and enjoy the beauty of the moment. ENTPs can help their partners become more assertive and independent of other people's opinions. ESFPs often say that their partners encourage them to stand up for themselves and to accept constructive criticism without taking it personally. ENTPs also help ESFPs look ahead so they are better prepared for the future.

The Frustrations

Despite their similarities, ESFPs and ENTPs are different in significant ways, one of which is their temperamental values. ESFPs are the ultimate realists, while ENTPs are dreamers and schemers. ESFPs are content to live in the present moment and enjoy it, while ENTPs are excited by possibilities and are always recruiting others to help them bring their many innovations to life. ESFPs sometimes grow weary of their partners' inattention to the moment, just as ENTPs find it frustrating that their partners don't respond enthusiastically to all of their many brainstorms. ESFPs enjoy repeating pleasurable experiences, while ENTPs are bored by repetition and are eager to start their next great venture. Communication can be a source of frustration, because ESFPs generally need accurate details presented in a step-by-step manner, while

ENTPs want a quick summary of the highlights so they can figure out the implications. When ESFPs and ENTPs argue over money, it is often because neither are especially good at budgeting and both tend to be impulsive spenders.

Another area of frustration for many ESFP and ENTP couples is their different decision-making processes. ESFPs are very sensitive, often emotional, and persuaded by the needs of others. They are easily hurt by a sharp tone or a dismissive comment. In contrast, ENTPs are convinced by logical and airtight reasoning and typically have a much thicker skin. ENTPs like nothing better than to debate subjects, and they love to play the devil's advocate on almost any issue. ESFPs find this stressful and dispiriting, since they can rarely outmaneuver their ENTP partners. When they are in an argument, ESFPs will frequently capitulate in favor of reestablishing harmony, holding their ground only if the issue is truly important to them. ESFPs often feel that their partners are more concerned with winning the argument than sharing their heartfelt views. ENTPs generally think that their partners take things way too personally. ESFPs do well to remember that ENTPs live to shake things up and get enormous intellectual stimulation from discussing change and controversy. And ENTPs need to keep from getting so caught up in the thrill of competition that they trounce their partners' feelings just to score a point.

How to Reach Your ENTP Partner

- Listen enthusiastically and supportively to your partner's many ideas, innovations, and suggestions.
- Try to step back and look at the big picture. Ask your partner to point out potential implications.
- Beware of your tendency to acquiesce, feel resentful, and later say "I told you so" when you feel you've been taken for granted.
- Stand up for yourself and speak your mind. Take some time to collect and organize your

thoughts so you'll feel prepared to effectively and calmly argue your position.
- Offer your insights about people's feelings as a way of helping your partner increase his or her personal and professional effectiveness.
- Don't question your partner's competence in public or point out the practical flaws in his or her latest brainstorm.
- Encourage your partner's pursuit of her or his own interests and friends.

How to Reach Your ESFP Partner

- Try to scale down your ideas (or the explanations of them) to realistic terms. Point out how these ideas will work and what the practical benefits will be.
- Pay attention to some of the details around the house. Pitch in when you see your partner beginning to feel overwhelmed. Take over and give your partner some free time.
- Be sympathetic and patient. Listen to how your partner feels and offer comfort rather than pointing out what you would do in his or her place.
- Appreciate the many things your partner does to make life comfortable and happy. Compliment your partner on tangible things such as his or her looks and financial contributions.
- Beware of your tendency to overwhelm, intimidate, or outgun your partner in discussions and ultimately get your way. Be fair and generous.
- Don't dismiss your partner's feelings simply because you don't share or understand them. Beware of your tendency to act intellectually superior.

ESFP with INTP

The Joys

ESFPs and INTPs share one type preference, so they are typically fairly relaxed and easygoing people. They like to act spontaneously and have very curious natures, so they sometimes share a spirit of adventure. Issues such as power and control, which create problems in many relationships, seem to cause fewer conflicts for most ESFPs and INTPs. Both are casual, flexible, and rarely interested in trying to control anyone. They prefer a more leisurely approach to life and have no trouble stopping what they're doing to participate in something that captures their interest. Essentially process-oriented people, ESFPs and INTPs are comfortable keeping several projects going at once and waiting for the inspiration or motivation to finish them, as opposed to being hurried and frantic to get them done. Their homes are often fairly messy, but neither partner really minds.

It is often ESFPs' and INTPs' differences that are the source of the initial attraction between them. ESFPs are often drawn to INTPs because of their creative, quick minds and their intellectual independence. ESFPs find their partners to be totally original and usually quite fascinating, if sometimes a bit complex. INTPs are often attracted to ESFPs' warmth, friendliness, and social ease. ESFPs are usually entertaining and great fun to be with, and INTPs find their accepting and nonjudgmental natures very refreshing.

Because of their many differences, ESFPs and INTPs have the opportunity to help each other grow and develop in important ways. Down-to-earth ESFPs often bring their intellectual partners "out of the clouds" by helping them notice and appreciate all the little, and especially sensual, pleasures in life. ESFPs also encourage their partners to become more aware of their feelings and more sensitive to others. For their part, INTPs are usually such excellent problem solvers that they help their partners see possibilities and solutions they might never consider. INTPs also help ESFPs become more assertive and independent, and they are particularly helpful in advising their partners about career decisions.

The Frustrations

Because ESFP and INTP couples are so different, it is no surprise that they experience frequent frustrations and some significant challenges. ESFPs are very gregarious people who enjoy being around others. In contrast, INTPs are among the most independent of all types and quite comfortable spending lots of time alone thinking their own thoughts and working on their own projects. While ESFPs are curious about a lot of things, especially people, INTPs tend to have narrower, more focused interests and consider it a waste of time to think about or participate in activities that don't appeal to them. ESFPs are very expressive and need to talk about things to figure out how they feel, but most INTPs are very private and uncomfortable sharing their vulnerabilities. They need to think, often for extended periods of time, to clarify their positions and make sense of their feelings. Only after they understand how they feel will they risk discussing their emotions.

Another challenge facing ESFP and INTP couples stems from the fact that ESFPs are very gentle and sensitive people who try hard to make their partners happy. But they are uncomfortable with disharmony and generally avoid confrontations and arguments. INTPs are superlogical and honest people who are also naturally critical and may not realize that they've hurt their partners' feelings. And since INTPs are so aloof, they can exclude their partners from their lives and not share what's going on with them.

Because they see and deal with the world so differently, it's no surprise that ESFPs and INTPs may have trouble communicating. ESFPs tend to accept things at face value and rarely see deeper meanings or hidden agendas. In contrast, INTPs are extremely analytical and tend to complicate things by searching for underlying meanings. This, of course, can be equally frustrating to both partners. ESFPs find gratification in enjoying the moment, especially regarding social or physical experiences, whereas INTPs get more gratification from intellectual stimulation and overcoming challenges. A common complaint of INTPs is that their partners dismiss their unusual ideas unless they have some immediate and practical utility. INTPs also think that their partners are too complacent and don't challenge themselves enough, especially in regard to their work. During discussions or arguments, INTPs usually get to the point very quickly and then want to move on. ESFPs, however, want to go step-by-step and share each and every impression. ESFPs may feel hurt that their partners appear bored and impatient, while INTPs often think that the conversation is too repetitive or tedious.

While both ESFPs and INTPs are easygoing and have little need for excessive structure or rules, they sometimes neglect to follow through on routine household chores. In reality, someone has to be responsible for paying the bills, keeping appointments, and organizing and coordinating family activities. Since neither partner enjoys doing these things, they usually fall on the more practical ESFP or on the woman. Understandably, this can become a source of resentment and result in conflict.

How to Reach Your INTP Partner

- Give your partner plenty of privacy and time alone without guilt or blame.
- Respect your partner's independent nature. Don't try to pressure him or her to accompany you to every social event.
- Don't expect your partner to respond to an issue right away, especially when it has to do with his or her feelings.
- Help your partner grow and develop by offering your insights and suggestions about people's feelings.
- Support your partner's career drive and aspirations.
- Try to learn more about some of the areas that interest your partner so you can discuss them intelligently.

How to Reach Your ESFP Partner

- Respect your partner's need for and love of fun. Try to accommodate him or her as much as possible.
- Give your partner your full attention when he or she is telling you how he or she feels. Don't dismiss your partner's feelings as overreactions just because you don't share them.
- Be willing to share what you're feeling and experiencing. Try writing notes.
- Encourage your partner to respond to life's opportunities spontaneously and to enjoy his or her free time.
- Watch your tendency to debate everything. Be willing to let some inconsistencies go without pointing them out.
- Be positive. Express your appreciation of the many things your partner does to make you happy.
- If your partner is the one responsible for maintaining the household, try to do your share and take over some of his or her tasks.

ISFP with ENTJ

The Joys

ISFPs and ENTJs have no type preferences in common, so there is great potential for growth and balance. But these relationships are challenging and exciting as well. As these couples learn to understand and appreciate each other, they usually find that they can better understand and deal more effectively with other people.

ISFPs and ENTJs are usually attracted to each other because of their very different styles and natures. ISFPs are often initially drawn to the sheer power of ENTJs' personalities. They are impressed with ENTJs' take-charge attitude, their ability to focus on the future and the big picture, and their skill at long-range planning. ISFPs admire ENTJs' amazing personal and professional confidence and find them to be stimulating conversationalists and partners. ENTJs are typically drawn to the warmth, gentleness, and sincerity of ISFPs. ENTJs like ISFPs' down-to-earth practicality, their calm steadiness, and their deeply affectionate, loyal, and loving nature. Above all, ISFPs are very patient and accepting and make ENTJs feel loved and even sometimes adored.

Because of their many fundamental differences, ISFPs and ENTJs have many opportunities to help each other grow and develop in important ways. ISFPs help their ENTJ partners develop the people skills — empathy, patience, forgiveness, and generosity — they often lack. These skills help ENTJs increase their personal competence, something they constantly strive to do. By learning to slow down and pay closer attention to the details of everyday life, ENTJs find that their lives are enriched and made more meaningful. And ISFPs also help ENTJs learn how to express their feelings more accurately and develop more compassion for others. For their part, ENTJs help ISFPs become more assertive and clearer about their needs and more objective so they don't get their feelings hurt quite so often. As ISFPs seek to raise their personal and professional standards, they often find that they can handle the pressures of life better and are more effective in leadership positions. ISFPs also credit their ENTJ partners with helping them communicate more directly and honestly.

The Frustrations

Despite their many opportunities for growth, ISFPs and ENTJs usually experience regular conflict. Growth rarely comes without a price, and for this couple that price can be high. The main areas ISFPs and ENTJs struggle with are control and communication. While both types desire autonomy, they have fundamentally different natures.

ISFPs are gentle free spirits who live in the moment and seek to experience as much of the beauty and joy of life as possible. ENTJs are intellectual perfectionists who strive to learn and master all that they attempt and always keep an eye on future implications. So, ISFPs sometimes feel that ENTJs take the fun out of experiences by pushing too hard or always trying to organize. In contrast, ENTJs often find ISFPs' desire to wait for life to unfold both disorderly and maddening. ISFPs are often repelled by their partners' bossy and superior attitudes, so they will often give in to their partners' wishes but then go and do just what they want anyway. Naturally, ENTJs find this infuriating and insulting.

Because ISFPs so dislike confrontation and avoid it at almost any cost, they are rarely as direct or assertive as their ENTJ partners may wish. ENTJs want to deal with issues head-on and find it confusing and frustrating to try to solve problems when their ISFP partners withdraw or won't speak their minds. Of course, the more ENTJs pressure ISFPs, the more they will back away. ISFPs tend to take everything very personally, especially criticism, so what ENTJs intend as constructive and helpful suggestions, ISFPs often perceive as a personal attack. To be sure, ISFPs are prone to being moody and sensitive and to holding on to hurts for a long time. For their part, ENTJs can be rather insensitive and impatient and sometimes take their easygoing partners for granted. When there is a conflict, ISFPs usually want to restore harmony as quickly as possible. Conversely, ENTJs are not only unfazed by but often enjoy the intellectual stimulation of a heated debate. ISFPs may agree to things they don't really want just to please their partners. ENTJs may be so uncertain about how to deal with fundamental emotions that they refuse to open up and risk vulnerability. ISFPs and ENTJs often have to work hard to develop communication strategies that serve them both and strengthen their relationships.

Finally, ISFPs and ENTJs may have sharply different values. ENTJs tend to value their professional accomplishments greatly, and their self-worth may be wrapped up in their professional image. ISFPs place more importance on their relationships and personal pursuits. And since they both like to immerse themselves in their own interests, they can each unintentionally leave their partners out of the things they care deeply about.

How to Reach Your ENTJ Partner

- Never undermine your partner's competence, especially in public.
- Compliment your partner on his or her great ideas, innovations, and recommendations for improvement.
- Respect your partner's need for order and routine. Don't change things without warning.
- Try to be accountable for the things you say you'll do.
- Speak up for yourself; don't capitulate just for harmony. Be clear, direct, and honest.
- Support your partner's professional efforts; be encouraging and complimentary. Take some of the load off at home, especially during times when your partner is stressed at work.

How to Reach Your ISFP Partner

- Be sure to respect your partner's need for quiet and solitude. Don't resist it or make him or her feel guilty for taking time alone.
- Look for signs that your partner is feeling stressed and step in to help in some tangible and thoughtful way.
- Express your feelings. Share your frustrations, fears, worries, and joys.
- Avoid placing too many unreasonable demands on your partner. Recognize and compliment the efforts your partner makes.
- Tell your partner how happy he or she makes you. Smile, sit close, hold hands, and be affectionate.

- Don't pressure your partner into attending social functions. When your mate does attend, introduce him or her to people.
- Play with your partner. Surprise him or her with small, thoughtful gifts and take time off to go on an adventure together.

ISFP with INTJ

The Joys

The one type preference ISFPs and INTJs share gives them a common need for quiet, depth, focus, and privacy. ISFPs and INTJs both tend to be very good and attentive listeners, and they respect and understand each other's needs for time away from other people to relax or pursue their individual interests. Privately affectionate, they often enjoy time alone together or with a small group of trusted friends. Most ISFPs and INTJs prefer small gatherings to large parties. They typically share a strong desire for autonomy, expressed in ISFPs as freedom to respond to the moment and in INTJs as independence from prescribed thinking.

ISFPs' and INTJs' many differences often are the source of their initial attraction to each other. ISFPs are drawn to INTJs because of their intellectual prowess, creative thinking, and originality. ISFPs also admire INTJs' ability to be logical, calm, and self-assured and their tendency to be determined and disciplined. For their part, INTJs are often attracted to ISFPs for their warmth, gentleness, and sweet demeanor. ISFPs provide a down-to-earth and emotional perspective that INTJs find stimulating, if sometimes confusing and irritating. INTJs are also intrigued by ISFPs' impulsiveness and playfulness.

Because of their many significant differences, ISFPs and INTJs have the opportunity to help each other grow and develop in important ways. ISFPs often help INTJs learn to stop and consider other people's needs and become more aware of their own feelings. INTJs often credit their partners with helping them become more sensitive and compassionate. For their part, INTJs help ISFPs become more assertive and better able to articulate their views and needs. Many ISFPs say that their INTJ partners help them see beyond the present to the larger implications of their actions. ISFPs also find that their partners help them become more objective so they don't get their feelings hurt so often. ISFPs and INTJs both encourage their partners to accept different perspectives. For ISFPs, that often means being open to new ideas; for INTJs, it means developing willingness to consider the human impact of their decisions.

The Frustrations

Despite their complementary qualities, ISFPs and INTJs have significant differences that are responsible for many of the frustrations they experience. One common area of irritation is their different needs for order and closure. ISFPs prefer a relaxed and unhurried pace so they can enjoy the moment and have time to appreciate the beauty around them. While ISFPs are eager to please others, they are rarely concerned about disorder or clutter and are content for their homes to be attractive and comfortable. INTJs, by contrast, are quite distracted by clutter and prefer their homes and lives to be well organized and their routines carefully maintained. So ISFPs often feel that their partners are too controlling and critical, while INTJs may find ISFPs too casual and sloppy for their tastes. ISFPs live fully in the moment, so they may lose track of time or become distracted on their way to an appointment. INTJs tend to be very punctual and are easily irritated by their partners' apparent lack of responsibility or consideration. Since ISFPs are so impulsive, they love to respond spontaneously to opportunities that present themselves and are often frustrated by their partners' unwillingness to change plans so that they can enjoy the moment.

Another area of frustration for many ISFP and INTJ couples is that ISFPs are practical and realistic, while INTJs are rather abstract and theoretical. Although many couples find this difference stimulating and intellectually challenging, it can be difficult for them to understand each other fully and consequently take a real interest in each other's pursuits and projects.

But perhaps the most fundamental conflict for ISFP and INTJ couples stems from their different ways of making decisions. ISFPs are usually people of great emotion, and they typically have very personal reactions to experiences, even if they tend to keep those feelings to themselves. They are extremely sensitive and quietly affectionate. In contrast, INTJs tend to be cool and outwardly aloof. Although they may have passionate reactions, they appear to be emotionally self-contained and on an even keel, and they are usually able to remain objective even regarding personal issues. ISFPs often feel that their partners don't understand them and have little patience for their feelings, while INTJs often think that their partners overreact and won't let go of minor hurts. What INTJs offer as an observation or a suggestion for improvement is often received as hurtful criticism by ISFPs. To be sure, INTJs can be impatient, just as ISFPs can take a long time to get over past offenses. Since INTJs generally dislike anything remotely contrived or artificial, they may consider some of their ISFP partners' expressions of affection too effusive or unnecessary.

Finally, ISFPs and INTJs tend to view arguments and conflicts very differently. For ISFPs, any conflict is uncomfortable and scary, so many ISFPs will avoid even healthy confrontation and are typically very eager to restore harmony, even if it means suppressing things that are really bothering them. Although INTJs enjoy a heated and spirited debate and are not upset by disagreements or conflict, they also avoid discussions that touch on their fears or vulnerabilities. As long as the debate remains on an intellectual level, INTJs are comfortable, but as soon as it becomes emotional, they tend to want nothing to do with it. But most ISFPs would prefer a real discussion of true feelings, even if it requires tears from them or their partners.

How to Reach Your INTJ Partner

- Respect your partner's routines, rituals, and practices.
- Don't interrupt your partner's train of thought. Be sure to respect his or her privacy and need for time to work through ideas alone.
- Listen attentively to your partner's ideas and ask questions to understand his or her vision better.
- Try to be accountable and dependable. Strive to be on time.
- Keep common areas of your home tidy and follow some of your partner's suggestions about how to organize household chores and functions.
- Never tease or question your partner's competence in public. Don't embarrass your partner by praising him or her too much in public.

How to Reach Your ISFP Partner

- Listen attentively and sympathetically when your partner expresses his or her feelings and reactions. Don't offer solutions to problems right away.
- Watch your tendency to be dismissive and arrogant about your partner's feelings or unwilling to discuss your own emotions.
- Be willing to share your fears and vulnerabilities.
- Receive the tenderness your partner wishes to give you.
- Try to go along with some of your partner's spontaneous and fun ideas and adventures.

ISFP with ENTP

The Joys

Because ISFPs and ENTPs share only one type preference — for a relaxed and casual lifestyle — they are both typically curious, adaptive, and fun loving. The homes of ISFP and ENTP couples are often informal and free of excessive rules or structure. They enjoy each other's openness and non-judgmental natures, and their relationships are usually accepting and easygoing.

The fundamental differences between ISFPs and ENTPs are often the source of their initial attraction. ISFPs are often drawn to ENTPs because of their high energy, enthusiasm, and confidence. Verbal and clever ENTPs amaze and impress ISFPs with their rapid-fire thinking, creativity, and ability to solve strategic problems in unusual ways. ISFPs love that their ENTP partners enthusiastically support their efforts and accomplishments. For their part, ENTPs are attracted to ISFPs because of their warmth, unpretentiousness, and genuine caring about other people. ENTPs often feel pampered by their affectionate ISFP partners, who demonstrate their devotion in many thoughtful and personal ways.

Because of their many differences, ISFPs and ENTPs have the opportunity to help each other grow and develop in important ways. ISFPs help their more high-energy and ambitious ENTP partners relax, slow down, and follow the important steps of a process. ENTPs often credit their partners with helping them to become more compassionate and sensitive to other people's problems and generally to be more careful with their words. ISFPs also help ENTPs notice and appreciate more of the beautiful details of life. For their part, ENTPs help ISFPs become more assertive, more willing to articulate their positions, and better able hear constructive criticism without taking it personally.

ISFPs also say that their partners help them take more action, accept things on faith, and look ahead with greater optimism.

The Frustrations

Despite the complementary aspects of their relationships, ISFPs and ENTPs face some substantial challenges. ISFPs are extremely realistic and down-to-earth people, while ENTPs are very theoretical and global thinkers. ISFPs pay close attention to the details of everyday life, while ENTPs love to imagine the future and see possibilities everywhere. ISFPs often find ENTPs too vague, and ENTPs sometimes find ISFPs too methodical and unimaginative. Whereas ENTPs love to debate concepts and ideas and enjoy the intellectual stimulation of verbal sparring, ISFPs usually find it exhausting and too contentious to be fun.

Another challenge arises from their different decision-making styles. ISFPs have strong personal values, chief among them their belief in kindness and compassion. They are always careful to be nice and to maintain harmony in their relationships. ENTPs are more analytical and tend to rely on sound logical principles to guide their choices. They can take a hard line when necessary and stay objective even in discussions about personal issues. When things heat up, ISFPs tend to back down or avoid saying things that sound hurtful, even when they need to be said. ENTPs tend to press hard to prove they're right and sometimes say things they don't really mean just to make a point or be clever. This strain is often exacerbated because ISFPs need and want time to think through their feelings and thoughts before discussing them, while ENTPs prefer to discuss things as they come up. In fact, it's very difficult for ISFPs to think out loud, but it's equally difficult for ENTPs not to. The more pressure ISFPs feel to respond, the more they tend to withdraw, and the more frustrated ENTPs feel, the more they push. ENTPs are naturally insightful and can often anticipate their partners' moods, but they may find it dispiriting when their partners can't read theirs in return.

Finally, ISFPs and ENTPs sometimes struggle over their different requirements for social stimulation. ISFPs tend to prefer quiet times spent with their partners or with a few very close friends. ENTPs have a much higher need for social interaction and typically have a wide and varied circle of friends. Almost all ENTPs love meeting new people and want to party more often and longer than their partners. ISFP and ENTP couples frequently need to compromise on how many social events they attend together and separately. And they need to be sure to shut out the world sometimes and spend time alone together.

How to Reach Your ENTP Partner

- Listen and respond enthusiastically to your partner's ideas. Avoid pointing out why they may not be immediately workable or practical.
- Share your thoughts and reactions readily. Don't withdraw without explaining that you need time to think things through.
- Act on your many good impulses. Take action and speak up for yourself.
- Don't hold back or worry that speaking your mind will hurt your partner's feelings.
- Stay calm and try to be clear and logical.
- Be willing to try some of the adventures or innovative solutions your partner suggests.

How to Reach Your ISFP Partner

- Be patient and quiet and maintain close eye contact during discussions or conflicts.
- Don't expect your partner to be able to read your mind. Be clear and explicit.
- Be affectionate, loving, and gentle. Compliment your partner on his or her efforts and for the thoughtful things he or she does for you.
- Listen attentively to your partner, especially about his or her problems with other people. Be

supportive, but don't try to fix problems immediately.

• Surprise your partner with romantic dinners or adventures alone together.

• Watch your tendency to have to be the expert.

ISFP with INTP

The Joys

Sharing two type preferences gives most ISFP and INTP couples a similar quiet, easygoing energy and casual lifestyle. In different ways, ISFPs and INTPs are fairly nonconformist and content to live their lives unfettered by the expectations and demands of the outside world. They both like to pursue their interests and treasured friendships in depth, are generally attentive listeners, and respect each other's need for solitude. Since ISFPs and INTPs aren't especially concerned about schedules and order, they rarely try to control each other. They are usually content to maintain a relaxed and unstructured home life and don't mind a certain amount of clutter.

It's often ISFPs' and INTPs' differences that are the source of the initial attraction between them. Many ISFPs are fascinated by INTPs' sharp minds and admire their originality, creativity, and fierce independence. INTPs usually are so unlike other people that ISFPs can't help but be impressed by their unique take on things. Also, ISFPs admire how emotionally self-contained and unflappable INTPs are even when stressed. For their part, INTPs find the gentleness and warmth of ISFPs very appealing. They are often drawn to ISFPs' affectionate and accepting nature, their devotion, and their great common sense. INTPs also respect ISFPs' gift for enjoying the simple pleasures of life.

Because of their differences, ISFPs and INTPs have the opportunity to help each other grow and develop in important ways. ISFPs are able to help INTPs become more compassionate and sensitive to the needs of other people. ISFPs often encourage INTPs to notice the joys and beauty of the moment and pull their partners out of their cerebral world to participate in social activities. In addition, ISFPs' common sense helps make INTPs' great ideas and innovations more workable. For their part, INTPs frequently can help ISFPs look beyond the known and accepted to see the connections between things and understand the larger picture. ISFPs often credit their partners with helping them become more assertive and articulate about their needs and better able to receive constructive criticism.

The Frustrations

The major frustrations for ISFPs and INTPs stem from their different ways of noticing and interacting with the world. ISFPs are so practical and realistic that they are sometimes frustrated by their partners' need to question even the most widely accepted conventional wisdom. INTPs tend to think that ISFPs accept too much at face value and buy into myths that don't serve them well. The interests the two types pursue are also quite different. Most ISFPs like to be either out in nature enjoying the physical world or engaging in crafts or hobbies with a practical end result. INTPs are rarely engaged for very long by anything repetitious, so they tend to have ever-evolving interests and areas of study. INTPs can lose themselves quite easily in their thoughts and may neglect to notice that an entire day has slipped away while they were reading or working at the computer. And since ISFPs tend to be very linear and straightforward, while INTPs are often abstract and somewhat vague, they can often find communication a challenge.

ISFPs and INTPs sometimes disagree about the importance of material belongings. ISFPs tend to take great care of their prized possessions. INTPs are rarely as interested in objects, and although they enjoy new technology and inventions of all sorts, they tend not to be very meticulous about maintaining them.

But the major source of frustration for most ISFP and INTP couples stems from the different criteria each trusts to guide their decisions. ISFPs are very emotional and sensitive people who tend to take most things to heart and are easily affected by the needs of others. INTPs are much more objective and aloof. Although they may have deep feelings, they are much more private about them and tend to find effusive praise or affection embarrassing and uncomfortable. INTPs are also naturally quite critical, and without meaning to, they often hurt their partners' feelings by offering constructive suggestions. ISFPs are among the least assertive of all types, so they tend not to speak up for themselves or challenge their partners even when it's in their best interests. INTPs are exceptionally honest but can be blunt and tactless at times, just as ISFPs are often less than direct in order to avoid confrontations. ISFPs may need to resist their tendency to compromise more than is good for them, and their INTP partners may need to soften their words.

How to Reach Your INTP Partner

• Listen enthusiastically to your partner's ideas and visions. Resist the urge to point out the factual flaws right away.

• Respect your partner's privacy and need for lots of uninterrupted time to work on his or her projects and ideas.
• Give your partner plenty of time to think about important issues before discussing them.
• Don't pressure your partner into being with your friends when he or she isn't interested.
• Be calm, clear, and direct about your needs. Be honest, and don't avoid discussing problems.
• Ask your partner for advice about how to manage complicated or new projects.
• Compliment your partner on his or her good ideas and innovations.

How to Reach Your ISFP Partner

• Express your thoughts, feelings, and reactions freely.
• Begin with the positive. Appreciate the many ways your partner brings warmth and happiness to your life and helps you find fun in everyday things.
• Smile, sit close, and touch your partner when talking, especially when you're discussing unpleasant topics.
• Listen attentively to the stories your partner tells, even if they are about people you don't know. Try to remember the personal details.
• Tell your partner when you need time alone so he or she doesn't misinterpret your absence or silence as rejection.

Chapter 10

Experiencers with Idealists: SPs with NFs

ESTP with ENFJ

The Joys

With only one of the four type preferences in common, ESTPs and ENFJs are very different people, but they share a love of action and social stimulation. They are high-energy, expressive, and enthusiastic people who like to spend time socializing with a variety of people. They often enjoy entertaining and spending time laughing and having fun with friends. Their outgoing styles complement each other: ENFJs usually express their feelings in words, while ESTPs often demonstrate their affection through thoughtful actions. And since they have such different perspectives, they usually find their relationships both challenging and exciting.

ESTPs and ENFJs are often initially attracted to each other because of their many differences. ESTPs are drawn to ENFJs because of their warmth, sophistication, and ability to articulate their thoughts and feelings. ESTPs admire ENFJs' ability to understand others' motivations and anticipate their needs. ESTPs also admire how creative, organized, and accomplished ENFJs can be. ENFJs are often attracted to ESTPs because they are so easygoing and generous. ESTPs make even the most mundane experiences fun and exciting, and ENFJs find their irreverence surprising, if sometimes a little shocking. ENFJs admire ESTPs' even-tempered demeanor and envy how spontaneous and ready for adventure they always seem to be.

Because of their many differences, ESTPs and ENFJs have the opportunity to help each other grow and develop in important ways. ESTPs help ENFJs temper their need to be perfect and encourage them to try to please themselves as much as they please others. ENFJs say that their partners help them become more aware of the details and realities of life and the options that are available to them. For their part, ENFJs are able to help ESTPs to become more sensitive and to consider how others will be affected by their behavior. ESTPs credit their partners with helping them get organized, finish more of the projects they start, and generally become more accountable.

The Frustrations

Despite their potential for mutual growth, ESTPs and ENFJs face some formidable communication challenges. ESTPs are ultrarealistic people who tend to speak directly and literally and focus on the facts, while ENFJs tend to leap from topic to topic, sometimes starting in the middle of a sentence. ENFJs are much more figurative and idealistic and search for the underlying meanings of things. ESTPs sometimes find ENFJs to be confusing and imprecise, while ENFJs may feel that their partners are too obvious and miss meaningful subtleties.

Another area of frustration for ESTP and ENFJ couples is the different ways they make decisions. Although ESTPs can be very charming and friendly, they are nonetheless analytical decision makers who can sometimes be blunt and insensitive. ENFJs are the ultimate diplomats, ever tactful and careful to avoid hurting people's feelings. But they also put such a positive spin on things that they aren't always completely honest. ENFJs will go to great lengths to avoid discussing problems frankly and openly. When ESTPs don't immediately understand their partners' deep feelings and dramatic reactions, they tend to dismiss them as overreactions. ESTPs also tend to try to solve problems expediently when their partners really need just a loving, patient listener.

Finally, ESTPs and ENFJs often experience frustration stemming from their different needs for order and closure. ESTPs are easygoing but also very distractible and impulsive. They often start projects they don't finish and fail to keep the promises they make. ENFJs like issues to be settled and plans to be made and followed, and they usually have trouble adapting to last-minute changes. ESTPs often feel that their partners try to pin them down and force decisions before they're ready. For their part, ENFJs often feel unnecessarily inconvenienced when their inconsiderate partners procrastinate and refuse to make (and stick with) even small decisions. To be sure, ENFJs can act bossy and controlling and insist that their way is the right way, just as ESTPs can be too nonchalant about their commitments. Since ENFJs take everything personally, they are easily offended and hurt, while ESTPs, who are more naturally thick-skinned, think that their partners blow small things out of proportion. In order to maintain a trusting and healthy relationship, ESTP and ENFJ couples need to work hard at honest yet loving communication and balance ESTPs' need for freedom with ENFJs' need for stability.

How to Reach Your ENFJ Partner

- Share your feelings, thoughts, reactions, and concerns in a loving and intimate way.

- Try to follow through on commitments and keep your promises. Resist the urge to give in to the temptation to follow your impulses, especially when your partner is counting on you.
- Be gentle and diplomatic when discussing problems. Praise and compliment rather than criticize.
- Be patient with your partner's complicated and dramatic stories. Don't dismiss your partner's feelings as overreactions.
- Listen sympathetically to your partner's problems and concerns. Don't try to fix problems or be dismissive about the intensity of your partner's feelings.
- Avoid too many surprises, especially those that require your partner to adapt his or her plans. Call before bringing people home for dinner.
- Do your share of the household chores. Pick up after yourself and finish projects you start.

How to Reach Your ESTP partner

- Do things and go places with your partner and participate in his or her interests and activities. Plan to be spontaneous.
- Stay calm and clear; be direct and honest. Don't tiptoe around problems.
- Be willing to let some things go. Strike a balance between overdiscussing and keeping important issues to yourself.
- Be patient with your partner's need to gather more information and check out options even after you think things are decided.
- Don't pin your partner down or insist that he or she account for every minute of his or her time. Recognize how important freedom is to your partner
- Get the facts straight and be prepared to supply the level of detail your partner needs.
- Watch your tendency to nag about chores and be rigid and bossy. Let little things go.

ESTP with INFJ

The Joys

Although ESTPs and INFJs have no type preferences in common, they find great joy in exposing each other to new ways of looking at things and new activities they would normally not experience. Not surprisingly, people who are so different are often attracted to the very qualities they lack in themselves. ESTPs are drawn to their partners' integrity, thoughtfulness, wide range of interests, and depth. INFJs are attracted to ESTPs because they're so playful, charming, and adaptable. For INFJs, life with an ESTP is a series of exciting, if sometimes hair-raising, adventures.

Because of their many differences, ESTPs and INFJs also have the opportunity to help each other grow and develop in important ways. Easygoing and casual, ESTPs help their partners be present in the moment and enjoy life's little pleasures. They also get them out in the world and help them relax some of their rigid opinions. For their part, the more introspective INFJs introduce their partners to more cerebral and sometimes artistic endeavors. ESTPs often admit that INFJs bring a depth, intensity, and richness of meaning they were missing on their own. Their different natural strengths can make this combination a good team. When entertaining, for example, INFJs prefer and are better at planning, while ESTPs often enjoy taking care of the physical needs of their guests and making sure they have a good time.

The Frustrations

Because ESTPs and INFJs are so different, they often face some significant challenges as a couple, chief among them their very social needs. Most ESTPs love a good party and will quickly drop what they're doing to do something fun with friends. INFJs are too aware of what is appropriate and too conscientious about meeting their obligations to feel comfortable acting so spontaneously. ESTPs and INFJs also have different communication styles. Whereas ESTPs like to talk about things as they occur to them, most INFJs prefer to consider things quietly before they respond. ESTPs often complain that their partners are too vague and theoretical, while INFJs often find that their partners are too detail-oriented and miss the big picture.

Because INFJs and ESTPs see the world so differently, it's common for them to have dissimilar views about a variety of issues ranging from politics to parenting philosophies. For instance, INFJs tend to be fairly conservative about money. They invest their money carefully and spend it judiciously on quality products and activities they value, such as theater tickets. ESTPs tend to be generous and spontaneous spenders, making purchases (often vacations, toys, or other things that will bring them pleasure and fun) as the spirit moves them.

INFJs and ESTPs also approach conflict very differently. INFJs try to avoid it whenever possible. Once they are forced into a confrontation, they usually push for a quick resolution. Since disharmony seldom causes ESTPs the same amount of discomfort, they're inclined to ignore it and hope the problem will take care of itself. But when ESTPs do become engaged, they may have difficulty controlling their tempers and explode in angry outbursts. Although venting their feelings may make them feel better, it does little to address the underlying problems. INFJs are more likely to want to engage in a substantive, if not always comfortable, discussion of the issues.

ESTPs' and INFJs' different temperaments may create additional challenges for them. ESTPs crave freedom and the ability to respond spontaneously to whatever exciting opportunities present themselves. They are not particularly impressed by authority and have no compunction about bending the rules as unnecessary. They're usually better at starting things than finishing them and are quick to change plans. But INFJs tend to be serious and conscientious. They like and respect order and have a hard time shifting gears when situations change. This dichotomy sometimes casts both partners in roles neither wants: the INFJ becomes the disciplining parent, and the ESTP becomes the mischievous child. They may need to work hard to reestablish balance and equity in their relationships.

How to Reach Your INFJ Partner

• Take an interest in your partner's passions. Be willing to attend events or read books he or she recommends.
• Be considerate and try to anticipate how your partner may perceive your actions. Be willing to accommodate his or her needs and feelings.
• When your partner feels stressed and overworked, lighten the load by doing household chores, watching the children, or providing him or her with some uninterrupted time to finish a project.
• Respect your partner's value system. Don't put your mate down or tease him or her about his or her values and opinions.
• Encourage intimacy by sharing your emotions.
• Express your appreciation in words and actions. Take the initiative and ask what's going on, then listen without critiquing or trying to fix the problem.
• Be considerate of your partner's space. Respect his or her need for order and neatness.
• Give your partner time to get used to changes in plans.

How to Reach Your ESTP Partner

• Resist the urge to analyze your partner and tell him or her what he or she is feeling.

• Give your partner plenty of space and freedom. Don't make your mate account for all his or her time and actions.
• Try to be spontaneous. Be willing to change plans or just wing it.
• Include your partner in your thought process. Let him or her know when something is bothering you.
• Recognize your partner's need to let off steam and relieve stress by doing something physical. Initiate physical intimacy and indulge your partner's need for sex at unusual times and in unusual places.
• Respect your partner's curiosity. Don't force your partner to make a decision before he or she is ready.
• Do physical things together, such as playing sports, walking, biking, giving each other back rubs or massages, and cuddling.
• Try not to be too judgmental or demanding. Strive to be flexible.

ESTP with ENFP

The Joys

ESTPs and ENFPs have two of the four type preferences in common, giving them similar energy and social ease. Friendly, talkative, and curious, they enjoy discussing whatever they notice, and usually have a wide circle of friends and associates with whom they like to spend time. ESTPs and ENFPs are very spontaneous and will usually drop what they're doing to jump into some unexpected and enticing experience. They are also both pretty casual, adaptable people who don't like to plan too far in advance or feel particularly committed to plans they do make. They seldom argue about the neatness of their homes, nor do they often experience conflict over control issues, since both tend to be tolerant of the other's behavior.

In addition to their similarities, they are often initially attracted to each other because of their differences. ESTPs are often drawn to ENFPs because of their creativity, sensitivity, and thoughtfulness. ENFPs are very nurturing and eager to please, and most ESTPs find that very appealing. ENFPs are often attracted to ESTPs because they're so much fun. ENFPs admire their partners' devil-may-care attitude and adventurous spirit.

Because of their differences, ESTP and ENFP couples have a great opportunity to help each other grow and develop in important ways. ESTPs are usually able to help ENFPs hear constructive criticism without getting their feelings hurt and to lighten up and enjoy the present moment. For their part, ENFPs often help their partners become more sensitive, genuine, and introspective. ESTPs say that their partners encourage them to be more open and expressive of their true feelings.

The Frustrations

While ESTPs and ENFPs are similar in two important ways, they also are different in two equally important ways. ESTPs are among the most realistic and pragmatic of all types. One of their greatest strengths is their ability to notice and remember details and to engage fully in whatever they are experiencing at the moment. But they are also somewhat skeptical about theories or ideas with which they have no firsthand experience. By contrast, ENFPs are driven to find new and unique ways of solving old problems. They follow their inspiration and gut instincts, are highly imaginative, and are often very idealistic. But they can also be a bit vague and abstract, making it hard for their partners to follow their convoluted trains of thought. ESTPs tend to become restless with too much discussion and prefer to get busy in the present rather than dwell on the future.

Another important difference lies in ESTPs' and ENFPs' different stands regarding how personally they view most decisions. Since ESTPs are naturally quite objective, they are quick to offer a comment or critique based on their impersonal observations. ENFPs tend to be diplomatic and careful not to hurt other people's feelings. They are also very sensitive to criticism, especially with regard to their ideas or deep beliefs. So ESTPs frequently, albeit inadvertently, hurt their partners' feelings, often without a clue as to how they did it. ESTPs often feel exasperated by the depth and intensity of their partners' feelings and how long they hold on to hurts.

ESTPs and ENFPs also deal with conflict very differently. ESTPs tend to deal with problems directly, though sometimes explosively. When ESTPs become upset or angry, they are likely to express their feelings vociferously and then resume their calm demeanor. ENFPs tend to withdraw emotionally, often feeling guilty regardless of whether they are responsible for causing the problem. Ultimately, ENFPs are motivated to understand what went wrong and to reach out to restore harmony with their partners.

ESTPs and ENFPs also face a formidable challenge regarding their values. ESTPs are often more conservative both socially and politically than their more naturally liberal ENFP partners. And ESTPs essentially take life as it comes and find their partners' endless search for meaning a waste of time and energy. ENFPs tend to idealize their important relationships, often yearn for a spiritual connection, and really want their partners to be their soul mates. ESTPs tend to be more content to accept life and their relationships as they are. But that may leave ENFPs feeling disconnected if they wish to deepen or explore new areas of their relationships.

Finally, since both ESTPs and ENFPs are pretty casual, they may experience conflict over responsibility for mundane chores such as organizing the household, paying bills, and making and confirming appointments. When both partners naturally dislike household chores, they often fall to the one who dislikes them less. And not surprisingly, most often the woman feels pressured to be the domestic one, a situation that is bound to cause resentment. This naturally flexible couple needs to be sure to stay open to making changes that are comfortable for both partners.

How to Reach Your ENFP Partner

- Try to be sensitive to your partner's needs. Be patient and gentle.
- Resist the urge to criticize or immediately point out factual errors in your partner's ideas.
- Express your appreciation of your partner's creativity. Support his or her need for artistic expression.
- Understand your partner's desire for close and deep friendships with friends and family members, even if you don't particularly like them.
- Let your partner know in words and actions how much you appreciate him or her.
- Realize that your partner has deep feelings about many things but may have trouble communicating them right away. Listen supportively when your partner shares his or her feelings.
- Give your partner plenty of physical contact, such as cuddling, that doesn't necessarily lead to sex.

How to Reach Your ESTP Partner

- Try to participate in activities your partner enjoys.
- Give your partner plenty of physical contact, such as back rubs and body massages.
- Buy your partner toys. Surprise him or her with treats.
- Try to enjoy your partner's desire for spontaneous lovemaking.
- Don't overschedule your partner's time or

impose too many restrictions on his or her freedom.
- Be clear, direct, and explicit, especially about things you want to change.

ESTP with INFP

The Joys

Because of the one type preference ESTPs and INFPs have in common, they often share a relaxed and easygoing style. They are both curious and adaptable people who enjoy responding to the moment without a lot of planning or structure. Neither especially like to make decisions but instead prefer to stay open to experiencing as much of life as possible.

In addition to their mutual desire for spontaneity, ESTPs and INFPs are often initially attracted to each other because of their many differences. ESTPs are drawn to INFPs' natural warmth, compassion, and nurturing style. They are impressed with INFPs' deep yet private devotion to the people and ideas they value. They also are intrigued, if not a bit mystified, by INFPs' rich imaginations and original takes on everyday experiences. For their part, INFPs are often attracted to ESTPs' charm, enthusiasm, and fun-loving natures. INFPs admire ESTPs' social ease and willingness to take risks. Most INFPs also respect ESTPs' ability to make the tough calls when necessary, to be realistic and practical, and to thoroughly enjoy the moment.

Because of their many differences, ESTPs and INFPs have the opportunity to help each other grow and develop in important ways. ESTPs often help INFPs enjoy outdoor or active physical experiences and take occasional physical risks. INFPs credit their partners with helping them be more objective so they don't take everything to heart and get hurt so easily. ESTPs also draw out their partners and encourage them to meet new people.

For their part, INFPs often help their ESTP partners slow down, focus some of their energy and attention, and see beyond the obvious. INFPs encourage their partners to be more compassionate and sensitive to the needs of others. Most ESTPs say that their partners help them develop emotional intimacy with the important people in their lives.

The Frustrations

Despite those opportunities for growth, ESTPs and INFPs also face some formidable communication challenges. ESTPs are generally busy, social, and talkative people, while INFPs are far more private and reflective. ESTPs frequently want and need more social interaction than their INFP partners, who usually commit themselves to only a few cherished people and guard their private time. ESTPs sometimes feel frustrated by INFPs' lack of initiative, while INFPs sometimes feel pressured to participate in more activities than they have energy for. Temperamentally, ESTPs and INFPs have different motivations: INFPs are driven to understand the deeper meaning of their lives, whereas free-spirited ESTPs simply want to live each moment as fully as they can.

ESTPs and INFPs tend to look at the world in very different ways. ESTPs are super-observant people who notice the facts, details, and realities of life and tend to accept things as they are. By contrast, INFPs are dreamy, idealistic people who pay more attention to the possibilities and seek meaning in everyday experiences. ESTPs sometimes have little patience for INFPs' vague and complicated thought processes, just as INFPs sometimes find ESTPs too simplistic and unwilling to look below the surface.

But the most serious challenge facing most ESTP and INFP couples is their opposite ways of coming to conclusions and making decisions. ESTPs are the ultimate pragmatists — ever logical and detached and able to give and receive con-structive criticism. INFPs are supersensitive people who tend to take everything personally. Whereas ESTPs are direct and honest, INFPs are diplomatic and gentle. ESTPs tend to deal with conflicts head-on (unless they are of a very personal nature), and INFPs tend to avoid confrontations but are usually eager to discuss emotional subjects at greater length. ESTPs often think their partners are too serious and generally blow things out of proportion, whereas INFPs find ESTPs too casual about people's feelings, sometimes even occasionally crude.

INFPs may outwardly appear calm and even cool, but they crave intense emotional connections with their partners. They often feel that their partners are impatient with the depth or intensity of their feelings and are unwilling to share their own emotions, reactions, and vulnerabilities. ESTPs resist when their partner press for too much intimacy or pry into their inner thoughts. Although ESTPs are often very charming and expressive, most don't feel comfortable disclosing highly personal information. ESTP and INFP couples may have to work hard to find a compromise that allows ESTPs enough freedom and independence and gives INFPs enough of an intimate connection. A combination of patience and commitment are essential for this couple to accept and appreciate each other.

How to Reach Your INFP Partner

- Share your feelings and intimate thoughts as much as you can.
- Show your love and concern for your partner and family members.
- Never dismiss your partner's feelings, even if you don't understand or share them.
- Listen attentively and supportively when your partner is sharing or is upset. Avoid scanning the room or appearing distracted or uninterested.
- Be willing to try some of the more unusual or

emotionally risky experiences your partner suggests. Stay open to the possibility of getting the help of a therapist to better understand and communicate with each other.

• Be willing to turn down some social invitations to spend quiet time alone with your partner.

How to Reach Your ESTP Partner

• Be explicit, literal, and direct. Don't expect your partner to read your mind.
• Be clear about your feelings. Be honest and up-front about problems as they arise.
• Try not to hold grudges. Instead, try to move forward with forgiveness.
• Be willing to occasionally try some of the more adventurous experiences your partner suggests. Relax and have fun.
• Encourage your partner to get the social stimulation he or she needs, even if you don't always participate.
• Try to keep the small things small and not to blow things out of proportion.

ISTP with ENFJ

The Joys

When couples have no type preferences in common, they have great opportunities for growth and learning. While most ISTP and ENFJ couples have difficulty communicating, they're also fascinated by what makes the other person tick. Not surprisingly, it is their differences that most often attract them to each other. ISTPs are attracted to ENFJs because of their high energy, enthusiasm, and warmth. ENFJs have quick minds and optimistic attitudes, and because most are very articulate, they often dazzle their more matter-of-fact ISTP partners with their eloquence and insight. ENFJs are often attracted to the cool, calm introspection of ISTPs, who are very down-to-earth, honest, and straightforward and exude a quiet confidence that ENFJs admire.

Because they are so different, ISTPs and ENFJs can help each other grow and develop in important ways. ISTPs help ENFJs learn not to take things so personally and to strike a balance between pleasing others and pleasing themselves. ISTPs' aptitude for living in the moment helps ENFJs slow down and enjoy more of the simple joys of life. For their part, ENFJs can help ISTPs better understand and deepen their relationships, both personal and professional, by increasing their sensitivity to people and learning to articulate their feelings. ISTPs also credit their partners with encouraging them to look for subtler, underlying meanings.

The Frustrations

Because of their many differences, ISTPs and ENFJs typically experience a host of frustrations that stem from their radically different values and reactions. ISTPs are down-to-earth, practical people who place a high value on personal freedom, whereas ENFJs are empathetic, idealistic people who strive to create harmonious relationships. ISTPs are very adaptable and have a pragmatic view of life. ENFJs are planners who naturally look for hidden motives and new possibilities. ENFJs are as concerned about living according to their personal values as ISTPs are about living free from unnecessary restraints.

ISTPs tend to feel that ENFJs make too big a deal out of just about everything, whereas ENFJs feel that ISTPs don't take enough initiative or responsibility for their actions. ENFJs want a deep emotional connection with their partners and corresponding physical intimacy. But for ISTPs, variety and spontaneity are the spice of life, and they don't see the need to endlessly remind their partners of how much they love them because to them it's self-evident. To be sure, ISTPs are very private and often remote people who can sometimes act insensitively. When ISTPs are bored with something, they tend to disappear physically or emotionally, or both. Since ENFJs are so verbal and expressive, they constantly have to prod their partners to share their feelings. ISTPs are more likely to show their love and appreciation through actions, such as giving back rubs, bringing home unexpected treats, and spending their money generously.

Other frustrations stem from these two types' different communication styles. When relaying a story, for example, ISTPs give all the details in sequential and logical order without a lot of repetition or exaggeration. ENFJs, by contrast, give the highlights and concentrate on the dramatic or personal elements of the story, often skipping over essential details in their enthusiasm. Also, when ENFJs experience a problem, they rarely want their partners to try to solve it immediately. What they need instead is a sympathetic ear. ISTPs like to figure out what, if anything, can be changed, to take action, and then to leave it alone. It's frustrating and boring for ISTPs to rehash things, especially those that are out of their immediate control.

ENFJs and ISTPs also struggle over the degree of order and neatness in their lives. ISTPs are extremely casual and easygoing people, while ENFJs are always on the go and driven to be productive. ENFJs usually want their homes to be organized because a neat home makes them feel calmer and because appearances really matter to them. But ENFJs can be rather bossy, insisting that things be done according to their timetables. ISTPs rarely share ENFJs' need for organization and sense of urgency. Instead, ISTPs are very curious people and need a lot more information before they make a decision or take action. They respond when they absolutely have to. And again, when ISTPs feel too controlled or intruded on, they tend to move farther away and communicate less. Finally, ENFJs also have a greater need to make and hold fast to plans, while ISTPs like to stay flexible and able to respond to the moment. It

takes a lot of commitment, patience, and accommodation for ISTP and ENFJ couples to achieve respect and satisfaction in their relationships.

How to Reach Your ISTP Partner

- When your partner is talking, stop what you're doing and focus, or you will miss opportunities to foster the closeness you want.
- Try not to exaggerate or be overly dramatic. Give the facts clearly and calmly.
- Go with the flow. Be willing to experiment and try new things. Be more selective about which issues are important and which aren't worth the struggle.
- Give your partner plenty of time to mull over issues rather than forcing a discussion. Ask your partner to help you see the logical consequences of your actions.
- Compliment your partner on how smart and competent he or she is.
- Be specific about what you want your partner to do, and say when you really need it to be done.
- Encourage your partner to pursue the activities and friendships that bring him or her pleasure. Don't make your mate feel guilty for wanting to pursue them without you.

How to Reach Your ENFJ Partner

- Never dismiss your partner's feelings as invalid, even if you don't understand them.
- Be patient with your partner's indirect and dramatic way of telling a story. In your own stories, include details about people as well as the drier facts.
- Take the initiative and finish chores and projects rather than waiting until you totally understand the underlying principles at work.
- Appreciate how supportive and insightful your partner is.
- Encourage your partner to seek the social stimulation he or she needs from other people. Be willing to accompany your partner at times.

- Express your feelings rather than assuming that your partner already knows how you feel.
- Try to be on time and to keep your promises and commitments. Call when you're going to be late.

ISTP with INFJ

The Joys

Since ISTPs and INFJs share only one of the four type preferences, they are very different kinds of people and may face some significant challenges in their relationships. Their common preference for quiet and a relatively peaceful and solitary life gives them an innate respect for each other's personal space. Both need plenty of time to think things through. Although INFJs place a high value on relationships, neither tend to need a lot of social stimulation. They like to have a circle of close friends with whom they enjoy similar interests and activities. Although they have different temperaments, ISTPs and INFJs are both fairly independent and nonconforming, so they understand those qualities in each other.

ISTPs and INFJs are often initially attracted to each other because of their many differences. ISTPs are often drawn to INFJs' creativity, originality, and strength of their convictions. ISTPs admire INFJs' compassion and are impressed by their ability to articulate their visions and global perspective. INFJs are often attracted to ISTPs because of their easygoing and playful natures. INFJs admire ISTPs' adaptability, varied skills, and free-spirited curiosity about the physical world.

Not surprisingly, ISTPs and INFJs have the opportunity to help each other grow and develop in important ways. For one thing, ISTPs help INFJs pay closer attention to the joys of the moment. Many INFJs say that their partners help them relax and learn not to take things so seriously or personally. For their part, INFJs help their partners become more aware of their feelings, pay more attention to the needs of others, and be more willing to communicate. ISTPs often credit their partners with adding depth and meaning to their lives.

The Frustrations

With so many significant differences, it's understandable that ISTP and INFJ couples experience a variety of frustrations. Miscommunication is often at the top of the list. Most ISTPs readily admit they are not great communicators because they often can't pinpoint how they feel about particular issues. ISTPs are often frustrated that their partners ask them endless questions for which they have no answers. INFJs place most of their experiences within a personal context, take all their relationships very seriously, and have a strong desire for an emotional connection with their partners. INFJs frequently feel that their partners seal themselves off and won't risk vulnerability by sharing their private feelings. INFJs often feel lonely and disconnected from their partners, while ISTPs feel pressured and uncomfortable. And when they do broach an important subject, conversation can be frustrating for both because ISTPs give short, matter-of-fact answers, while INFJs go into great depth, sometimes repeating themselves or being vague and abstract. ISTPs are so objective that INFJs often get their feelings hurt by what seems to them to be a lack of caring. For ISTPs, the mere fact that they are in the relationship is evidence of their commitment. Words alone won't make their devotion stronger, just as the lack of them doesn't imply they care less. For most INFJs, however, words are very important.

Many ISTP and INFJ couples experience conflicts stemming from their different temperamental natures. ISTPs tend to be impulsive and physical people who are happiest when they are enjoying the moment. INFJs are seekers of personal meaning who love thinking about and sharing their unique vision of how the world ought to be. ISTPs like to adapt and respond to life, while INFJs prefer to plan ahead. ISTPs are people of action, while INFJs are people of many complex ideas and careful deliberations. It's no surprise, then, that ISTPs and INFJs are rarely passionate about each other's activities and find it more satisfying to pursue their own interests.

Finally, ISTPs and INFJs experience conflicts because of their different needs for order and closure. ISTPs are very spontaneous and adventurous people who prefer to keep their options open and their lives free of rules. INFJs are always looking ahead and trying to make the best plan, in sync with their strong personal values. And once they make a plan, INFJs like to stick with it. ISTPs don't appreciate it when their INFJ partners press their agendas, and INFJs are frustrated by their ISTP partners' unwillingness to make a commitment and follow through on it. INFJs and ISTPs also frequently disagree about the importance of organization. INFJs like their homes neat and clutter-free, while ISTPs like their prized possessions nearby and easily accessible, even if that means keeping their kayak in the living room!

How to Reach Your INFJ Partner

- Try to express your reactions and feelings in words.
- Don't shut down and walk away when you're upset or angry. Tell your partner how you feel or that you need some time to process it.
- Give your partner time to adjust to changes in plans or directions. Don't surprise him or her too often.
- Try to be on time and to follow through on the projects you start.
- Never dismiss your partner's feelings or the intensity with which he or she responds to things. Remember that your partner's beliefs and values are of central importance to him or her.

How to Reach Your ISTP Partner

- Accept that your partner may not have much to say on a subject and isn't intentionally withholding anything important.
- Demonstrate your affection and appreciation in actions as well as words.
- Surprise your partner. Bring home an unexpected treat or gift.
- Encourage your partner to spend time alone puttering with his or her projects without having to account for this time or prove that it is productive.
- Be willing to try some of the spontaneous adventures your partner suggests.
- Beware of your tendency to assume that you know what your partner is thinking or feeling without checking with him or her first.
- Resist the urge to moralize. Don't overanalyze your partner or the relationship.

ISTP with ENFP

The Joys

ISTPs and ENFPs share only one type preference, preferring an informal and relaxed lifestyle, a casual and easygoing household, and a fairly non-judgmental approach to dealing with other people. Neither partner is especially interested in trying to control the other, and they both like to take advantage of spontaneous opportunities and experiences as they come up.

In addition to their playful natures, ISTPs and ENFPs are often attracted to each other because of their differences. Typically, ISTPs are attracted to ENFPs' warmth, humor, creativity, and open-mindedness. ISTPs frequently admire ENFPs' enthusiasm, social ease, and wealth of creative ideas. ENFPs are often drawn to ISTPs' calm, easygoing, and independent attitude. ENFPs find ISTPs' natural physicality and adventurousness exciting.

While ENFPs are very verbally expressive, ISTPs tend to demonstrate their affection in actions.

Because of their many differences, ISTPs and ENFPs have the opportunity to help each other grow and develop in important ways. ISTPs help ENFPs relax and not worry so much about the future or about other people's opinions of them. ISTPs encourage ENFPs to enjoy the moment, take some risks, and more fully experience the physical world. By learning to be more logical in their decision making, ENFPs often find that they are able to take things less personally. For their part, ENFPs help ISTPs look beyond their immediate experiences to see patterns and consider the future implications of their actions. ISTPs often credit their ENFP partners with helping them share more openly, become more sensitive to other people's needs, and take the time to cultivate and deepen their important relationships.

The Frustrations

Despite their opportunity for growth and balance, ISTPs and ENFPs face some formidable communication challenges. ISTPs are very private people who say little to begin with and repeat themselves rarely. ENFPs, however, are very verbal and have a strong need to discuss and express their feelings, reactions, and ideas. ISTPs often feel that their partners are prying, while ENFPs feel that they are being shut out. ISTPs are logical and analytical people who are almost always dispassionate and calm, even if others around them are upset and emotional. By contrast, ENFPs usually have very personal reactions and want and need to talk through their feelings for longer periods of time. ISTPs and ENFPs also have different views on intimacy. ISTPs tend to look for physical and sexual intimacy as an avenue for emotional sharing, while ENFPs usually want emotional closeness before sexual intimacy.

ISTPs and ENFPs have different social needs as well. ISTPs are comfortable being alone or with a few close friends, actively engaged in things they all enjoy. ENFPs have a much wider circle of friends and like to spend much more of their time socializing. Like many couples, ISTPs and ENFPs often find that it makes sense to encourage each other to pursue their own friendships while occasionally participating in each other's interests. When it comes to communication, ISTPs and ENFPs may have trouble finding common areas of interest. ISTPs typically become restless when discussing either theoretical or personal subjects, while ENFPs are often bored with anything that lacks depth, creativity, or a personal context.

ISTPs and ENFPs view risk taking differently. ISTPs are more likely to play the odds. They live for the thrill, the challenge, and physical danger. Although some ENFPs enjoy an element of risk, most are more physically conservative because they think in terms of possibilities and see the potential for disaster everywhere. ENFPs are more comfortable taking intellectual, emotional, or professional risks. They call for caution in general and try to protect their partners, who end up ignoring or resisting them. That often leaves ENFPs feeling that their partners don't respect their fears. But ENFPs need to remember that physical challenges are central to ISTPs' core value of experiencing life fully.

Finally, while ISTPs and ENFPs are most comfortable in a relaxed and unstructured environment, they often have different standards for the neatness of their homes. ENFPs typically hate housework, don't mind clutter, and are especially bored by routine and repetitive tasks. Many ISTPs, ruled as they are by logic, may want their homes to be a bit more orderly. When neither person especially likes handling domestic chores, the burden often falls to the woman, regardless of her type preferences. It's important for the person who wants order and neatness to be equally responsible for maintaining it. Accountability, promptness, and follow-through are qualities both ISTPs and

ENFPs need to work on to avoid unnecessary conflicts. Also, rather than avoiding discussing problems, they need to be willing to share what's on their minds and listen fully and respectfully to each other's needs.

How to Reach Your ENFP Partner

- Share the details and events of your day. Offer your feelings and reactions.
- Avoid reminding your partner that you have already covered a topic. Let him or her think out loud, even if it's repetitive.
- Compliment your partner on his or her many original ideas.
- Express your gratitude for the meaning your partner brings to life and all the ways he or she nurtures and cares for you.
- Be patient with and attentive to your partner's stories. Try to remember some of the important people details he or she shares.
- Tell your partner when you need time alone and explain that this isn't a personal rejection.

How to Reach Your ISTP Partner

- Resist the urge to coddle or smother your partner. Accept as fundamental his or her need to experience the adrenaline rush of life.
- Try to wait some things out. Give your partner time to explain things in his or her own time.
- Remember that to ISTPs, actions speak louder than words. Do thoughtful things and resist the urge to point them out to your partner.
- Watch for the ways your partner shows you affection and be appreciative.
- Listen completely and attentively when your partner speaks. Stop whatever else you're doing and look at your partner.
- Be calm and succinct. Try not to repeat yourself or go on and on about things.

ISTP with INFP

The Joys

The two type preferences ISTPs and INFPs have in common are most closely related to lifestyle choices. Both types tend to be quiet, thoughtful people who generally prefer an unhurried pace. Neither has especially high energy or needs a lot of external stimulation. Rather, they like being alone or spending time with each other or a few close friends. They are also different in significant ways and support each other's needs to pursue their own, often divergent, interests.

In addition to their similarities, ISTPs and INFPs are often initially attracted to each other because of their differences. Many ISTPs are attracted to INFPs' creativity, emotional availability, and warmth. ISTPs appreciate the rich, creative dimension INFPs bring to their lives. INFPs are often drawn to the calm, confident, self-contained nature of ISTPs. They are impressed by their skill at physical activities and refreshed by their lack of pretense and ability to enjoy the moment.

Because ISTPs and INFPs are so different, they have the opportunity to help each other grow and develop in important ways. ISTPs are often able to help their partners relax some of their high expectations about other people, be less prone to disappointment, and feel free to experience the simple pleasures of life. For their part, INFPs are often able to help their partners find greater meaning in their experiences, increase their sensitivity to others, and improve the quality and depth of all their relationships.

The Frustrations

The primary cause of frustration between ISTPs and INFPs is their different styles. ISTPs are the ultimate pragmatists, supremely logical and dispassionate. While they may have deep feelings for their partners, they rarely feel compelled to express them verbally. Instead, they may do considerate things or surprise their partners with nice treats or adventures. Most ISTPs are people of few words. To them, their commitment is self-evident, and it's not only unnecessary but also uncomfortable to be pressured to expose themselves emotionally. The more they are pressed, the more they tend to close down.

In contrast, INFPs need lots of affection and reassurance of their partners' commitment. They take things very personally and have strong emotional reactions, even to things that don't affect them directly. When they feel hurt, they tend to withdraw and often have a hard time getting over even small offenses. For INFPs, a strong, harmonious, and intimate emotional connection is essential to their happiness, and they're hurt when their ISTP partners don't or won't share their feelings, for without that connection, INFPs feel lonely and misunderstood. In contrast, ISTPs are often frustrated by what they see as their partners' overly emotional reactions and their need to talk issues to death. And they sometimes find INFPs to be too intense, as well as a bit morally righteous. Flexible in small ways, INFPs can be inflexible when it comes to their cherished values.

Temperamental differences can present a serious challenge to ISTP and INFP couples. ISTPs are keenly aware of the present moment and have a gift for enjoying whatever they happen to be doing at the time. They take things at face value and feel little need to analyze or change them. But for INFPs, everything has meaning, and they are prone to overanalyze many things. Finding common areas of interest can be a real challenge, since this couple is often drawn to very different pursuits. The activities ISTPs like are often too competitive, physical, or mechanical for INFPs, and the more artistic or expressive interests of INFPs are usually too theoretical or emotional for most ISTPs.

Communication is another area of frustration for many ISTPs and INFPs. ISTPs are direct, lit-

eral, and judicious in their choice of words. INFPs tend to elaborate and repeat themselves, and they are much more circuitous in their thought processes. It's no wonder that ISTPs and INFPs often fail to understand each other. ISTPs also tend to have more conservative values, while INFPs tend to be more liberal, which can create tension and ongoing frustration.

Finally, although these couples tend to be very relaxed about rules, order, and time, they can run into trouble when no one throws anything away and no one takes the lead in starting (or finishing!) household chores.

How to Reach Your INFP Partner

- Talk a lot; share how you feel and volunteer your reactions. Let your partner draw you out.
- Listen to your partner's feelings. Let him or her talk without interruption.
- Listen carefully and supportively to your partner's concerns. Resist immediately trying to fix your partner's problems.
- Try to be gentle and sensitive and to avoid becoming impatient — even if you've heard it all before.
- Compliment your partner on his or her innovations and original ideas. Be willing to try the alternative approaches your partner suggests.
- Don't walk away from unpleasant discussions. Strive to reach a compromise and make up after disagreements.

How to Reach Your ISTP Partner

- Give your partner plenty of freedom and space. Be sure your partner doesn't have to account for how he or she spends his or her spare time.
- Don't nag. Be clear, calm, and direct about what you need or want, then let your partner do it (without reminders).
- Let your partner play — and be willing to play with him or her.

- Compliment your partner's looks. Tease your partner to keep things light and let him or her tease you, too.
- Be selective about which issues you are compelled to work out. Once something is resolved, don't rehash it.

ESFP with ENFJ

The Joys

Because of the two type preferences ESFPs and ENFJs have in common, they typically enjoy a relationship that is active, busy, and loving. ESFPs and ENFJs are generally high-energy, expressive people who like to talk about their experiences. Outgoing and friendly, they are quite social and derive great energy from being around a variety of people. Caring, warm, and sensitive, they enjoy a close emotional connection because they express their feelings and strive to understand their partners better. They usually share similar values regarding the importance of being kind to others and place helping people high on their lists of priorities. Affectionate and thoughtful, ESFPs and ENFJs are careful to avoid hurting each other.

In addition to their similarities, ESFPs and ENFJs are often initially attracted to each other because of their differences. ESFPs are drawn to ENFJs because of their creativity, their insight into themselves and others, and their ability to make unique connections quickly. ESFPs admire how articulate, confident, and organized ENFJs are and feel that their partners' optimism for the future gives them both confidence to face the unknown. ENFJs are often attracted to ESFPs because they are so carefree. They admire how gracefully ESFPs roll with the punches and how eager they are to help others. ESFPs are also very sensible, down-to-earth, and practical, all qualities their more imaginative and idealistic partners find appealing and grounding.

Because of their differences, ESFPs and ENFJs have the opportunity to help each other grow and develop in important ways. Typically, ESFPs help ENFJs pay more attention to the realities of life and enjoy the beauty of everyday experiences. ESFPs encourage their partners to take some reasonable risks, be less rigid, and balance their need to be productive with their need to rest. For their part, ENFJs help ESFPs raise their personal and professional standards and become better organized so they get more accomplished. ENFJs inspire their partners to consider new alternatives, think ahead about the possible consequences of their actions, and become more accountable and dependable.

The Frustrations

One of the chief sources of frustration for ESFPs and ENFJs is their different ways of looking at the world. ESFPs notice realities and details, while ENFJs see patterns and possibilities. ESFPs may think that their partners are careless about important facts and skip over vital steps. They get confused when their partners are vague and abstract and focus on what might be instead of what is. ENFJs sometimes feel frustrated with their ESFP partners' inability to generalize or accept information that falls outside their immediate experience. While ESFPs like to experience and discuss the present, ENFJs want to fantasize and plan for the future.

ESFPs and ENFJs differ temperamentally as well. ESFPs are more playful and impulsive than ENFJs and often take risks that their partners find unsettling. ENFJs are constantly searching for the personal meaning in every situation and experience and are forever trying to determine their special mission in life. In contrast, ESFPs quickly adapt to whatever situation they find themselves in and rarely understand the wanderlust and discontent their partners experience. They also tend to believe that their ENFJ partners blow things out of proportion and look for hidden meaning where there is none. And since both ESFPs and ENFJs are so sensitive, they tend to take everything personally, especially their partners' dissatisfaction. As a result, they tiptoe around conflicts and avoid discussing important but unpleasant subjects in an effort to maintain harmony.

Finally, ESFP and ENFJ couples have very different needs for order and closure. ESFPs are very curious people who often are more interested in starting projects than finishing them. ENFJs like things settled but may hurry through experiences just to get them completed. In their zeal to be on time and organized, ENFJs can be inflexible and push their partners to make decisions before they feel they've gathered enough information. For their part, ESFPs can be messy and disorganized and tend to postpone decisions so long that they miss important deadlines. Since ENFJs tend to like their homes neat and tidy, they often do more than their fair share of household chores, which they attribute to their partners' lack of concern. Naturally, this makes them resentful. But since ENFJs don't always address their concerns in a direct way, they may ascribe motives to their partners that simply aren't there. While ESFPs feel things very deeply, they don't always express their feelings as freely as their more articulate ENFJ partners. ENFJs need to remember that ESFPs' devotion runs at least as deep as their own, even if their partners don't express it. ESFP and ENFJ couples need to commit to regular, frank discussions that allow both partners the chance to air their grievances and find satisfying compromises.

How to Reach Your ENFJ Partner

- Express your feelings in words as well as actions. Tell your partner why you love him or her.
- Work hard to fulfill commitments. Strive to be where you say you will, when you say you will. Call if you're running late.

- Put things away when you're finished with them. Pick up after yourself.
- Once you've made a decision or selected a course of action, try not to make sudden changes or impulsively go off in another direction.
- Compliment your partner on his or her great ideas and innovations, as well as the depth of meaning he or she brings to your life.

How to Reach Your ESFP Partner

- Watch your tendency to blow things out of proportion or let your imagination get the better of you. Accept your partner's devotion as fact.
- Be totally direct and explicit in explaining your needs and wants. Show your partner what you like.
- Be willing to wait to finish projects so you can participate in some of your partner's spontaneous suggestions.
- Look for the humor in the moment and enjoy it with your partner.
- Surprise your partner. Bring home treats or occasionally do some funny or outrageous thing.
- Respect your partner's need to gather a lot of information before making a choice; don't force decisions.

ESFP with INFJ

The Joys

The central emotional connection between ESFPs and INFJs often serves as the glue that holds these couples together. They share a strong desire for harmony in all their personal relationships. Both take a very personal approach to life and usually place each other's needs ahead of outside distractions. For ESFPs and INFJs, satisfaction lies in feeling safe and encouraged to be emotionally vulnerable to each other.

Despite these similarities, it's often the differences between these types that are the source of their initial attraction. ESFPs are drawn to the gentle warmth, calm, and sophistication of INFJs, who are often great wordsmiths and express themselves in unique ways. ESFPs respect INFJs' creativity and ability to think in abstract ways. INFJs are often drawn to the lighthearted, outgoing, and adventurous natures of ESFPs. Most INFJs also admire that ESFPs are so down-to-earth, unpretentious, and enthusiastic.

Because of their many differences, ESFPs and INFJs have the opportunity to help each other grow and develop in important ways. ESFPs help broaden the horizons of INFJs by encouraging them to get out in the world and enjoy some of the pleasures of nature and everyday life. INFPs say that their partners encourage them to pay closer attention to important details and release some of their need to strive for perfection. For their part, INFJs often help their more realistic partners see new solutions to old problems. ESFPs often credit their partners with helping them slow down and focus so they can finish more of the projects they start.

The Frustrations

Most of the frustrations ESFPs and INFJs experience come from their differences. ESFPs and INFJs typically disagree about the necessity of planning: ESFPs prefer to jump into life and worry about consequences later, whereas INFJs generally want to plot things out well ahead of time. Also, ESFPs are much more likely to create messes and be content with clutter than are INFJs, who are often pretty formal people and prefer that things are tidy and in their place. INFJs also tend to hear a decision being made when their partners are only voicing options, so ESFPs often feel that their partners are too rigid and even authoritarian. Since INFJs are frequently unwilling or unable to change their plans, they often miss opportunities that arise

spontaneously. On the other hand, ESFPs' lack of planning usually results in a hectic pace and the need to constantly respond in a crisis mode. INFJs also find that because their casual ESFP partners are so easily distracted (especially by social opportunities), they can be somewhat reckless, irresponsible, and unable to follow through.

The different amount of talk each prefers is another area of frustration for many ESFP and INFJ couples. Most ESFPs want to talk about options and observations at great length, while INFJs want a great deal more private time and the opportunity to think things through. When INFJs have something important to consider, they usually need even more time to reflect so they can express themselves clearly and diplomatically. But while they are processing, they are also being noncommunicative, which is confusing and frustrating to ESFPs, who like to discuss things on the fly. Since ESFPs tend to tell it like it is, their INFJ partners can find their sometimes unpolished style a bit offensive. ESFPs often complain that INFJs agonize over everything and work even the simplest idea or project to death with endless revisions. For ESFPs that takes all the fun out of it, while for INFJs the ruminating process *is* the fun. Most ESFP and INFJ couples find that pursuing different projects in their own styles and asking for the specific kind of feedback or advice they need can reduce the frustration in their relationships.

How to Reach Your INFJ Partner

- Try to tie things together rather than talking only about the specifics. Try to offer a framework for your thoughts.
- Respect your partner's need for quiet time to concentrate on projects he or she cares about.
- Avoid changing plans without giving your partner some notice.
- Be where you say you will, when you say you will.
- Avoid accumulating piles of clutter, especially in

your partner's line of vision (such as on counter-tops or his or her desk).

- Make an effort to join your partner in pursuing the causes and interests that are meaningful to him or her.
- When your partner is under stress, offer simple, loving expressions of your support, such as back rubs, a cup of tea, or fresh flowers.

How to Reach Your ESFP Partner

- Be sure to pay close attention during discussions. Focus on the moment and look your partner in the eyes.
- Give spontaneous physical expressions of your appreciation and affection, such as back rubs, hand-holding, or lovemaking.
- Watch that you don't moralize or speak in a condescending tone.
- Participate in activities your partner considers fun. Be willing to try new things.
- Appreciate your partner for all the little things he or she does to make life more joyful, fun, and beautiful.
- Don't disappear. When you have a lot on your mind, tell your partner you need some time to think. Be sure to make it clear you aren't quiet because you're mad at him or her.
- Don't force decisions. Give your partner options and time to check them out before committing.
- When your partner is under stress, remember to stop what you're doing, listen carefully to his or her story, and offer gentle and manageable possibilities.

ESFP with ENFP

The Joys

ESFPs and ENFPs share three type preferences, giving them a very playful, fun, and easygoing relationship. Both partners tend to be energetic and friendly, and they enjoy the company of lots of friends and acquaintances. Enthusiastic, curious, and spontaneous, ESFPs and ENFPs like to stay open to opportunities and are ready to drop whatever they're doing to help out a friend. Gentle and sentimental, both care deeply about the needs and feelings of others. They enjoy a strong emotional connection because both feel safe to share their vulnerabilities with each other. Neither type is especially rooted in tradition, so these couples are often unconventional and irreverent, finding humor and fun almost anywhere. Ever flexible and resourceful, ESFPs and ENFPs share a desire to experience as much of life as possible.

In addition to their many similarities, ESFPs and ENFPs are often initially attracted to each other because of their differences. ESFPs are often drawn to ENFPs because of their optimism and irrepressible creativity. ESFPs are excited by ENFPs' wealth of ideas and their ability to see new and interesting possibilities everywhere. ESFPs also admire ENFPs' ability to grasp complex subjects and instantly see underlying connections between things. ENFPs are typically drawn to ESFPs because of their happy-go-lucky attitude and ability to have a good time no matter what they're doing. ENFPs find ESFPs refreshingly down-to-earth and guileless, and they admire their willingness to take risks and experience life fully.

Because of their differences, ESFPs and ENFPs have the opportunity to help each other grow and develop in important ways. ESFPs help ENFPs lighten up, enjoy the moment, and spend less energy worrying about potential problems. They also help their partners pay closer attention to details so they make fewer factual mistakes and remember important steps in the process. ENFPs often credit their partners with encouraging them to try more physical experiences and take more risks. For their part, ENFPs help ESFPs look beyond the obvious to see the potential implications of their actions. ESFPs often say that partners help them open up to new ideas and consider the future.

The Frustrations

Despite their many similarities, ESFPs and ENFPs experience frustration stemming from their different ways of noticing the world. ESFPs are super-realistic and practical, while ENFPs are highly imaginative and creative. ESFPs notice the details and realities of experiences, whereas ENFPs focus on the possibilities and what could be. Therefore, ESFP and ENFP couples sometimes have trouble understanding each other. ESFPs complain that ENFPs jump around from subject to subject and often begin conversations in the middle of a sentence. While ESFPs often think that ENFPs are too vague and random, ENFPs often think that ESFPs are too literal and specific and insist on telling stories sequentially, including every detail. Some of ENFPs' wildly imaginative ideas seem unrealistic and unworkable to ESFPs, who can easily become bored with abstract theories. For their part, ENFPs are sometimes frustrated by their partners' lack of enthusiasm for their ideas and their habit of pointing out factual errors. Because ESFPs don't immediately grasp the possibilities, ENFPs sometimes grow impatient and feel unappreciated.

Since ESFPs live so completely in the present, they are seldom as interested in discussing future events as ENFPs, who find it tedious and boring to limit their focus to the present. ENFPs also worry more than ESFPs, especially about matters of safety and health. ESFPs are prone to overindulging in spontaneous pleasures, giving ENFPs even more to fret about.

Although both types are loving and appreciative of each other, they also are prone to take any criticism and rejection personally. And when they feel upset, they tend to keep their feelings to themselves and may need time alone to calm down and sort

out their emotions. It's important that they work out their problems before too much time passes, however, and the chasm between them widens.

Another area of frustration for ESFPs and ENFPs is their lack of interest in planning or maintaining order around them. They both like to keep as many options open as possible, and frequently they put off decisions so long that they miss out on opportunities or have to rush to meet important deadlines. They may play a game of hot potato when it comes to making decisions, balancing the checkbook, or following up on appointments. They also dislike feeling controlled or limited in any way, but because someone has to keep track of their finances, there is bound to be tension between them when only one partner decides how their money will be spent. ESFPs and ENFPs also may struggle with neatness if one partner is more put off by clutter than the other. Generally, however, these couples tend to be pretty flexible about small matters, even as they are firm in relation to things they care deeply about.

Finally, since ESFPs and ENFPs are so energetic and busy, they can overextend themselves with work or other projects and neglect their quiet time together. Because they are both expressive and talkative, they may not listen as attentively or respectfully as they should. They need to slow down, share their feelings, and reestablish the emotional connection they both cherish.

How to Reach Your ENFP Partner

• Give your partner's ideas a fair hearing. Resist the urge to point out why they may not be realistic or practical.

• Compliment your partner on his or her creativity and ability to see possibilities.

• Encourage your partner to share his or her feelings, and listen attentively and respectfully.

• Don't tell your partner that he or she is worrying needlessly.

• Be willing to go into depth about subjects with your partner. Don't always stay on the surface of things.

How to Reach Your ESFP Partner

• Be patient with your partner's impulsivity. Be willing to try some of the physical adventures and experiences your partner enjoys.
• Work hard to be careful about details, money, receipts, and facts.
• Express your affection in words and deeds. Give your partner plenty of physical affection.
• Watch your tendency to rush through explanations or to generalize. Be patient with your partner's attempts to understand your theories.
• Clearly identify when you are changing subjects or making a transition.

ESFP with INFP

The Joys

Because of the two type preferences ESFPs and INFPs share, they are usually gentle, expressive, and compassionate people who have a relaxed responsiveness to life. They also share a common goal of cultivating harmonious relationships. Curious and flexible, they are generally willing to listen supportively and are eager to understand each other's needs and feelings.

In addition to their important emotional connections, ESFPs and INFPs are often initially attracted to each other because of their differences. ESFPs are drawn to INFPs because of their creativity, originality, and spiritual natures. They love INFPs' quiet intensity and ability to find deeper meanings in things. INFPs are drawn to ESFPs because of their social ease, unpretentiousness, and happy-go-lucky attitude. INFPs are instantly cheered by ESFPs' playfulness and

delighted by their sense of adventure. ESFPs tend to do thoughtful little things in response to their partners' needs of the moment. In contrast, INFPs often express their devotion in words, either written or spoken.

Because of their differences, ESFPs and INFPs have the opportunity to help each other grow and develop in important ways. ESFPs help INFPs take life a little less seriously, take occasional risks, participate in social or physical adventures, and generally appreciate the joy of everyday experiences. For their part, INFPs strive to find deeper meanings, to strike a balance between privacy and social involvement, and to help their partners look to the future with optimism.

The Frustrations

One of the most common sources of frustration for ESFP and INFP couples is their different ways of noticing and responding to the world around them. ESFPs typically enjoy life fully and are easily caught up in the fun and action of the moment. INFPs are generally more cautious and reflective. ESFPs tend to accept things as they are, and they become frustrated and bored with INFPs' seriousness and need to analyze things in depth. ESFPs feel that life is a gift that ought to be enjoyed, but most INFPs feel that an unexamined life is not worth living, so their ESFP partners can seem superficial and impulsive. While both ESFPs and INFPs take things personally, idealistic INFPs take things so completely to heart that they are easily hurt and disappointed when their ESFP partners don't notice their subtle signals.

Another area of frustration for ESFPs and INFPs is that since neither are especially organized, life can quickly get hectic and out of control. Their mutual lack of planning means that ESFPs and INFPs often either run late and miss deadlines or one of them is forced to carry an undue burden. Accountability and follow-through are hot-button issues for this couple, especially when the INFP is a woman. INFPs naturally look ahead, see the larger picture, and forecast the needs of their families, whereas ESFPs are more apt to respond to immediate concerns. But INFPs may quickly tire of always having to remember to buy milk or mail in the mortgage payment.

Whereas ESFPs are often very physically active, INFPs are often more cerebral and intellectual. Also, ESFPs have a greater need for social activity and the stimulation of talking and playing with lots of people. ESFPs tend to be constantly on the go, while INFPs tend to want more depth and focus and can feel stressed by the amount of activity ESFPs create.

The biggest area of conflict for these couples is that both have strong needs for harmony and a tendency to avoid healthy confrontation. Rather than talk about problems immediately, they often ignore them and hope they'll just go away. Sometimes they do, but for the most part avoiding them lets resentment fester, which inevitably leads to the criticism that both ESFPs and INFPs find so poisonous. INFPs are more likely to imagine criticism where it does not exist or to get so lost in their own thoughts or projects that they ignore or neglect their partners' needs. ESFPs are more likely to be inadvertently insensitive to the depth of their partners' feelings and the amount of time and privacy they need to work things through.

How to Reach Your INFP Partner

- Take the time to put your feelings and appreciation into words.
- Avoid criticism. Be honest but also gentle and diplomatic.
- Be patient with your partner's slower reaction time.
- Encourage your partner to spend time alone. Don't require your partner to participate in activities he or she isn't up for.

- Try to be on time and not neglect the things you've committed to do.
- Watch your tendency to jump at social opportunities and unintentionally ignore your partner.

How to Reach Your ESFP Partner

- Try to relax and go with the flow.
- Be clear and specific about what you need or want and when you need or want it.
- Don't assume that your partner's light attitude implies a lack of deep feelings.
- Avoid criticism. Be loving yet specific and clear.
- Be patient with your partner's slower process for seeing the big picture. Patiently help him or her understand what you mean.
- Encourage your partner to participate in the many activities and opportunities he or she desires, even if they don't always include you.

ISFP with ENFJ

The Joys

ISFPs and ENFJs share only one of the four type preferences, but since they may share many of the same personal values, they often enjoy a strong emotional connection. ISFP and ENFJ couples are usually warm, loving, and expressive. Supportive and understanding, they are sensitive and concerned about each other's needs and share a strong desire to maintain harmony in their relationships.

In addition to their mutual interest in a strong relationship, ISFPs and ENFJs are often initially attracted to each other because of their many differences. ISFPs are drawn to ENFJs because of their drive, ambition, and impressive urge to make things happen. ISFPs are dazzled by ENFJs' articulate expressiveness and their great organizational skills and productivity. ISFPs also like being able to trust ENFJs to follow through. ENFJs are often attracted to ISFPs because of their accepting and accommodating natures. ENFJs find ISFPs' gentle unpretentiousness refreshing and appreciate how their free-spirited partners help lighten them up and make life more fun.

Because of their many differences, ISFPs and ENFJs have the opportunity to help each other grow and develop in important ways. Typically, ISFPs help ENFJs slow down and enjoy the moment by paying more attention to the details and simple beauty of life. ENFJs credit their partners with getting them to relax and have fun instead of always trying to please others, often at the expense of their own happiness. For their part, ENFJs help ISFPs see the big picture and anticipate the consequences of their actions. ISFPs often say that their ENFJ partners help them follow through on projects and encourage them to set and reach goals. ISFPs also may learn to express themselves more freely and become more willing to speak up for themselves.

The Frustrations

Since ISFPs and ENFJs have so many differences, it's understandable that they may experience frequent frustrations. ENFJs typically feel that their naturally impulsive and playful ISFP partners are so casual that they are sometimes reckless. To be sure, ISFPs don't look ahead and do take more physical chances than the more purposeful and cautious ENFJs. But ENFJs can be bossy, attempt to control their partners, and unintentionally act as if they know best. It is especially discouraging to ISFPs when their partners appear to be dissatisfied with their lives and when they wonder aloud about possibilities that may never come to pass.

ISFPs and ENFJs also have very different communication styles and often struggle to understand each other fully. ISFPs can get frustrated when trying to follow their more theoretical partners, because ENFJs have the tendency to skip important steps and be careless with details. By contrast, ENFJs find it frustrating when their literal-minded partners get mired in details rather than seeing the big picture. ISFPs and ENFJs also have to work hard to find energy for each other's interests. They tend to have different hobbies: ISFPs often enjoy quiet activities with close friends, while ENFJs have much stronger needs for social stimulation and variety. ISFPs often enjoy being in nature or participating in activities that have some element of physical risk, while ENFJs are more likely to enjoy discussing intellectual or spiritual issues. ISFPs also need more time to think about things before acting on them and prefer to conserve their energy until action is imperative. In contrast, ENFJs get an idea and run with it. ENFJs sometimes feel frustrated at the apparent lack of drive in their mellow partners, while ISFPs sometimes find their partners' incessant rushing around unnecessary and stressful.

Another common frustration for ISFP and ENFJ couples stems from their different needs for order and closure. ISFPs love to surround themselves with their prized possessions, while ENFJs find excessive clutter distracting and annoying. ISFPs don't have the same need for neatness and start many projects but fail to finish those they begin. ENFJs' strong drive to settle issues sometimes causes them to pressure their partners to make decisions before they feel ready to do so. Whereas ENFJs sometimes make hasty decisions, ISFPs are prone to procrastination and leaving things to the last minute.

Finally, since neither ISFPs nor ENFJs are especially good at managing conflict, they may need to work hard to discuss problems as soon as they come up. Both partners are especially sensitive to criticism, so they may have to force themselves to be truthful and direct while still being loving and gentle with each other. Rather than allow small irritations to fester and grow, they need to agree to have regular frank discussions and be open to making changes to keep the relationship healthy.

How to Reach Your ENFJ Partner

- Try to finish some of the projects you start. Put things away when you're finished using them.
- Do your share of the household chores. Pitch in and help out when your partner needs to get things whipped into shape.
- Be up-front and direct about your needs and feelings. Don't withdraw and wait for your partner to figure out what's bothering you.
- Try to be on time and follow through on promises.
- Compliment your partner on his or her many great ideas and suggestions for change. Support his or her professional goals.
- Resist some of your impulses and the tendency to get distracted and not be where you say you will be.
- Try not to change plans suddenly. Give your partner as much notice as possible.

How to Reach Your ISFP Partner

- Slow down and enjoy the moment with your partner. Resist the urge always to have an agenda.
- Be willing to adapt your plans or abandon what you're doing to participate in some of the spontaneous activities your partner enjoys.
- Be patient when explaining your more abstract ideas or complicated projects. Don't talk too fast or leap from topic to topic.
- Watch your tendency to be critical and judgmental about your partner's choices or to assume you know better.
- Consider relaxing some of your standards for neatness and respect your partner's desire to be surrounded with the possessions he or she loves.
- Be careful not to become so overcommitted to outside projects and work that you don't spend quiet time with your partner.
- Don't pressure your partner to participate in every social event with you.

ISFP with INFJ

The Joys

ISFPs and INFJs have two type preferences in common and often enjoy a close emotional connection. They are quiet, thoughtful, and gentle people who tend to spend a lot of time alone, with each other, or with a few very close and trusted friends. ISFPs and INFJs strive to create loving relationships and are typically very sensitive to each other's needs and feelings. Both work hard to avoid conflict and quickly restore harmony when they do have disagreements. Quietly expressive, ISFPs and INFJs usually tell their partners how much they love them and are very appreciative of the ways their partners demonstrate their support.

In addition to their similarities, ISFPs and INFJs are often initially attracted to each other because of their differences. ISFPs are drawn to INFJs because of their strength of character, strong beliefs, and unshakable integrity. ISFPs admire how articulate, creative, and imaginative their partners are and marvel at how quickly they come up with original insights. INFJs are often attracted to ISFPs' sweetness and their down-to-earth, nonjudgmental nature. INFJs feel totally accepted by ISFPs and often admire their ability to respond positively to life and find fun in everyday experiences.

Because of their differences, ISFPs and INFJs are often able to help each other grow and develop in important ways. ISFPs help INFJs pay closer attention to details, which helps them make fewer factual mistakes and create more workable projects. INFJs say that their playful and easygoing partners help them relax and take everything a little less seriously. ISFPs also nudge INFJs out of their interior worlds and encourage them to participate in more physical and outdoor activities. For their part, INFJs help ISFPs anticipate future needs so they don't find themselves poorly prepared or mired in details. ISFPs credit their partners with exposing them to new ideas and encouraging them to consider new approaches to old problems. By helping ISFPs become savvier about other people's motivations, INFJs help their partners avoid being taken advantage of or disillusioned by people who aren't what they appear to be.

The Frustrations

Despite their essentially warm and close relationships, ISFPs and INFJs experience frustrations that stem from their differences. ISFPs are essentially free-spirited and playful, while INFJs are usually very serious and intense. Although ISFPs are very sensitive, they sometimes don't understand fully the complexity of their partners' emotions or reactions. In contrast, INFJs may not appreciate fully how their partners can live so utterly in the present and take life as it comes. ISFPs rarely spend a lot of time trying to change people or worrying about things that are out of their control. They often wish that their INFJ partners would be more able to let some things go and enjoy the moment. For most INFJs, it is the search for meaning in experiences that gives life its rich texture, and they sometimes feel disappointed by their partners' lack of interest in growing, improving, or taking on personal challenges.

Another related frustration for many ISFP and INFJ couples is the different ways they see the world around them. ISFPs are super-observant and notice details, especially those about other people or the beauty of the natural world. INFJs are more interested in the connections between things and see possibilities rather than realities. INFJs also are usually interested in going deeper in conversations or areas of study, while ISFPs are more curious about a variety of things and more interested in helping people in practical ways. They also tend to get bored and restless with too much inactivity or with their partners' complicated theories.

ISFPs and INFJs sometimes struggle with issues of order and decision making. ISFPs strive to create comfortable, warm, and happy homes but are characteristically relaxed about clutter. INFJs like their environments to be free of distractions and can be particular about keeping things orderly. While ISFPs don't usually mind repetitious household chores, especially if doing them pleases their partners, they are easily distracted and tend to leave things half-finished. INFJs find this very annoying, and even though they may not enjoy housework of any kind, they tend to complete household tasks quickly and efficiently. ISFP and INFJ couples also may struggle with decision making, since ISFPs want a lot of information before making decisions, and INFJs usually make decisions quickly. INFJs feel frustrated by how long it takes their partners to decide and how frequently they change their minds afterward. ISFPs find their partners' inflexibility and somewhat arbitrary decision-making style irritating.

In general, ISFPs have fewer strong opinions, so they sometimes feel that their INFJ partners are trying to impose their views and moral positions on them. When it comes to money, INFJ and ISFP couples may disagree about spending. INFJs tend to be careful and even frugal, while ISFPs are usually generous and impulsive. INFJs usually want to research and plan purchases in advance, while ISFPs tend to get caught up in the excitement of spending money on fun toys and activities. Since both ISFPs and INFJs are very uncomfortable with confrontation and disharmony, they tend to avoid having open and honest discussions until little problems become major issues. By agreeing to be direct but gentle with each other, they can keep their relationships healthy and strong.

How to Reach Your INFJ Partner

- Be respectful and accommodating of your partner's routines and rituals. Don't interrupt or change plans suddenly.

- Try to keep careful track of the money you share and be respectful of your partner's desire to save and follow a budget.
- Try to come to conclusions and stick with decisions rather than leave things up in the air for too long or repeatedly change your mind after selecting a course of action.
- Compliment your partner on his or her creativity and unique ideas. Listen to your partner's visions and theories with respect and resist the urge to point out factual flaws.
- Try to finish projects you start and pick up after yourself. Pull your own weight when it comes to household chores.
- Speak up. Don't rely on your partner to figure out how you feel.

How to Reach Your ISFP Partner

- Never underestimate your partner's need for physical contact and affection. Hold and stroke your partner often, especially when he or she is stressed or upset.
- Listen fully, attentively, and sympathetically to your partner's feelings and troubles. Sit close and maintain eye contact.
- Don't impose your ambitions or values on your partner or assume a superior attitude that implies you always know what's best.
- Relax and be willing to stop what you're doing to participate in some of the spontaneous activities your partner enjoys.
- Don't try to control or limit your partner's activities or spending habits. Encourage your partner's innate desire for freedom.
- Try not to force premature decision making. Respect your partner's need to gather a lot of information and consider choices fully before making a commitment.

ISFP with ENFP

The Joys

ISFPs and ENFPs have two out of the four type preferences in common and share a desire for harmony and flexibility in their relationships. They tend to be loving, supportive, and affectionate couples with strong and sustaining emotional connections. Naturally empathetic, they are understanding and forgiving with one another and are usually eager to share their easily accessed feelings and values. They are both good listeners who want to help sort out each other's feelings. Responsive and compassionate, ISFPs and ENFPs are usually eager to accommodate each other's differences in order to make life easier and more enjoyable for each other. Since both partners are fairly relaxed in their approach to everyday life and in their dealings with other people, neither is especially interested in trying to control the other. Although they hold strong and inviolate values, they are typically easygoing about the little things and quite adaptable to change.

In addition to the qualities they share, ISFPs and ENFPs are often drawn to each other because of their differences. ISFPs are fascinated by ENFPs' creative minds and impressed by how quickly they come up with original ideas. ISFPs also admire ENFPs' offbeat humor, high energy level, and ease in social situations. ENFPs are often drawn to ISFPs' genuine warmth, kindness, and devotion to people and animals. They especially admire ISFPs' lack of pretense and down-to-earth style. ISFPs are usually great fun to be with, and they make ENFPs feel loved and accepted.

Because of their differences and their mutual desire to support each other, ISFPs and ENFPs have the opportunity to help each other grow and develop in important ways. Typically, ISFPs help ENFPs become more attuned to the moment so they can enjoy the delights of everyday life, especially those involving the physical world, such as nature and touch. ENFPs especially like ISFPs' ability to focus their attention and really be with their partners in the moment. For their part, ENFPs often help ISFPs see the less obvious connections between things, consider new ideas, look ahead to the future, and generally broaden their horizons. ISFPs often credit their partners with encouraging and supporting their efforts to step out into the social world more frequently and with more confidence.

The Frustrations

Their different social needs may create some frustrations for ISFP and ENFP couples. Most ISFPs are content to maintain a small group of close and trusted friends and need less human interaction than their very social and high-energy ENFP partners. ENFPs thrive on meeting new people, reconnecting with old friends, and generally being engaged in a variety of activities. ENFPs often have difficulty refusing any interesting opportunity, especially one that involves other people, so they may spend more time out of the house or on the telephone than with their partners, who may feel hurt and left out. Since they aren't especially assertive, ISFPs may suffer in silence. For their part, ENFPs may feel frustrated by their partners' lack of initiative and their tendency to resist invitations, especially those that come after a busy day. ENFPs sometimes pressure their partners to accompany them to events or stay longer at parties than their partners want to. These couples should allow each other the time and space they need for either rest or activity.

Another area of difference between ENFPs and ISFPs is their communication styles. ISFPs are attentive, focused, and sympathetic listeners. They also take a while to formulate their thoughts, especially if the subject is important or unpleasant and they wish to be tactful. While ENFPs care deeply about understanding their partners, they tend to interrupt, especially when they anticipate what their partners are trying to say. Although their intention may be to help, this can be a little intimidating and overwhelming to some ISFPs.

ISFPs' realism and ENFPs' imagination can lead to conflicts. New approaches or theories that are particularly energizing to ENFPs are generally much less interesting to their ISFP partners, especially if these ideas have little or no practical purpose. ENFPs sometimes feel unappreciated when their many inventive ideas are not met with enthusiasm. Misunderstandings also may occur because ISFPs are so literal and accurate about facts and details and ENFPs are often quite theoretical and vague. For example, dropping by a friend's house for a "quick" visit means a two-hour stopover to ENFPs and a fifteen-minute chat to ISFPs.

Finally, ISFPs and ENFPs avoid discussing areas of conflict as immediately, frankly, and openly as they should for fear of hurting each other's feelings. And since neither needs a lot of order or is especially good at planning, they may find themselves late on deadlines, swamped by chores, or overwhelmed by large projects. ISFPs and ENFPs need to find equitable ways of dividing up the tasks nobody wants to do so neither partner feels burdened and unappreciated.

How to Reach Your ENFP Partner

- Try to cultivate an interest in some of the things your partner cares about. Participate by asking questions and making informed comments.
- Ask your partner for his or her insights about the hidden connections or meanings of things.
- Compliment your partner on his or her many innovative and unusual ideas. Don't take the wind out of his or her sails by pointing out why these ideas won't work.
- Try some of your partner's ideas for new ways of doing things or solving problems or for out-of-the-ordinary experiences.

• Encourage your partner's desire to meet new people and keep lots of relationships alive. Make sure your partner feels free to socialize even if you aren't in the mood.

How to Reach Your ISFP Partner

• Listen fully and completely. Give your partner your undivided attention.
• Maintain close personal contact, especially when discussing unpleasant subjects or working out problems.
• Initiate lots of loving, physical affection, including massages and holding hands.
• Compliment your partner on his or her empathy for people and his or her devotion to relationships.
• Encourage your partner's desire to experience things firsthand and to learn by doing.
• Don't pressure your partner into going to social events with you.

ISFP with INFP

The Joys

With three of the four type preferences in common, ISFPs and INFPs are alike in many respects. Both are loyal, gentle, and sensitive people who make devoted partners and strive to have harmonious relationships. Thoughtful and considerate, ISFPs and INFPs prefer a leisurely pace and enjoy spending quiet time together or with a few close friends. Accommodating and flexible, they have a "live and let live" attitude toward their partners and others. And because neither is overly concerned about keeping their living spaces neat and tidy, they seldom argue over chores or whether both are pulling their weight around the house.

In addition to their many similarities and the natural comfort they often feel with each other, ISFPs and INFPs are also attracted to each other's differences. ISFPs are drawn to the more complex, artistic, and utterly original natures of INFPs. ISFPs find their partners a little mysterious and intriguing, if sometimes baffling. INFPs find ISFPs refreshingly accepting and easygoing. They admire how fun loving, spontaneous, and sensual their ISFP playmates are. INFPs also envy their partners' ability to be thoroughly engaged in what they're doing at the moment.

These differences provide the opportunity for ISFPs and INFPs to grow and develop in important ways. ISFPs help their partners lighten up, pay more attention to the moment, and enjoy life's sensual pleasures. For their part, INFPs often expose their partners to new ideas and ways of looking at things and to seeing connections they might ordinarily miss.

The Frustrations

Probably the greatest challenge for ISFP and INFP couples stems from the fact that both are intensely sensitive people who are absolutely driven by their deeply held personal values. When their values are in sync, they feel connected and united. But if either has a strong conviction that the other opposes, conflict is likely. For as flexible as they are in everyday matters, they can dig in their heels and become quite stubborn about issues that are important to them. And for a couple that strives for and thrives on harmonious relationships, even the small conflicts cause anxiety and tension. ISFPs and INFPs tend to blame themselves and avoid problems or dissension. In addition, ISFPs and INFPs are both very private people who sometimes have trouble sharing their complicated feelings unless they have time to think them through and feel totally safe and supported.

Another source of friction is that INFPs tend to idealize their relationships, and ISFPs sometimes feel guilty and frustrated when they can't live up to these fantasy expectations. For ISFPs, life is a series of adventures, and they don't spend much time worrying about things they can't control. For

INFPs, life is a search for meaning, and because they have such active imaginations, they are prone to worry about lots of things. INFPs and ISFPs often have different interests as well. ISFPs tend to enjoy physical, hands-on activities, such as sports, crafts, enjoying nature, or caring for animals. INFPs enjoy more artistic or intellectual pursuits, such as reading or writing. It can be frustrating for both partners when they don't share each other's interests. Sometimes INFPs also wish that they had more of a spiritual connection with their partners, while ISFPs wish that their physical connection was more intense.

Different communication styles can be a source of frustration for these couples. ISFPs are very literal communicators. They think and speak in specifics and are careful not to leave out any details or steps. INFPs think in terms of the big picture and are frequently more interested in the connections between things than in the facts. Where ISFPs are detailed and repetitive, INFPs are often abstract and vague.

Finally, neither partner particularly enjoys performing the mundane tasks necessary to keep a household running smoothly. Sparks may fly when things such as maintaining major appliances, registering cars, and paying bills on time always fall to the partner who dislikes doing them less or to the woman. Both INFPs and ISFPs can be impulsive spenders, which may cause the more thrifty partner some anxiety.

How to Reach Your INFP Partner

- Appreciate and compliment your partner on his

or her unique and accurate perceptions of other people.
- Accept your partner's occasional moodiness. Be supportive and loving, but don't assume that you are the cause.
- Try to become familiar with issues or activities that interest your partner so you can discuss or experience them together.
- Appreciate your partner's complexity and creativity. Compliment his or her good ideas.
- Listen patiently to your partner's sometimes obscure or convoluted stories.
- Appreciate the ways your partner's vision adds depth and meaning to your life or helps you plan for the future.

How to Reach Your ISFP Partner

- Appreciate your partner's gift for being in and enjoying the moment. Participate as often as you can.
- Recognize and support your partner's need to experience things firsthand and to learn by doing.
- Play with your partner. Especially do physical things together.
- Accept some things for what they are and resist the urge to analyze them and find a deeper meaning.
- Be specific and clear, especially about things that are conceptual or esoteric. Be patient with your partner's slower grasp of your abstract ideas.
- Be specific and include all the pertinent details.
- Be affectionate. Give your partner plenty of physical contact, such as lovemaking, massages, and hand-holding.

Chapter 11

The Conceptualizers²: NTs with NTs

ENTJ with ENTJ

The Joys

As with other couples who have all four preferences in common, ENTJs have little trouble understanding their partners. Both are logical, decisive, and strategic people who share many of the same values, such as being competent, working hard to succeed, and reaching their goals. People who naturally take charge of any situation, ENTJs are quite ambitious and are especially driven in their careers, sometimes even putting their work ahead of personal or family obligations. But because they share these priorities, they are usually very supportive and encouraging of each other's efforts to get more education or take advantage of career advancement opportunities.

ENTJs are active, high-energy people who have a wide range of interests, which they often enjoy sharing with their partners or with other people. ENTJs share the ability to quickly grasp underlying meanings, far-reaching implications, and less obvious relationships between things. Intellectually curious and strongly opinionated, ENTJs are stimulated by lively discussions or heated debates of topics they consider interesting. And since ENTJs like being around and interacting with a lot of people, these couples often have busy schedules and a lot of friends.

ENTJs are among the most straightforward and direct of all types. Their naturally logical way of thinking enables them to make objective decisions and practically compels them to try to implement them! They can be extremely critical and insensitive, but because they share these characteristics, they rarely hurt each other's feelings. Similarly, they don't communicate their feelings easily, but neither do they need lots of reassurance that they are loved.

Because ENTJs value competence, intelligence, and ambition, they are often attracted to and feel comfortable with people who share those qualities. And since ENTJs are motivated by the accumulation and exercise of power, the idea of aligning oneself with an equally powerful mate can be appealing and self-validating.

Because of their many similarities, ENTJs can help each other grow and develop in important ways. They can encourage one another to pay more attention to cultivating their personal relationships and enjoying their free time. They may get each other to slow down, live in the moment, and be more gentle and accepting of other people.

The Frustrations

Since ENTJ couples share the same strengths, they also share many of the same weaknesses. ENTJs avoid detailed, repetitive tasks such as household chores and maintenance. When these tasks routinely fall on the partner who dislikes them less, or on the woman in the couple, resentment can build over the unfair distribution of labor. And since ENTJs tend to be perfectionists, they are likely to be critical when their high standards are not met.

ENTJs are also naturally competitive. This can be an advantage when they are paired in a tennis match, but it also means that they compare and measure their success in other areas, such as their careers. Neither partner is generally eager to give up or postpone his or her (and it is usually *her*) career to raise a family.

Although ENTJs are highly verbal and articulate, they are considerably less adept at dealing with the needs or feelings of others. They tend to avoid situations that make them feel anything less than completely competent or in charge. They analyze conflict coolly, logically, and impersonally, but they also avoid exposing their insecurities or vulnerabilities, even to their partners. They may run the risk of not resolving problems because they ignore the underlying causes or refuse to admit they are wrong.

Advice for ENTJs

• Recognize that when something your partner does bothers you, it is probably because you are seeing a quality or behavior that you don't like in yourself.
• Consider reevaluating your priorities with regard to conflicts between career aspirations and home responsibilities.
• Commit to spending quiet time together without a plan or agenda.
• Take time to express your appreciation to your partner. Share your personal feelings and reactions.
• Watch your tendency to compete. Be willing to lose an occasional argument.
• Be willing to let down your guard and express the full range of your feelings to your partner.
• Understand that being competent in dealing with your relationship is just as important as being competent in your career.

• Take turns managing household chores. Create a fair yet flexible arrangement.

ENTJ with INTJ

The Joys

With three type preferences and temperamental values in common, ENTJs and INTJs are similar in many significant ways. Both are driven by a need for knowledge, competence, and power, and both set very high standards for themselves and their partners. Similarly, they are energized by intellectual stimulation and are usually quite ambitious. They are also great sources of support for each other. These couples see the world in a similar, global way and frequently share common interests and passions. They are perpetual learners who spend some of their most pleasurable times together studying or engaging in lively discussions. They may even like to attend professional conferences in each other's fields just so they can share something new with their partners. Since both ENTJs and INTJs are highly imaginative and quite logical, they tend to be excellent problem solvers who love to apply their creativity to difficult challenges.

In addition to their similarities, ENTJs and INTJs are often initially attracted to each other because of their different energy levels and social needs. ENTJs are drawn to INTJs' calm and ability to focus internally, just as INTJs are attracted to ENTJs' social confidence and verbal skills.

Both partners have an opportunity to help each other grow and develop in important ways. ENTJs can help their partners get out in the world, discuss concerns more freely, and experience new people and places. INTJs can help their partners focus some of their energy, take time to explore issues in more depth, and be more selective about where they invest their considerable energy.

The Frustrations

Because INTJs and ENTJs are so similar, they can unwittingly serve as reminders of each other's flaws. For instance, both have very high standards, and they like to live in an orderly home. Although they rarely have conflicts about neatness, neither partner is likely to be very interested in mundane housework or the highly detailed tasks necessary to run a home. But someone has to do these things, so these jobs are often divided along gender lines — the woman takes care of the house, and the man is responsible for fixing things and for the finances. When the division of labor is not equitable or one partner's effort doesn't satisfy the other's high standards, it can cause friction.·

ENTJs and INTJs usually have very different social needs. Typically, ENTJs desire a lot of social contact, while INTJs like more time alone. Similarly, ENTJs often want more conversation, and INTJs want more quiet. When these partners do not share common interests, INTJs may make themselves unavailable by spending hours at a time on the computer, reading, or engaged in some other solitary activity, which makes ENTJs feel shut out. Similarly, when ENTJs require their partners to do too much socializing, INTJs may feel exhausted and resentful.

Both ENTJs and INTJs are very independent people (INTJs are generally considered to be the most independent of all types) with strong opinions. As a result, neither are willing to yield their positions. And since ENTJs and INTJs tend to be competitive and career-driven, serious conflicts can result when an opportunity arises that will advance one partner's career at the expense of the other's. This is especially true when the woman feels pressured to give up her career to have a family and finds many of her more domestic responsibilities unrewarding.

Although INTJs and ENTJs are good abstract problem solvers, they are often on shaky ground when it comes to dealing with their emotions or those of others. They are often critical, but they can also be defensive about their own weaknesses. And because they are not naturally tuned in to their own emotional undercurrents or those of their partners, they can be unaware of a problem until it becomes serious. Neither ENTJs nor INTJs are naturally empathetic and may feel unsupported in times of stress or crisis. When they are upset and unable to view a situation with their normal cool objectivity, they may retreat angrily from the conflict and from their partners, frustrated by their inability to figure out an effective solution. Regular, honest, and understanding communication is necessary for them to maintain a sense of connection and intimacy.

How to Reach Your ENTJ Partner

• Try to go out more or invite people to your house to socialize.
• Ask your partner to think about a problem you're having and offer his or her insights.
• Compliment your partner on good points he or she makes in an argument.
• Initiate intimacy and discussions.
• Ask for the space you need, but try not to wall yourself off for extended periods of time.
• Try to pick up on clues that something is bothering your partner. Be open to a discussion of his or her feelings, although that might be uncomfortable for you.

How to Reach Your INTJ Partner

• Give your partner plenty of time, space, and quiet.
• Don't ask your partner to do more than one thing at a time. For example, don't try to carry on an important conversation while your partner is cooking a meal.
• Compliment your partner on his or her ideas before evaluating or critiquing them.
• Try not to be too bossy or controlling.

- When something is bothering you, let your partner know and make an "appointment" to discuss it. Give your partner plenty of time to think about it first.
- If you can afford it, hire a housekeeper or someone else to do the tasks neither of you enjoys or is good at.
- Recognize that you and your partner may not be comfortable discussing your feelings, so be sensitive to this and supportive of each other.

ENTJ with ENTP

The Joys

The primary and sustaining connection between ENTJs and ENTPs is their similar independent natures and their strong intellectual curiosity. ENTJs and ENTPs share three out of the four preferences, so they understand and communicate with each other easily. They are both independent and often ambitious people who are eager to learn new things and constantly strive to increase their personal and professional competence. ENTJ and ENTP couples tend to be staunch supporters of each other's pursuits and interests, even when those interests are completely separate from their own.

Many ENTJ and ENTP couples are initially attracted to each other's creativity and intellectual curiosity. They also find each other refreshingly up-front and confident and not easily intimidated. They respect one another's quick thinking and ability to see long-range implications. It's their differences, however, that provide the intrigue. ENTJs are drawn to the playful, irreverent natures of ENTPs, while ENTPs often admire ENTJs' decisiveness and impressive organizational abilities.

Such differences provide these couples with the opportunity to help each other grow and develop in important ways. ENTJs help their partners focus some of their considerable energy on fewer projects so more of them succeed. For their part, ENTPs

help their decisive partners make better choices by collecting more information. ENTPs also can push their partners to experiment and take more calculated risks. Both partners can help each other become more sensitive to emotional undercurrents, express their appreciation, and clarify their own values.

Naturally articulate, ENTJs and ENTPs love to debate and have an impressive grasp of many issues. Their competitive spirit tends to pervade all areas of their lives, so they often find themselves playing one-upmanship, which can be stimulating and energizing — up to a point. No matter what the subject, ENTJs and ENTPs deal with things directly, if not always tactfully or gently. Although they are both very honest, they sometimes avoid the real and painful sources of conflict.

The Frustrations

Because most ENTJs and ENTPs feel strongly about their views and are stimulated by opposition, they can become somewhat bullheaded. Their habit of trying to best each other can escalate into a less-than-friendly or loving activity. And neither type is inclined to admit to hurt feelings, so ENTJs and ENTPs need to balance their banter with heartfelt expressions of their affection. ENTJs and ENTPs also need to set aside quiet, private time to discuss their relationships and make sure they understand each other's values and hopes.

The most common source of frustration for ENTJ and ENTP couples is their different attitudes about order, decision making, and structure. ENTJs are often irritated by how long it takes their partners to make a decision and how much discussion and research goes into even the simplest choice. ENTPs talk about many improvements they are thinking of making, but they often follow through on only a fraction of them. They may feel that their partners are too quick to come to conclusions and miss great opportunities because they are locked into their plans and schedules. And

ENTJs often hear a decision being made when their partners are only brainstorming. ENTJs also like a neat and orderly home, so they find it stressful and annoying to be around the clutter and half-finished projects of their ENTP partners. To be fair, ENTPs frequently neglect to pick up after themselves. ENTJ and ENTP couples need to find creative and workable ways of balancing ENTPs' need for a relaxed and comfortable atmosphere with ENTJs' need for order and organized systems.

How to Reach Your ENTP Partner

- Don't make a decision, then leave it up to your partner to implement it.
- Never criticize your partner's competence in public.
- Encourage your partner's freedom and curiosity. Be patient with the number of questions he or she asks.
- Try to relax your schedule occasionally. Be willing to act on some of your partner's spontaneous suggestions.
- Listen to your partner's many ideas and brainstorm possibilities together.
- Don't take offense when your partner asks for other people's opinions after you've given yours.

How to Reach Your ENTJ Partner

- Clean something, organize something, or tidy up.
- Make a decision and stick with it.
- Respect and try to follow your partner's systems. Remember to record checks in the register and keep track of shared property and resources.
- When you feel the need to debate the merits of every option, consider bending a friend's ear.
- Never criticize your partner's competence in public.
- Call when you're going to be late, and try not to change plans at the last minute.

- Respect your partner's rituals and routines.

ENTJ with INTP

The Joys

ENTJs and INTPs share two of the four type preferences and many of the same fundamental values and motivations. They both have a natural drive for competence and a thirst for knowledge and learning, and they are independent, freethinking people. Most ENTJs and INTPs find that the core of their relationships is an intellectual connection. They enjoy discussions about a wide range of subjects and share even radically different points of view with respect and intensity. Books, movies, theater, and art often provide excellent fodder for their spirited and even heated debates. As long as ENTJs resist being obstinate and INTPs avoid switching sides too often simply to "stir the pot," these couples may enjoy great satisfaction.

ENTJs and INTPs often strive to create and maintain an equal partnership unbounded by society's conventions or gender role limitations. Both are deeply interested in any kind of learning and are open to trying new things. It's their differences, however, that are most frequently the source of their initial attraction. ENTJs are attracted to INTPs' independence, great ideas, and calm and self-contained energy. INTPs are usually very accepting people, so ENTJs (especially female ENTJs) may feel comfortable being the assertive and ambitious people they are. INTPs are often attracted to ENTJs' strength, decisiveness, political savvy, and utter confidence.

ENTJ and INTP couples' differences give them the opportunity to grow and develop in important ways. ENTJs help INTPs make more of their innovations a reality by encouraging them to follow through on some of the many projects they start. ENTJs also help INTPs get out in the world, meet new people, and become more socially confident.

For their part, INTPs often help ENTJs slow down, gather more information before making decisions, and relinquish some of their need to be in charge. Together, they can help each other become more aware of the realities of life and more open and vulnerable with each other.

The Frustrations

Typically, it is the everyday irritations caused by their differences that frustrate both ENTJs and INTPs. Neither are particularly interested in or satisfied by mundane chores, so they may both avoid necessary housework. Given their natural compulsion to complete projects and have things in order, ENTJs are more likely to take on this workload, but their sense of fairness will eventually force them to point out the inequity. ENTJs also become annoyed when their INTP partners lose interest in a task as soon as the creative challenge is over. INTPs rarely have the same zeal for finishing projects as they have for starting them. And most INTPs are so relaxed about meeting deadlines that they often act quite irresponsibly. On the other hand, ENTJs typically have such extremely high standards for how things ought to be done that they can be too demanding and rigid.

Another area of frustration for ENTJs and INTPs is their different social needs. ENTJs are usually much more active and enjoy the stimulation and energy they get from other people, travel, and varied experiences. INTPs want and need much more privacy and uninterrupted time alone to think and work on projects that interest them. As long as ENTJs and INTPs have adequate time to enjoy mutually interesting activities and to pursue their own interests, they can be quite content living fairly independent lives.

Although ENTJs and INTPs are usually very supportive of each other's career aspirations, they are also naturally competitive and may debate issues past the point where it is fun. It may be hard for them to admit they're wrong, so what starts as an intellectual exercise may become unpleasant when neither partner feels safe enough to surrender. Because ENTJs and INTPs are usually so uncomfortable being vulnerable, they tend to avoid getting into the scary emotional territory that can help them grow and deepen their trust in each other. They need to be willing to tackle life's problems together rather than always dealing with them separately.

How to Reach Your INTP Partner

- Give your partner plenty of space and time to think things through without interruption. Respect your mate's need to become immersed in his or her projects.
- Allow your partner to work on tasks alone without comment or even the physical proximity of another person.
- Encourage your partner's need for independence, and don't hover. INTPs need lots of privacy and the freedom to come and go as they please.
- Try not to force decisions. Give your partner the chance to mull things over and carefully consider issues.
- Talk less but be willing to discuss things when your partner wants to talk. Try waiting for a quiet time, then gently ask for your partner's opinion.
- Choose your battles carefully. Your partner is much more likely to come out and share if the atmosphere isn't too intense.

How to Reach Your ENTJ Partner

- Initiate discussions, physical intimacy, household chores, and activities of all sorts.
- Try to participate in activities and social events that are important to your partner.
- Share what you're thinking, feeling, and want. Remember, it's really important to your partner to have regular discussions of substance, depth, and importance.

• Ask your partner's advice and invite his or her input and opinions.

• Try to be patient with your partner's slower adaptation time. Give him or her as much notice of a change in plans as possible.

• Try to be prompt. Strive to finish more of the projects you start.

INTJ with INTJ

The Joys

Because they share all four type preferences, INTJ couples are usually very compatible and find their relationships to be fairly easy and calm. An intense intellectual connection between INTJs accounts in great part for their attraction and satisfaction. At its core, it's an attraction of the minds. Both partners usually enjoy intellectual debates and the free exchange of ideas. Creative and original, they like to compare and contrast theories, drawing out the best in each other and offering constructive suggestions for improvement. Since they both value personal and professional competence highly and share a strong desire for independence and constant challenge, they tend to respect each other's pursuits and ideals. Because neither is especially romantic, it comes as a great relief that they do not expect each other to be overly sentimental.

Most INTJs have a great need for privacy and large blocks of time alone to concentrate. Perhaps one of the most frustrating experiences for INTJs is to be interrupted and unable to explore subjects in depth. Since both partners share this fundamental need, they can protect each other's time. When they're ready, INTJs bring a wealth of fresh and well-considered opinions to any discussion and take great pleasure in sharing different points of view, even if they are contradictory. Since INTJs are very objective, they are typically able to have intellectually passionate debates without getting their feelings hurt. They continuously search for meaning and truth in any discussion, so while they do tend to have trouble backing down from a position, they can be won over by sound logic.

INTJ couples often enjoy experiencing new things together and talking them through afterward. Above all, they love being challenged to think in new and deeper ways. Many INTJs have many of the same interests and derive great satisfaction from their partner's offbeat sense of humor.

Because of their shared strengths and blind spots, INTJ couples have the opportunity to help each other grow and develop in important ways. With effort and commitment, they are able to open up emotionally and become more sensitive to their partners and others. Together, INTJs can pay closer attention to the more mundane and repetitive tasks of daily life and make fewer factual mistakes. They can also encourage each other to relax, accommodate the unexpected, and enjoy more of life's pleasures.

The Frustrations

One common area of frustration for INTJ couples is that they both have very strong opinions about how to run their lives, from the way they like their homes organized to what time they like to eat breakfast. These preferences are very clear, and neither partner is particularly flexible. Since most INTJs are quite regimented — even a bit set in their ways — they find it very hard to adapt to changes in plans or schedules. Given their propensity for stubbornness, these couples come to impasses regularly. Women INTJs are no more likely to give up their plans or independence than are their male partners. Creative thinking and compromise are required to resolve these pesky issues fairly.

INTJ couples tend to be critical and demanding of themselves, each other, and other people. But even INTJs can feel uncomfortable watching their partners respond harshly or impatiently with others. Perhaps the biggest challenge for INTJ couples is to feel comfortable expressing their deep feelings, fears, or vulnerabilities. INTJs tend to withdraw into their own private worlds, and these couples may have to work especially hard to maintain an emotional connection. They may overanalyze problems and make assumptions rather than really communicate with their partners. Talk is essential for these couples, and they need to find time every day to share with each other so they don't let too much space grow between them. Dependence, even if it's mutual, is very difficult for INTJs. They may find it hard to ask for or give help without feeling some sense of disdain for their own or their partners' weakness. They can be very critical of each other, holding their partners to impossibly high and unyielding standards.

Advice for INTJs

• Give each other plenty of privacy and space to pursue your own interests.
• Avoid "I told you so," and don't correct each other in public.
• Take time to talk openly about your feelings, fears, and vulnerabilities. Share your insights and ideas. (Consider writing to each other.)
• Set aside time on a regular basis to spend together. Try to relax your schedules and make room for spontaneity.
• Give your partner your total attention when he or she is talking.
• Be willing to explore new ways of developing and deepening emotional and physical intimacy.

INTJ with ENTP

The Joys

INTJs and ENTPs share two type preferences and a temperamental drive to understand the world and be competent in all they attempt. They have a thirst for knowledge and enjoy all sorts of intellectual stimulation. One of their favorite activities is engaging in spirited debates, almost without

regard to the topic. Since they tend to be highly career-focused, they can be encouraging and supportive of each other. INTJs and ENTPs are very independent people, so these couples often choose to lead fairly separate lives. Some find keeping their finances separate preferable, since their attitudes about money and spending can be quite different (ENTPs are typically more impulsive than their INTJ mates). When these couples have disagreements, they are usually able to analyze the situation objectively and use their excellent problem-solving skills to arrive at a mutually satisfactory solution.

INTJs and ENTPs also derive satisfaction from their shared view of the world. They tend to see possibilities, take a global view of issues, and understand the interrelatedness of subjects. This important connection gives them great insight into each other. In addition to their similarities, they are initially attracted by each other's differences. INTJs admire ENTPs' charm, wit, and ease in social situations, while ENTPs are often drawn to the strength, brilliance, and depth of INTJs.

These differences often enable INTJs and ENTPs to help each other grow and develop in important ways. INTJs help ENTPs focus some of their enviable energy, become more organized, and hence become more productive, effective, and accountable. For their part, ENTPs often help the more serious INTJs lighten up, encouraging them to stay open to new experiences and to relax, play, and laugh.

The Frustrations

Although they share some strong similarities, INTJs' and ENTPs' differences present appreciable challenges. Both types usually have very high standards, but INTJs' standards can be nearly unachievable. INTJs are often perfectionists who have little patience for things not done the "right" way. As a result, they can be perceived as rigid and demanding partners. Because ENTPs often see myriad possibilities, they are often at odds with their partners as to how, and especially when, a particular task should be completed.

The majority of conflicts these couples experience revolve around the fact that INTJs like things decided and settled and want their homes and workspaces to be neat and orderly. By nature, ENTPs are more adaptable and responsive, but they are also notoriously messy. Although ENTPs are often inspired to start innovative projects, they rarely finish them. Conflict arises when the organized INTJs meet the more disorganized ENTPs. INTJs want to stick with a plan, while ENTPs are ever ready to shift gears and respond to a more interesting opportunity.

INTJs and ENTPs frequently have different notions about time as well. INTJs tend to be very prompt and believe that when they make a commitment, it ought to be honored. ENTPs tend to run behind schedule because they are more easily distracted by opportunities they find along the way. To be sure, ENTPs often make promises they can't or don't keep, while INTJs can be a bit inflexible. These different approaches may result in ENTPs feeling that they are being controlled by INTJs, while INTJs think that ENTPs are not trustworthy or reliable.

Another potential source of conflict for these couples is that ENTPs usually need a lot of social interaction and often have a wide circle of friends and acquaintances. In contrast, INTJs are not usually comfortable in large social gatherings because the talk is often so superficial. But INTJs can sometimes feel neglected when their ENTP partners choose to be out with others instead of at home with them.

When conflicts arise, INTJs and ENTPs often prefer to deal with them in different ways. ENTPs want to talk things out right away, while INTJs generally want to think about things before responding. When issues are ignored for too long, ENTPs are likely to explode and act irrationally, while INTJs are more likely to withdraw, let their anger percolate, and give their partners the silent treatment. Because neither ENTPs nor INTJs may be in touch with their deep feelings about any issue, they may have trouble being sensitive to their partners and to other people.

Finally, both INTJs and ENTPs like to focus on the future and possible implications, so they may miss some important details or some of the pleasures of the moment. They need to find ways of reminding themselves and each other to stop, enjoy, and be grateful for what they have.

How to Reach Your ENTP Partner

- Never criticize or question your partner's competence in public.
- Encourage your partner's independent social life but attempt to participate in some of his or her social activities. Make an effort to meet and like his or her friends.
- Try to be flexible. Practice letting the small annoyances go.
- Plan surprises for your partner. Arrange for periodic dates away from home and work. Try new things.
- Give your partner a few choices but be sure to offer ones that you can live with.
- Don't try to nail your partner down before he or she has considered all the options and maybe even asked other people for their opinions.

How to Reach Your INTJ Partner

- Try to stick with the agreements and plans you make together. Introduce changes slowly, giving plenty of warning if possible.
- Compliment your partner on his or her achievements. Never question your partner's competence in public.
- Don't ask your partner to do or focus on more than one thing at a time. If you have a complaint, choose a time to discuss it when you aren't interrupting your partner's work or thoughts.

- Try to help your partner relax. Find fun activities that appeal to his or her interests and initiate physical intimacy.
- Don't force or expect too much socializing. Consider bringing two cars to social events so your partner can leave early.
- Give your partner plenty of space and time to think about things before expecting a response.
- Try to follow rules and routines that are important to your partner.

INTJ with INTP

The Joys

With three of the four type preferences in common, INTJs and INTPs are similar in many ways. Both are logical, creative, and highly independent people whose primary motivation is to be competent in all that they do, so they set very high standards for themselves and each other. Global thinkers, INTJs and INTPs crave intellectual stimulation, constantly seek new challenges, and enjoy discussing and debating a wide range of issues. They focus on the larger implications of issues and rarely get mired in the details. Naturally reserved and private, both partners enjoy spending lots of time thinking or spending time alone or with each other, but usually not with a large number of people.

Because INTJ and INTP couples are similar in so many ways, they report a high degree of comfort in their relationships. They seem to understand each other well, and day-to-day communication tends to be easy. As reflective and objective people, they take an intellectual approach to problem solving and seldom hurt each other's feelings. Because they value their own professional achievements and competence, they are usually very supportive of each other's career aspirations and efforts. Finally, it is not surprising that two such independent people are content to lead fairly separate and autonomous lives.

Because INTJs and INTPs place such a high value on intellectual prowess and competence, it's understandable that they would be most impressed by and attracted to people they consider their intellectual equals. In addition to that important commonality, INTJs and INTPs are also attracted to each other because of their different attitudes about order and closure. INTJs often find their partners' more casual, spontaneous, and flexible natures appealing, just as INTPs admire their partners' organizational abilities, drive to get things done, and decisiveness.

Because of their differences, INTJs and INTPs have the opportunity to help each other grow and develop in important ways. INTJs are able to help INTPs prioritize and then eliminate some of their options so they move ahead and finish the projects they start. INTPs often credit their partners with helping them adopt time management and organizational strategies that make them more effective. For their part, INTPs encourage INTJs to resist the urge to make decisions too quickly and absolutely. INTJs say that their partners help them relax and stay open to spontaneous opportunities that arise.

The Frustrations

The chief source of frustration for most INTJs and INTPs is their different needs for order and closure. For organized INTJs, time is a precious resource, something that must be used judiciously and never wasted. Most INTJs like to make and adhere to schedules in both their personal and professional lives. INTPs are considerably more spontaneous and often feel that their partners' insistence on planning takes the fun out of experiences. INTPs are generally much better at starting things than finishing them and can usually find a compelling reason to stop what they're doing to pursue something more challenging or interesting. This tendency grates on the nerves of INTJs, who are determined to complete whatever tasks they start. INTJs sometimes complain that their partners are too messy and disorganized, while INTPs just as frequently feel that their partners are too serious, inflexible, and bent on controlling everything and everyone around them.

With great strengths often come great weaknesses. Because neither INTJs nor INTPs are particularly comfortable or skillful when dealing with emotions, they may fail to explore the underlying causes of conflicts and therefore never really resolve them. By not getting at the root of the problem, resentment can build until it erodes their connection with each other. Although both types are logical and analytical, INTPs are usually a bit more emotionally and physically demonstrative than their INTJ partners. Neither may take the time to express their appreciation for their partners, however. Although their intellectual discussions are usually a source of great stimulation and enjoyment, these two types are naturally quite competitive and may be so convinced that their own perspectives are superior that they debate past the point of having fun.

Finally, since neither INTJs nor INTPs are especially realistic or practical, they may not pay close attention to factual details or may skip uninteresting steps in projects. They can become so focused on their individual interests that they neglect more mundane but important events happening around them. Things such as maintaining communication with relatives and friends may not appeal much to either partner, and the one who is forced to assume these roles may come to resent it.

How to Reach Your INTJ Partner

- Be sure to give your partner the time and space he or she needs to think things through without interruption.
- Honor your commitments. Work at being prompt and following through on chores.
- Try to pick up after yourself and leave common areas neat.
- Initiate outings. Don't allow other things to interfere with time set aside for the two of you.

- Try to make decisions and not leave issues unsettled for too long.
- Respect your partner's schedules, routines, and rituals.

How to Reach Your INTP Partner

- Try to accommodate your partner's need for spontaneity. If necessary, plan for it in advance.
- Schedule downtime for the two of you to get away. Be willing to leave plans open and respond to the moment without having an agenda or predetermined destination.
- Watch your tendency to point out flaws in your partner's ideas or feel compelled to improve on them.
- Try not to impose too many rules or too much structure on your partner. Encourage his or her freedom and need to question the status quo.
- Respect your partner's curiosity and need to consider many options before making a decision.

ENTP with ENTP

The Joys

Couples who share all four type preferences have almost no trouble understanding each other. This is especially true of ENTPs because they are naturally curious and insightful about people and are driven to understand others. Also, because they are typically very outgoing and social and usually have had a wide variety of relationships, they are often particularly perceptive about their current ones. ENTPs are engaging and charismatic and usually love meeting new people and keeping friendships alive. They like coming up with and sharing ideas, seeing new possibilities, and finding creative ways to solve problems. And because they are so similar, they often enjoy spending time together and pursuing many of the same activities and interests.

What usually attracts ENTPs to each other is that they both feel free to be themselves. Naturally competitive, ENTPs often encourage and stimulate each other's pursuit of excellence. ENTPs also can help each other grow and develop in important ways, such as learning to pay attention to important facts and details, slowing down to become more patient and sensitive listeners, and being accountable and sticking with plans.

The Frustrations

Partners who mirror each other's strengths also accurately reflect each other's weaknesses. Because ENTPs pride themselves on their competence, they don't like to be confronted with their shortcomings or to acknowledge them. ENTPs can be very critical, and when their criticism is directed at their partners, it can be hurtful and destructive. ENTPs often exude charm, which they use to their great advantage. However, their persuasiveness and gift of gab can make others question their genuineness. Naturally, the same trait can foster suspicion about their partners' motives and sincerity.

One potential frustration for ENTP couples is that neither partner is particularly attentive to details or naturally very organized. In reality, someone has to make sure the bills get paid on time and appointments are made and kept. But since neither partner enjoys or is particularly good at these activities, they often fall on the person who dislikes them less or feels pressured into doing them. Women are more likely to shoulder the burden, especially when it comes to parenting and household tasks. These couples need to find innovative ways of sharing or trading off on these chores.

Another common frustration stems from the fact that neither person is naturally inclined to give careful consideration to how others may feel about their decisions or actions. Because they are so competitive by nature, ENTP couples often find themselves engaged in a kind of one-upmanship, frequently debating issues beyond the point where it is still fun. ENTPs are typically very ambitious and career-focused, so they can sometimes be accused of acting selfishly. And since ENTPs can be very impulsive about spending money, both may take unnecessary risks or ignore budgets that interfere with their fun. Because these partners are uncomfortable reining in each other — and being reined in themselves — they run the risk of getting into real financial trouble. Likewise, ENTP couples' love of the possible rather than the practical can result in their squandering energy and money on plans that don't work out.

When it comes to resolving conflicts, ENTPs may be very good at analyzing problems and trying to arrive at innovative solutions, but they may fail to explore and deal with underlying emotional causes. And because they strongly need to appear capable and competent at all times, they may have trouble revealing their vulnerabilities to each other.

Advice for ENTPs

- Be sure to consider how your partner will feel about your actions rather than rushing into something new.
- Share the responsibilities and tasks that neither of you likes to do. When it's your partner's turn, make sure he or she knows that you appreciate his or her efforts.
- Praise your partner's competence, good ideas, and clever solutions without feeling the need to improve on them.
- Celebrate your partner's victories. Try not to see his or her success as something you have to match.
- Take turns wearing a watch so you'll be on time for important appointments and not inconvenience others.
- Find time to spend together so you can deepen your emotional connection.

ENTP with INTP

The Joys

A shared intellectual connection is the source of great and sustaining satisfaction for many ENTP and INTP couples. Since they have three out of four type preferences in common and share the same temperament, they often have easy and comfortable relationships based on mutual respect. Many ENTPs and INTPs enjoy fascinating, engaging, and in-depth discussions about a variety of issues and global topics. They tend to be interested in politics and the arts, and they have a common desire to learn and excel. ENTPs and INTPs are very independent people, so their closeness is almost always balanced by their separate and rewarding lives. They both have vivid imaginations and a desire to apply their creativity to all aspects of their lives. They are ambitious, curious, and ever eager to add to their impressive storehouse of knowledge and experiences. Since ENTPs and INTPs are flexible and adaptive, they follow their inspiration wherever it takes them, whether down a career path or on a spontaneous vacation. They need little planning and almost no structure to have a great time. In fact, the homes of most ENTPs and INTPs are very relaxed and informal places. The few rules they do have tend to maintain respect, fairness, and equality.

Most ENTPs and INTPs are not threatened by differences but instead see them as sources of excitement and stimulation. ENTPs are often drawn to the intensity, calm, and fierce independence of INTPs, while INTPs admire the social skills, charm, and charisma of ENTPs. Because of this difference, ENTPs and INTPs have the opportunity to help each other grow and develop in important ways. Typically, ENTPs help draw INTPs out into the social world and encourage them to share their ideas and innovations with others. As a result, many

INTPs say that they are more comfortable interacting with people and are exposed to a wider range of experiences. For their part, INTPs help their ENTP partners channel their energy into fewer projects so they get better results. ENTPs also credit their INTP partners with helping them balance their need for socializing with the satisfaction of a few meaningful relationships. As they grow together, ENTPs often find that they become more compassionate and sensitive to others, and INTPs find that they are more realistic and pragmatic.

The Frustrations

Like many very similar couples, ENTPs and INTPs may experience frustrations caused by their shared characteristics. Since they tend to put their careers first, they may become so involved in their work that they lose touch with each other and neglect the relationship. Also, even though they enjoy regular intellectual debates, they can become too competitive and sacrifice closeness for the sake of winning. Rather than express their true feelings of devotion and appreciation, they tease, kid, or bait each other. And since neither partner is comfortable admitting when he or she is hurt, the verbal sparring often continues past the point of fun and stimulation. When ENTPs and INTPs turn their naturally critical eyes on each other, the situation can turn nasty and hurtful.

Another similarity that causes friction between ENTPs and INTPs is that neither is especially accurate about facts and details or good at finishing projects. Yet they may both find it frustrating to have so many projects left undone — especially those belonging to their partners! They enjoy creative problem solving but quickly tire of anything routine. And since INTPs generally need more time than ENTPs to consider options before acting on them, the partners may clash when considering purchases, both major and minor ones.

The biggest source of conflict between ENTPs

and INTPs is their different needs for social stimulation. ENTPs are true social animals; they thrive on meeting and talking with new people and like to be involved in a wide range of projects. INTPs are much more private people who prefer a lot of time alone to immerse themselves in projects that interest them. ENTPs are often frustrated by the amount of time their INTP partners spend inside their own heads, while INTPs often feel that their partners invade their space and simply talk too much! ENTP and INTP couples need to find ways for both partners to get the private time they need, whether that time is spent together or alone.

How to Reach Your INTP Partner

- Try not to overpower your partner when you're debating or having a discussion. Remember that winning isn't everything.
- Surprise your partner with small, unusual gifts that show you understand her or him.
- Give your partner plenty of privacy.
- Don't push for discussions or decisions. Respect your partner's need to think things through fully and gather a lot of information before acting.
- Educate yourself on the topics that interest your partner so you can discuss them intelligently.
- Suggest a discussion time in advance so your partner will have time to clarify his or her feelings. When your partner is talking, listen carefully and respectfully.
- Ask for your partner's opinions and creative solutions to complex or difficult challenges.

How to Reach Your ENTP Partner

- Surprise your partner with unexpected get-togethers. Be willing to drop by to see friends.
- Encourage your partner to go out with friends and continue to meet new people even if you don't accompany him or her.
- Respect your partner's need to gather information by talking to a lot of people even after you've offered your opinion.

- Brainstorm with your partner. Remember that he or she needs to talk to clarify his or her positions, so listen with enthusiasm.
- Listen patiently to your partner's sometimes long-winded and dramatic stories.

INTP with INTP

The Joys

Since INTP couples share all four type preferences, they tend to have very easygoing, amicable relationships based on mutual respect for their individuality. INTPs are characteristically serious, intellectual, and intense people with rich inner lives and vivid imaginations. INTP couples usually respect each other's needs for peace, quiet, and the time to focus on projects that captivate their interests. Since independence is a central and highly valued characteristic of INTPs, they often make special allowances for each other's pursuits and relish the fact that they are not exclusively responsible for each other's happiness and fulfillment.

One of the most prominent features of INTP relationships is the couple's intellectual connection. They typically derive great pleasure from discussing theoretical subjects or global topics in depth. Both are superior debaters, so they often enjoy the back-and-forth of a heated argument, and they rarely get their feelings hurt. Since neither partner is prone to take things personally, INTP couples can give and receive constructive criticism and generally trust each other to be totally honest with them. Both are driven to excel and master their areas of study, which makes them strong supporters of each other's professional growth and development. INTPs also are casual, flexible, and easygoing people. They tend to reject any convention or expectation that doesn't make logical sense, and they often operate without regard to society's gender roles.

Given their similarities, it's no surprise that

INTPs are often attracted to each other. They are a rare breed in American culture, accounting for only about 3 percent of the population, and INTP women especially appreciate the freedom from convention that a relationship with another INTP affords. Because they understand each other so well, INTP couples have the opportunity to help each other grow and develop in important ways. Typically, INTPs encourage each other to pay closer attention to details, facts, and realities so they can become even more competent. By deepening their emotional connection to each other, they often become more patient and appreciative of the needs and feelings of others. They may even encourage each other to broaden their social horizons and meet new people.

The Frustrations

One of the biggest frustrations for INTP couples is their mutual blind spots and shortcomings. Specifically, since INTPs tend to lose interest in projects after the creative phase is completed, they tend not to follow through and often leave chores half-finished. It's annoying to trip over your partner's projects, even if yours are cluttering up the other half of the living room. INTPs try to keep their options open for as long as possible in case something more intriguing pops up. This means that they often miss important deadlines or have to rush to get someplace on time. Keeping in touch with friends may be difficult because INTPs often resist committing to a place or activity in advance. And running a household becomes complicated when neither partner remembers to shop for groceries or pay the bills. INTPs need to find fair and reasonable systems that accommodate their need for flexibility.

Another source of frustration for INTP couples is their naturally logical and critical approach to problem solving. Since they both tend to see the flaws or inconsistencies in an idea, they may fail to appreciate each other's contributions. In their drive

to be honest, INTPs also can be blunt and insensitive. And when they turn their critical eye and demanding standards on their partners, they may sometimes be harsh or sarcastic.

Finally, since INTP couples are so independent and focused on their own interests, they can get so deeply involved in projects that they risk losing the connection with their partners. Because both partners are so autonomous and rarely need much reassurance, this may not seem like a big problem. But over time, these aloof and somewhat detached people may begin to feel more like roommates and professional colleagues than lovers and romantic partners. It's important that they take the time and be willing to risk the vulnerability that comes with sharing their feelings, concerns, and fears.

Advice for INTPs

- Don't compare your relationship with anyone else's or with society's ideal of what a perfect relationship ought to be.
- Be willing to discuss your feelings and fears with each other. Listen attentively and respectfully when your partner shares.
- Strive to be as competent in understanding and working with your partner as you are in your professional life.
- Find common interests so you don't become too disconnected. Ask about your partner's day and share stories and details.
- Take turns managing boring or mundane household chores. Figure out a fair and equitable distribution of labor.
- Be willing to participate in each other's activities and events. Look at this as a way of understanding your partner better.
- Watch your tendency to be critical, sarcastic, or too competitive with each other or to debate issues past the point where it is fun for both partners.
- Enjoy your mutual desire to debate and argue but realize that you don't always need to win.

Chapter 12

Conceptualizers with Idealists: NTs with NFs

ENTJ with ENFJ

The Joys

While ENTJs and ENFJs have one major difference between them, they share three type preferences, so they also have a lot in common. Typically, these couples are high-energy, friendly, and social people with a great number of friends, associates, and acquaintances. They both enjoy being involved in their communities and their work, so they are often busy with a variety of work-related and volunteer commitments. ENTJs and ENFJs are big talkers, so they tend to enjoy lengthy and involved discussions on any number of subjects. Their favorite topics include global issues, possibilities, theories, spiritual questions, and other subjects that engage their vivid imaginations and highly developed intuition. They tend to enjoy dreaming about and planning for the future, and they are eager to learn new things and experience a variety of cultural and artistic offerings, which provide additional food for thought and discussion.

ENTJs and ENFJs also share a preference to have things settled, planned, and organized. They tend to be tidy people who are prompt, organized, and responsible about their chores. They like to research their options quickly, make almost instant decisions, and move on to the next challenge.

Although their common traits are usually the source of their initial attraction, their differences

create the spark that fuels their passion. ENTJs are often attracted to ENFJs' positive energy, warmth, compassion, and nurturing spirit. ENTJs sense that their ENFJ partners' hearts are perpetually open to them, and they find their partners' charm and emotional vulnerability a source of delight. ENFJs are often drawn to ENTJs' energy, strength, confidence and intelligence. ENTJs seem to approach life as a series of fascinating challenges and are always eager to respond with creative solutions. ENTJs often impress ENFJs with their leadership abilities, while ENFJs win over ENTJs with their humanity.

These couples' differences can be the catalyst for helping them grow and develop in important ways. ENTJs almost always credit their ENFJ partners with helping them become more sensitive to other people, enhance their communication skills, and increase their compassion. ENFJs say that their ENTJ partners help them become less intimidated by the opinions of others and approach challenging situations — especially those fraught with emotion — with confidence and objectivity.

The Frustrations

The fundamental difference between ENTJs and ENFJs is how they approach decision making. ENTJs are very analytical people who are ruled by logic and reason. They find it virtually impossible to accept what does not make sense. They are consistent and impartial, and they value honesty and competence above all else. By contrast, ENFJs are deeply sensitive people who trust their very personal values more than objective information. ENFJs live by their feelings and values and are personally affected by almost everything they experience. They work hard to maintain harmony in all their relationships and are compassionate and empathetic people.

When ENTJs and ENFJs disagree or misunderstand each other, the issue is almost always whether a decision is logical or humane. ENTJs are often confused and frustrated by ENFJs' subjective reasoning, and ENFJs are often hurt and offended by the apparent coldness of ENTJs' choices. These couples also may struggle over who gets to be in charge. ENTJs are more likely to have strong opinions about the most logical way to do things, whereas ENFJs are more likely to argue for the compassionate choice. In their zeal to get things done, they may occasionally make hasty decisions, especially if neither partner is slowing the process down to consider the facts.

Finally, ENTJs typically need and want fewer expressions of affection and appreciation than do ENFJs, who need a strong and sustained emotional connection with their partners to feel trusting and open. These couples must work hard to establish fair and clear boundaries for discussions and listen carefully to each other to avoid frequent and painful miscommunication. They also need to protect their private time together so that they can nurture the trust and intimacy between them.

How to Reach Your ENFJ Partner

- Listen even when you are tired. Be patient with your partner's long-winded or repetitive style.
- Be sensitive to the impact other people's problems have on your partner. Remember that everything has a personal context for ENFJs.
- Be careful not to disregard the importance your partner places on how things look, especially if other people are involved.

- Dote on your partner. Be tender and offer regular pampering.
- Share your feelings frequently. Repeating how much you care is never overkill to an ENFJ.
- Appreciate your partner for the meaning and insight he or she brings to your life.

How to Reach Your ENTJ Partner

- Try to be consistent in your positions and clear and direct in your communication. Try not to exaggerate.
- Stand up to your partner. Don't be intimidated and back down when something is really important.
- Try not to take things personally. ENTJs offer constructive criticism with the best of intentions.
- Tell the truth about how you feel and what you need. Don't let your natural diplomacy override your ability to be totally honest.
- Encourage your partner to pursue his or her own interests. Compliment your partner on his or her achievements, status, and competence.
- Ask your partner's advice and listen respectfully.

ENTJ with INFJ

The Joys

ENTJs and INFJs share two of the four type preferences, so they are interested in possibilities and stimulated by new ideas. Although they may not always agree, they usually have little trouble understanding each other. They are also alike in that they think about the future, focus on the big picture, and easily see how events are related. They tend to be decisive, like to make and keep plans, and find comfort in structure and order. Naturally organized, ENTJs and INFJs like their homes to be neat and tidy and seldom struggle over household chores. These couples are especially productive; not only are they good at dreaming up projects, but they also are driven to complete them!

In addition to their similarities, ENTJs and INFJs are often initially attracted to each other because of their differences. ENTJs are often drawn to INFJs' quiet intensity, thoughtfulness, creativity, and integrity. They admire their partners' warmth and fierce compassion for the people and things they care about. INFJs are often attracted to ENTJs' competence, self-assurance, and high energy level. Being natural leaders, ENTJs tend to be powerful people who inspire confidence and respect.

Because of their differences, ENTJs and INFJs are able to help each other grow and develop in important ways. ENTJs are often able to help INFJs become bolder and more comfortable taking risks. Many INFJs say that their partners help them receive constructive criticism better and avoid getting their feelings hurt so easily. For their part, INFJs are able to help ENTJs become more sensitive, thoughtful, and introspective, allowing them to express more fully their appreciation of others.

The Frustrations

One of the common frustrations between ENTJs and INFJs is their very different needs for social activity. Typically, ENTJs want to be out of their homes meeting and working with a large number of people. INFJs are less social, but, ironically, they are often the ones who are left to initiate gatherings with friends and take care of the social niceties, such as acknowledging special occasions, sending gifts, and responding to invitations.

Another big difference between these types is that ENTJs usually run at or close to top speed, while INFJs prefer a more thoughtful and deliberate pace. This can result in INFJs feeling pressured and rushed and ENTJs chafing at the bit to get moving. INFJs also are much more home- and family-centered than ENTJs, who are usually very career-driven and are more likely to be workaholics. This difference, especially when there are children involved, can become a continual source of conflict for these couples.

The difference that causes the most painful frustration for ENTJs and INFJs is how they come to conclusions and make decisions. Although ENTJs are very honest and direct, they can also be critical and condescending. Their bluntness can unintentionally hurt their partners' feelings, often without even realizing it. In contrast, INFJs often have emotional reactions that their partners find overblown and illogical. To be sure, ENTJs can be dismissive of reactions or feelings they don't share, and INFJs are prone to take everything very seriously and rarely let even small offenses go. ENTJs are typically sure their positions are more logical and intellectually sound. Meanwhile, INFJs are convinced they're right based on their strongly held personal and moral beliefs. So both partners sometimes become intractable, and they can find themselves at a painful impasse.

When conflicts arise, ENTJs generally want to deal with them head-on by logically analyzing and debating the issue and coming quickly to a reasonable resolution. But because INFJs seek harmony and need to think about things before acting on them, they often retreat to reflect on their feelings privately. As ENTJs become more frustrated, they may exhibit angry outbursts. This threatens and overwhelms INFJs, and they withdraw even more. Both types want to resolve issues quickly, but they go about it in very different ways. A careful balance of honesty and gentleness is important for them to restore equilibrium to their relationships.

How to Reach Your INFJ Partner

- Be sensitive to your partner's feelings. Recognize that he or she doesn't like confrontation, so avoid angry outbursts.
- Give your partner time to think and process his or her feelings.
- Express your appreciation of all the nurturing

things your partner does to deepen and cultivate your relationship.

- Listen patiently and attentively. Resist the urge to bring the conversation back to you, fix the problem, or come up with a solution.
- Recognize that your partner's vision and values are very important and cannot easily be compromised. Don't ask your partner to bend on those things.
- Fight the urge to respond or especially to criticize your partner immediately. Think things through, then edit them for diplomacy.
- Express your feelings. Say "I love you" a lot!

How to Reach Your ENTJ Partner

- Support, appreciate, and compliment your partner on his or her accomplishments and achievements.
- Recognize how important your partner's career aspirations are and support them whenever you can.
- Never criticize or question your partner's competence in public.
- Strive to be more flexible on the little things. Prioritize issues and focus on those that are really critical.
- Try to lighten up and not insist on a deep emotional connection all the time.

ENTJ with ENFP

The Joys

ENTJs and ENFPs share two important type preferences that provide great satisfaction and connection. Both partners are friendly, active, high-energy people with lots of interests, friends, and commitments. They are quite verbal and expressive, and they share a sense of humor that is a source of considerable enjoyment. ENTJs' and ENFPs' homes are typically filled with activity and friends working or playing together with great gusto. These couples enjoy talking about their experiences and sharing their ideas. They readily see implications and possibilities, so they like to discuss politics or the arts, easily leaping from one topic to another. ENTJs and ENFPs understand each other's ways of seeing the world and tend to support each other's passions, even if they don't always share them.

In addition to their similarities, ENTJs and ENFPs are often initially attracted to each other because of their differences. ENTJs are drawn to the warmth, empathy, and spontaneity of ENFPs. They admire their partners' insight into people and feel very nurtured by them. ENFPs are often drawn to the strength, calm, and natural leadership of ENTJs, and they respect their partners' ambition and self-confidence.

Because of their differences, ENTJs and ENFPs have the opportunity to help each other grow and develop in important ways. ENTJs typically help ENFPs accomplish their many good ideas by encouraging them to follow through on complicated tasks. ENTJs also help ENFPs step back, take things less personally, and be open to constructive criticism. For their part, ENFPs encourage their ENTJ partners to work hard to deepen the emotional connection between them by sharing their feelings. ENFPs also help ENTJs become more sensitive to and appreciative of the important people in their lives. In the process, ENTJs learn how to listen more patiently, express their feelings more readily, and generally become more compassionate.

The Frustrations

The two most common sources of frustration for ENTJs and ENFPs are their different decision-making styles and their different needs for structure. ENTJs are typically calm, cool, and logical, while ENFPs are much more emotional and have more personal reactions to issues. ENTJs are bottom-line people, convinced only by logical reasoning. ENFPs are compassionate people, persuaded by the human impact of choices and a desire for harmony and understanding. Often neither feel that their partners truly understand or respect their perspectives. During moments of conflict, ENFPs are likely to use emotional appeals and arguments that may be illogical but are heartfelt. ENTJs tend to pull back and take a more detached approach, focusing on what they perceive as fair, even if it sometimes means hurting their partners' feelings.

ENFPs tend to feel that their partners dismiss their feelings or accuse them of overreacting, while ENTJs often think that their partners allow their emotions to cloud issues or they try to get their partners' cooperation by using guilt. ENTJs and ENFPs experience the greatest satisfaction when they establish fair and compassionate ground rules for discussions that allow both to speak their minds without fear of criticism.

ENTJs have a strong temperamental drive to be competent in all that they do and to find opportunities to demonstrate how much they know. ENFPs are driven by an equally passionate desire for understanding themselves and other people. Most ENFPs are constantly searching for meaning and harmony in their relationships. These couples need to be careful to find private time together to talk and share their lives so they don't become too disconnected.

The other major area of frustration for many ENTJ and ENFP couples is that they require different amounts of order and planning in their lives. ENTJs like things to be organized and to complete projects quickly and efficiently, while ENFPs can be masterful procrastinators. Both tend to work on things that inspire them, but ENFPs often become bored and distracted after they solve the interesting challenges, and they neglect to follow through — something ENTJs find infuriating. ENFPs are much more adaptive and easygoing about changes in plans and find their ENTJ part-

ners' inflexibility frustrating, especially when it prevents them from taking part in some intriguing new opportunity. Also, ENTJs tend to have strong opinions and are generally not concerned about how others view them. In contrast, ENFPs are considerably more tentative, harder to nail down, and very diplomatic when sharing their views. As a couple, ENTJs and ENFPs need to work at listening respectfully to each other without trying to change each other's minds.

How to Reach Your ENFP Partner

- Explain that you need to think emotional issues through privately and discuss them only after they make sense to you.
- Be patient with and respect your partner's feelings, even if you don't share them.
- Express your appreciation and affection spontaneously with messages, notes, cards, and little gifts.
- Watch your tendency to put being right above being loving or understanding.
- Respect your partner's curiosity and tendency to change his or her mind. Encourage your partner to pursue his or her interests and spend time alone with friends.
- Try to find situations where you can give in or back down. Remember that the process is just as important as the product.

How to Reach Your ENTJ Partner

- Initiate and complete chores around the house.
- Tell others how much you respect and appreciate your partner's accomplishments. Objective, third-party compliments are especially credible to ENTJs.
- Watch your tendency to run late or get distracted and not fulfill promises.
- Be direct, calm, and honest about how you feel. Don't mince words or be less than totally honest.
- Understand your partner's strong passion for perfection. Try to finish jobs you take on.

ENTJ with INFP

The Joys

ENTJs and INFPs have one of the four type preferences in common, and theirs is often a strong intellectual and creative connection. Since they share a passion for new ideas and novel theories, they typically enjoy in-depth discussions of current events or global concerns. ENTJs and INFPs appreciate each other's vivid imaginations and easily understand each other's desire to consider the long-range implications of issues or actions. As a couple, they often enjoy thinking about and planning their future together. ENTJs and INFPs notice unusual possibilities and take great pleasure in each other's creativity and original sense of humor. Because neither tends to be especially rooted in tradition, both are usually open to considering new options and are often strong supporters of their partners' efforts for personal and professional development.

ENTJs and INFPs may be initially attracted to each other because of their differences. ENTJs are often drawn to INFPs because of their warmth, gentleness, and uncanny insight into people. ENTJs admire their partners' ability to understand the subtleties of human behavior and their eagerness to please and nurture others. ENTJs also appreciate INFPs' willingness to accommodate their partners' agendas and needs. INFPs are often attracted to ENTJs' drive, ambition, and natural leadership capabilities. They admire ENTJs' enormous personal energy and confidence, as well as their ability to manage very large or complex projects and get so many things done.

Because of their many differences, ENTJs and INFPs have the opportunity to help each other grow and develop in important ways. Typically, ENTJs help INFPs become more assertive and willing to bear the tension they feel when speaking their minds. INFPs say that their partners help them manage disappointments better and generally learn not to take things quite so personally. By becoming better organized, INFPs can become more accomplished and gain more self-confidence. For their part, INFPs can help ENTJs slow down and appreciate the people and joy in their lives. They become better able to express the full range of their feelings, become more sensitive to others, and become less critical and more patient and appreciative.

The Frustrations

Given their many differences, it's no surprise that many ENTJ and INFP couples experience frustration on a regular basis. Temperamentally, ENTJs are naturally driven to learn and increase their competence, while INFPs are more concerned with personal expression and developing meaningful relationships. INFPs sometimes feel that their partners place too much importance on their careers and professional success, while ENTJs think that their partners are far too idealistic and easily disillusioned.

Another frustration for ENTJs and INFPs stems from their different social needs. ENTJs are big talkers who like and need to be with a large variety of people on a regular basis. They tend to be active and busy and may sometimes get overextended with outside projects. INFPs are much more private, reflective people who need a lot of time alone or with a few close friends. INFPs feel frustrated when their partners don't listen attentively or when they interrupt and finish their sentences. ENTJs and INFPs also have different needs to be busy and active. ENTJs tend to move quickly from one challenge to the next, rarely pausing or enjoying much downtime. INFPs, by contrast, need more time to ponder their choices and tend to become tired or overwhelmed when too many things are competing for their attention at once.

ENTJs and INFPs also have different needs for order and closure. ENTJs like to have things settled and to make decisions quickly without angst or equivocation. But they sometimes miss important facts because they are in such a hurry. INFPs need much more information before they feel prepared and confident to make decisions, so they tend to ask a lot of questions and postpone decisions. ENTJs sometimes consider their partners indecisive and inconsistent, while INFPs find their partners intimidating and demanding. ENTJs also like their homes to be orderly and well organized, while INFPs are much more concerned about personal comfort and the freedom to linger over whatever they are doing. ENTJs and INFPs sometimes struggle over household chores and argue about clutter and unfinished projects. ENTJs often think that their partners aren't pulling their weight, while INFPs frequently feel that their partners are too rigid and controlling.

The biggest source of frustration for most ENTJs and INFPs is their different communication styles. ENTJs are logical and objective, and they strive to make sound, rational decisions. INFPs are ever conscious of the human impact of their choices and try to ensure that their actions are in harmony with their personal values. ENTJs tend to want to fix problems as they come up, but their no-nonsense style often seems critical and dismissive to their very sensitive INFP partners. Although ENTJs are very direct and truthful, they sometimes lack tact. INFPs tend to respond emotionally and personally to almost everything, which ENTJs find confusing and inconsistent. When INFPs are hurt or upset, they withdraw and avoid even healthy and honest discussions of issues. Both partners need to make it a priority to have regular opportunities to share their feelings and reconnect on an emotional level.

How to Reach Your INFP Partner

• Listen completely and attentively to your partner. Don't interrupt or express impatience with his or her sometimes convoluted or repetitious stories.
• Find points of agreement and areas of harmony before pointing out differences or disagreements.
• Be supportive, and don't rush to explain how your partner might fix his or her problems.
• Be willing to change your plans or stop what you're doing to participate in some of your partner's spontaneous activities.
• Watch your tendency to speak harshly of others and your need always to be right. Keep heated debates to a minimum.
• Be gentle and express your feelings. Tell your partner how much you care about him or her.
• Don't force your partner to participate in more social events than he or she wants.

How to Reach Your ENTJ Partner

• Try to remain calm when you're expressing your feelings. Try not to repeat yourself or become overly emotional.
• Tell your partner directly when you need him or her to listen supportively.
• Listen for the constructive suggestions in your partner's critiques. Remember that they are usually offered with good intentions.
• Strive to finish some of the projects you start. Don't leave things unsettled or up in the air for too long. Don't leave piles or clutter in the common areas of your home.
• Try not to change plans abruptly. Let your partner know when you are going to be late or are unable to meet as planned.

INTJ with ENFJ

The Joys

With two preferences in common, INTJs and ENFJs have some strong similarities and some equally clear differences. Because they both focus on the big picture, they see the world in much the same way, and focus their attention on the future. They like new ideas and possibilities and want to understand the connections between things. INTJs and ENFJs have a strong need to understand why things are as they are. Another area of commonality is that they are both very organized and like their lives and homes to be run in an orderly way. And since both INTJs and ENFJs are quite goal-oriented, they can help each other accomplish great things if they share or support each other's visions.

But it is frequently the differences that attract INTJs and ENFJs to each other. INTJs usually admire ENFJs' positive energy, enthusiasm, and sophisticated social skills, while ENFJs find INTJs' depth, intellectual prowess, and independence appealing. Because of their differences, they can help each other grow and develop in important ways. Being excellent, creative problem solvers, INTJs can help ENFJs gain objectivity and sometimes reframe an issue so they can see solutions where there were only emotions before. INTJs also can help ENFJs slow down and listen with more perspective and patience. For their part, ENFJs can help INTJs better understand their own and other people's feelings so they can become more sensitive and more effective in their personal and professional relationships. ENFJs also can help their partners clarify what is really important to them.

The Frustrations

To ENFJs, all relationships are important, but their relationships with their partners are clearly a priority. Most ENFJs expend enormous energy trying to understand, communicate with, and please their partners. Creating a harmonious, supportive, and loving relationship is their primary goal. But INTJs frequently have different priorities. They are extremely independent people who are often preoccupied with their own ideas and projects. Many INTJs are so focused on feeding their intellectual appetites or advancing their careers that they don't pay nearly as much attention to nurturing their relationships as their ENFJ partners want or need them to.

Being extremely sensitive, ENFJs tend to take things personally and typically wear their hearts on their sleeves. INTJs almost always know how their ENFJ partners feel because ENFJs tell them. But INTJs are much more private people, especially when it comes to sharing their feelings. ENFJs can find this hurtful and isolating, while INTJs can feel suffocated when pushed into getting too close emotionally. Since nurturing does not come naturally to most INTJs, they can easily dismiss their partners' feelings as illogical. Their occasionally patronizing attitudes only serve to undermine the trust ENFJs need to feel in their relationships. INTJs also use their critical thinking skills to critique their partners and find arguing an intellectually rewarding exercise. Most ENFJs, however, find debates confrontational and unpleasant. These differences, if not understood, can put a serious strain on the relationship.

ENFJs are very social creatures who enjoy spending time with others. Most INTJs find social gatherings uncomfortable and draining, especially if they don't know, respect, or care about the people attending. And whereas ENFJs are great conversationalists, unless INTJs find the subject compelling, they are not easily engaged in conversation.

Conflicts can arise if these partners do not share similar values. Since INTJs tend to be very career-driven, they may be tempted to put their career needs above their partner's. ENFJs may acquiesce and take second place for the sake of harmony, but this can cause lingering resentment. Whereas ENFJs may be upset and shaken by tension, INTJs may not even notice it. And unfortunately, ENFJs and INTJs tend to approach conflict resolution in very different ways. Most often, ENFJs will go to great lengths to restore harmony, but if their partners are unresponsive, they can become cold and antagonistic. INTJs are more likely to retreat, become even more uncommunicative, and withhold their approval or affection. Because both partners want a certain amount of control, they often are at loggerheads. Without mutually constructive and supportive discussions, they may find themselves at a resentful and painful stalemate.

How to Reach Your INTJ Partner

- Recognize your partner's need for independence and give him or her plenty of space and privacy.
- Compliment your partner on his or her ideas and accomplishments. Try to be especially supportive of your partner's career needs.
- Convey how important conversation and sharing are to you, then give your partner your undivided attention. Listen without making value judgments.
- Don't misinterpret your partner's silence for a lack of caring. Just because your partner doesn't say it, that doesn't mean he or she doesn't feel it.
- Don't force too much social contact on your partner.
- Watch your tendency to become impatient with your partner's longer processing time.

How to Reach Your ENFJ Partner

- Never dismiss your partner's feelings, even if they don't make sense to you.
- Reexamine your priorities. Try to balance your family and work lives. Don't automatically put work first.
- Cuddle your partner and show your affection in other ways.
- Allow your partner to help you learn to share your feelings.
- Express your appreciation of the many thoughtful and loving things your partner does. Make regular romantic gestures.

- Let your partner know when you need space and uninterrupted quiet time.
- When discussing problems, be gentle and positive. Avoid becoming confrontational or intimidating.

INTJ with INFJ

The Joys

Because INTJs and INFJs share three type preferences, they often have a lot in common. Naturally quiet, intense, and serious people, they are selective yet passionate about their interests. They need lots of time alone to process their ideas, so they understand and respect each other's privacy. INTJs and INFJs typically share a strong intellectual connection based on their common love of ideas and possibilities. They usually enjoy discussing theories or potential implications of issues. Both are highly creative, imaginative, and original, and they often feel especially close when they are planning the future together or discussing their unique visions.

INTJ and INFJ couples share a common preference for having things orderly and decided. They like to keep their homes neat and their routines in place without sudden changes, interruptions, or surprises. They typically have strong opinions about almost everything and feel energized by making decisions and getting things done.

In addition to their many similarities, INTJs and INFJs are often initially attracted to each other because of their different decision-making styles. INTJs are drawn to INFJs because of their compassion, warmth, and concern for others. They also admire the communication skills that come so naturally to most INFJs. INFJs are attracted to INTJs because of their calm objectivity and natural strategic and critical thinking abilities. INFJs also admire their partners' independence and willingness to stick by their principles in the face of opposition or pressure.

Because of their differences, INTJs and INFJs are often able to help each other grow and develop in important ways. INTJs help INFJs become more logical and less prone to taking everything so personally. INFJs often credit their partners with helping them learn not to sacrifice truthfulness for diplomacy. For their part, INFJs help their INTJ partners develop more patience and compassion for others. INTJs routinely say that their partners encourage them to consider and express their feelings rather than keep them to themselves.

The Frustrations

Since INTJs and INFJs use different criteria to make decisions, they sometimes find themselves on opposite sides of issues. INTJs tend to be naturally analytical and critical, and they may make comments or judgments that fail to take into account how other people feel. In contrast, INFJs are usually acutely aware of how others may feel about their actions or choices, and they may even compromise their positions to please others. This can make them inconsistent, a quality that is irritating to their INTJ partners. INTJs also think that their partners overreact and are unnecessarily hurt by constructive criticism, while INFJs frequently feel that their partners are overly critical and either impatient with or dismissive of their feelings. INFJs can also be embarrassed when their partners argue with or speak harshly to other people.

Some of the common frustrations INTJs and INFJs experience result from their similarities. Both partners, but especially INTJs, can be rather single-minded perfectionists. They tend to think first and foremost about their own positions and convenience. When they get involved in their own projects and run on autopilot, they may become self-involved. Whereas INFJs are drawn into the outside world by their desire to connect emotionally with their friends, INTJs are prone to get lost in their internal worlds and end up acting remote and disconnected from their partners and families.

Finally, since both INTJs and INFJs like order and structure and have very strong opinions about the "right" ways to handle things, they may become engaged in power struggles. INTJs often take a superior attitude, while INFJs tend to take a morally righteous one, and neither partner is especially willing to back down. While INFJs are more likely to broker an agreement that reestablishes harmony, INTJs can hold their ground almost indefinitely, which can drive a wedge between them. Because they both tend to get stuck in their ways, they may refuse to change or postpone their plans in order to take advantage of spontaneous opportunities. And since neither partner likes details and both lose interest in anything repetitive or mundane, they may sometimes neglect household chores or be careless about maintaining their possessions. When one partner (often the woman, regardless of her type) ends up doing more than his or her fair share of the work, resentment can build. As long as INTJs and INFJs share the burden, however, they can operate as an efficient and hardworking team.

How to Reach Your INFJ Partner

- Be patient and accepting of your partner's feelings, even if you don't understand them or they seem illogical to you.
- Ask your partner's advice and insights about other people, especially about others' feelings, needs, or motivations.
- Listen attentively to your partner's stories, especially those about people and about his or her other relationships.
- Support your partner's professional efforts, especially concerning changes that are difficult or scary. Encourage your partner to stretch.
- Try to express your feelings, reactions, and appreciation. Don't clam up, because your partner may think you're mad at him or her.
- Smile, be gentle, and ask how your partner is feeling.

How to Reach Your INTJ Partner

- Tell your partner straight-out what you want him or her to do to please you or what things you wish were different in your relationships. Don't make your partner play guessing games.
- Ask your partner for his or her opinions on issues rather than assuming you know how he or she feels.
- Respect your partner's expertise and knowledge. Never question your partner's competence in public.
- Respect your partner's need for time alone to pursue his or her own projects, then genuinely give it without implying that you feel left out or lonely.
- Help your partner express his or her feelings and work through his or her frustrations with other people.

INTJ with ENFP

The Joys

Although INTJs and ENFPs share only one type preference in common, it is perhaps the most important one since it is a common and imaginative view of the world. Both partners generally focus on the big picture, are excited by possibilities, and see implications and how things affect each other. And as people who naturally question why things work as they do, they are likely to understand the dynamics in relationships. Both are typically intrigued with global issues such as politics and the arts, and they enjoy sharing each other's perspectives. Their shared creativity is a strong and enduring connection between them.

Yet INTJs' and ENFPs' differences are often the source of their initial attraction. INTJs are drawn to ENFPs' warmth, enthusiasm, and social ease. They admire ENFPs' ability to improvise and respond to the needs of other people. And INTJs

also enjoy ENFPs' irreverent humor, their playful, accepting natures, and their unconventional approach to overcoming obstacles. ENFPs are attracted to INTJs' calm and their commitment to their intellectual passions. They also admire how INTJs are able to step back and remain objective even in the face of great emotion or tumult and still handle projects productively and efficiently.

Because of their differences, INTJs and ENFPs help each other grow and develop in important ways. INTJs help ENFPs focus and commit themselves to fewer projects so they don't scatter their impressive talents on too many ventures at once. ENFPs often say that their partners help them to stick with a time-management plan and follow through more carefully with their commitments. With their partner's influence, many ENFPs are able to benefit from constructive criticism. For their part, ENFPs are generally able to soften the exterior of INTJs and encourage them to be more sensitive and compassionate. ENFPs help INTJs to better understand and share their own feelings and to become more patient. And INTJs often say that their partners get them to relax, enjoy life, and not take things quite so seriously.

The Frustrations

As with any couple with several differences in type preference, frequent frustrations are experienced by both partners in this combination, the most striking being that ENFPs are among the most social of all types and INTJs are often among the least. While INTJs are perfectly content to spend time alone, ENFPs delight in meeting new people and become bored and restless with too much time by themselves. Most INTJs prefer to maintain a few close relationships, while ENFPs typically enjoy a wide circle of friends. When an unexpected social opportunity presents itself, ENFPs love to be able to respond, but their INTJ partners generally need considerably more time to come around, if they decide to participate at all.

INTJs and ENFPs also have very different communication styles. Most INTJs process their ideas and reactions first in their heads and rarely speak unless they have something specific and well conceived to say. In contrast ENFPs are big talkers; they need to talk in order to think things through. Since maintaining harmony and feeling emotionally connected to their mates is so important to ENFPs, they are constantly asking their partners how they are feeling. But to many INTJs this is an unnecessary exercise at best and an annoying intrusion at worst. Most INTJs don't necessarily know how they feel about something unless they mull it over first, and then they simply don't have as many emotional reactions to things as ENFPs do.

While INTJs are logical and objective, they can also be critical and a bit insensitive to their partners' feelings. They set very high standards for themselves and others and can be demanding about people living up to their expectations. When conflicts arise, this couple tends to respond in different ways; INTJs may react angrily at first, while most ENFPs generally avoid a confrontation at all cost or try to quickly reestablish harmony.

Another source of frustration experienced by INTJ and ENFP couples revolves around their different needs for closure. INTJs prefer things to be decided and settled. They find comfort in structure and predictability, making plans, and knowing what to expect. As a result, they are typically deliberate, organized, and productive and want a neat environment. In contrast, ENFPs prefer a more open-ended, spontaneous lifestyle. They often resist making plans for fear of missing out on some future opportunity. They also like surprises and frequently change plans at the last minute — an act that understandably frustrates their partners. INTJs sometimes view such behavior as impulsive and even irresponsible, while ENFPs complain that their partners are too rigid and controlling.

How to Reach Your ENFP Partner

- Try to talk and share your feelings freely with your partner. Don't close down or dismiss your partner's reactions.
- Try to participate in more social events. Resist the urge to retreat into your work, a book, your computer, etc.
- Give your partner your undivided attention, and be especially attentive when he or she is sharing emotional concerns.
- Notice, comment, and be appreciative when your partner does something nice for you.
- Admit when you're wrong, and recognize there are other "right ways" of doing things besides your own. Don't impose your standards on your partner.
- Let your partner know when something is bothering you. Don't wait for the resentment to build until it explodes.
- Try not to criticize your partner. Begin with and emphasize the positive.

How to Reach Your INTJ Partner

- Give him or her plenty of emotional and physical space. Don't try to discuss things as soon as your mate gets home from work.
- Respect your partner's very independent nature and need for ritual and routine.
- Don't force your partner into too many social situations. Opt for small gatherings of close friends, or encourage participation in small discussion or book groups.
- Try to learn more about the things that are of particular interest to your partner.
- Do what you say you'll do. Strive to be prompt and accountable.
- Schedule time for the two of you to spend time together. Don't expect your partner to drop what he or she is doing to play with you spontaneously.

INTJ with INFP

The Joys

INTJs and INFPs share a strong intellectual connection, which is often a source of great satisfaction. Both tend to have vivid imaginations and rich inner lives. Their mutual interest in possibilities and their ability to see how things relate give them a shared perspective that most find very stimulating. Essentially, both partners have a deep curiosity about theories, a great facility with complex ideas, and a tendency to focus on the new and the future. Discussing abstract concepts or global issues makes them feel in sync with each other. Additionally, INTJs and INFPs share a strong need for privacy and independence within the relationship. They understand and respect each other's desire for time alone and the chance to concentrate deeply and think things through fully. Since neither type tends to need a lot of outside stimulation, they often meet their social needs by spending time with a small group of close friends or colleagues.

INFPs and INTJs tend to be quiet, intense couples who place a high value on respect and individuality. When conflicts arise, they tend to mull things over separately first, then discuss things calmly and quietly. At their best, they are willing to listen fully and respectfully to each other and share their well-considered viewpoints.

INTJs and INFPs are also attracted to each other because of their differences. INTJs are drawn to the warmth, compassion, and gentleness of INFPs, while INFPs are often attracted to the sense of purpose, conviction, and confidence of INTJs. Also because of their differences, they have the opportunity to help each other grow and develop in important ways. INTJs help INFPs become more objective in their decision making and more organized, which helps them complete more of their projects. Many INFPs also credit their partners with helping them become more

assertive. For their part, INFPs often help INTJs see the human impact of their decisions and develop an increased sensitivity and patience in all their relationships. INTJs frequently say that their partners add a rich and deeply intimate dimension to their lives and make it easier for them to understand and express their feelings.

The Frustrations

Generally, the most common conflicts for INTJs and INFPs stem from their different needs for closure. Issues about order, time, and accountability tend to dog this couple. INTJs can be real sticklers for neatness, while INFPs usually don't care about or even notice the clutter on the kitchen counter, the piles of books beside the bed, or the missing check in the checkbook. INTJs are often exacting and even controlling about the ways things ought to be maintained, insisting that chores be completed in order and finances be carefully controlled. Different attitudes about time also create tension for these couples. INTJs tend to be prompt and focused on work and productivity, while INFPs have a more leisurely and easygoing approach to life, accommodating extenuating circumstances and enjoying spontaneous opportunities in everyday life. But INFPs also find themselves running late and struggling to be better organized. Although INTJs usually have plenty of advice for eliminating inefficiency, INFPs are rarely interested in actually implementing any of the logical time management strategies INTJs recommend. And since INFPs tend to take everything very personally, they quite easily and frequently get their feelings hurt by their naturally brusque and critical INTJ partners.

Because INFPs value emotional connection and intimacy in their relationships above all else, they often feel lonely or disconnected from their partners when they are unwilling (or unable) to open up and share their personal feelings. Since most INTJs want to feel competent and in control at all times, they are seldom as comfortable sharing their feelings of confusion and fear as readily as their partners may wish or even demand. So INFPs typically feel that INTJs are too critical and demanding, and INTJs feel that INFPs rely on guilt or emotional blackmail to force a connection. Unfortunately, this can leave both partners feeling belittled and unappreciated. Ultimately, INTJs and INFPs need to fully and calmly think through their positions before coming together to discuss and share their feelings openly. They also need to make the time to hear each other out without criticism or judgment. Then they can engage their powerful intuition to find unique and satisfying solutions to challenges.

How to Reach Your INFP Partner

- Focus on the positive. Start by acknowledging and complimenting, not criticizing.
- Share your feelings, concerns, and fears — don't hide them or bottle them up. Be gentle and tactful.
- Try to temper your natural competitiveness — with yourself and everyone else!
- Try not to impose too many rules and too much structure on your partner.
- Organize spontaneous activities just for the two of you. Surprise your partner.
- Listen without judgment. Your partner will see that as a sign of affection.

How to Reach Your INTJ Partner

- Take a step back and try to see constructive criticism as a suggestion, not an attack.
- Initiate discussions and be patient with your partner's initial reluctance to share feelings. Demonstrate and model how to frame issues in a personal context.
- Be careful with money and talk about purchases before you make them.
- Appreciate your partner's good ideas. Thank your partner for his or her creativity.

- Try to be where you say you will be, when you say you will be. Call your partner when you are going to be late. (Wear a watch.)
- Be honest and direct; don't skirt around issues.
- Take on household chores. Your partner will see that as a sign of affection.

ENTP with ENFJ

The Joys

The primary and most sustaining connections for many ENTPs and ENFJs are often their imaginations and their interest in understanding the meaning of their experiences. Because they share two type preferences, they both enjoy the intense intellectual stimulation they get from each other and from other people. They like talking about possibilities, theories, and ideas and tend to enjoy a wide variety of discussions with far-reaching implications. As a couple, they love to dream about their individual and combined goals, are genuinely excited about each other's pursuits, and are supportive of the challenges each takes on.

Many ENTP and ENFJ couples also experience a strong spiritual or philosophical dimension to their relationships. Both tend to be very articulate, so they share their thoughts and reactions easily. Socially, they are poised and confident and tend to enjoy a wide circle of friends and acquaintances.

In addition to their areas of commonality, ENTPs and ENFJs are often attracted to each other because of their differences. ENTPs are drawn to ENFJs' warmth, emotional and intellectual depth, and eagerness to nurture and please others. ENTPs admire their partners' eloquence and poise in dealing with people, as well as their organizational skills and productivity. ENFJs are often attracted to ENTPs' humor, wit, and quick, creative minds. ENFJs admire ENTPs' playfulness, irreverence, and ability to improvise and find ways of overcoming almost any obstacle.

Because of their differences, ENTPs and ENFJs have the opportunity to help each other grow and develop in important ways. ENTPs help their ENFJ partners take some risks and free themselves from other people's expectations. By encouraging them to ask more questions, ENTPs help ENFJs make better decisions and avoid getting locked into things they don't really want to do. ENFJs also credit their ENTP partners with helping them be more forthright. For their part, ENFJs help their ENTP partners become better organized and focus more of their creative energy. ENFJs also help ENTPs deepen their commitment to people and projects and stay true to their values and priorities. ENTPs often credit their ENFJ partners with helping them become more sensitive to the needs and feelings of others.

The Frustrations

Although ENTPs and ENFJs are skillful in dealing with people, they have the tendency to be less than totally honest — ENTPs because they know what others want to hear, and ENFJs because they are so diplomatic and want to avoid unpleasantness, disharmony, and conflict. When these couples stay on the surface of things for too long, both partners pretending everything is fine, they may jeopardize their relationships. Often they let things fester until they blow up. And since neither ENTPs nor ENFJs are especially eager to admit that they're wrong, they may argue a point they don't believe in just to win the argument.

A more common frustration stems from ENTPs' and ENFJs' different needs for order and closure. ENTPs don't like to be locked into a plan, because they want to be free to follow their inspiration and experience whatever strikes their fancy. In contrast, ENFJs want to know the plan in advance so they can move efficiently and productively through the day. As a result, ENTPs frequently feel hemmed in and controlled, while ENFJs feel exasperated and up in the air. ENFJs tend to press their ENTP partners to make decisions before they have enough information. ENTPs have the tendency to ask for their partners' opinions, then ask several other people what they think. Ultimately, they may come around to the same position, but ENTPs' need to solicit so many different points of view insults ENFJs.

Another frequent bone of contention between ENTPs and ENFJs is that ENFJs want things neat and organized, and they feel pressured to put work before play. ENTPs are much more casual about everything and are usually delighted when people stop by unexpectedly, even if there are piles of clean laundry on the couch. ENFJs are embarrassed when they are caught unprepared or not looking or behaving their best.

But the most serious source of frustration for ENTPs and ENFJs is their different ways of making decisions. Logical and objective about most things, ENTPs have a strong need for decisions to make sense and be rational. They often don't understand their ENFJ partners' more emotional reactions and choices. ENTPs also tend to point out how their partners might have avoided a dilemma or can fix a particular problem. But ENFJs are usually looking only for an empathetic ear, and because they tend to take things quite personally, especially when they are upset, they rarely see the value of even the most constructive criticism. And just as ENTPs tend to criticize rather than appreciate, ENFJs tend to find fault with many of their partners' ideas. This is especially true when an idea is not particularly well thought out or when the ENTP partner springs it on the ENFJ when he or she is busy. It really takes the wind out of ENTPs' sails when their ENFJ partners feel compelled to point out all the reasons the idea will never fly rather than stopping to support their inspiration and applaud their inventiveness.

How to Reach Your ENFJ Partner

• Be patient with your partner's need to share feelings and emotional reactions, even if you've already heard these things before.

• Pitch in and initiate household chores. Take the burden off your partner and demonstrate that you want to help relieve his or her stress.

• Follow through on your commitments. Be where you say you will be, when you say you will be.

• Be patient with your partner's hesitancy to act spontaneously. Try to be supportive rather than critical.

• Appreciate the many ways your partner nurtures you and takes care of you, including performing the many important maintenance and sustenance details of life.

• Never dismiss your partner's feelings or try to talk your mate out of how he or she feels.

How to Reach Your ENTP Partner

• Listen without judgment or reservation to your partner's many ideas. Stop yourself from immediately pointing out why these ideas are unrealistic.

• Express your enthusiasm for your partner's vision. Be supportive of his or her efforts to move ahead professionally.

• Don't nag or complain about chores that don't get finished. Try to praise your partner for the things that do get done.

• Try to be spontaneous and go with the flow of your partner's ideas for adventure.

• Try not to push too hard for decisions and closure. Whenever possible, let some things stand open.

• Occasionally be willing to debate your partner. Stay calm, and don't take the debate personally.

ENTP with INFJ

The Joys

Although ENTPs and INFJs have only one type preference in common, their vivid imaginations form the basis for a strong connection. Both view the world in unusual ways, seeing not what is or has been but what could be. When these couples focus their considerable intuitive powers on possibilities, their dreaming knows no bounds. Their discussions soar to higher and higher levels, both adding inspiration and energy to the fire of innovative thinking. Theirs is a heady and often intoxicating combination. The heat and light they generate together fuels and maintains this pair of very different people.

In addition to their similarities, ENTPs and INFJs may be attracted to each other for their differences. ENTPs are often drawn to the powerful vision and unimpeachable integrity of INFJs, whose natural idealism and commitment appeals to ENTPs in part because they represent an ability to focus that ENTPs frequently lack. INFJs are often attracted to ENTPs' energy, optimism, and enthusiasm about the future. ENTPs also are easygoing, confident, and charming, and those qualities are seductive to the more serious and often formal INFJs.

Because of their differences, ENTPs and INFJs have the opportunity to help each other grow and develop in important ways. ENTPs bring out the more playful and adventurous sides of INFJs and encourage them to relax and open up to new experiences. INFJs say that their partners encourage them to be more objective so they get their feelings hurt less often and more easily make choices that are right for them even if others don't like them. For their part, INFJs often help ENTPs better understand the emotional impact their actions have on others. Since ENTPs are already keenly perceptive about people, the increased sensitivity to others makes their observations more accurate. INFJs also help ENTPs slow down, get organized, and focus their considerable talents, making them even more effective and productive.

The Frustrations

The most common source of frustration for ENTPs and INFJs arises from their different needs for order and neatness. ENTPs often are irritating to INFJs because they constantly mess up rooms and plans, leaving a trail of disorder in their wake. Because ENTPs aren't very realistic about how long it takes to get things done, they continually make promises they simply can't keep. They have great energy for starting a variety of projects but rarely have as much energy for finishing them. And they may leave their partners and families waiting while they explore some new distraction. Although INFJs are not especially realistic either, they are more time conscious and productive. They can easily lose themselves in their thoughts and projects, but they are generally more efficient than their ENTP partners. In their zeal for closure, however, INFJs may try to force their partners into premature decisions or impose their value judgments on them. For ENTPs, INFJs' absolute moral positions can be exasperating. ENTPs are, above all, curious, possibilities-oriented people, and they feel hemmed in when they are limited in talking about and exploring other options. They often complain that their INFJ partners insist on coming up with quick solutions or judgments rather than simply listening and encouraging them in a free-flowing, dynamic exchange. But ENTPs' constant need to talk can interrupt their partners' train of thought or prevent them from working on important projects in their own style — quietly and thoughtfully.

ENTPs and INFJs make decisions based on very different criteria. ENTPs are logical and detached when confronted with a decision, and they can unwittingly and unintentionally be insensitive to their INFJ partners' feelings. This often comes as a shock to INFJs, who have seen how insightful, skillful, and charming ENTPs are with others. And ENTPs are equally surprised by the degree to which INFJs are offended. Since everything has a personal effect on INFJs, what for ENTPs begins as a recreational debate can quickly turn into an argument about morals and values. This is both exhausting and annoying to most ENTPs and hurtful to INFJs. And when ENTPs lose interest in something, their tendency is to just move on.

Most ENTPs have enormous energy for social activities and enjoy a wide and varied group of friendships. INFJs are much more selective and allow only a small group of kindred souls into their hearts. These relationships are generally long lasting and deeply meaningful. Most ENTP and INFJ couples do best when they maintain their own friendships and allow for plenty of social independence within the relationship. They also need to find regular time to be alone and reconnect using their shared imaginations.

How to Reach Your INFJ Partner

- Listen with your full attention when your partner is sharing something important.
- Beware of your tendency to flirt. Be genuine and sincere with your partner.
- Pitch in around the house on a regular basis. Take the initiative with chores rather than waiting to be asked to help. Finish some of the projects you start.
- Never dismiss your partner's feelings as overreactions. Don't ask your partner to compromise on his or her values or strong beliefs.
- Be on time, follow through, and don't make promises you can't keep.
- Use your rational and logical approach to problem solving gently when it involves issues about which your partner is sensitive. Watch your tone of voice; don't be condescending.

How to Reach Your ENTP Partner

• Bring up concerns or issues immediately and calmly. Don't let them lie dormant until they — or you — explode.

• Make time to talk with your partner about ideas and intellectual interests.

• Be willing to be spontaneous; try to go with the flow. Initiate physical intimacy and *plan* to surprise your partner.

• Keep communicating. Don't withdraw when you feel hurt; explain your feelings.

• Be willing to stop what you're doing and listen to your partner's ideas and visions without criticism or insisting that he or she make them all a reality.

• Be willing to engage in good-natured debates. Try not to take these discussions personally.

ENTP with ENFP

The Joys

ENTPs and ENFPs share three type preferences, so they have a lot in common and usually enjoy a high degree of satisfaction in their relationships. ENTPs and ENFPs are very outgoing and love meeting new people. They are easygoing, fun-loving, and active people who are eager to try new things and experience as much of life as possible. Flexible and spontaneous (if somewhat impulsive), ENTPs and ENFPs share an irreverent sense of humor and a love of words and puns. They often enjoy high-spirited times filled with jokes and laughter, as well as enthusiastic discussions on a wide range of subjects.

The strongest connection between ENTPs and ENFPs is their shared intuition. These two curious people see possibilities everywhere and are eager to talk about their many ideas and innovations. They are usually extremely insightful, highly creative, and rarely deterred by obstacles that threaten

to keep their ideas from becoming a reality. ENTP and ENFP couples often enjoy each other most when they're discussing their ideas, brainstorming possibilities, and fantasizing about their future together.

In fact, many ENTPs and ENFPs are drawn to each other because it is familiar, fun, and energizing to be with someone who is so much like oneself. ENTPs and ENFPs typically describe themselves as best friends as well as lovers and partners. But in addition to their similarities, ENTPs and ENFPs are often initially attracted to each other because of their differences. ENTPs admire ENFPs' compassion, self-awareness, and warmth. ENFPs are often drawn to ENTPs' confidence, calm logic, and ability to shrug off rejection and criticism.

Because of their differences, ENTPs and ENFPs are able to help each other grow and develop in important ways. ENTPs help ENFPs ignore the pressure to please other people and instead learn to speak their minds with honesty and confidence. For their part, ENFPs often help ENTPs cultivate more genuine compassion and sensitivity to people and commit themselves more fully to their important relationships.

The Frustrations

A chief source of frustration for ENTPs and ENFPs is that they have the same blind spots. They are often unaware of facts and details and share a general disregard for structure and plans. So while these couples often have great fun together, conflicts do arise when neither partner takes the initiative to maintain order and complete household chores. Often the more mundane or repetitive tasks fall on the shoulders of the woman, regardless of her desire or aptitude, and this naturally causes resentment. Also, because both ENTPs and ENFPs are so social and busy, they may become overextended and put other people and activities ahead of their relationships. As a result, they may unintentionally neglect to spend time together just relaxing and enjoying each other's company.

Another source of conflict for ENTPs and ENFPs is conflict itself. ENTPs tend to be much more confrontational and blunt than ENFPs, who are naturally diplomatic and sensitive. So ENTPs sometimes hurt their partners' feelings without meaning to, and ENFPs are sometimes less than completely honest or direct when dealing with problems. ENFPs have a more powerful need for harmony than ENTPs, who often find it energizing to engage in heated debate. But what begins as a purely intellectual exercise for ENTPs can quickly turn into a contentious argument over what seems to ENFPs like meaningless hairsplitting. Also, some ENTPs are more ambitious and driven by success than their ENFP partners. When this is the case, ENTPs may be impatient and critical of their partners' desire to find meaningful, but not necessarily lucrative, work.

Perhaps the most common source of frustration for ENTPs and ENFPs lies in their different ways of making decisions. Although many ENTPs are charming and highly insightful about others, they are primarily logical people and strategic decision makers. In contrast, ENFPs are deeply emotional people who base their opinions and decisions on their heartfelt personal values. So ENTPs sometimes get frustrated by the extent to which their ENFP partners take things personally and how frequently they get their feelings hurt. For their part, ENFPs often feel that their partners discount their emotional reactions and their need to be understood and supported. Whereas ENTPs can be demanding and critical, ENFPs can be overly dramatic. When they feel overwhelmed, ENFPs' small issues may escalate into large and totally unrealistic ones. Therefore, although ENTPs and ENFPs tend to be compatible, they need to be patient, clear, honest, and sensitive with each other when they communicate. Refocusing their attention on

the possibilities and future usually helps them feel reenergized and optimistic.

How to Reach Your ENFP Partner

- Be patient with your partner's deep and intense feelings.
- Listen patiently while your partner talks, even if his or her ideas seem illogical or disorganized.
- Take seriously your partner's desire to please others and nurture all his or her many relationships.
- Be sure to establish harmony and closeness before expecting sexual intimacy.
- Focus on the positive. Start with appreciation before offering constructive criticism.
- Don't place other relationships and friendships ahead of the one you share with your partner.

How to Reach Your ENTP Partner

- Compliment your partner on his or her accomplishments, intelligence, and competence.
- Be calm and direct in your communication, especially when discussing problems.
- Encourage your partner to maintain friendships outside your relationship.
- Ask your partner to help you see the logical consequences of your actions.
- Never question your partner's competence in public.
- Take constructive criticism in the helpful spirit in which it is intended. Step back and try to be objective.

ENTP with INFP

The Joys

ENTPs and INFPs have two of the four type preferences in common, making them both creative, nontraditional, and open-minded people who are typically interested in many things. Since they are curious about new ideas and often eager to gain a deeper understanding of issues, they tend to have a similar take on things, which is a source of great satisfaction. ENTPs and INFPs are usually more concerned about their own individuality and creative expression than they are about anyone else's standards. They both enjoy thinking about and discussing possibilities, especially their insights into other people.

Adaptable, playful, and willing to try new things, ENTPs and INFPs often have lots of fun together. But in addition to their many similarities, ENTP and INFP couples may be initially attracted to each other because of their differences. ENTPs are drawn to INFPs because of their independence, openness, emotional availability, and intensity. INFPs are attracted to the captivating energy, charm, and confidence of ENTPs.

Because of their differences, ENTPs and INFPs have the opportunity to help each other grow and develop in important ways. ENTPs say that their INFP partners encourage them to slow down and purposefully cultivate deeper emotional connections with the people they love. ENTPs find that under the influence, they are able to balance their impulsiveness with the need to make choices that are in harmony with their personal values. INFPs usually credit ENTPs with helping them become less intense and judgmental. Increased objectivity helps INFPs avoid getting their feelings hurt quite as often and keeps them from being constantly disillusioned and disappointed by others.

The Frustrations

Most of the common frustrations ENTP and INFP couples experience stem from their differences. Typically logical and objective, ENTPs often think that INFPs are too moody and blow small disappointments or offenses out of proportion. INFPs feel that their ENTP partners do not always consider them first and are frequently distracted,

insensitive to their feelings, and impatient for them to "snap out of it." Also, since ENTPs place the highest value on their personal competence, they tend to be quite career-driven. INFPs are essentially seekers of inner balance and truth, and they place the most importance on harmony in their personal relationships. As a result, INFPs can become intractable about their values or moral positions. ENTPs constantly seek varied social and intellectual stimulation, even if that pursuit takes them out of the house a lot, whereas INFPs make establishing a more intimate connection with their partners a priority. Consequently, ENTPs can sometimes feel a bit smothered, and INFPs can sometimes feel a bit neglected. And while a sense of exclusivity and faithfulness is what generates trust and satisfaction for INFPs, ENTPs want their independence to be respected and to know that their partners trust them. This can set up an uncomfortable paradox and an ongoing challenge for these couples.

Finally, since neither ENTPs nor INFPs are especially interested in or good at following through on mundane tasks and chores, they can experience conflict about everyday household jobs. This can be especially problematic if they fall into stereotypical gender roles, since neither type wants to be responsible for the domestic management of the home. Happily, ENTPs and INFPs are also very flexible and usually willing to find imaginative ways of getting things done. Any task that becomes too repetitive, however, is likely to be neglected or forgotten, or done with resentment. The same is true for decision making, since both partners are much more interested in checking out possibilities than ruling out options. They may end up waiting so long to make a decision that they reduce or eliminate their choices or miss out on opportunities. Again, ENTPs and INFPs need to find a flexible and fair way of sharing the more unpleasant tasks of everyday life.

How to Reach Your INFP Partner

- Never dismiss your partner's feelings, even if they don't make sense or seem too extreme to you.
- Watch your tendency to be distracted and impatient when your partner is talking. Give him or her your full attention.
- Make sure you spend time alone with your partner rather than always including other people.
- Express your appreciation for the emotional support and nurturing your partner readily gives you.
- Be willing to forgo an occasional social opportunity to stay home and spend quiet, intimate time with your partner.
- Share your feelings, fears, and insecurities to deepen your connection to your partner. Respect your partner's privacy.

How to Reach Your ENTP Partner

- Keep it fun. Try not to get stuck in a serious mood for too long.
- Watch your tendency to become judgmental and disapproving.
- Express your appreciation of your partner's excellent problem-solving skills and many creative ideas.
- Compliment your partner on his or her accomplishments and innovations.
- Make sure your partner has plenty of opportunities to socialize, both with and without you.
- Initiate discussions about problems as soon as they come up. Don't hold things in and avoid frank discussions.

INTP with ENFJ

The Joys

INTPs and ENFJs share only one of the four type preferences and usually experience a primary connection through their imaginations. Both are driven by a unique perspective and somewhat idealistic vision of how the world could be. They frequently share a passion for the arts, for innovation, and for creative expression in their lives. Some of their best times together are spent discussing their ideas or enjoying a concert, movie, museum, or lecture.

The source of their initial attraction is often their many and significant differences. INTPs are often attracted to ENFJs' warmth, optimism, and enthusiasm for life. They admire their partners' energy and social confidence and respect their insights and understanding of what makes people tick. ENFJs are often drawn to INTPs' independence, creativity, and calm way of dealing with crises. Many ENFJs admire their partners' resourceful ways of solving problems and find their original ideas exciting and stimulating.

The many differences between INTPs and ENFJs offer them the opportunity to help each other grow and develop in important ways. INTPs help ENFJs become less dependent on other people's opinions and better able to remain objective when making decisions. ENFJs credit their partners with helping them gather more information before forming their opinions. For their part, ENFJs help INTPs become more aware of their feelings and more willing to express them, as well as more sensitive to the needs of others. Many INTPs say that their ENFJ partners bring a joyful dimension to their lives that they didn't know before.

The Frustrations

Despite their shared intuitiveness, couples of this combination have some big differences. Typically,

INTPs need much more privacy and the opportunity to think things through at their own pace. By contrast, ENFJs crave social experiences with friends, the stimulation of meeting new people, and the opportunity to share their feelings and opinions. ENFJs need to talk things out to work them through, and INTPs need to think things through before they can work them out. ENFJs also tend to avoid conflict for as long as possible, then ambush their partners with a laundry list of complaints. INTPs typically retreat, either waiting for the issues to go away or working to effect a change to avoid having to actually talk about them again. Generally, ENFJs feel that they are constantly trying to get their partners to open up and share, and INTPs often feel nagged and crowded.

Perhaps the most fundamental area of discontent results from these couples' different decision-making styles. ENFJs are usually very diplomatic and want to be treated with kindness and tact, while INTPs prefer direct, even blunt, honesty. Above all, ENFJs need an emotional connection with their partners, which must precede any kind of physical intimacy. When ENFJs feel cut off, hurt, or threatened, they may turn to passive-aggressive tactics, such as bringing up old issues that have already been settled. Conversely, INTPs are superlogical and sometimes very detached people. It takes a real effort and risk for INTPs to articulate their true feelings, even to their partners. When they either are unsure of how they feel or aren't comfortable sharing, they tend to close themselves off and say nothing. Not naturally empathetic, they frequently don't understand their partners' feelings and tend to write them off as overreactions. But dismissing ENFJs as hypersensitive is like questioning INTPs' competence: it undermines trust in the relationship and forces a widening gulf.

Finally, INTP and ENFJ couples tend to experience regular conflicts about order and neatness in their homes. ENFJs are genuinely concerned about what other people think and may be resentful of or embarrassed by their INTP partners' lack of initiative or follow-through on household chores. Non-conforming and independent INTPs have little interest in meeting other people's expectations, whether about housekeeping or dress or work habits. ENFJs also may feel taken advantage of when they are forced to pick up constantly after their absentminded mates. For their part, INTPs feel criticized and nagged about details they see as irrelevant or silly — and that sends them into a retreat faster than almost anything else. ENFJs and INTPs need to agree on how to maintain common areas of the home and allow each other to keep their private spaces in whatever way they choose.

How to Reach Your INTP Partner

- Give your partner genuine compliments, especially about the creativity and value of his or her ideas. Ask for your partner's opinions, especially concerning creative or technical issues.
- Respect your partner's desire and need to be alone. Spend some quiet time together.
- When your partner is listening, be careful not to "wear out your welcome" by talking too much.
- Pursue your high social needs on your own. Don't pressure your partner to join you.
- After you express your needs or dissatisfaction calmly, wait and see what happens. Your partner is more likely to take action without further discussion.
- Don't criticize your partner's competence publicly or ambush him or her with huge emotional outbursts.
- Watch your tendency to put other people's needs ahead of your partner's.

How to Reach Your ENFJ Partner

- Talk, talk, and talk some more! Try to remember some of the people details of your partner's stories to show that you are really listening.

• If you need to disengage, let your partner know that's what you're doing so he or she won't take it personally.

• Offer your partner a periodic "weather report" about how you are feeling. Let him or her know if you're still mulling something over and need more time before talking about it.

• Apologize when you know you've hurt your partner's feelings. Don't dismiss his or her feelings, even if they don't make sense to you.

• Offer gentle suggestions rather than blunt criticism. Begin with a positive statement.

• Try to be prompt and to finish some of the projects you start.

INTP with INFJ

The Joys

INTPs and INFJs share two of the four type preferences, and they often enjoy complementary and interesting relationships. They have a common need for solitude and concentration, so they respect each other's privacy. But perhaps the strongest connection between INTPs and INFJs is their shared intuitiveness and the similar ways they view the world. They both readily see possibilities and usually enjoy discussing global issues and future implications of current events. Many INTPs and INFJs have an unusual sense of humor and enjoy each other's unique ways of expressing themselves. The degree to which they both feel understood is often a source of great satisfaction.

In addition to their shared sensibility, INTPs and INFJs are often initially attracted to each other because of their differences. Typically, INTPs are drawn to INFJs because of their warmth, integrity, and emotional availability. Many INTPs credit their INFJ partners with bringing about a deeper connection in their relationships. INFJs are often attracted to the intelligence, dry sense of humor, and quiet confidence of INTPs. They admire their partners' independence and find their honesty refreshing.

Because of their differences, INTPs and INFJs can help each other grow and develop in important ways. INTPs often help INFJs increase their personal and professional confidence and competence. INFJs come to develop a more logical approach, which helps them remain objective and be less likely to get overwhelmed. For their part, INFJs help INTPs become more aware of their genuine feelings and encourage them to articulate and share those feelings. Many INTPs also credit their partners with helping them become more compassionate, sensitive, and patient with the sometimes complex reactions of other people.

The Frustrations

Perhaps the greatest source of frustration for INTP and INFJ couples comes from their very different needs for sharing and intimacy. INTPs are ultra-private and independent people, while INFJs crave strong emotional connections with their partners. For most INFJs, there simply can't be too much sharing, talking things through, and establishing harmony and agreement. Most INFJs also have very strong moral beliefs, and their insistence on the "right" way can feel confining or patronizing to their INTP partners. For INTPs, their commitment to their partners is largely self-evident, and they're seldom comfortable, or even able, to express their feelings as freely or eloquently as their partners. Also, by nature, INTPs are calm and unemotional, and they occasionally find that their INFJ partners are too intense and reactionary. But the more disconnected INFJs feel, the more they push to reestablish harmony. And the more INTPs feel pressured to share their feelings, the more they pull back.

Another common frustration stems from the fact that both INTPs and INFJs tend to avoid conflict, though for different reasons. INTPs spend so much time in their own worlds that they're often unaware that problems are brewing, especially when the problems result from inadvertent insensitivity to their partners' feelings. INTPs have difficulty admitting that they don't have everything under control or that they feel weak or vulnerable in any way. For their part, INFJs tend to put a rosy glow on things. Both INTPs and INFJs may avoid talking about problems until they've become big. To keep small issues from becoming destructive, both partners need to be sensitive to their partners but honest about their own needs.

INTP and INFJ couples also have very different needs for order, neatness, and sticking with a plan. INFJs feel that they do more than their fair share of the household chores and that they are constantly picking up after their partners. INTPs may feel nagged and prodded into doing chores according to their partners' timetables or to please other people, neither of which is especially motivating for them. Because INFJs have such a strong need for closure, they often impose their sense of urgency on their partners and press for decisions before INTPs feel that they've gathered enough information. In addition, INFJs almost always have a plan and want to stick with it rather than be spontaneous. By contrast, INTPs like to stay open to new opportunities. INTPs may resist plans, while INFJs tend to insist on them, creating frequent conflict between them.

How to Reach Your INFJ Partner

- Talk! Share your feelings and your personal reactions to events.
- Offer your opinions and demonstrate that you are really listening to your partner. Give him or her your undivided attention. Sit close and maintain eye contact.
- Offer expressions of affection — words or physical touching that is affectionate but not necessarily a prelude to sex.

- Be sure to include your partner in some of your projects or activities. Share what's going on and solicit his or her insights.
- Never dismiss your partner's feelings as illogical or overblown.
- Pitch in to initiate and finish household chores, especially after you offer to.
- Be where you say you will be and try not to be late.
- Compliment your partner on his or her good ideas and creativity.

How to Reach Your INTP Partner

- Respect your partner's needs for privacy and independence.
- Be careful not to become so involved in the needs of other people that you spread yourself too thin and don't have any energy left for your partner.
- Encourage your partner to relax and enjoy some downtime.
- Be direct, honest, and calm about problems or issues. Try not to exaggerate or repeat yourself.
- Keep your partner's confidences. Never talk about his or her private issues with your friends.
- Try not to nag or make smug comments about how much work you are doing compared with how much your partner is doing.
- Be willing to adjust your timetable or agenda to accommodate your partner's ideas and spontaneity.
- Appreciate your partner's accomplishments and competence.

INTP with ENFP

The Joys

INTPs and ENFPs often have playful, creative, and fun relationships due to the two type preferences they share. Their rich imaginations and forward thinking gives them similar frames of reference, as they both love to consider possibilities and new ideas. INTPs and ENFPs often enjoy fantasy, discussing theoretical or global issues, and investigating anything out of the ordinary. Given their shared sense of adventure, these couples love to hop in the car and head out in search of some new experience. INTPs and ENFPs rarely have any interest in maintaining the status quo and they share an irreverent sense of humor. They often enjoy creative pursuits, including art, theater, museums, and exploring the Internet. Since neither partner has a strong need to control the other, they are usually quite supportive of each other's needs to make changes and to grow professionally.

INTPs and ENFPs are often attracted to each other because of their easygoing natures and their unconventional lifestyles and attitudes. But some of their differences also draw them together. INTPs are attracted to ENFPs' warmth, nurturing energy, and accurate insights into people (especially their INTP partners). INTPs are impressed with their partners' social skills and ability to articulate their feelings clearly and passionately. ENFPs are often drawn to the wit and creative independence of INTPs, are fascinated by their creative minds, and enjoy their casual yet intense style.

Because of their differences, INTPs and ENFPs are often able to help each other grow and develop in important ways. INTPs help their partners increase their overall competence in foreseeing the logical consequences of their actions. INTPs also help ENFPs slow down, become more selective, and fine-tune their ideas by focusing some of their tremendous energy. For their part, ENFPs help broaden their partners' social horizons and encourage them to participate more fully in the world outside themselves. Many INTPs also say that their partners help them articulate their feelings and become more patient with and sensitive to other people.

The Frustrations

The frustrations INTP and ENFP couples experience usually stem from their different decision-making processes. INTPs are especially logical people, convinced only by objective, rational reasoning. Although they can almost always assess the logical consequences of their actions, they are often unclear about other people and their feelings. By contrast, ENFPs are driven to understand others and maintain harmony in their relationships, especially those that are closest to their hearts. ENFPs are very sensitive and empathetic people. They are insightful and even prophetic in their understanding of what makes people tick, but they are not particularly objective. Whereas INTPs can be detached, remote, and unaware that they have been insensitive, ENFPs can be blinded by emotion and overly sensitive to criticism, even when it is offered as constructive feedback.

This difference is exacerbated by the fact that ENFPs tend to hold on to grievances for a long time, even though they are generally much more willing and eager to talk about issues than are their INTP partners. INTPs are extremely private people who resent any invasion of their private time and space. When a conflict arises, INTPs tend to withdraw so they can think the issue through logically and objectively before discussing it. ENFPs may pull away initially, but they usually want to talk and resolve issues quickly. For most ENFPs, sharing their experiences and thoughts is an essential part of their lives. Without this sharing, they feel cut off and lonely. These characteristics also play a role in INTPs' and ENFPs' different social needs. INTPs tend to prefer fewer, more intimate gatherings and more spontaneous and free-flowing events. ENFPs like lots of interaction and will usually play along with almost any game or activity.

Finally, INTPs and ENFPs may experience frustration that results from the fact that neither partner is especially organized or decisive or likes to be in charge. Although this makes for a very easygoing household, opportunities are often missed and practical concerns ignored because no one is watching the clock or the calendar. Eventually, bills must be paid and groceries purchased, routine chores often fall either to the person who dislikes them less or is less inept, or to the woman in the couple. This can breed a good deal of resentment, which is likely to be held in and allowed to fester. Since both INTPs and ENFPs tend to abandon projects once the interesting, challenging, or creative part is worked out, these couples need to find innovative and flexible ways to share the burden so they can stay on top of responsibilities.

How to Reach Your ENFP Partner

- Share your feelings and experiences and the events of your day. Respond to your partner and make sure he or she knows you are involved.
- Don't dismiss your partner's reactions or feelings as overly dramatic or illogical simply because you don't share them.
- Take time to listen to your partner's concerns without immediately making suggestions for how to fix them.
- Initiate household chores and follow through on the ones for which you are responsible.
- Be sure to encourage your partner to get together with his or her friends and socialize as much as he or she wants, with or without you.
- Compliment your partner for his or her creativity and insights. Appreciate the warmth and harmony your mate brings to your life.
- Express your feelings. Say "I love you" a lot!

How to Reach Your INTP Partner

- Respect your partner's privacy and need for plenty of uninterrupted time alone.
- Listen completely to your partner's ideas before jumping in to offer your ideas or to finish his or her sentences.

- When your partner is sharing his or her thoughts, be careful not to assume that you know how he or she feels. Try not to interrupt.
- Never force your partner into the spotlight or discuss private matters with other people without his or her permission.
- Compliment your partner on his or her achievements and innovations. Recognize your partner's good ideas and intellect.
- Follow through on household chores that are your responsibility; don't nag your partner when he or she forgets to do his or her chores.

INTP with INFP

The Joys

INTPs and INFPs share three of the four type preferences, so they often have a lot in common. They are both private, quiet people who need plenty of time to themselves pursuing things that they find interesting or personally meaningful. Both are interested in personal growth and development — whether of an intellectual, emotional, or spiritual nature — and tend to be supportive of each other's individual pursuits. They frequently have a similar take on things, are interested in exploring deeper meanings and subtle connections, and enjoy the creative stimulation they get from movies, art, music, or theater. They focus on the big picture and enjoy having deep and substantive discussions about a variety of topics. Relaxed and flexible about most things, INTPs and INFPs are typically curious about and open to each other's views and thoughts. Neither is especially interested in trying to control the other, and both prefer to lead unstructured, casual lives. They are supportive listeners and generally have little need for a lot of outside stimulation or input.

Understandably, INTPs and INFPs are often attracted to each other not only because of their many similarities but also because of their differences. INTPs are typically drawn to INFPs' warmth and genuine desire to nurture and share with their partners. INFPs also are deeply compassionate and devoted people who look for the best in their partners. For their part, INFPs are attracted to INTPs because they're so unique, confident, calm, and independent. INTPs are usually utterly unpretentious and especially honest about themselves — a quality INFPs find refreshing.

Because of their differences, INTPs and INFPs have the opportunity to help each other grow and develop in important ways. INTPs often say that their partners help them open up and share the emotional side of their lives. INTPs find that their partners encourage them to be more compassionate and also more sensitive to other people's feelings. Many INFPs credit their INTP partners with helping them become more objective, especially about themselves. They learn to take fewer things personally and generally become more assertive and independent.

The Frustrations

The chief frustration INTPs and INFPs experience involves communication and their radically different ways of making decisions. INTPs are superlogical people and are rarely convinced by anything that doesn't make rational sense to them. By contrast, INFPs are intensely sensitive people who base most of their decisions on personal values. INTPs unintentionally hurt their INFP partners' feelings by being critical and detached, and INFPs often feel shut out from their partners' reactions, which makes them feel lonely. Sharing a deep, meaningful, and emotionally intimate connection with their partners is paramount to INFPs. INTPs are often baffled by the reactions, or overreactions, of their INFP partners. They believe that their commitment is self-evident and don't understand why their partners take offense at their honesty or their efforts to help their partners improve by pointing out flaws or mistakes. Their intentions

are honorable, and they can't see why their partners can't accept constructive criticism in the spirit in which it is given. INFPs often complain that their partners don't share their feelings and thoughts with them as much as they want and need. For their part, INTPs often feel that their partners are too dependent on them and press them to share when they aren't ready.

When conflicts arise, INTPs tend to withdraw and act even cooler, while INFPs withdraw and brood. Compounding the problem is the fact that neither INTPs nor INFPs discuss problems immediately. INTPs are reluctant to express their fears and be vulnerable, so when they aren't completely sure how to state their feelings, they take time to think about it. For their part, INFPs may avoid confrontation because they don't want to face the reality that there are problems. Since INFPs also want to express their feelings diplomatically, they frequently ruminate about things longer than they should. INTPs and INFPs often find it beneficial to set regular times to talk about their relationships, giving both partners time to think about things ahead of time.

While INTPs and INFPs may like intellectual discussions, INTPs enjoy the stimulation and tension of debates. But INFPs find that tension stressful because they equate arguments with disharmony. So discussions that begin as interesting and fun can turn uncomfortable when INFPs begin to take things personally and INTPs try to prove they're right. Although INTPs and INFPs are usually flexible and casual about small matters, INTPs can be sticklers about their principles, and INFPs can be rigid when their values are challenged.

Finally, since neither INTPs nor INFPs pay close attention to routine or mundane details, they can both neglect important practical matters such as paying bills or maintaining their homes. They tend to be very relaxed about deadlines and follow-through, and they may play a game of hot potato when it comes to making decisions or finishing projects. As with many couples, there is often an unfair distribution of household labor when the woman, regardless of her type, feels pressured to take on more than her fair share of the cleaning and organizing.

How to Reach Your INFP Partner

- Don't put off discussing important things, but do so gently and lovingly.
- Watch your tendency to be overly critical and analytical and to find fault with your partner's reasoning.
- Sit close to your partner when talking about conflict. Touch and smile. Start by expressing the positive things before the negative.
- Express your gratitude and appreciation of all the ways your partner nurtures and supports you. Do it in writing if that's easier for you.
- Compliment your partner's *efforts* in all things, such as finishing projects, initiating plans, and striking out independently.

- Don't dismiss your partner's feelings, even if you don't understand them.
- Never ask your partner to compromise on his or her personal values and beliefs.

How to Reach Your INTP Partner

- Tell your partner you need a break to calm down and become rational again. Then go back and discuss things calmly and honestly.
- Present your views logically and rationally. Try not to repeat yourself.
- Give your partner time to think about how he or she feels about things before expecting a response.
- Appreciate the effort your partner makes to share with you. Compliment him or her on the stimulation he or she brings to your life.
- Initiate discussions of new and complex subjects.
- Don't question your partner's competence or put him or her on the spot publicly.

Chapter 13

The Idealists²: NFs with NFs

ENFJ with ENFJ

The Joys

Since ENFJ couples share all four type preferences and the same temperament, they tend to have a tremendous amount in common and usually enjoy an intimate, emotional connection. Most ENFJs place their relationships with their partners at the top of their list of priorities, followed by their relationships with other family members and friends. ENFJ couples are high-energy people with a desire to be productive. They usually have a wide variety of friends and associates and a strong need for social interaction and stimulation. Above all, their work and relationships must complement their deeply held personal values and beliefs, and they must feel free to pursue personal and professional growth. Diplomatic and skillful with people, ENFJs like harmony and want to help other people reach their full potentials. They also share a strong penchant for organization and order and tend to work together to keep their homes neat and attractive. They love to discuss the future and plan their time in order to be as efficient and productive as possible. Expressive, appreciative, and loving, ENFJ partners are each other's best and most enthusiastic cheerleaders.

But just as ENFJ couples share many of the same strengths, they also share the same weaknesses. Their strong drive for personal awareness and growth gives them many opportunities to help

each other develop in important ways. ENFJs often provide a safe atmosphere that helps the other learn to speak the truth instead of saying what they intuitively know others want to hear. By trusting each other, they can learn to resist their natural urge to avoid confrontation and instead build healthier relationships with all people, based on honesty and authenticity. Learning to apply logic and objectivity to their decisions makes ENFJs less likely to take everything personally and frees them from the pressure of having to please everyone else. Also, ENFJ couples can support each other's efforts to be more realistic and accurate with facts and details and encourage each other to pay closer attention to the present rather than focusing only on future possibilities. Finally, ENFJ partners can help each other slow down and relax.

The Frustrations

Chief among the sources of frustration for ENFJ couples is that they both have strong opinions and need to be in charge. Each of them has a clear and firm agenda, and they frequently jockey for position, sometimes being less than generous about helping their partners get their needs met. When either feels unsupported, they tend to act a bit cold, stubborn, and unwilling to compromise.

Another challenge for ENFJ couples is that because they share a strong desire for harmony, they avoid even honest discussions about potentially uncomfortable issues. They tend to be quite emotional and often have trouble hearing even constructive criticism. Sweeping things under the rug may work temporarily, but ultimately it can undermine the connection they feel to each other. Most ENFJs can't go too long bearing the weight of unhappiness between them and are eager to make up and move ahead. The solution for them is to take the time to talk honestly about underlying issues. ENFJs also tend to take absolute moral positions on most subjects, and if one partner finds those beliefs in conflict with the other's, they can have real difficulty reconciling. ENFJs rarely compromise their values and usually find it painful to live with the distance conflicting beliefs create.

ENFJs also need to be careful not to become so overextended by outside or work-related activities that they become exhausted. Finding a balance between being with and helping other people and improving the quality of their relationships is essential. They are generally happy to schedule private time with their partners to focus on each other in order to remain connected.

Advice for ENFJs

- Slow down. Resist the urge to get involved in so many projects that you become exhausted.
- Take time on a regular basis to discuss the relationship — where you think it is going and how you might make constructive changes.
- Be truthful and direct with each other. Be sure to spend time sharing both the positive and the negative with tact and honesty.
- Don't avoid healthy confrontations and discussions. Don't run away when there's a problem or put off speaking your mind.
- Go on vacations alone together. Encourage each other to relax and not be productive for periods of time.
- Encourage each other's independence and individuality. Pursue your own interests and support each other's growth.

ENFJ with INFJ

The Joys

Because they share three of the four type preferences, ENFJs and INFJs are similar in many significant ways. They often feel a powerful kinship, trust, and commitment because they understand each other so well. ENFJs and INFJs value good communication and pride themselves on their ability to express themselves accurately and lovingly. Diplomatic, warm, and affectionate, ENFJs and INFJs are typically very supportive of each other and their individual needs for self-expression, individuality, and personal and professional growth. They both seek deep emotional intimacy and share their private thoughts and feelings. They are appreciative of each other's originality and respectful of each other's values. Since ENFJs and INFJs are both decisive and organized, they often work well together and derive great pleasure from dreaming and planning their future. Finally, many ENFJs and INFJs are free of restrictive gender expectations, and the woman of the couple is likely to find that her partner is much more emotionally accessible than many of the other men she's known.

Not surprisingly, because ENFJs and INFJs are so similar, they often find it easy and comfortable to be together, but they are also attracted to each other because of their differences. ENFJs often admire INFJs' intensity, unshakable integrity, and thoughtfulness. ENFJs appreciate what sensitive and attentive listeners their INFJ partners are. For their part, INFJs are often drawn to ENFJs' enthusiasm, boundless energy, social ease, and poise. INFJs admire their partners' ability to make things happen and get things done with charm and confidence.

Because of their differences, and especially because of their mutual desire for growth and understanding, ENFJs and INFJs have the opportunity to help each other develop in important ways. Typically, ENFJs are able to help INFJs broaden their horizons, pulling them out of their own worlds and encouraging them to participate in a variety of activities. INFJs often credit their partners with helping them act on more of their many interesting ideas. INFJs are often able to help their ENFJ partners slow down and focus on fewer projects to greater effect. ENFJs credit their INFJ partners with helping them be more selective about where they devote their attention and improve their ability to listen. ENFJs and INFJs help each other be more logical in their decision making and pay closer attention to the details and delights of everyday life.

The Frustrations

The main source of frustration for most ENFJ and INFJ couples is their different energy levels. ENFJs are active, talkative, and social, while INFJs are much more reserved, private, and selective about their pursuits. ENFJs tend to jump into things without a lot of forethought, which can be irritating to their partners. On the other hand, INFJs' need to think things through first and their slower response time can be exasperating to ENFJs. Also, ENFJs usually want a lot of conversation, even after a busy and stressful day. But INFJs need time to unwind and reenergize by being alone, reading, thinking, or resting. INFJs often feel pressured to participate in activities or discussions and may resent ENFJs' seemingly insensitive intrusion into their personal space. ENFJs are left feeling shut out if their INFJ partners are not immediately available. And while most INFJs want to socialize and share experiences with their partners, they usually prefer the interaction to be quieter and more intimate. ENFJs are also annoyed by their INFJ partners' tendency to moralize and their rather egocentric focus. INFJs find it irritating and hurtful when ENFJs put other people's needs ahead of their partners'.

Another potential problem for many ENFJs and

INFJs is that since they both like and want to be in control, they sometimes struggle over how things should be done. They see issues in rather black-and-white terms and have trouble shifting gears and responding to spontaneous opportunities. Also both ENFJs and INFJs hold very strong opinions and they each arrive at conclusions based almost exclusively on their personal values. So both partners are loath to violate or even occasionally compromise those values. And since ENFJs and INFJs are so sensitive, they tend to take criticism as a personal affront. This sets up a difficult challenge for these couples, because as they strive for harmony, they also avoid conflict and healthy confrontation. So they need to be vigilant about discussing small problems openly and honestly before they grow, breeding resentment that can poison an otherwise satisfying relationship.

How to Reach Your INFJ Partner

- Recognize and accept your partner's need for private space and quiet time, especially if he or she is under a lot of pressure.
- Encourage your partner to pursue his or her own interests, activities, and friendships.
- Listen fully and completely when your partner is talking. Don't do anything else but look right into his or her eyes.
- Compliment your partner on his or her many great ideas and visions.
- Accept your partner's need to opt out of some of the social activities you want to pursue. Don't try to pressure him or her into attending.
- Try not to get overinvolved in outside commitments. Continue to put your partner first.

How to Reach Your ENFJ Partner

- Share your reactions, thoughts, and feelings right away. Try not to withdraw.
- Encourage your partner to pursue his or her own interests, friends, and activities.

- Try to accompany your partner to as many social events as you can, but admit when you're tired so your partner won't take it personally.
- Be careful not to become so tired from outside activities that you have nothing left for your partner.
- Encourage your partner to think out loud. Be a receptive and attentive sounding board.

ENFJ with ENFP

The Joys

Because ENFJs and ENFPs have three type preferences in common and share the same temperamental values, they often have very compatible relationships and understand each other well. Confident, warm, and enthusiastic, ENFJs and ENFPs seem to be on a perpetual quest for the meaning of life, and they take a very personal approach to all interactions and projects. As a couple, they enjoy thinking about and especially talking about their unique perspectives on world events, future possibilities, and other people. ENFJs and ENFPs value their relationships most highly and spend lots of energy trying to improve and deepen the connection they feel with their partners. They communicate in intimate, loving, and expressive ways and are eager to discover new or unusual sides to their partners. ENFJs and ENFPs usually lead active social lives and have lots of meaningful friendships. As a couple, they may choose a somewhat nonconventional lifestyle and are often most concerned with things of a spiritual nature.

In addition to their many areas of commonality, ENFJs and ENFPs are attracted to each other because of their complementary strengths. Generally, ENFJs are drawn to ENFPs because they are so fun, irreverent, and genuinely caring. ENFJs enjoy and are stimulated by ENFPs' creativity and the fact that they are rarely deterred or discour-

aged by obstacles. ENFPs are attracted to ENFJs because they are highly motivated, organized, and often ambitious. ENFPs admire how expressive, warm, and charming ENFJs are, and ENFJs' enormous desire to please makes ENFPs feel nurtured and supported.

Because of their differences, as well as their strong desire to support each other, ENFJs and ENFPs have the opportunity to help each other grow and develop in important ways. ENFPs often credit their partners with helping them become more selective, organized, and productive so they don't scatter their efforts among too many projects. They say that their partners make them feel safe enough to share their feelings. ENFPs are often able to help ENFJs lighten up and become more relaxed and flexible. ENFJs often say that their partners help them slow down and reduce their intense need to do things just to please others. ENFJs help their partners really be themselves, even if that means they are not always cheerful and helpful.

The Frustrations

Because ENFJs and ENFPs have different decision-making styles, they frequently experience frustration about order, structure, and closure. ENFJs like things organized and settled, whereas ENFPs are happier leaving their options open. ENFPs don't like to feel restricted, so they sometimes avoid committing themselves to one course of action. ENFJs often feel frustrated by their partners' unwillingness to commit, while ENFPs often feel pressured and rushed into making decisions without adequate information. ENFJs hear a plan being made when ENFPs are merely thinking out loud or brainstorming. ENFJs then feel irritated and inconvenienced when their partners change "plans" to pursue another opportunity that pops up.

For the most part, ENFJs like their surroundings to be neat, because to them clutter represents things to be done and they can't relax when their work is unfinished. ENFPs, however, are generally unaffected by clutter and disorder and even enjoy having several projects going at once. When it comes to doing ordinary and mundane chores, ENFPs tend to become bored with repetition much faster than ENFJs. ENFPs either don't notice or find another way to occupy their time when the dishwasher needs to be emptied or the clean laundry needs to be put away. By contrast, many ENFJs are neat freaks and drive their partners a little crazy with their frantic need to tidy up or keep their homes looking nice in case unexpected company drops in.

Another set of frustrations for ENFJ and ENFP couples stems from their common blind spots. Since neither tends to notice details, they also don't enjoy doing practical chores such as paying bills and balancing the checkbook. The one who hates it less or the partner who is more compelled to have it finished (usually the ENFJ) ends up doing the task. But whenever one person is required to do more than his or her fair share of unpleasant chores, resentment can brew. ENFJs are especially prone to feeling overworked, since they are driven to get things done and tend to keep a mental scorecard in their heads. Rather than speak up about their dissatisfaction, they may express their frustration in passive-aggressive ways. Since both ENFJs and ENFPs tend to avoid confrontation and the ensuing disharmony, they need to find ways of honestly and openly discussing the minor irritations that arise before they develop into larger problems.

How to Reach Your ENFP Partner

- Temper some of your strong opinions. Resist the urge to vehemently express your likes or dislikes immediately.
- Try to be flexible about plans. Don't take it personally when your partner decides to change course.

- Encourage your partner to pursue his or her many friendships and interests.
- Be honest and open about what's bothering you. Don't avoid or cover up small problems or always try to put a good face on things for other people's sakes.
- Be willing to change plans or leave things unfinished so you can participate in some of the spontaneous adventures your partner suggests.
- Be an enthusiastic and attentive listener of your partner's many ideas. Don't immediately point out why they may not work.

How to Reach Your ENFJ Partner

- Listen to your partner's feelings and reactions with concern and support. Don't immediately point out why it might not make sense to feel the way he or she does.
- Pull your own weight with household chores. Offer to help with or initiate projects that need doing. Pick up after yourself.
- Try to keep track of money and take care of the possessions you and your partner own together.
- Try not to change plans at the last minute. Give your partner as much warning as possible when you decide to bring people home.
- Strive to follow through on more of the many projects you start.

ENFJ with INFP

The Joys

Because ENFJs and INFPs share the same temperament, their strongest connection is usually their deeply felt values and mutual desire for a close, emotional connection. Highly idealistic, ENFJs and INFPs are concerned with each other's happiness and supportive of each other's personal growth. They each have a set of inviolate personal values on which they base most of their decisions, and since both partners typically want to discuss everything, they tend to have strong communication skills. ENFJs and INFPs are empathetic, gentle, and loving people who are eager to share themselves and apply their creativity and originality to all areas of their lives. They also share an interest in developing or exploring their spiritual identities. ENFJs and INFPs are engaged in a lifelong search for meaning and understanding, and they often share both intellectual curiosity and a strong aesthetic sensibility.

ENFJs and INFPs are often attracted to each other because of their differences. ENFJs often find the playful gentleness and unique insights of INFPs appealing. INFPs always push for more intimacy, rarely letting their sometimes more superficial ENFJ partners off the hook. Instead, they insist that ENFJs really share what is going on with them. Most ENFJs find true openness both exhilarating and scary and usually credit their INFP partners with adding depth, spontaneity, and profound sharing to their relationships. For their part, INFPs are usually drawn to ENFJs' warmth, enthusiasm, and charm. Typically, INFPs are grateful for ENFJs' expressiveness, optimism, and energy. ENFJs are usually staunch supporters of their INFP partners and help them realize some of their many aspirations.

Because of their differences, ENFJs and INFPs are able to help each other grow and develop in important ways. Together, they help each other take the time to enjoy their senses. Many couples find that they are much more likely to notice and participate in their physical surroundings through shared activities such as hiking, soaking in a hot tub, or preparing good food.

The Frustrations

The most common source of irritation and frustration for ENFJ and INFP couples is usually their different needs for order and closure. ENFJs want things decided and like to make and adhere to plans. INFPs prefer to wait and see how things go.

ENFJs usually have a higher energy level than INFPs, who are happy to spend more time and energy on one thing at a time. ENFJs tend to notice immediately what needs to be done, so they want chores performed quickly and projects finished. Typically, ENFJs care more about how things look than do their INFP partners. ENFJs want their homes neat, since they are often concerned about what is appropriate and pleasing to others. Consequently, ENFJs often feel that they are responsible for a disproportionate amount of the normal household maintenance. This feeling is especially common when the ENFJ is a woman. In contrast, INFPs are generally less concerned about what other people think and more interested in what makes them comfortable. Natural pack rats, they are likely to leave piles around the house, not noticing or being bothered by the clutter. INFPs are more focused on the process than on the end product and feel that ENFJs are entirely too concerned about appearances. They watch their ENFJ partners scurrying around, frantically trying to get too much done and becoming increasingly controlling and bossy. The more ENFJs do, the more INFPs tend to back away, exhausted and overwhelmed by the sheer force of energy ENFJs generate. Naturally, the more INFPs withdraw, the more anxious ENFJs feel because not only are they responsible for everything, but they also feel alone and unappreciated.

Finally, both ENFJs and INFPs may avoid confrontation and honest discussion of problems, or they may hold back what they are really feeling. They need to resist this tendency and trust that the strength of their connection will support the weight of all of their feelings. It's important for both partners to speak lovingly, gently, and without blame and criticism, but they also must force themselves to be totally honest with each other. If they conceal their real frustrations or fears, they may allow resentment and mistrust to corrode the integrity of their relationships. Finally, although they understand each other exceptionally well, they need to guard against assuming that they know exactly what the other person is thinking or feeling.

How to Reach Your INFP Partner

- Prepare your partner for important plans. Frame them in terms of how important they are to you.
- Curb your tendency to criticize and nag your partner about following through.
- Relax and go at your partner's pace. Try to be spontaneous rather than so project- or time-driven. Watch your tendency to be so much "on a mission" that you begin to act cold and controlling.
- Respect your partner's need for quiet and inactive time. Don't talk too much or invade his or her space.
- Express your honest feelings right away. Do so gently but directly.
- Be careful not to put other relationships or outside activities above your partner.
- Try to be more flexible about the little things. Let your partner help you lighten up.

How to Reach Your ENFJ Partner

- Acknowledge the many things your partner does to please you. Thank your mate for his or her efforts and praise your partner's high energy and productivity.
- Be aware of your tendency to be inflexible about things that upset you.
- Don't withdraw when you're feeling hurt. Express your feelings gently but also honestly and immediately.
- If writing suits you better than talking, make a list of the things your partner does that you appreciate. Share the list with your partner.
- Respect your partner's need for social stimulation. Go to events when you can and encourage your partner to go to others without you.

INFJ with INFJ

The Joys

Like all couples who have all four type preferences in common, INFJs understand each other very well. Not only do they have similar styles, but they also share a strong natural drive to understand and connect with others. It's not surprising that some INFJ couples describe their first encounter as "soul mates at first glance." The initial attraction for this type (which represents a small percentage of the population) is often a feeling of being truly understood — sometimes for the first time in their lives. In addition to sharing the same values, and frequently many of the same interests, INFJs are also visionary people who love to brainstorm and look to the future. They see the world in a broad context and enjoy discussing theories, complexities, and their views of the way the world ought to be. They often derive great pleasure from long, involved, intimate conversations about a variety of subjects they care deeply about.

INFJ couples also need harmony in their relationships to feel satisfied and comfortable. They tend to be polite, gentle, and considerate and enjoy doing thoughtful things for each other. And because INFJs like having things settled and keeping their environments neat and tidy, they rarely have conflicts over how organized the house is. They are quick to follow through on their chores, and since they both like to plan ahead, they rarely leave their partners in the lurch. Most INFJs are also pretty careful with their money and investments. They are very goal-oriented, and if their goals are in sync, they are fervently supportive of each other and committed to helping each other accomplish great things. Because of their similarities and their desire to grow and develop, they can help each other cultivate a more relaxed attitude, a willingness to slow down and consider alternatives, and a more tolerant view of different values and beliefs.

The Frustrations

Typically, INFJs are not particularly interested in or attentive to the realities of daily life. Focused as they are on the future possibilities, they may fail to notice when they're out of groceries or the oil in the car needs to be changed. Predictably, these undesirable tasks typically fall on the partner who dislikes them less or is expected to do them, which may result in resentment. Similarly, since both partners are more interested in dreaming and planning ahead, they may fail to appreciate many of the positive things in their day-to-day lives. And because they are also not especially aware of the present moment, they can spend huge amounts of time caught up in their unrealistic fantasies and then become overwhelmed when too many details are thrown at them all at once.

Typically quite self-contained and involved in their private projects, INFJs rarely initiate social contact. Unless the more social of the pair makes a real effort to draw them out into the world, they may miss out on opportunities and experiences they might enjoy and benefit from. They also have a tendency to look for hidden motives and meanings in every situation and often overanalyze problems or rehash issues even after they've been settled.

INFJs are very independent, focused, and persistent people who characteristically possess uncompromising integrity. They are driven by their inner vision, and if that vision is at odds with their partners', it can cause serious conflict. They can be quite determined and also single-minded and unyielding as they stand by their moral positions.

Fortunately, there is a natural counterbalance to this dynamic: both prefer a harmonious relationship. But when they are engaged in an emotional argument, it can be difficult for them to put their feelings aside and really hear each other. And when they reach an impasse, they may withdraw and stop communicating, which is the last thing

either partner wants. Interestingly, they have the tendency to be somewhat judgmental, so INFJs who dislike this quality in themselves may be particularly sensitive to it in their partners.

Advice for INFJs

- Appreciate and remind each other of this rare opportunity to be with someone who really knows how you feel.
- Spend quality time together doing things you both enjoy but also allow your partner to have his or her own space and interests.
- Recognize and appreciate your partner's great ideas without feeling the need to improve on them.
- Let your partner know your true feelings. In the heat of an argument, take a breath, step back, and try to listen objectively to what your partner is saying.
- Try not to be too judgmental or too quick to provide the "right" answer.
- Pay attention to what is happening with your partner and in your life at the moment.
- Encourage each other to be more flexible, engaged in the present, and open to spontaneous adventures.
- Take the initiative to organize social experiences you know your partner will like.

INFJ with ENFP

The Joys

Because INFJs and ENFPs share temperamental values and two of the four type preferences, they seek emotional intimacy, harmony, and mutual support. Naturally expressive and empathetic, they work hard to understand their partners' perspectives and feelings, and they are generally successful. The energy they put into understanding themselves and each other helps them create a meaningful connection. They may express their devotion not only in words but also in thoughtful actions and notes. They often share strongly held values, similar social and political views, a rich and vivid imagination, and an offbeat sense of humor.

Gentle, loving, and generally open with their feelings, INFJs and ENFPs are usually very nurturing and expressive parents. They often have similar philosophies about child rearing and may enjoy an egalitarian distribution of household labor. Since they are both intellectually curious, they share a love of new ideas and are usually willing to consider trying new ways of handling old tasks, especially boring or repetitious ones. They are staunch supporters of each other's goals and dreams.

INFJ and ENFP couples are often drawn together by their similarities, but they also are attracted by their differences. INFJs are attracted to ENFPs' warmth, playfulness, and innate social confidence. Most ENFPs have such a wide range of interests that they make fascinating and stimulating partners. ENFPs are drawn to INFJs because of their calm, depth, and maturity. Most INFJs exude an integrity, trustworthiness, and stability that ENFPs admire. Both ENFP and INFJ men are often much more emotionally available than men of other types — a quality many women find especially attractive.

INFJs and ENFPs have the opportunity to help each other grow and develop in important ways. Both are very interested in personal development, and their mutual support helps them make difficult adjustments. INFJs often help their ENFP partners focus their considerable yet scattered talents. By learning to be more selective and resist some of the temptations around them, ENFPs are more effective in making their many great ideas a reality. ENFPs also say that any experience is deeper and more meaningful when shared with their INFJ partners. For their part, ENFPs help INFJs relax some of their often ferocious need to be productive and stick to their plans and schedules. ENFPs urge their partners to get out in the world, try new things, and broaden their horizons. Many INFJs credit their partners with helping them enjoy life by responding to more sudden opportunities.

The Frustrations

The common frustrations INFJs and ENFPs experience stem primarily from their different attitudes about order and closure. INFJs really want things settled and decided and often make what their partners consider hasty decisions. Because ENFPs want to keep their options open for as long as possible, INFJs often have to deal with issues or plans left up in the air — or worse, from their perspective, changed without notice! Issues of control and commitment are typical, as INFJs want to stick with plans, and ENFPs want to feel free to take advantage of opportunities that present themselves. ENFPs' more casual attitude about order and neatness also causes frequent conflicts. INFJs often feel that they are doing more than their fair share of household chores because they notice what needs to be done and are compelled to do it. ENFPs don't mind clutter and are rarely driven to clean anything they don't really need to.

Typically, most INFJs end up doing more of the tasks that require attention to detail, such as paying bills and balancing the checkbook. But they don't usually enjoy it, and resentment can build. Although ENFPs feel controlled by INFJs tight fiscal policies, they are usually unwilling to take over the tasks. Without compromise, honest discussions, and plenty of expressions of appreciation, this can lead to ongoing tension. Both ENFPs and INFJs are very sensitive, and their fear of hurting their partners' feelings can sometimes prevent them from having frank discussions. The regular airing of little annoyances is imperative so they don't build and threaten the health of these relationships.

Finally, INFJs and ENFPs tend to experience common frustration about their different needs for socializing and time alone. ENFPs have a powerful need to be around other people, maintain all sorts of relationships, and spend a lot of time out in the world. INFJs need less stimulation from others and often find themselves exhausted from too much activity or interaction. ENFPs need to respect and make allowances for their partners' desire to rest or be alone, and INFJs should encourage their partners to seek the interaction they crave. Both need to be sure to protect the quality time they spend together.

How to Reach Your ENFP Partner

- Listen enthusiastically to your partner's ideas and brainstorms. Accept that much of the fun is in the imagining, not only in the doing.
- Try to stay open to some of your partner's more outlandish ideas.
- Be sure to give your partner plenty of freedom to explore possibilities and meet new people.
- Be willing to participate in some of the things your partner is interested in.
- Ask questions and listen attentively to your partner's responses.
- Follow some of your partner's inspirations and be willing to sometimes leave what you're doing to go on an adventure.
- Don't withdraw when you're upset. Be direct when asking for the time you need to think something through so your partner doesn't think you are rejecting him or her.
- Make allowances for your partner to keep his or her treasures in a special place.

How to Reach Your INFJ Partner

- Listen completely and with your full attention. Don't finish your partner's sentences or interrupt, even when you know where the conversation is going.
- Be patient with your partner's longer processing time. Respect his or her need to work and rework things.

- Help out around the house. Finish some of your partner's chores so he or she will be free to do something else.
- Respect your partner's need for peace and quiet, especially during and after busy social or work times.
- Try to accommodate your partner's schedules and keep a fairly neat and organized home.
- Be willing to occasionally forgo some interesting outside activities to stay home and enjoy quiet time with your partner.

INFJ with INFP

The Joys

With three out of four type preferences in common, INFJs and INFPs often recognize each other as kindred spirits. For both, finding another person who is so familiar is a rare thing, especially since both INFJs and INFPs are relatively uncommon types in American culture. INFJs and INFPs often enjoy a sense of total acceptance and deep, harmonious connection, and they describe their partners as soul mates. INFJs and INFPs typically have a similar take on things, find humor in offbeat and unusual places, and share rich and vivid inner lives. Deeply sensitive and empathetic people, they are ruled by strong personal values, chief among them personal and professional growth and the search for meaning in all things. They strive to maintain a happy family life and are especially attentive to each other's needs. INFJs and INFPs are typically respectful, supportive listeners and enjoy talking about global issues and finding the personal meaning in all their experiences. Since INFJ and INFP couples typically understand and respect each other's need for solitude, they often protect those quiet times so they are better able to enjoy their time together as a couple.

In addition to their many areas of commonality, INFJs and INFPs are often attracted to each other because of their differences. INFJs are often drawn to INFPs' calm and gentleness, especially INFP men, who are especially rare. INFPs are so loving and nurturing that INFJs are practically intoxicated by them. INFJs also admire INFPs' inner balance and unyielding devotion to the people and causes important to them. For their part, INFPs are often drawn to INFJs' verbal expressiveness and eloquence. Many INFPs admire their partners' ability to get things accomplished and their unshakable personal integrity.

Because of their differences, INFJs and INFPs have the opportunity to help each other grow and develop in important ways. INFJs are often able to help INFPs make tough decisions so they can commit to and finish some of their projects. INFPs derive enormous satisfaction from seeing their unique vision realized, and the encouragement they receive from their INFJ partners bolsters their confidence and assertiveness. For their part, INFPs are often able to help INFJs relax a bit so they aren't in such a hurry that they miss out on fun or interesting opportunities. Sometimes it is only their INFP partners who are able to coax INFJs out of their rigid schedules and persuade them to treat themselves to spontaneous pleasures.

The Frustrations

A potential challenge for INFJ and INFP couples is that they may come to take their relationships for granted because they are so easy and low maintenance. Neither partner typically needs or wants a lot of outside stimulation, so they can get in a rut if they don't seek out adventures and opportunities to grow as individuals and as a couple. Also, since both are easily overwhelmed and exhausted when they take on too many projects, they may have little energy left by the time they return home. This is especially true of INFJs, who are driven to be especially productive.

Interestingly, the strength of their personal values sometimes causes conflicts for some INFJ and INFP couples. INFJs have such strong opinions about appropriate behavior that they may seem quite judgmental to INFPs. For many INFJs, what is morally right is crystal clear, so their opinions can be absolute and their attitudes superior. Although most INFPs are pretty easygoing about the choices other people make and about deadlines and schedules, they can be surprisingly inflexible and unyielding when it comes to issues involving their own personal values. INFPs also tend to be very sensitive and easily hurt. When they feel attacked or criticized in any way, they withdraw and hold on to those feelings for a long time.

Typically, INFJs' and INFPs' different needs for order and closure result in most of their conflicts. INFJs can get especially frustrated with INFPs' lack of initiative and follow-through and with their reluctance to speak up for themselves in public. INFPs generally prefer to wait for inspiration before making a move and don't like to be pressured or forced to respond to artificial deadlines. For their part, INFJs have good intentions but can come across as intimidating and controlling. INFPs are frustrated by their partners' need to fit into social convention, even if it isn't really right for them. And INFJs' sense of appropriateness and strict adherence to schedules is not always shared by the more nonconformist INFPs.

Finally, INFJs and INFPs may experience conflict over the importance of a well-kept home. INFJs feel distracted and bothered by clutter, whereas INFPs tend not to notice it. INFPs are more interested in maintaining a comfortable home, not necessarily a neat one, especially if keeping things tidy means adding unnecessary stress. INFJs frequently do more than their fair share of the mundane practical chores and can come to resent the inequity.

How to Reach Your INFP Partner

- Listen respectfully and attentively. Watch that impatience and judgment don't creep into your voice, and resist the urge to moralize.
- Take time to pamper your partner. Spend a whole day devoted to demonstrating your affection and devotion.
- Be patient with the mess and clutter. Work with your partner to finish boring chores.
- Accept your partner's need to move through projects slowly and his or her propensity to change directions in midstream.
- Support your partner's deep feelings.
- Don't pressure your partner to participate in anything too formal or contrived.

How to Reach Your INFJ Partner

- Try to move outside yourself to give your partner the verbal feedback and response he or she needs and wants.
- When you need time to think about something, let your partner know so he or she won't take your silence personally.
- Try to be where you say you will be and work toward being on time. Call if you're running late.
- Watch out for piles and clutter; try to keep common areas of your home clean and neat.
- Ask for your partner's advice, then listen respectfully to his or her opinions.

ENFP with ENFP

The Joys

Anytime two people share all four type preferences, they have a very easy time understanding each other. This can be especially true of two ENFPs, who are naturally insightful and driven to understand others. ENFPs typically find these relationships relaxed and familiar, which is often one

source of their initial attraction. ENFP couples share many of the same values, an irreverent sense of humor, and a tendency to be nonconformists. Most ENFPs are loving, fun, easygoing, and flexible. They are usually eager to try new things and are willing to drop whatever they're doing to respond to an intriguing possibility or to help a friend. As parents, they tend to agree on most important issues and run a very relaxed and playful household.

Two ENFPs also share a strong desire for a deep and meaningful emotional connection and will devote a great deal of time, energy, and care to establishing it. Gentle, affectionate, and compassionate people, they are eager to help their partners grow and develop. Male ENFPs are often much more expressive than men of other types, and female ENFPs are usually delighted to find partners who are so comfortable and willing to share their emotions. Most ENFP couples are sensitive to each other's feelings and eager to please.

ENFP couples share a strong need for social stimulation, which they satisfy with a large and constantly growing circle of friends. They enjoy meeting new people and get a real kick out of putting people together who wouldn't ordinarily meet, whether for business purposes or just for fun. They love parties and spontaneous get-togethers and are often involved in numerous projects outside the home.

The strongest connection for most ENFP couples is their genuine and passionate love of ideas and possibilities. Curious and open, ENFPs love to brainstorm and fantasize about the future together. They are usually full of suggestions to help each other make positive changes in their lives and eager to consider any kind of solution to a problem or to overcome any obstacle.

One of the benefits for people who understand each other so well is that they can often help each other grow and develop in important ways. Most ENFP couples find that they encourage each other to develop the organizational skills that make some of the routines of their lives more bearable and efficient. Also, they help each other become more assertive about their needs and more willing to stand up for things that are important to them, regardless of how others may feel. Rather than sweep conflicts under the rug, as is their tendency, ENFPs can help each other deal with them more directly, honestly, and constructively. And, ironically, ENFPs may learn to leave some things alone and focus on enjoying their lives in the present moment.

The Frustrations

The source of most everyday frustrations for ENFP couples is that they have the same blind spots. Neither person is inclined to read the fine print, nor do they generally do a lot of planning. Given their rather impulsive natures, they may find themselves gleefully off on an impromptu vacation with no reservations, no gas in the car, and no money in their wallets. Since structure isn't appealing to most ENFPs, one or both partners are quick to abandon plans when something new, better, or more intriguing comes along to divert their attention. Since ENFPs don't relish confrontation, they may erroneously assume that they know what's bothering their partners and avoid frank discussions of unpleasant subjects in order to keep things sunny and harmonious.

Another area of frustration for ENFP couples is that because they are so outgoing and talkative, they frequently compete for airtime as the center of attention. And finally, since most ENFPs have minimal interest in mundane chores, they tend to put off things such as mowing the lawn or doing the laundry until they have to — or until the other person does them. Typically, the woman ends up doing more than her fair share of unappealing chores such as making car pool arrangements or balancing the checkbook. Not only does she feel unduly burdened, but if she does keep track of

details and expenditures, her partner may feel controlled and restricted. ENFP couples need to use their impressive ability to find creative solutions to problems and their eagerness to support and help each other in order to avoid needless conflict.

Advice for ENFPs

- Take turns being responsible for necessary chores and keeping your lives organized.
- Don't dance around conflict. Push yourselves to bring things up. Stay honest and don't be afraid to say how you really feel or what you wish or need to be different. Work slowly toward the center of the issue.
- Be sure to give each other plenty of freedom and opportunities to socialize with friends or to do things separately. Maintain your own interests and friendships.
- Surprise your partner. Share funny little stories or oddities to bring you closer when your relationship is strained.
- Discuss matters of the heart, issues of spirituality, and other areas of personal growth.
- Be tolerant of each other's lack of follow-through. Work together to get boring but necessary tasks finished so they don't fall on one person.
- If possible, hire someone (bookkeeper, accountant, housekeeper, gardener, travel agent, mechanic) to help with some of the details.

ENFP with INFP

The Joys

ENFPs and INFPs share three of the four type preferences. Their greatest joy is their emotional connection, which is generally far stronger than that which they experience with most other people. That ENFPs and INFPs share a rather unique and often nonconformist view of the world is also a source of great comfort, because both feel that the rest of the world rarely understands them. In these relationships, both partners are not only understood but totally accepted for who they are — often for the first time in their lives. They feel safe to express themselves fully because their partners eagerly encourage their personal growth. Because they believe that relationships are more important than almost anything else, they are usually willing to be emotionally vulnerable to each other. They typically delight in each other's imaginations and have great patience with and support for each other's need for change.

ENFPs' and INFPs' different energy levels are often the source of their initial attraction. ENFPs are attracted to INFPs' inner strength and sense of balance. ENFPs admire how fiercely devoted and committed their partners are to their beliefs. INFPs are often attracted to the high energy, creativity, enthusiasm, and social confidence of ENFPs. Because of their differences and their shared commitment to personal growth, they can help each other develop in important ways. ENFPs can draw INFPs out, exposing them to new people and experiences. INFPs help ENFPs slow down, focus their energy, and become even more aware of their feelings. Since neither ENFPs nor INFPs tend to be very logical, they can help each other pay more attention to details and realities.

The Frustrations

Couples with so many personality characteristics in common typically experience a tremendous sense of ease and familiarity. But they also tend to have the same blind spots. Since both ENFPs and INFPs desire harmony, neither are very good at dealing with conflict or confrontation. Small annoyances may go unattended as they carefully try to avoid hurting each other's feelings. By not being completely honest and forthcoming, however, they can unwittingly jeopardize the health of their relationships. Additionally, since neither partner is especially realistic or practical, no one takes the initiative to organize mundane chores such as getting the car serviced, balancing the checkbook, and maintaining the house. This can become a problem if one partner begins to blame the other for not pulling his or her weight. Often these tasks get dumped on the person who is better at doing them or the partner (often the woman) who is expected to do them. Taking time to create and stick with a household plan and budget and dividing up chores fairly can lessen the burden. Since neither partner is especially interested in planning, these couples may find themselves frequently late or rushing to meet deadlines and as a result feeling stressed-out. Finally, because both ENFPs and INFPs are naturally idealistic, they are susceptible to becoming overwhelmed by and depressed about financial or career dissatisfaction.

The most common source of frustration for many ENFP and INFP couples is their different social needs. Typically, ENFPs want much more social interaction than do their INFP partners. ENFPs also like and need to talk, while INFPs need to think through their responses first. Eager and enthusiastic ENFPs may inadvertently crowd or overwhelm INFPs with ideas, activities, and the need for an immediate response. Other conflicts occur because INFPs are extremely sensitive and take everything personally. They hold on to grievances long after the offenses, and they retreat from confrontation more often than their ENFP partners do. When INFPs are upset, they shut down and avoid conversation or intimacy. ENFPs and INFPs need to test the strength of their connection by discussing problems honestly, openly, and regularly.

How to Reach Your ENFP Partner

- Initiate discussions and intimacy. Don't always wait for your partner to do it.
- Share your feelings or explain that you are still mulling something over. Give your partner an emotional "weather report."

- Pay attention to your tendency to avoid or ignore issues and then explode later.
- Listen to your partner's many ideas without criticism. Let your partner ramble when he or she needs to think an idea through out loud.
- Express your gratitude for the extent to which you are free to be yourself. Thank your partner for challenging you and keeping you from stagnating.
- Try not to take things too seriously. Look for the humor in life.

How to Reach Your INFP Partner

- Wait before offering advice, comments, or opinions.
- Don't put your partner on the spot publicly.
- Sit in silence with your partner; enjoy the peace and quiet. Give your partner space even when you are doing things together.
- Slow down. Use a quiet and gentle tone of voice.
- Express your appreciation. Be reassuring during difficult times. (A silent hug is great.)
- Be patient as your partner slowly becomes aware of what is bothering him or her. Just because you may immediately see the connection between things, your partner may need more time to think through what he or she wants to say.
- Express your gratitude for being encouraged to be who you are.

INFP with INFP

The Joys

Whenever two people have all four type preferences in common, they experience a familiarity and ease together that other couples rarely share. INFP couples often derive profound satisfaction from the way they understand each other's strengths and weaknesses. Their communication is typically easy, intimate, and satisfying. Many feel,

often for the first time in their lives, free and safe to accept themselves completely, even the sides they normally hide from others. They often describe their connection as us against the world. Many INFP couples feel that they can glean their partners' feelings, reactions, and needs from a simple facial expression.

Another source of mutual satisfaction for many INFP couples is that they share similar values and feelings. Both have a rather offbeat sense of humor, similar political and social views, and generally the same reactions to events and people. For INFPs, internal harmony and balance are lifelong goals, so these couples enjoy sharing and talking about their values with each other. Most INFPs are happy to spend plenty of quiet time as a couple or family. They understand and respect each other's need for peace, quiet, and time to concentrate on rewarding projects. As a result, they may not have a strong need to socialize except with a small group of close friends. The sense of having found one's soul mate is often cited as the basis for their attraction. Each is drawn to the other's natural warmth, kindness, and compassion.

These shared qualities provide INFP couples with the opportunity to help each other grow and develop in important ways. They are each other's greatest teachers, as they learn to take everything a little less personally and become more realistic and better organized.

The Frustrations

Two people who are so much alike also tend to share the same shortcomings. Two INFPs often take everything so personally that even the slightest insensitivity is perceived as criticism. Although they rarely insult or hurt each other intentionally, they may offend one another easily, and tend to imagine the very worst reasons for it. Because they avoid conflict and disharmony, they may stay silent about resentments rather than bringing them up immediately and dealing with them directly. In fact, most INFP couples find that the greatest challenge for them is to be completely honest with each other, especially if doing so will hurt their partners' feelings. Conquering this challenge has great rewards, since their willingness to sweep problems under the rug can pose a serious threat to the long-term health of their relationships.

Another potential source of conflict for INFP couples is that although most INFPs are flexible in small matters, they can be very firm or even rigid about their personal values. So if they disagree about an important issue, such as parenting philosophies or important religious or social beliefs, this trait can result in serious conflicts.

INFP couples may have to force themselves to get out in the world and avoid becoming too insular. Invariably, one partner has a stronger need for human interaction, so the other may have to work at understanding his or her partner's wish to socialize with friends. Some INFP couples may need to work to achieve a healthy balance of togetherness and time apart.

Finally, since neither partner is especially well organized or likes to plan ahead, they may be a bit careless with money, facts, and the important steps in a project. Neither partner really wants to return phone calls, initiate household chores, or perform mundane or uninteresting tasks. Like many couples, they may need to figure out how to get the important tasks done in a fair and flexible way so one person (typically the woman) doesn't end up feeling overburdened.

Advice for INFPs

- Avoid nagging each other. Find a fair and reasonable division of labor and try to stick with it.
- Tell the whole truth, even if you're worried it will hurt your partner's feelings.
- Be willing to deal completely with crucial issues right away. Never allow things to fester.
- Give each other space and time alone.
- Recognize your partner's efforts and accomplishments.
- Don't assume that your partner knows how much you appreciate him or her. Express your appreciation regularly.
- Remember that when you are angry, it's often because you're hurt. Tell the truth about how you feel.
- Try writing letters if you find it difficult to express your complicated feelings orally.

Chapter 14

Where Do We Go from Here?
Final Thoughts, Recommendations, and Resources

At this point, you have discovered your type and your partner's type, read about your combination, and, we hope, found the insights useful and encouraging. Personality Type will do that for you: it will give you energy and optimism because it validates who you are. In the next section, you'll find an exercise that will personalize this experience even more and help you and your partner begin some important conversations.

But perhaps after reading about your combination, you feel a little discouraged. That's normal, too. Relationships are hard — really hard — and mercurial. Some days it's all you can do not to bolt for the door, while other days you feel like the luckiest person alive. If your relationship feels safe, supportive, fun, interesting, stimulating, and stable, you have much to be grateful for. But even great relationships sometimes feel off-kilter. Often a little perspective can help.

We learned so much by researching and writing this book, but by far the most important insights came from couples of all type combinations who have been together for a long time, in some cases as long as fifty years. And we thought, what better way to end this book than by sharing the observations and advice of the *real* experts — those couples who, metaphorically, have been down in the trenches and up on the mountaintops and are still here to talk about it.

So, with apologies if they sound like platitudes, here are some of the wise observations these generous couples have shared in the hope that we can

all learn from their mistakes and gain some of their invaluable perspective.

- No relationship is perfect, nor is there only one perfect person out there somewhere for you (regardless of what the fairy tales say!). If you're holding out for someone with whom you'll have no conflicts, be prepared to wait a long, long time.

- There's a lot to be said about commitment and your willingness to work hard on your relationship every day. Relationships are damaged and strengthened in small ways, when we turn either toward our partners or away from them. Working hard means making a conscious decision to try to please your partner — to become aware of the things he or she appreciates most and to try to provide them as often as possible. It also means becoming aware of things that irritate your partner and trying not to do them quite so often. As is true of so much in life, it turns out that the little things really do mean a lot. And quite naturally, different types will feel differently about which little things mean the most. For Extraverts, it might mean letting a little annoyance go without saying anything about it, especially when you're dying to! For Introverts, it might mean speaking up when you're upset instead of giving your partner the silent treatment. For the task-minded Judger, it might mean quietly unloading the dishwasher when it's not your turn — or for a Perceiver, being sure to unload it before your partner gets home when it *is* your turn. And for Thinkers, maybe you can remember to ask about your spouse's co-worker who is sick, because you know your partner is really concerned. While the little things are different in every relationship (we're sure your partner will be happy to provide you with a list of his or hers!), over time, paying attention to those things creates the atmosphere of generosity and mutual support that couples of all types say is so important to them.

• Every relationship is unique, just as every individual is unique. The perfect relationship for you may be *very* different from that for your neighbor or even your best friend. But we all fall into the trap of expectations. For example, Traditionalists (SJs) have a strong tendency to pattern their relationships after their parents' — regardless of how good or bad those relationships were. Idealists (NFs) are particularly susceptible to media images of the ideal wife, husband, and relationship. Ignore what others tell you your relationship should be like and create the one *you* want and need.

• A long marriage (or relationship) is really like a lot of little marriages. Every relationship has its times of closeness and distance — of ebb and flow. Sometimes the key is to just wait faithfully for the tide to turn. As one couple explained, "Every couple has something they're good at together. Maybe it's entertaining, or parenting, or traveling, or just working on the house together. Find that something. And then when times are difficult, do it. Do it while you pass the time and one of you figures out what else to do or until things shift on their own. They often do, you know."

• Acceptance isn't settling. Accepting another person's differences and limitations is not the same

thing as selling out. This may be harder for some types to do than others. For example, Conceptualizers (NTs) may find it difficult not to continually notice and point out flaws, while Idealists (NFs) may struggle to keep their expectations about themselves and their partners realistic. Try to keep in mind that the qualities or habits you sometimes find so annoying may be the very same ones that attracted you to your partner in the first place!

• The bottom line — and we heard this from practically every couple we spoke with — is that you can never *really* change anyone else. All you will do by trying is to make that person feel misunderstood and unappreciated. But what you *can* do — and Personality Type is a wonderful tool for helping you do this — is learn to understand, accept, and ultimately appreciate your partner for exactly who he or she is and the many gifts he or she brings to the relationship.

So, in a way, we end this book where we began — talking about how important understanding and communication are to a satisfying relationship. We hope that learning about Personality Type has given you some valuable new insights into yourself, your partner, and how the two of you are as a couple. Perhaps these insights will enable you to communicate better and help you create the relationship you've always wanted. We wish you the best of luck on your journey!

Just Your Type: An Exercise for Couples

Here's a great exercise to do with your partner. Below are some questions that will really get at the heart of your relationship. We asked the hundreds of couples we interviewed for this book these questions, and most of them told us that the experience of thinking about and discussing their answers with their partners was unusually revealing and extremely helpful.

There are several ways to approach this exercise, and different types will inevitably be more comfortable with different ways. Talk about it with your partner and choose the way that works best for you. One suggestion is for both of you to find some quiet time and a place where you won't be interrupted and take turns answering the questions. Or you may prefer to make two copies of the questions and go off on your own to think about them. It may be helpful to write your answers down and let your partner read them before you have your discussion. Whichever way you choose to do the exercise, it's a good chance to use what you've learned about Personality Type and communication.

A final note: although the prospect of discussing some of these questions may initially feel a little scary, the overwhelming number of couples who did the exercise found that the rewards far outweighed any imagined risks, and they emerged with a new appreciation for each other. Always keep in mind your purpose in doing this exercise: to share with each other what you need and want from the relationship and each other. So try to be as open, nondefensive, and uncritical of your partner's answers as possible.

1. What initially attracted you to your partner?

2. What are some words that accurately describe your relationship?

3. What would you say is the best thing about your relationship?

4. What would you say is the biggest challenge in your relationship?

5. What are the most common areas of conflict?

6. How do you two typically resolve most conflicts? How do you *wish* you resolved conflicts?

7. What are three things you do that bring the two of you closer?

8. What are three things you do that push the two of you farther apart?

9. What are three things your partner does to bring the two of you closer?

10. What are three things your partner does that push you farther apart?

11. If you could change anything about your relationship, what would it be?

12. What does your partner do that demonstrates that he or she really appreciates you?

13. What do you do to demonstrate that you really appreciate your partner?

Tips for Finding a Marriage Counselor

Perhaps you feel that you and your partner would benefit from talking to a marriage counselor but don't know how to go about finding a good one. There are many options available. Firsthand referrals from friends, family members, co-workers, clergy, your primary care physician, or other people whose judgment you trust are often good places to start. But knowing whether a particular therapist is qualified to help you with your specific problem or whether he or she will be right for you may take a little work. Here are a few things that can help you in your search.

Not all therapists specialize in working with couples, and not all couples therapists have the same philosophy or training. One excellent source for finding someone with specialized training is the **American Association for Marriage and Family Therapy (AAMFT)**, a professional association dedicated to marriage and family issues with more than 23,000 members throughout the world.

AAMFT Clinical Members must meet stringent training and education requirements, which include a minimum of a master's degree in marriage and family therapy or a related field and two years of supervised clinical work after completing their graduate degrees. Their training often includes live supervision by experienced marriage and family therapists (MFTs), and all AAMFT Clinical

Members must agree to abide by the association's code of ethics. To locate a therapist in your geographic area, either call the association or check out its Web site.

American Association for Marriage and Family
   Therapy (**AAMFT**)
1133 Fifteenth Street NW, Suite 300
Washington, DC 20005-2710
Phone: (202) 452-0109
Fax: (202) 223-2329
www.aamft.org

Other practitioners believe that effective couples therapists should be psychologists who have broad-based training and experience dealing with a wide range of issues. The **National Register of Health Service Providers in Psychology** is the largest credentialing organization for psychologists. It evaluates the education, training, and experience of licensed psychologists and lists on its Web site members in different geographic areas of the country.

National Register of Health Service Providers
   in Psychology
1120 G Street NW, Suite 330
Washington, DC 20005
Phone: (202) 783-7663
www.nationalregister.com

In your search for a therapist, you will discover that many social workers specialize in working with couples. The **National Association of Social Workers (NASW)** is the largest organization of professional social workers in the world and represents 155,000 social workers in 55 chapters throughout the United States and abroad. NASW members constitute about 50 percent of the nation's social workers, and about half of the members are clinical social workers, many of them psychotherapists in private practice. Therapists who are social workers focus on the environmental forces that create or contribute to people's problems.

The NASW maintains the Register of Clinical Social Workers, a list of professionals who have met national standards for education, credentials, and experience established by the NASW. Clinical social workers at two levels of experience and expertise are listed: Qualified Clinical Social Workers and NASW Diplomates in Clinical Social Work. You can find a member nearest you by visiting the association's Web site.

National Association of Social Workers
   (**NASW**)
750 First Street NE, Suite 700
Washington, DC 20002-4241
Phone: (202) 408-8600
Fax: (202) 336-8311
TTD: (202) 408-8396
www.naswdc.org

Another resource for locating a therapist who may also have extensive experience with Personality Type is the **Association for Psychological Type (APT)**. To receive a referral, call the APT office or visit its Web site.

Association for Psychological Type (**APT**)
9140 Ward Parkway
Kansas City, MO 64114-3313
Phone: (816) 444-3500
www.aptcentral.org

As you can see, there are many ways to find a therapist. Regardless of the method you use to locate one, or that person's particular orientation or training, it is always advisable to interview him or her over the phone to see if he or she will be a good match for you. Remember that you may find the best person in the world for you on your first try, or you may need to try more than one person. It may help you to think of a therapist as you would any other consultant — a person with a certain expertise whom you hire to help you with a problem. Always remember that you are the consumer and you have the final decision about whom you feel comfortable working with.

Other Alternatives

Although many couples benefit greatly from working with a counselor, others may find educational or support groups helpful. A wide variety of courses are offered in most metropolitan areas through community organizations such as the YMCA and through churches and synagogues.

Probably the best-known group is **Worldwide Marriage Encounter,** which has offered support to more than two million people over the past thirty years. Operating in eighty-eight countries and representing Catholic and eleven Protestant faiths, the group focuses on weekend retreats.

The Marriage Encounter Weekend experience is designed for married couples who have a good marriage and want to make it even better. Spouses are given time to be alone together without everyday distractions and learn a technique of communication that helps build mutual intimacy and understanding.

The group also offers a weekend program designed to help and renew troubled marriages called the Retrouvaille Weekend. *Retrouvaille* means "rediscovery," and the program offers couples the chance to rediscover themselves, their spouses, and their loving relationships. The emphasis in this experience is on learning new and effective communication techniques. Contact the group to find out more about programs near you.

Worldwide Marriage Encounter
2210 East Highland Avenue, Suite 106
San Bernardino, CA 92404-4666
Phone: (800) 795-LOVE (5683) or
   (909) 863-9963
Fax: (909) 863-9986
E-mail: office@wwwme.org

A marriage encounter organization for non-Christians is **Jewish Marriage Encounter (JME).** Though spiritual in nature, JME is not a religious program. Its weekends are conducted within the context of Jewish values, but non-Jewish and religiously mixed couples have participated with great success. JME was founded in 1972 and is for couples whose marriages are essentially good but who need to improve and deepen their communication. It is open to couples, regardless of age, who have been married for two or more years. JME weekends are held in various locations in the greater Los Angeles area.

Jewish Marriage Encounter
P.O. Box 4494
West Hills, CA 91308-4494
Phone: (818) 225-0099

Type-Related Organizations and Resources

Now that you've found out how useful Personality Type can be in your relationship, you may be interested in learning how to apply its insights to other parts of your life. You can use Type to help you find a satisfying career or job, in parenting (especially if your children are very different from each other or from you and your spouse), and to improve your communication effectiveness at home and at work.

We've assembled a short list of books, journals, training opportunities, and organizations to assist you in these endeavors. You will find an expanded list of resources on our Web site, www.personalitytype.com.

Organizations

Communication Consultants, LLC
20 Beverly Road
West Hartford, CT 06119

Phone: (800) YOUR-TYPE
Fax: (860) 232-1321
www.personalitytype.com

Communication Consultants, LLC, with principals Paul Tieger and Barbara Barron-Tieger, provides specialized training for career professionals from introductory to advanced programs. We also offer sales and management training based on *The Art of SpeedReading People,* and parent effectiveness workshops based on *Nurture by Nature.* Programs can be arranged for organizations and companies, by contacting us through our Web site.

Association for Psychological Type (APT)
9140 Ward Parkway
Kansas City, MO 64114-3313
Phone: (816) 444-3500
www.aptcentral.org

APT is an international organization open to all people interested in Type. It conducts training workshops, publishes the *Bulletin of Psychological Type* and the *Journal of Psychological Type,* and conducts training programs for the Myers-Briggs Type Indicator. APT sponsors international and regional conferences, as well as local groups throughout the country and around the world that meet to share information about Type.

Center for the Applications of Psychological
 Type (CAPT)
2815 Northwest Thirteenth Street, Suite 401
Gainesville, FL 32609
Phone: (800) 777-CAPT
www.capt.org

CAPT provides training programs in Type for professionals and the public, offers consulting services for training and research, publishes Type-related books and materials, compiles research to advance the understanding of Type, does computer scoring of the Myers-Briggs Type Indicator, and maintains the Isabel Briggs Myers Memorial Library.

Recommendations for Further Reading

After reading this book, you may want to read other books about couples and relationships. To assist you, we've asked many experienced marriage and family therapists which resources their clients find most helpful. Their suggestions are listed below. For a more comprehensive list, please visit our Web site: www.personalitytype.com.

Books about Couples

Campbell, Susan. *The Couples Journey.* San Luis Obispo, Calif.: Impact Publishers, 1987 (out of print).

Henrix, Harvel. *Getting the Love You Want: A Guide for Couples.* New York: Harper Perennial Library, 1992.

Kroeger, Otto, and Janet Thuesen. *16 Ways to Love Your Lover.* New York: Delacorte Press, 1994.

Lerner, Harriet. *The Dance of Anger: A Woman's Guide to Changing the Patterns of Intimacy.* New York: HarperCollins, 1989.

Pines, Ayala Malach. *Couple Burnout: Causes and Cures.* New York: Routledge, 1996.

Rubin, Lillian B. *Intimate Strangers: Men and Women Together.* New York: HarperCollins, 1990.

Scarf, Maggie. *Intimate Partners.* New York: Ballantine Books, 1996.

Soloman, Marion. *Narcissism and Intimacy: Love and Marriage in an Age of Confusion.* New York: W. W. Norton, 1992.

Wegsheider-Cruse, Shawn. *Coupleship: How to Build a Relationship.* Deerfield Beach, Fla.: Health Communications, 1988.

Books about Personality Type

General Introduction to Personality Type

Brownsword, Alan. *It Takes All Types.* Herndon, Va.: Baytree Publication Company, 1987.

Duniho, Terence. *Patterns of Preference.* Providence, R.I.: Career Designs, 1993.

Giovannoni, Louise C., Linda V. Berens, and Sue A. Cooper. *Introduction to Temperament.* Huntington Beach, Calif.: Cooper, Berens, 1986.

Hirsh, Sandra, and Jean Kummerow. *Lifetypes.* New York: Warner Books, 1989.

Keirsey, David. *Please Understand Me II: Temperament Character Intelligence.* Del Mar, Calif.: Prometheus Nemesis, 1998.

Kroeger, Otto, and Janet A. Thuesen. *Type Talk.* New York: Delacorte Press, 1988.

———. *Type Talk at Work: How the 16 Types Determine Your Success on the Job.* New York: Delacorte Press, 1992.

Myers, Isabel Briggs. *Introduction to Type: A Description of the Theory and Application of the Myers-Briggs Type Indicator.* Palo Alto, Calif.: Consulting Psychologists Press, 1987.

Myers, Isabel Briggs, and Mary H. McCaulley. *Manual: A Guide to the Development and Use of the Myers-Briggs Type Indicator.* Palo Alto, Calif.: Consulting Psychologists Press, 1985.

Myers, Isabel B., with revisions by K. Myers and L. Kirby. *Introduction to Type.* Palo Alto, Calif.: Consulting Psychologists Press, 1993.

Myers, Isabel Briggs, with Peter Myers. *Gifts Differing.* Palo Alto, Calif.: Consulting Psychologists Press, 1980.

Myers, Katharine D., and Linda K. Kirby. *Introduction to Type Dynamics and Development.* Palo Alto, Calif.: Consulting Psychologists Press, 1994.

Quenk, Naomi L. *Beside Ourselves: Our Hidden Personality in Everyday Life.* Palo Alto, Calif.: Consulting Psychologists Press, 1993.

Saunders, Frances. *Katharine and Isabel: Mother's Light, Daughter's Journey.* Palo Alto, Calif.: Consulting Psychologists Press, 1983.

———. *Katharine and Isabel.* Palo Alto, Calif.: Consulting Psychologists Press, 1991.

Tieger, Paul D., and Barbara Barron-Tieger. *Do What You Are: Discover the Perfect Career for You Through the Secrets of Personality Type,* rev. ed. Boston: Little, Brown, 1995.

The Type Reporter. Published eight times a year. Contains articles and information on various topics of interest concerning psychological type. Susan Scanlon, editor, 524 North Paxton Street, Alexandria, VA 22304.

Yabroff, William. *The Inner Image: A Resource for Type Development.* Palo Alto, Calif.: Consulting Psychologists Press, 1990.

Personality Type and Counseling/Relationships

Duniho, Terence. *Personalities at Risk: Addiction, Codependency and Psychological Type.* Gladwyne, Pa.: Type & Temperament, 1992.

———. *Understanding Relationships.* Providence, R.I.: Life Patterns Institute, 1988.

Faucett, Robert, and Carol Ann Faucett. *Intimacy and Mid-Life: Understanding Your Journey.* New York: Crossroads Publishing, 1990.

Grant, Richard D. *Symbols of Recovery: The 12 Steps at Work in the Unconscious.* Gladwyne, Pa.: Type & Temperament, 1990.

Hartzler, Margaret. *Using Type with Couples.* Gaithersburg, Md.: Type Resources, 1988.

Isachsen, Olaf, and Linda V. Berens. *Working Together: A Personality-Centered Approach,* 3rd ed. San Juan Capistrano, Calif.: Institute for Management Development, 1995.

Milner, Nan Y. B., and Eleanor S. Corlett. *Navigating Mid-life: Using Typology as a Guide.* Palo Alto, Calif.: Consulting Psychologists Press, 1993.

Provost, Judith A. *A Casebook: Applications of the Myers-Briggs Type Indicator in Counseling.* Gainesville, Fla.: Center for Applications of Psychological Type, 1984.

Stein, Murray, and John Hollwitz, eds. *Psyche at Work: Workplace Applications of Jungian Analytical Psychology.* Wilmette, Ill.: Chiron Publications, 1992.

Ward, Ruth McRoberts. *Blending Temperaments: Improving Relationships — Yours and Others.* Grand Rapids, Mich.: Baker Book House, 1988.

Appendix: About the Research for *Just Your Type*

♥

There has been much speculation among people interested in Personality Type about the connection between Type and relationship satisfaction. To learn more definitively about the connection, we conducted the most comprehensive research on the subject to date. We were most interested in discovering the most common sources of satisfaction as well as the most frequent causes of conflicts for couples of each type combination.

There were four components to the research. The first involved interviews with several therapists who specialize in working with couples to identify the key issues that cause problems in their clients' relationships. The second was an extensive survey questionnaire comprising primarily multiple-choice answers, filled out by over 2,500 individuals, of which 1,040 were included in the analysis. One main objective of the study was to determine the most satisfying aspects of a relationship and the most common sources of conflict for individual members of every type combination. The third component consisted of an open-ended, thirteen-item questionnaire designed to collect more anecdotal data. Among the topics covered were what each partner does to bring the other closer, push him or her farther away, and show appreciation. Participants were also asked about the secrets of a satisfying relationship and what advice they would give to another couple of the same type combination to improve their relationship. Seven hundred fifty participants filled out this extended questionnaire. The fourth component consisted of in-depth, primarily telephone, interviews with hundreds of couples. Participants were sent a list of questions and given the opportunity to discuss the answers with their partners prior to the interview. Questions included how the couple met, what initially attracted them to each other, what they like most and least about their relationship, what the most common sources of conflicts are and how they typically try to resolve them, how the relationship has changed over time, and what advice they would give to couples of the same type combination.

Important demographic data collected included each participant's type, age, gender, marital status, ethnic background, religious preference, number of times married, number of past long-term relationships, birth order, educational background, number of children, political philosophy, occupation, and income range.

To ensure that our research would be most useful to the largest number of people, a vigorous effort was made to recruit participants who would reflect a cross section of the American population. Recruitment methods included placing advertisements in the *Bulletin of Psychological Type,* a mailing campaign to chapter leaders of the Association for Psychological Type, making the survey available on our Web site (www.personalitytype.com), and engaging a large network of colleagues and associates, representing several varied businesses and educational organizations, to promote the survey to their constituents.

Respondents represented a wide range of ages, education levels, incomes, ethnic backgrounds, time in the relationship, and political attitudes. Perhaps most important, they represented all four temperaments and all sixteen types. Respondents came from all fifty states and dozens of foreign countries. The survey was available only to participants who had access to the Internet. Although initially concerned that this might create a sampling problem, we were surprised at how few requests we had from people wanting to take the survey in paper form.

We used a variety of methods to ensure that each respondent knew his or her personality type, including querying respondents on how they became familiar with Personality Type, how sure they were that they had correctly identified their types, and offering them the opportunity to take an on-line quiz and read profiles to verify their types.

Following is a summary of some of the highlights of the research and our comments on what they mean and how they can help people have more satisfying relationships.

Two Key Findings

Our findings demonstrate a strong link between Personality Type and relationship satisfaction. Respondents said that effective communication is an extremely important — perhaps the single most important — component of a satisfying relationship.

- Ninety-two percent of respondents considered good communication the "most important" aspect of a satisfying relationship.
- The more satisfied they were with the quality of their communication, the more satisfied they were with their relationships.

Here's another finding that confirmed our belief that similarity between partners is directly related to the level of satisfaction couples feel in their relationship:

- The more type preferences a couple had in common, the higher they rated their satisfaction with the quality of their communication.

But we're quick to point out that this does not mean that people with fewer or no preferences in common can't still have great relationships. In reality, most couples do not share all four preferences. As previous studies have established and our research confirms,

- about 10% of couples share all four preferences in common
- about 20% share three preferences in common
- about 35% have only two of the same preferences (the most common occurence)
- about 25% have one preference in common
- 10% have no preferences in common

So while sharing preferences does not *guarantee* couples a satisfying relationship, the survey and our extensive interviewing did confirm that people with fewer preferences in common may have to work much harder at their relationships.

Other Important Findings

- The more similar people were to their partners, the more satisfied they were with their relationships. Fifty-two percent of those who were satisfied described themselves as "similar" to their partners, compared with the 22 percent who were satisfied but who said they were different from their partners.

This finding suggests that although opposites may attract, the more similar people are, the easier time they have understanding and being able to communicate with each other.

- Those people most satisfied with their careers were also more satisfied in their relationships.

This "spillover" effect is not surprising, but it can help all couples — especially those who are experiencing difficulty — understand how much strain job dissatisfaction can place on a relationship.

Dispelling the Gender Myth

In an effort to confirm or refute several popularly held beliefs about differences between men and women, we analyzed the data to see what, if any, effect gender has on specific behaviors and attitudes. In the majority of items analyzed, gender appears to have little influence. And in several instances, results suggest that people's behavior is often influenced more by one's personality type than by one's gender. Following are two examples.

Participants ranked several qualities in order of importance in a satisfying relationship. Slightly more women than men considered intimacy most important. But far greater differences occurred between Thinkers and Feelers. About 60 percent of Thinkers (both men and women) considered intimacy most important, compared with 75 percent of Feelers (both men and women). And slightly more male Thinkers than female Thinkers considered it most important.

We also asked them to rate the importance of intellectual stimulation. Contrary to what one might expect, by a wide margin (58% vs. 45%) more women than men considered it most important. And predictably, more Thinkers than Feelers considered intellectual stimulation most important. But by a very significant margin (63% vs. 41%), more women Thinkers than male Feelers considered it most important. These results — typical of many of our findings — suggest that Type preferences, especially Thinking and Feeling, have more influence on behavior and attitudes than gender.

Aspects of a Satisfying Relationship

The survey looked at twenty-two aspects of satisfying relationships to determine which were most important to people of different types. The items were intimacy, sexual compatibility, communication, shared values, shared interests, security, trust, mutual respect, companionship, shared religious beliefs, financial security, similar parenting styles, being listened to, intellectual stimulation, having fun together, accepting each other's differences, mutual commitment, fidelity, mutual support, humor, spending time together, and spiritual connection. Participants were asked to rank each of these aspects according to how important it was to them (1 = most important, 2 = important, and 3 = less important).

Following are those aspects that the clear majority people indicated were *most important*.

1.	Trust	95%
2.	Communication	92%
3.	Mutual respect	92%
4.	Mutual commitment	86%
5.	Fidelity	82%

This list reminds us that some things are important to people of all types. Even partners who are very different from each other can have a deep connection when they share these core values.

Here are the aspects that significantly fewer people indicated were *most important*.

1.	Shared religious beliefs	18%
2.	Financial security	27%
3.	Shared interests	28%
4.	Similar parenting styles	33%
5.	Spiritual connection	34%

The list of the aspects rated less important helps debunk some of the myths about the causes of potential problems in relationships. For example, couples (especially young people) are often warned about the dangers of marrying outside their faiths. But in our survey, only 18 percent felt that shared religious beliefs were most important to them.

Clearly, some types value certain characteristics more than others. Looking at which aspects are considered most and least important to different types can help us predict where problems might arise for different pairings. For example, 81 percent of INFPs rated intimacy as most important, but only 52 percent of ISTPs rated it that high. It is reasonable to assume that ISTP and INFP couples might experience conflict, or at least tension, around issues of intimacy. This information can help couples identify potentially problematic issues, recognize that it's normal for different partners to have different values, and develop an appreciation for what is most important to their partners.

Here are some other examples of disparate ratings for aspects of a satisfying relationship. The percentages reflect how many people said these aspects are most important.

Sexual compatibility	ESTP 64%, ISFP 32%
Shared values	ISTJ 77%, ESTP 46%
Security	ISTJ 61%, INTP 31%
Companionship	ESFJ 74%, INTJ 56%
Similar parenting styles	ENFJ 45%, ENTP 32%
Intellectual stimulation	ENTP 67%, ISFJ 28%
Having fun together	ESTP 91%, ISTJ 66%
Mutual support	ISFJ 86%, ISTP 52%
Spending time together	ENFJ 65%, ESTP 18%
Spiritual connection	ENFP 45%, ISTJ 27%
Shared interests	ENTJ 37%, INFP 18%
Being listened to	ENFJ 89%, ISTP 52%
Accepting each other's differences	INFJ 69%, ISFP 57%
Shared religious beliefs	ENTJ 29%, ESFP 13%
Fidelity	ESTJ 88%, INTJ 73%
Humor	ENFP 71%, ISFJ 48%

The Judging/Perceiving Conundrum

Because many people believe that differences in Judging and Perceiving are the source of the most conflicts in relationships, we examined how similarities or differences on this dimension affect relationship satisfaction. We found almost identical levels of satisfaction for people who were alike and different on the Judging/Perceiving scale.

But when we examined combinations of Thinking/Feeling (T/F) with Judging/Perceiving, we noted some dramatic differences. Following are the combinations reporting the *most satisfaction*.

TJ with TJ	74%
FJ with FJ	72%
TJ with TP	71%
FP with FP	70%

Three out of these four combinations were the same on both the T/F and J/P scales. These combinations were probably most satisfied because all three pairs (TJ with TJ, FJ with FJ, and FP with FP) are similar in important ways. For example, both TJ partners tend to be logical and rather thick-skinned and live fairly structured lives. Both FJ partners tend to be highly sensitive to each other and like their homes neat, so there are not likely to be many complaints about sloppiness — a common marital complaint. And both FP partners tend to be gentle and adaptable, and neither needs to control the other.

But it is equally interesting to learn which combinations of T/F with J/P were the *least satisfied*:

FJ with TJ	58%
TP with FJ	55%
TJ with FJ	49%
TP with TP	46%

FJ with TJ pairs were probably less satisfied because FJs tend to be extremely sensitive and may feel that their honest but sometimes blunt TJ partners are insensitive or dismiss their feelings as not being important. TPs with FJs may find their partners to be too sensitive, judgmental, and controlling. And TJs with FJ partners may have similar issues, plus the additional factor that TJs are logical and impersonal when dealing with others, while FJs express their feeling and emotions readily with others and try hard to please them. It is more challenging to explain why TPs with TP partners were dissatisfied. One possible, though certainly not proven, explanation is that TPs are both critical by nature and are constantly on the lookout for exciting new possibilities, which may lead them to be less appreciative or satisfied with their current partners.

A Look at Temperament Groups

Since temperament reflects core values, we examined how temperamental similarities and differences might influence relationship satisfaction. Respondents of similar and different temperament combinations were asked to rate, on a scale from 1 to 5, their satisfaction with their relationship (1 = very dissatisfied to 5 = very satisfied). Here are the results, ranked from most to least satisfied, with the reporting partner's temperament first.

SJ with SJ	79%	SP with SP	59%
NF with NF	73%	NT with NT	59%
SP with NT	73%	SJ with NF	58%
SJ with SP	71%	NT with SP	54%
NT with NF	65%	SP with NF	54%
NF with NT	64%	NT with SJ	52%
SP with SJ	63%	NF with SP	51%
SJ with NT	62%	NF with SJ	46%

We suggest that the reason SJs with SJ partners reported being most satisfied has to do with their traditional natures and the importance they place on commitment. The second-highest ranking was NFs with NF partners. We know that NFs invest a lot of time and energy in trying to improve their relationships and that they also rate communication high among their cherished values. Significantly fewer (59%) NTs with NTs said they were satisfied. Perhaps it is because both partners tend to be naturally critical and have exceptionally high standards. In other words, they may just be harder to please.

Adding Thinking and Feeling to the Mix

Only 59 percent of SPs with SPs also reported being satisfied. One explanation might be that SPs are so busy actually living their lives that they don't spend much time thinking or worrying about the quality of their relationships. But we suspected that one's preference for Thinking or Feeling might alter these results. So we looked deeper at STPs with STPs and discovered that only 33 percent were satisfied, while 80 percent of SFPs with SFPs were satisfied. As our research and experience suggest, STPs are generally among the least concerned about the quality of their relationships and SFPs are generally among the most concerned. Again, Feelers tend to be more concerned about pleasing their partners and strive to communicate well. When paired with another SFP, they find those concerns and efforts reciprocated and, therefore, feel more satisfaction.

It is interesting to note that some temperament combinations reported similar levels of satisfaction regardless of which partner reported. For example, 51 percent of NFs with SPs were satisfied, and 54 percent of SPs with NFs were satisfied. Other combinations, however, were quite different. Seventy-three percent of SPs with NTs were satisfied, but only 54 percent of NTs with SPs were satisfied with their partners.

Because SJs with SJ partners were the most satisfied (79%) and NFs with SJ partners the least satisfied (46%), we looked at how satisfaction would be affected if we also factored in a person's preferences for Thinking/Feeling and Judging/Perceiving. Here are the results, ranked from most to least satisfied for the SJ and NF combinations:

SFJ with NFP	86%	NFP with SFJ	53%
SFJ with NFJ	67%	NFJ with STJ	49%
STJ with NFJ	58%	STJ with NFP	45%
NFJ with SFJ	57%	NFP with STJ	42%

The most satisfied combinations were SFJs with NFPs (86%) and SFJs with NFJs (67%). Again, a likely explanation may be that both types are committed to pleasing their partners and making their relationships work. The least satisfied were NFPs with STJs (42%) and STJs with NFPs (45%). This is particularly interesting, since according to our research, a high percentage of NFPs and STJs form relationships. Although it's impossible to know for sure, this finding might be further evidence that opposites really do attract — but they don't always have the most satisfying relationships. A likely explanation for their mutual dissatisfaction: NFPs often feel controlled, criticized, and stifled by their much more conservative STJ partners, and STJs are often uncomfortable with their partners' unpredictability, emotionality, and lack of follow-through.

We found that the more preferences factored in the analysis, the more insightful and useful the findings. For example, 44 percent of all SPs considered fidelity a most important aspect of a satisfying relationship, but almost twice as many SFPs (63%) than STPs (33%) considered it most important.

Quite possibly this is because the supersensitive SFPs are more tuned in to the pain that is caused and the damage done when one or both partners are unfaithful. These results underscore the importance of making the distinction between Thinkers and Feelers when interpreting findings that focus on temperament.

Common Sources of Conflict

Since conflict is inherent in all relationships, people's ability to understand, anticipate, and deal with conflict constructively can have a significant influence on their satisfaction with their relationships. According to our survey, people experienced conflict around the following issues *most frequently*:

1. Communication
2. Power and control
3. Intimacy
4. Money
5. Quality time together

Once again, these results underscore the importance of communication in relationships. A more complex statistical analysis explained about 25 percent of the variation in levels of satisfaction. And conflict in the areas of communication, intimacy, and power and control accounted for nearly one-third (!) of all couples' satisfaction with their relationships.

The issues around which people experienced conflict the *least frequently* were as follows:

1. Drug or alcohol use/abuse
2. Blended family relationships
3. Religious or cultural differences
4. Political differences
5. Age differences

These findings may serve to dispel some popularly held misconceptions. People contemplating or involved in relationships in which one partner is considerably older than the other may be relieved to learn that only 2 percent of people experienced conflict because of age differences. Likewise, only 3 percent had conflict because of religious or cultural differences. Also worthy of note — and contrary to popular belief — gender differences appeared to play no part in explaining sources of conflict.

The Judging/Perceiving Connection in Conflict

Although Judging/Perceiving differences alone did not appear to affect couples' satisfaction with their relationships, they do seem to be related to several potential sources of conflict. For example, when the issue of power and control was examined from the J/P perspective, the percentages for those reporting that they frequently experienced conflict around this issue were quite different.

Perceivers with Judging partners	46%
Judgers with Perceiving partners	36%
Judgers with Judging partners	29%
Perceivers with Perceiving partners	22%

While 22 percent of Perceivers with Perceiving partners frequently experienced conflict around the issue of power and control, more than twice as many Perceivers with Judging partners (46%) experienced it frequently. The reason almost half the Perceivers with Judging partners frequently experienced conflict around this issue is no doubt because Perceivers prefer to live a spontaneous life, while Judgers like to make and keep plans.

Another potential source of conflict, household chores, yielded similar results. Here are the percentages of people who frequently experienced conflict around this issue.

Perceivers with Judging partners	33%
Judgers with Judging partners	25%
Judgers with Perceiving partners	24%
Perceivers with Perceiving partners	16%

While only 16 percent of Perceivers with Perceiving partners frequently experienced conflict around the issue of household chores, more than twice as many Perceivers with Judging partners (33%) experienced it frequently. Again, these results are understandable and even predictable. Because they like closure and generally have a strong work ethic, most Judgers are driven to complete their work (in this case, household chores) before they can relax and enjoy themselves. But because they're more comfortable leaving things open and have more of a play ethic, Perceivers are more apt to put off tasks that aren't fun, reasoning that they can always complete them later.

Some Final Thoughts About the Practical Implications of This Study

The four components of this research — interviews with couples therapists, an on-line questionnaire, an open-ended questionnaire, and in-depth interviews with hundreds of couples — confirmed scientifically much of what we had suspected intuitively based on anecdotal evidence collected over twenty years of working with Personality Type on a daily basis.

Understanding individual behavior is difficult enough, but gaining insight into the multitude of dynamics that account for conflict and satisfaction in a relationship between two people is truly a daunting task. Although personality type is only one piece of a complex puzzle, this study demonstrated conclusively that it is a very important piece. Our hope and expectation is that this work will have lasting benefits for couples in helping them to understand natural sources of conflict and to develop ways of resolving conflicts so they can have the most satisfying relationships possible.

Because all research has limitations, especially that involving as complex a subject as this, we encourage other psychological researchers to continue exploring the powerful connection between personality type and relationship satisfaction, and we are eager to provide whatever assistance we can.

For more information about the research and questionnaire used in this study, please contact us through our Web site, www.personalitytype.com.

Index

Who do you have to get along with?

What if you could instantly know what people are thinking, what they care deeply about, their likes and dislikes? During a job interview or in everyday life, you'd know best how to pique their interest, strike a great bargain, or simply put them at ease.

Get what you want by knowing what others want. *The Art of SpeedReading People* helps you quickly (sometimes instantly) identify and understand key personality characteristics in others, and gives you a powerful advantage in communicating with all kinds of people.

In *The Art of SpeedReading People,* you'll learn how to:

- Make dynamite first impressions
- Instantly "read" and impress job interviewers
- Get along better with everyone — even your in-laws!
- Negotiate more effectively
- Be more persuasive with co-workers, employees, and your boss
- Sell your ideas, products, or services like never before

Find yourself at
www.personalitytype.com
The newest and most complete Web site about Personality Type in the universe

Hardcover ISBN 0-316-84525-6
Paperback ISBN 0-316-84518-3
Available at bookstores everywhere
Little, Brown and Company

"My kids are wonderful. But until I read *Nurture by Nature*, raising them was a huge stress on our marriage."

Let's face it, arguments over parenting decisions can be devastating to a marriage and to kids. Parents who really understand what makes their children tick are able to work together as a team, and that makes the job of co-parenting easier and much more rewarding.

This one-of-a-kind guide shows you how to use Personality Type to understand your child as never before. And because *Nurture by Nature* is the only parenting book written specifically about *your* child, you'll be amazed by how accurately it describes your child and how well its strategies work.

Find yourself at
www.personalitytype.com
The newest and most complete Web site about Personality Type in the universe

Nurture by Nature helps you:

- Discover your child's one true personality type and understand how best to motivate him or her
- Reduce stress between you and your partner caused by different parenting styles
- Nurture your children emotionally, using strategies that really work
- Instantly reduce sibling rivalry and the power struggles that drive you crazy

Whether your child is a toddler, a teen, or somewhere in between, *Nurture by Nature* gives you the powerful insights to raise healthy, loving, and responsible children, and create a more peaceful home for you, as well!

ISBN 0-316-84513-2
Available in paperback at bookstores everywhere
Little, Brown and Company

CPSIA information can be obtained at www.ICGtesting.com
Printed in the USA
LVOW110151201112

308044LV00004B/63/P